Fodor's Kenya & Tanzania

MW00330462

Fodor's Travel Publications, Inc.
New York • Toronto • London • Sydney • Auckland

ISBN 0–679–02309–7

Grateful acknowledgment is made to North Point Press for permission to reprint "Aloft over Africa," formerly titled "Message from Nungwe," from *West with the Night* by Beryl Markham. Copyright © 1983 by Beryl Markham. Published by North Point Press.

Fodor's Kenya & Tanzania

Editor: Conrad Little Paulus
Editorial Consultant and Chief Contributor: Delta Willis
Contributors: Deborah Appleton, Terry Burke, Marti Colley, Kathy Eldon, Paula Hirschoff, Michael Pennacchia, Marcy Pritchard, Ann Reilly, Terry Stevenson, Daniel Stiles, Phoebe Vreeland, Richard Wilding
Researchers: Julie Galosy, Holland McKenna
Creative Director: Fabrizio La Rocca
Cartographers: David Lindroth, Maryland Cartographics
Illustrator: Karl Tanner
Cover Photograph: E. G. Degginger/Animals, Animals
Design: Vignelli Associates

Special Sales

Contents

Foreword

While every care has been taken to ensure the accuracy of the information in this guide, the passage of time will always bring change, and consequently, the publisher cannot accept responsibility for errors that may occur.

All prices and opening times quoted here are based on information available to us at press time. Hours and admission fees may change, however, and the prudent traveler will avoid inconvenience by calling ahead.

Fodor's wants to hear about your travel experiences, both pleasant and unpleasant. When a hotel or restaurant fails to live up to its billing, let us know and we will investigate the complaint and revise our entries where the facts warrant it.

Send your letters to the editors of Fodor's Travel Publications, 201 E. 50th Street, New York, NY 10022.

Highlights and Fodor's Choice

Highlights

During the first half of 1991 the Persian Gulf War caused many American and British travelers to postpone their safari plans, and a travel warning on Tanzania further discouraged Americans. Several major tour operators felt the pinch (one went bankrupt), and some airlines, including Kenya Airways, trimmed the number of flights out of London. But the industry recovered, buoyed by Europeans who didn't skip a beat and a wave of Yanks and Brits who booked again as soon as the war was over. The numbers are not back up to the post-*Out of Africa* peak, and as we go to press, the postwar atmosphere of confidence is being dissipated by political problems and corruption in Kenya. Nevertheless, the development plans inspired by the late '80s boom are slowly becoming a reality.

Extraordinary growth is visible in Tanzania, whose government proclaimed tourism the number-one priority for 1990. There is a new highway running south from Arusha, and a number of renovated lodges in Tanzania's Northern Circuit, which includes the Serengeti, Lake Manyara, and Ngorongoro Crater. Tarangire and Arusha National Parks are becoming more popular, as are the Selous Game Reserve, Ruaha and Mikumi National Parks, which form a Southern Circuit in more adventurous terrain.

The most rapid growth is in the east, on the Indian Ocean island of Zanzibar. Until very recently, this Tanzanian island was only for the intrepid. There were few decent places to stay, and transportation from Dar es Salaam was unreliable. Now there are daily flights on Air Tanzania, and a sleek new hydrofoil, *Sea Express*, offers a first-class section for a fast, comfortable journey from Dar. Zanzibar can also be reached by direct flights from Mombasa, Kenya, on Kenya Airways.

Zanzibar's Stonetown is bustling with renovation; historic buildings are undergoing spectacular face-lifts: The intricate carvings traditional to this Swahili culture are being restored, and some buildings are being converted to museums. There are many good guest houses, and massive hotels are in the planning stages. There's been such an influx of Italians that local teenagers say *"Ciao!"* as often as *"Jambo!"*—which is not necessarily a good sign, if you've made the trip to experience the Swahili culture of this ancient Arab isle.

Eco-Tourism Growth in tourism is not always good news. Kenya's Amboseli National Park, north of Kilimanjaro, became a center of controversy as erosion began to turn it into a desert, or "a disaster," as Richard Leakey, the new head of parks and wildlife, termed it. *National Geographic* and

Condé Nast Traveller covered the Amboseli dilemma in 1991 feature reports. While some blamed elephants for damaging trees, part of the problem was too many tourist vans in a hurry. Many people flew in for day trips from the coast and pushed to see as much game as possible. Drivers ventured off the roads, destroying the grass and sending up trails of dust. With increasing interest in conservation and ecology, responsible tour operators avoid such crowded parks as Amboseli. Eco-tourism, always a good idea, quickly became a selling point, and to limit the damage in Amboseli, a one-way circuit has been paved and off-road driving strictly forbidden.

While Kenya leaders like Leakey made great strides toward protecting elephants in a highly publicized war on poaching (and Nairobi National Park actually recorded an increase in the rhino population), many wilderness habitats of endangered species remain threatened. Kenya is the fastest-growing nation in the world, and nomadic people are beginning to settle down on small farms, building fences that halt natural wildlife migration out of the parks. Now the great challenge is to diminish conflict between people and wildlife, and a strange but perhaps inevitable price tag has been put on the heads of elephants: Each one is said to be worth $20,000 in tourist income. To benefit locals and provide an incentive for conservation, park entrance fees have been substantially increased in both Kenya and Tanzania.

In Tanzania, camping on the floor of Ngorongoro Crater was halted at the end of February 1992, because of concerns about environmental damage. Some tour operators plan to camp at sites along the crater rim instead. Game drives will still be permitted in the crater. Some travel programs, like those of the New York Zoological Society, offer visitors a chance to see their conservation efforts in the field, with lectures by ecologists included in the itinerary. Visits to Roland Purcell's Mahale Mountain Camp near Lake Tanganyika include an opportunity to observe chimpanzees in the wild, and a new tented camp on the Tana River Delta, north of Malindi, offers excellent birdwatching via boats that meander through the mangroves.

As nature lovers moved away from the vehicles that crowd not only Amboseli, but the Masai Mara and Tanzania's Ngorongoro Crater, small, discreet lodges sprang up, offering panoramic beauty and privacy. Accommodations like Ol Donyo Wuas, on the edge of Kenya's Chyulu Hills, find advantage in locations outside national parks, where you can get out of your vehicle and get a little exercise.

But uncluttered views can mean an increase in prices, with some operators charging as much as $1,200 per person per day (the rate for a safari in the Selous). Camel safaris in northern Kenya remain relatively inexpensive, less than $75 per person per day. Bargains are more difficult to find nowadays, but the rustic cabins, or *bandas*, at Shimba Hills National Reserve and in Tsavo East cost less than $10 a night.

The move away from crowded parks sent many visitors north, into Samburu country and the Mathews Range, to the Ol Pejeta Reserve, near Mt. Kenya, or on fishing trips to Rusinga Island, on Lake Victoria. And as growth moved north in Kenya, intrepid operators moved south in Tanzania, into the Selous Game Reserve.

Aldabra, the remote Southernmost island of the Seychelles, drew scuba divers with the live-aboard vessel *Fantasea*, renowned for its dive program in the Red Sea. Many Seychelles hotels underwent face-lifts and expansion, but the government has proclaimed a lid of 4,000 beds throughout the country, to ensure that Mahé will never resemble Miami Beach. So far, so good; the Republic of Seychelles (a pioneer in conservation before the word "ecotourism" was invented) remains exotic and breathtaking.

Hotel Developments In Kenya: Windsor Hotels built the lavish Victorian **Windsor Golf & Country Club,** just outside Nairobi, with health club and conference facilities. Lonrho, the firm that renovated Nairobi's famous Norfolk Hotel, bought Adnan Khashoggi's 108,000-acre ranch and turned his former home into **Ol Pejeta Lodge,** with spa facilities. Former hunting grounds now serve as a rhino sanctuary, and visitors see plenty of elephant from nearby **Sweetwater's,** a luxury tented camp with a first-class restaurant. The new **Tana River Delta** tented camp is reached by a motorized wooden dhow named the *African Queen*. **Kitich** tented camp in the Mathews Range has had some management problems, but the remote swimming hole and a chance to walk in the footsteps of a Dorobo tracker make the trip worthwhile.

Peponi's maintains its status as *the* first-class hotel on the island of Lamu, with excellent lobster in the dining room, bungalows with a view, and a lively bar and grill. The **Kiwayu** resort, on Kiwayu Peninsula, and the new **Kipugani Lodge,** on the remote tip of Lamu island, offer private beaches and large thatched bungalows ideal for honeymooners. North of Malindi new cottages are being constructed at Che Shale. The most luxurious accommodation in Malindi is also the most private. No sign marks the driveway to the **Indian Ocean Lodge,** an elegant seashore mansion with private terraces that overlook the coral reefs. In Zanzibar, the **Narrow Street Motel** and **Malindi Guest House** are among the most charming places to stay in Stonetown, and both cost around $20 per person a night. The **Palm Beach Inn** in the fishing village of Bwejuu on the east coast charges $10 per person a night. In Tanzania: **Lobo** and **Seronera** lodges in the northern Serengeti are under new management, as is the newly expanded **Ndutu Lodge,** near the southern border of the park. All feature substantially improved cuisine, especially Ndutu, which is managed by the same people who made Gibbs Farm a gourmet luncheon stop. **Tarangire National Park,** south of Arusha off the new highway, has a luxury permanent tented camp, with a pool and wonderful baobab trees.

Several new guest houses and small lodges have sprung up just south of Arusha, including the **Ngare Sero Mountain Lodge,** with trout fishing on the property. The old Momela Lakes Hunting Lodge, in Arusha National Park, has been renovated and granted a name change—it is now the **Momela Lakes Wildlife Lodge**—reflecting changing times, though hunters are still welcome in southern Tanzania, where they are charged stiff fees to shoot buffalo in the Selous.

The new **Karibu Hotel,** north of Dar es Salaam, is worth the drive out of town, as is the partly renovated **Oyster Bay Hotel,** because most hotels in downtown Dar scream for a decorator, and some lack even a pool. It doesn't take many Campari and sodas at the new **Casanova** restaurant ($7 a shot) to get that ripped-off feeling in Dar, and some cab drivers try to charge too much; fix a sum before you get in. The beaches can be dangerous, with muggings and robberies, so don't waste time and money in Dar; the rest of Tanzania is too beautiful. Some operators plan to whisk travelers into the Selous and out to Zanzibar by air, with no overnight stay in the capital.

Travel Advisories The U.S. State Department provides taped travel advisories (tel. 202/647–5225) with cautionary advice for Americans traveling abroad. Of the three types of advisories, the Caution and Notice Categories are not meant to deter travel and usually cover only minor items. "Warnings" recommend that Americans either avoid all travel or all nonessential travel to all or part of a country.

Most operators and travel agents feel that while advisories may be alarmist, they should inform their clients about them and let travelers make up their own minds. If there is an advisory that sounds serious, consult a trusted travel agent or tour operator, who will have reports from returning clients and can fax your questions to its Africa-based colleagues. You should ask your tour operator about its refund policy in the event a Warning is issued.

A Warning was issued for Kenya in March 1992 regarding travel to the Masai Mara National Reserve, where attacks on single vehicles were reported. At press time there is a Caution on travel in Tanzania, in which you are told to beware of street crime in the cities, advised not to trade currency in the illegal black market, told that there are severe restrictions on photography around harbors, airports, and military installations, and that beaches in the Dar area can be dangerous. We include such precautions, which match the reports of our field correspondents, in relevant sections of this book.

Fodor's Choice

No two people will agree on what makes a perfect vacation, but it can be fun and helpful to know what others think. We hope you'll enjoy some of Fodor's Choices while visiting East Africa and the Indian Ocean. For detailed information about each entry, see the relevant sections in this guidebook.

Uniquely Africa

Sundowners on the Norfolk Terrace

The Great Rift Valley escarpment

Horseback riding at Lewa Downs, Kenya

The snows of Mt. Kilimanjaro

The annual wildebeest migration as seen from a hot-air balloon over the Masai Mara

The overnight train from Nairobi to Mombasa

An aerial view of the coral patterns around the outer Seychelles

Romantic Spots

Sunrise at Lake Baringo Island Camp, with fishermen singing in the distance

A private tented camp overlooking flocks of flamingos on Lake Manyara, Tanzania

The elegant shoreline of La Digue Island, Seychelles

Moonlight dhow voyage off the Kenya coast

Ol Donyo Wuas Lodge in Kenya's Chyulus

Taste Treats

Shrimp piri piri at the Tamarind, Mombasa

Grilled venison carved on to your plate at the Carnivore Restaurant, Nairobi

Curries at the Supreme Hotel, Nairobi

Chauve souris (flying foxes), Seychelles

Fresh lime juice, mango, coconut milk, and passion fruit throughout East Africa

Brunch at the Hilton, Nairobi

A cold Tusker beer

Boat Trips

The *African Queen* on the Tana River

Cruising the Steigler's Gorge of the Selous

Water-skiing on Lake Baringo, Kenya

Lake Victoria day tour, via the ferry from Kisumu

Dhow dinner trip from the Tamarind, Mombasa

Deep-sea fishing from Hemingway's, Watamu

The new sailing shuttle from Dar es Salaam to Zanzibar

Moonlight canoe trips from Kiwayu, Kenya coast

For Children

AFEW Giraffe Center, Langata

Nairobi National Park and Orphanage, Nairobi

National Museums of Kenya and Snake Park, Nairobi

Lions in the trees, Lake Manyara, Tanzania

Vallee du Mai, Praslin, Seychelles

Sports

Deep-sea fishing at Watamu or Shimoni, Kenya

Horseback riding at Mount Kenya Safari Club

Windsurfing and snorkeling at Diani Beach

Fly-fishing in the Aberdares

Climbing Mt. Kenya and Mt. Elgon

Scuba diving and sailing around Seychelles

Off the Beaten Track

A visit to the gallery of artist Michael Adams, near Anse aux Poules Bleues, Mahé, Seychelles

Koobi Fora Museum, East Turkana, Kenya

A camel safari in Samburu country, Kenya

Climbing Mt. Kenya or Mt. Kilimanjaro

Bird Island, nesting site of a million sooty terns, Seychelles

Olorgesailie, prehistoric site just south of Nairobi

The Arabic village of Siyu on Lamu Island explored on donkey or on foot

Dining

Kenya Horseman, Karen *(Expensive)*

Ibis Grill, Norfolk Hotel, Nairobi *(Expensive)*

Tamarind, Mombasa *(Expensive)*

Minar, Nairobi *(Moderate)*

Tanzania Gibbs Farm, Northern Circuit *(Moderate)*

Seychelles Kyoto, Victoria *(Moderate)*

Marie Antoinette's, Victoria *(Moderate)*

Lodging

Kenya Indian Ocean Lodge, Malindi *(Very Expensive)*

Kiwayu Safari Village, Lamu *(Very Expensive)*

Norfolk Hotel, Nairobi *(Very Expensive)*

Nairobi Safari Club, Nairobi *(Very Expensive)*

Ol Donyo Wuas, Chyulu Range *(Very Expensive)*

Windsor Golf and Country Club, Nairobi *(Very Expensive)*

Peponi's, Lamu *(Expensive)*

The Hotel Boulevard, Nairobi *(Inexpensive)*

Tanzania Gibbs Farm, Northern Circuit *(Moderate)*

Ndutu Safari Lodge, near Serengeti *(Moderate)*

Ngare Sero Mountain Lodge, Arusha *(Moderate)*

Tarangire Tented Camp *(Moderate)*

Seychelles Fisherman's Cove, Mahé Island *(Very Expensive)*

Maison des Palmes, Praslin Island *(Moderate)*

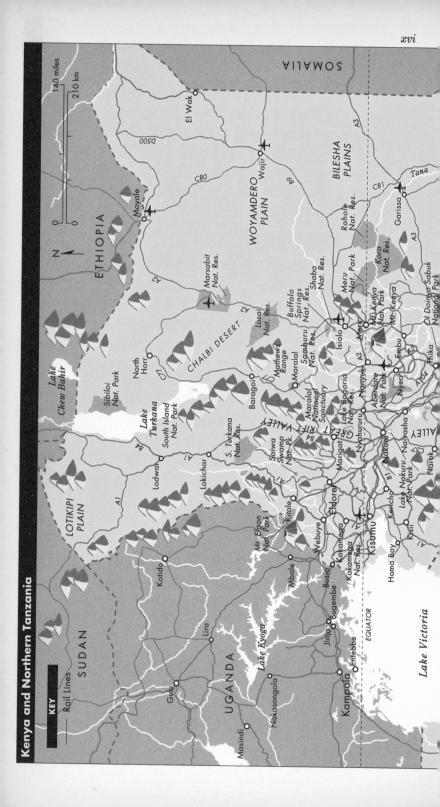

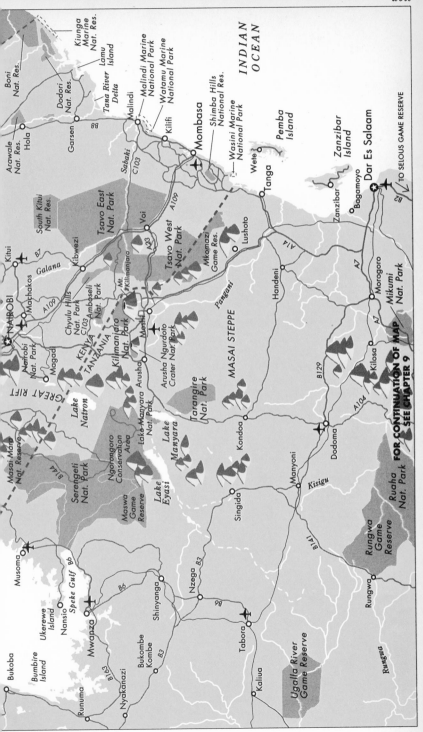

World Time Zones

Numbers below vertical bands relate each zone to Greenwich Mean Time (0 hrs.).
Local times frequently differ from these general indications,
as indicated by light-face numbers on map.

Algiers, **29**	Berlin, **34**	Delhi, **48**	Istanbul, **40**
Anchorage, **3**	Bogotá, **19**	Denver, **8**	Jerusalem, **42**
Athens, **41**	Budapest, **37**	Djakarta, **53**	Johannesburg, **44**
Auckland, **1**	Buenos Aires, **24**	Dublin, **26**	Lima, **20**
Baghdad, **46**	Caracas, **22**	Edmonton, **7**	Lisbon, **28**
Bangkok, **50**	Chicago, **9**	Hong Kong, **56**	London (Greenwich), **27**
Beijing, **54**	Copenhagen, **33**	Honolulu, **2**	Los Angeles, **6**
	Dallas, **10**		Madrid, **38**
			Manila, **57**

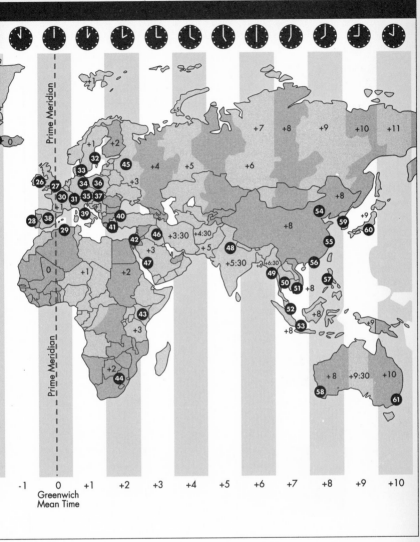

Introduction

By Delta Willis

Formerly associated with the "Survival" wildlife documentaries for television, Delta Willis is a writer/ photographer with a special interest in natural history. While researching her book The Hominid Gang *she lived in Kenya. She has also traveled in Tanzania and Seychelles.*

The first time I went to Africa, I headed straight to the Nairobi suburb of Karen, pulling into a long, circular driveway and stopping the car in front of a farmhouse that was so familiar, I half expected a dog to greet me. I knew the house from a black-and-white photograph in Peter Beard's book, *The End of the Game.* I also knew it from the stories of Isak Dinesen, the pen name for writer Karen Blixen, after whom this community is named. It was a place where minds met, where the Prince of Wales (later Duke of Windsor) dined, and where a passion for this country and its people began in a most unlikely setting of colonial sophistication and civilized rigor—meaning polished silver, fine furniture, and books.

The front of the farmhouse is simple enough, with a long veranda and a large clock centered over the entrance. Behind the great sloping lawn loom the Ngong Hills, purple and distant. "Here I am, where I ought to be," Karen Blixen wrote in *Out of Africa;* and that is the way I felt about this setting—as I would in other terrain often described as "hostile," such as the deserts of Kenya's northern frontier, where camels are the best form of transportation.

The horizons are vast here, the air thick with dust, and the nomadic people imbued with an enviable elegance and grace. Water is scarce, but desert beauty abounds, and I love this spare setting as much as the domestic one at Karen. In fact, there is no place in East Africa where I don't feel at home. From the dusty ravines at Olduvai Gorge to the lush forest of Valle du Mai in Seychelles, East Africa not only satisfies my wanderlust, but also affords me that special sense (both restful and inspiring) of being a part of nature.

My first journey to Nairobi was in 1977, long before Baroness Blixen's home was made into a museum and nearly a decade before Meryl Streep and Robert Redford would bring the characters in *Out of Africa* to the screen. I've since encountered many people who ventured to this country on the same sort of pilgrimage, just as others came here to walk in the footsteps of Hemingway and Huxley. We saw Karen as a base camp, as we would our tent in the bush, for it was the rest of the landscape that held us—the drama of the Great Rift Valley, the majesty of a herd of elephants, the light in a lion's eyes, and the very shape of a baobab tree. We were mesmerized, and we wondered at the story all these shapes and sounds had to impart.

People fall in love with East Africa and everything about it. Few people come here only once. My friends and I have returned again and again; some of us have chosen to live here for a while because we found a sense of self here that could not be forgotten when we returned to our city desks.

It was as if we were in search of a challenge, as if we needed to stand at a frontier—which East Africa remains. Fossils that might explain the mystery of human origins continue to emerge here with every rainfall, and the efforts to protect wildlife and halt desertification in this region are seen as a testing ground for what might prevail in the rest of the world. Nairobi, after all, is the international headquarters for UNEP, the United Nations Environmental Programme. When you read of pioneers like Louis Leakey (or see the wonderful films on his work on *National Geographic* television specials), you gain some sense of the pioneering spirit that prevails in his legacy.

L egacy is central to exploring this region. Alex Haley's *Roots* inspired many Americans to consider their own ancestry, and in East Africa you can take that search back in time, by visiting the coastal towns of Mombasa or Bagamoyo or excavation sites Olorgesailie or Koobi Fora. You can also wonder at the contrast of both plants and animals on the Seychelles archipelago, which has often been called the Galápagos of the Indian Ocean. What would Charles Darwin have written had he seen this infinite variety of life? In the same way that the Galápagos feature life so different from that on the South American mainland, so life on the Seychelles remains distinct from that of mainland East Africa. The islands are the remains of Precambrian bedrock, a thin spine of earth that managed to remain above the surface of the turquoise waters when Africa split from Indian and Asian tectonic plates.

"Zinj" is the ancient Arabic word for the East African coast, and the first hominid skull that Mary Leakey found at Olduvai Gorge in 1959 was given this name by her husband, Louis. It was an appropriate name because Dr. Leakey's discovery shifted the Cradle of Mankind from South Africa to East Africa. Many people visit East Africa today only for game drives on the savannas, failing to visit the coast. But it is here that you can find the origins of Islam in Africa, represented by the Swahili culture that began on Zinj and Zanzibar. At Lamu, you can also find exquisite crafts, from the beautiful Lamu doors to the elegant dhow boats. Modern and primitive art abound, as does good music—the kind that inspired Paul Simon's album "Graceland"; just listen to the local radio stations as you drive along, or sample some of the indigenous discos in Nairobi or Mombasa. Many tented camps and lodges offer tribal dancing and singing around a campfire in the evening. The experience is magical.

As a journalist, I frequently find myself burdened by my camera gear and tape recorder, too much in a hurry to capture the moment. At times I've felt that the camera lens has

imals) must think of me. During your stay, you, too, may
want to take a day off from your hard work as a visitor, lay
the gear aside, put the camera and the wallet away and try
out a few words of Swahili. When someone tries to sell you a
beaded gourd, venture, "How did you make it?" or "What is
it for?" Carry a postcard of your home terrain and offer it
for review. Give the gift of courtesy, and you may find that
you have created one of the most invaluable memories of
your journey. Relish the moment, for the traditional way of
life here is just as endangered as are the elephant and rhino.

Nonetheless, there are healthy plans afoot to benefit both
the people and the wildlife of Africa. The efforts of Dr.
Richard Leakey, who has temporarily relinquished his ca-
reer in fossil research to organize an all-out war to protect
Africa's wildlife, are well known. His efforts often make
headlines. Less well known, Cynthia Moss arrived in Kenya
20 years ago as a reporter on vacation and decided to stay to
study elephants in Amboseli. She had no scientific training,
but she had the will and the dedication that have since made
her one of the world's foremost experts on elephant behavior. Cynthia told me that the elephant herds in Tanzania's
Selous National Park have been in only a few years reduced
by 75%. Not surprisingly, there are many who come to East
Africa only to find that they cannot leave this kind of problem behind. There are too many beautiful settings in East
Africa that say, This, beyond all else, is what matters. This
was Blixen's backyard.

During my first visit to Karen House, I meandered
around the back lawn, once the setting for an especially romantic evening between Blixen and bush pilot Denys Finch-Hatton. I studied the overgrown garden
with an eye toward pruning, as if this were my domain and
by pruning I could bring such a moment back to life with
blossoms. I wondered at the clock over the veranda, which
had stopped at 3:30, and decided (without real historical
reason) that it had failed at 3:30 AM, the time of night when
lions can be heard in the distance. Such resonance should stop
a clock, as it does the heart.

A few years later I rented my own house in a Nairobi suburb,
complete with a garden I surveyed and a dog that greeted me
whether I'd been away on a brief safari or gone for a full season or two back to the United States. After sunset my attention centered on a typewriter or on friends around a dining
table who contributed stories to my empty pages.

The telling of stories is paramount in Africa. Without television programs consuming the evening, people deliver the
most extraordinary renderings. Some tales have to do with a
happening on a city street or a handshake along a remote
road. Mostly they have to do with an encounter with an animal, when we learn who is boss. The twist to the story is often
one of irony and dilemma: How do you capture what you want
of the land and not become an intruder? Can you refrain from

pressing the trigger on your camera any more than Hemingway could refrain from pulling the trigger on his gun? If you take of Africa, what of the Western world do you impart in turn?

The dinner parties at my house were rich fodder. My guests included scientists working with gorillas in Rwanda and primatologists studying baboons north of Mt. Kenya. There were ecologists working to give Masai people their fair share of tourism's returns, and there were people who discovered hand axes made by our ancestors. There were bureaucrats, from the museums and such institutions as the World Bank and the United Nations Environmental Program, saying, We are here, but asking, What have we done and what have we done wrong? There were photographers from *National Geographic* and journalists who wrote for *Time*. We were all trying to piece it together. We were tourists with pads and plenty of film. We proposed to be objective, to give a fair portrait, but with our hearts unabashedly attached to our work, we hoped the rest of the world might take notice of what we had seen. We were, in a sense, the new missionaries. Yet we hoped to come and go, not leave a mark on the landscape.

It left a mark on us. Around 3:30 AM, the lions began to roar. Most were probably nearby in Nairobi National Park, but after a time of learning—discerning low coughs from more distant appeals—I could know which ones were less than half a mile away.

It was this sense of accessibility that inevitably led to another safari. Sometimes, these were simple shortcuts, for on any Saturday or Sunday I could drive to the Nairobi National Park, a mere 10 minutes away, and see great cats.

But I often found myself sleeping out under the stars, and I was delighted to wake and find that lions had walked through the camp during the night. But there was an edge to this romance, a sharp reminder of reality that said, Grasp it, for it is soon gone.

1   Essential Information

Before You Go

Government Tourist Offices

Contact the **Kenya Tourist** offices.

In the United States: 424 Madison Ave., New York, NY 10017, tel. 212/486–1300; Doheny Plaza, Suite 111–112, 9100 Wilshire Blvd., Los Angeles, CA 90212, tel. 213/274–6635.

In the United Kingdom: 13 New Burlington St., London W1X 1FF, England, tel. 01/839–4477 or 4478.

There is no Kenya Tourist Office in Canada, but you can contact the **Kenya Diplomatic Mission** (Gillia Bldg., Suite 600, 141 Laurier Ave., East Ottawa, Ont. K1P 5J3, tel. 613/563–1773) for travel information.

Tour Groups

Few people head into the wilds of Africa without the assistance of an experienced tour operator. Given Kenya's magnificent coast, endlessly fascinating interior, and vast array of tour options, the problem is sorting out which package to take. Aside from the questions of how much time and money you will spend, consider your personal style. Do you like roughing it, or can't you get along without a hot shower? Is your idea of base camp a cluster of pup tents in a clearing, or a four-poster bed under tastefully draped mosquito netting?

There are two basic types of safari: *lodge safaris*, in which you are based in a resortlike lodge and venture out daily for game viewing; and *tented safaris*, in which you sleep under canvas in a secluded campsite. Lodge safaris are generally less expensive. *Wing safaris* use light aircraft to shuttle groups from reserve to reserve, cutting the time spent in transit. The companies listed below are respected, experienced operators, offering a variety of tour options. *See also* Choosing a Safari, *below*.

When considering a tour, be sure to find out the number of people in your group; the exact expenses included (such as tips, taxes, side trips, additional meals, and entertainment); the type and quality of accommodations; cancellation policies for both you and the tour operator; and the single supplement, if you are traveling alone. Most tour operators request that bookings be made through a travel agent, and there is no additional charge for doing so.

General-Interest Tours   **Abercrombie & Kent International** (1420 Kensington Rd., Oak Brook, IL 60521, tel. 312/954–2944 or 800/323–7308) was founded in Nairobi in 1962. There is no Abercrombie; Mr. Kent simply liked the status associated with the outfitters Abercrombie & Fitch, "and it puts us first in the telephone listings," says Geoff Kent. A & K have classic tented safaris in Kenya and Tanzania, as well as lodge tours.

Olson-Travelworld, Ltd. (1334 Parkview Ave., Suite 210, Manhattan Beach, CA 90266, tel. 310/546–8400 or 800/421–2255) offers a variety of safaris and tours ranging from 16 to 29 days, and takes you to your local airport in a private limousine. That level of service is maintained throughout the 18- or 23-day

"East Africa Discovery" in Kenya and Tanzania. An affiliate, **Olson Tours,** offers a lower-priced safari (around $2,000 per person, without airfare, which is $500 to $2,000 less than typical trips.

Pan African Travel Organization, Ltd. has a U.S. representative that will design an itinerary based on your needs (Bruce Baum, Kenya Consultants, Box 21C, Mt. Tremper, NY 12457, tel. 914/688–5951 or 800/541–2527).

Park East Tours, with offices in New York and Nairobi (1841 Broadway, New York, NY 10023, tel. 212/765–4870 and Box 42238, Nairobi, tel. 2/28168), runs reasonably priced group tours that are good value, traveling via plane or minivan and staying in lodges and permanent camps.

United Touring International (400 Market St., Suite 260, Philadelphia, PA 19106, tel. 215/923–8700 or 800/223–6486) offers a varied selection of tour packages and prices. It owns a number of first-class hotels and lodges, and runs fleets of safari vehicles into the game reserves.

Cheli & Peacock Ltd. (Box 39806, Nairobi, tel. 222551/2; fax 22553) and **Ker & Downey** (Box 41822, Nairobi, tel. 2556 466; fax 552 378) run luxury tented safaris.

Captain Doug Morey (Box 15098, Nairobi, tel. 2/891 309; fax 2500 845 or 882 723) an American-born bush pilot with a decade of experience in East Africa, organizes off-the-beaten-path safaris with air connections.

Richard Bonham Safaris Ltd. (Box 24133, Nairobi, tel. 2/882521, fax 2/882728; U.S. agent A.K. Taylor Int., 2724 Arvin Rd., Billings, MT, 59102, tel. 406/656–0706, fax 406/252–6353), run by the son of the late game warden Jack Bonham, specializes in walking and horseback safaris with movable tents, in remote areas like the Chyulu Hills and the Selous Game Reserve.

Special-Interest Tours
Adventure

While most people would consider any African safari an adventure, **Sobek's International Explorers Society** (Box 1089, Angels Camp, CA 95222, tel. 209/736–4524 or 800/777–7939) runs tours that are a little more daring. The "Kenya Walking Safari" is a walking tour of bush country, guaranteed to avoid tourist crowds. "Great African Outdoors" treks over Mt. Kenya and through the bird sanctuary at Lake Naivasha and to the Masai Mara, ending with a camel trip in the northern desert. **Mountain Travel** (6420 Fairmount Ave., El Cerrito, CA 94530, tel. 415/527–8100 or 800/227–2384) offers trekking trips on Mt. Kenya and Mt. Kilimanjaro and walking safaris in Masailand. Prices are in the mid to high range.

Honeymoon

The Seychelles are a popular honeymoon retreat, as is Kipugani Lodge, on the island of Lamu.

Ornithology

United Touring International (*see* General-Interest Tours, *above*) and **Micato Safaris** (15 W. 26th St., 11th floor, New York, NY 10010, tel. 212/545–7111) offer tours with special emphasis on bird-watching.

Scientific/Ecological

Museums and zoological societies organize many special-interest tours; for example, New York's **American Museum of Natural History** (Central Park West at 81st St., New York, NY 10024; tel. 212/769–5700 or 800/462–8687) features scientists as guides for its Discovery Tours to East Africa. **Nature Expedi-**

tions International (Box 11496, Eugene, OR 97440, tel. 503/484–6529 or 800/869–0639) runs a number of wildlife and walking tours, conducted by scientists. Tours focusing on eco-tourism are organized by **Members Afield** (217 E. 85th St., New York, NY 10028, tel. 212/879–2588 or 908/362–7744), who design programs for members of the New York Zoological Society.

Personal Guides
Kenya

(For dialing direct, the country code for Kenya is 254, the city code for Nairobi is 2. Kenya is eight hours ahead of EST in the U.S. The circuits are heavily used, and you must be persistent; it is best to call or fax midnight–6AM, EST, or fax 5–6 PM EST.)

Allen Safaris (Box 14712 Nairobi, tel. 60365 and 27 Stafford Terr., London W8 7BL, tel. 071/937–2937) are private tented safaris run by Kenya pilot David Allen, the preferred guide for journalists and photographers.

Tor Allan Safaris (Box 41959, Nairobi, tel. 891 190, telex: Compass 22963) are expensive private tented safaris via four-wheel drive vehicle.

Flame Tree Safaris Ltd. (Box 82, Nanyuki, Kenya, tel. 176/22053, fax 176/23302; U.S. agent Members Afield), expensive private safaris led by Chrissie Aldrich, are especially good for walking tours and horseback riding off the beaten path.

Rob Carr Hartley (Box 24669, Nairobi, tel. 2/882 816, fax 2/216 553) is a professional safari guide and consultant.

Lynne Leakey (c/o Abercrombie & Kent, or Box 24638, Nairobi, tel. 2/749 378) is an American-born guide for special safaris.

Package Deals for Independent Travelers

The best price for a package tour of Kenya can be found in Nairobi. "Tourist's Kenya," a free booklet that is updated weekly and available in all hotels, lists about 100 tour companies and their packages. Write to "Tourist's Kenya," Saver's Cards Limited (Box 40025, Nairobi, Kenya) for a copy. Once you've selected your safari, a travel agent can make arrangements for you or you can do it yourself by telex or in writing. (The Kenya Airways London office always has this booklet on hand, and it is worth a quick visit for this information.)

Born Free Safaris (4734 Greenbush Ave., Sherman Oaks, CA 91423, tel. 818/981–7185 or 800/372–3274) specializes in custom tented safaris for small groups.

The **East Africa Safari Company** (250 W. 57th St., Suite 1222, New York, NY 10107, tel. 212/757–0722 or 800/7–SAFARI) specializes in custom tented safaris for individuals and small groups, as well as walking safaris and accommodations at private ranches and homesteads. Most of the companies named above also offer special independent packages.

Safaritravel Kenya Ltd. (tel. 212/888–7596 or 800/882–5537) specializes in reasonably priced minivan/lodge and luxury permanent-tented safaris for as few as two people.

Tips for British Travelers

Passports and
Visas

You will need a valid 10-year passport (cost: £15). You do not need a visa unless you are of Asian origin or have spent more than 90 days in South Africa. You will need a vaccination certificate for yellow fever if you arrive within six days from or via endemic areas. Immunization against malaria, typhoid, yellow fever, and polio is recommended.

Customs Visitors 16 years or older can take in 200 cigarettes or ½ pound of tobacco; one bottle of wine or one bottle of spirits; and one pint of perfume. Firearms and ammunition require a police permit or a temporary import license for a bird-shooting safari.

In returning to the United Kingdom, you may take home, if you are 17 years or older: (1) 200 cigarettes or 100 cigarillos or 50 cigars or 250 grams of tobacco; (2) two liters of table wine with (a) one liter of alcohol over 22% by volume (most spirits), (b) two liters of alcohol under 22% by volume (fortified or sparkling wine), or (c) two more liters of table wine; (3) 50 grams of perfume and ¼ liter of toilet water; and (4) other goods up to a value of £32.

Insurance We recommend that you insure yourself against health and motoring mishaps. **Europ Assistance** (252 High St., Croydon, Surrey CR0 1NF, tel. 01/680–1234) is one firm that offers this service. It is also wise to take out insurance to cover lost luggage (check that such loss isn't already in any existing homeowners' policies you may have). Trip-cancellation insurance is also a good idea. **The Association of British Insurers** (51 Gresham St., London EC2V 7HQ, tel. 071/600–3333) will give you comprehensive advice on all aspects of holiday insurance.

Tour Operators Here is a selection of companies that offer package tours to Kenya. Check with your travel agent for the latest information:

Abercrombie & Kent Travel (Sloane Square House, Holbein Pl., London SW1W 8NS, tel. 071/730–9600).
Bales Tours Ltd (Bales House, Junction Rd., Dorking, Surrey RH4 3HB, tel. 0306/885991).
British Airways Holidays (Atlantic House, Hazelwick Ave., Three Bridges, Crawley, W. Sussex RH10 1NP, tel. 0293/611611).
Cosmosair (Ground Floor, Dale House, Tiviot Dale, Stockport, Cheshire SK1 1TB, tel. 061/480–5799).
Flamingo Tours of East Africa (Livingstone House, 167 Acton La., Acton, London W4 5HN, tel. 081/995–3505).
Premier Holidays (Westbrook, Milton Rd., Cambridge CB4 1YQ, tel. 0223/355977).
Thomson Holidays (Greater London House, Hampstead Rd., London NW1 7SD, tel. 081/200–8733).
Wexas International (45 Brompton Rd., Knightsbridge, London SW3, 1DE, tel. 071/581–8632, fax 071/589–8418).
Worldwide Journeys & Expeditions (146 Gloucester Rd., tel. 071/370–5032, fax 071/244–7783).

Airlines and Airfares Airlines flying to Kenya include **British Airways, Kenya Airways,** and **KLM.** At press time the low-season return APEX fare was £550.

Thomas Cook Ltd. can often book you on very inexpensive flights. Call the Cook branch nearest you and ask to be put through to the Airfare Warehouse. Be sure to call at least 21 days in advance of when you want to travel.

Also check the small ads in magazines such as *Time Out* and *City Limits* and in the Sunday papers, where flights are offered for as low as £375.

When to Go

The tourist year divides into high, middle, and low seasons, but there are differences in opinion on the precise periods covered by these divisions. Abercrombie & Kent, a leading safari firm knowledgeable about the country and the U.S. trade, sets it out as follows: **High season:** December 1 to March 31, and June 1 to August 31. **Low season:** April 1 to May 31, and September 1 to November 31.

The weather in Kenya is pleasant throughout the year, with the seasons differentiated mainly by the amount of rainfall. The "long rains" generally fall from April through May and the "short rains" from October through November. It seldom rains all day during the short rains; it may rain briefly and then turn sunny for the rest of the day.

Because they are influenced by the wind currents of the Indian Ocean, the rains arrive at a different time in southern Tanzania. In the Selous Game Reserve, for example, it is usually dry until the end of October; January is wet, and the month of July (which is wet in Kenya) is spectacular in the Selous. For detailed maps of the rains, see Jonathan Kingdon's book *Island Africa*.

The rains can turn roads into muddy, rutted tracks, especially in the highlands of the Aberdares, around Mt. Kenya, and in parts of Masailand. Sometimes roads are closed in the mountain parks. In Tsavo, apart from the odd rainy day, the tracks are passable. At the coast, rains are characterized by a downpour followed by a break in the clouds for a long, bright interval. Many insiders actually prefer the short rains. The landscape then is more spectacular—blooms among the vivid green, with dramatic skies for an interesting backdrop to photographs. It's also the affordable season, when most tour operators and hotels offer more reasonable rates. The high season is an expensive time to visit Kenya, and beds are at a premium, especially in the safari lodges and camps.

Another factor to consider in planning when to take a safari is the timing of the mass migrations of animals. The most photogenic, with up to 2 million plains animals crossing from the Masai Mara into the Serengeti in Tanzania, takes place from mid-August to the end of September, in Kenya.

Climate The following are average daily maximum and minimum temperatures for cities in Kenya, Tanzania, and Seychelles.

Mombasa, Kenya	**Jan.**	87F	31C	**May**	83F	28C	**Sept.**	82F	28C
		75	24		74	23		72	22
	Feb.	87F	31C	**June**	82F	28C	**Oct.**	84F	29C
		76	24		73	23		74	23
	Mar.	88F	31C	**July**	81F	27C	**Nov.**	85F	29C
		77	25		71	22		75	24
	Apr.	86F	30C	**Aug.**	81F	27C	**Dec.**	86F	30C
		76	24		71	22		75	24

Nairobi, Kenya	Jan.	77F 54	25C 12	May	72F 56	22C 13	Sept.	75F 52	24C 11
	Feb.	79F 55	26C 13	June	70F 53	21C 12	Oct.	76F 55	24C 13
	Mar.	77F 57	25C 14	July	69F 51	21C 11	Nov.	74F 56	23C 13
	Apr.	75F 58	24C 14	Aug.	70F 52	21C 11	Dec.	74F 55	23C 13

Tsavo, Kenya	Jan.	84F 50	29C 10	May	72F 52	22C 11	Sept.	76F 47	24C 8
	Feb.	84F 51	29C 11	June	70F 48	21C 9	Oct.	80F 51	27C 11
	Mar.	81F 53	27C 12	July	69F 49	21C 9	Nov.	81F 51	27C 11
	Apr.	77F 57	25C 14	Aug.	72F 48	22C 9	Dec.	81F 50	27C 10

Arusha, Tanzania	Jan.	84F 50	29C 10	May	72F 52	22C 11	Sept.	76F 47	24C 8
	Feb.	84F 51	29C 11	June	70F 48	21C 9	Oct.	80F 51	27C 11
	Mar.	81F 53	27C 12	July	69F 49	21C 9	Nov.	81F 51	27C 11
	Apr.	77F 57	25C 14	Aug.	72F 48	22C 9	Dec.	81F 50	27C 10

Dar es Salaam, Tanzania	Jan.	87F 77	31C 25	May	85F 71	29C 22	Sept.	83F 67	28C 19
	Feb.	88F 77	31C 25	June	84F 68	29C 20	Oct.	85F 69	29C 21
	Mar.	88F 75	31C 24	July	83F 66	28C 19	Nov.	86F 72	30C 22
	Apr.	86F 73	30C 23	Aug.	83F 66	28C 19	Dec.	87F 75	31C 24

Victoria, Seychelles	Jan.	86F 71	30C 21	May	85F 72	29C 22	Sept.	81F 72	27C 22
	Feb.	87F 71	31C 22	June	83F 72	28C 22	Oct.	83F 71	28C 22
	Mar.	87F 73	31C 23	July	79F 72	26C 22	Nov.	85F 71	29C 22
	Apr.	87F 72	31C 22	Aug.	80F 71	27C 22	Dec.	85F 71	29C 22

Festivals and Seasonal Events

The Easter Safari Rally and December 12, Independence Day, are the top annual events. In addition, fishing festivals are held on the coast between November and January. More information is available from the **Kenya Tourist Office** (424 Madison Ave., New York, NY 10017, tel. 212/486–1300).

Jan.: International Bill Fish Competition, Malindi.
Feb.: Mtwapa Off-shore Power Boat Race, Mtwapa, Malindi.

Feb.: Mombasa Fishing Festival, Mombasa.
Easter weekend: The Safari Rally, sponsored by Kenya Safari Rally Ltd., is the country's biggest sporting event.
June 1: Madaraka Day, anniversary of self-government.
Mid-June: Nakuru Agricultural Show.
Late Aug.: Mombasa Agricultural Show.
Late Sept.: Nairobi International Show.
Oct. 20: Kenyatta Day, anniversary of the arrest of the late president, Jomo Kenyatta, by the British.
Nov.: Malindi Sea Festival.
Dec. 12: Independence (Jamhuri) Day, anniversary of the day Kenya became independent in 1963.
Public holidays are New Year's Day, Good Friday, Easter Monday, Labor Day (May 1), Madaraka Day, Kenyatta Day and Jamhuri Day.

What to Pack

Be sure you have the essential documents, of course—passport with valid visa (for U.S. citizens), tickets, traveler's checks, credit cards, and driver's license (whether you plan to drive or not). Don't overload yourself. You can usually get clothes washed and pressed in Kenya unless you're on a frantic, whistle-stop tour. Take one fairly large suitcase, which can be left in the base hotel, and a smaller bag for short safaris. Bring lightweight, drip-dry casual wear, not necessarily the Hollywood-style khakis festooned with epaulets and button-down pockets, but the clothes you feel comfortable wearing on a summer day back home. The basics should include several sets of jeans, slacks, or culottes; shirts and blouses, both short-sleeved and long-sleeved to protect against insect bites; a sweater or two; sturdy walking shoes or ankle boots, sneakers, and shoes to wear in the evening; and good sunglasses and a sun hat. You'll also need an umbrella and a jacket or sweater for evenings. If you're going to the forest lodges in the Kenya highlands, you'll need a set of heavier clothes, including wool or corduroy slacks and a thick sweater. It can get very cold at night, even in Nairobi. You'll also need sports clothes, depending on your plans to swim, fish, golf, or mountain climb.

Generally, no one pays much attention to what you wear in Kenya, except on the coast, where topless sunbathing is verboten and there is a large Muslim population. You can dress casually as long as you don't look outrageous or indecent. For sunbathing or swimming at the coast you need at least a minimal bikini and some sort of cover-up. The traditional Swahili sarongs are ideal: *kikois* and *kangas* and a white, flowing, neck-to-ankle gown called a *kanzu*. At the elegant hotels, you may want to dress up in the evening for a dinner-dance or disco. Guests often wear jacket and tie or cocktail dresses, but casual clothes are perfectly acceptable. Pack all the toiletries and cosmetics you'll need; they're expensive in Kenya. Also take oils and lotions and any prescription medicines you might need. Bring a camera, film, binoculars for spotting animals, and an adaptor if you're packing an electrical appliance such as a shaver or hair dryer.

A few extras we always find useful are: pocket packs of tissues or moist towelettes; transparent tape; a utility jackknife with a corkscrew; a small flashlight; zip-close plastic bags; and a pocket calculator.

Taking Money Abroad

Traveler's checks and major U.S. credit cards are accepted in Nairobi, Mombasa, and the safari lodges. You'll need cash to spend in small towns and in many smaller restaurants and shops. For safety and convenience, it's always best to take traveler's checks. The most recognized traveler's checks are American Express, Barclays, Thomas Cook, and those issued through major commercial banks, such as Citibank and Bank of America. Some banks issue the checks free to established customers, but most charge a 1% commission. Since lodgings must be paid for in dollars (or other foreign currency), and you will always be given your change in Shillings, which cannot be exported, you'll find the local currency accumulating. For this reason and to avoid having to cash a large check at the end of your trip, buy your traveler's checks in small denominations. Remember to take with you the addresses of offices where you can get refunds for lost or stolen traveler's checks. In Kenya, banks are the best places to change money. Hotels, safari lodges, and private exchange firms offer significantly lower exchange rates.

Getting Money from Home

There are at least two ways to get money from home while you're traveling in Kenya: (1) Have it sent through a large commercial bank with a branch in Kenya; however, if you don't have an account with the bank, you'll have to go through your own bank, a slower and more expensive process. (2) If you have a gold or platinum American Express card with a line of credit, you can get a cash advance on your account in the American Express offices in Nairobi or Mombasa. If you have an American Express card, you can also cash a personal check or a counter check at an American Express office for up to $1,000; $200 will be in cash and $800 in traveler's checks. There is a 1% commission on the traveler's checks. In an emergency, you can place a collect call to Global Assist of American Express (tel. 202/783-7474). Western Union does not wire money to Kenya.

Kenyan Currency

The units of currency in Kenya are shillings (Kshs.) and cents. The bills are in 200, 100, 50, 20, 10, and 5 shilling denominations. The 5 shilling bill is being phased out in favor of the 5 shilling coin. Coins are 5 shillings, 1 shilling and 50, 10, and 5 cents. The Kenyan shilling is a floating currency with no fixed exchange rate. At press time, the exchange rate was Kshs. 24 = U.S. $1, Kshs. 19.5 = Canadian $1, and Kshs. 74 = £1.

What It Will Cost

Prices in Kenya have increased with the growth of tourism in recent years. Also, much of the travel within Kenya is away from the big cities, so hotels and lodges have the added costs of bringing food and comfort into the bush. If you are on a budget and plan to see a lot of the country in two weeks, $2,000, after airfare, should get you to a game park and down to the coast for three or four nights. Kenya can also be extremely expensive.

Restaurants are still a good bargain by Western standards, even the expensive ones. Spirits and wines, which are imported, tend to be costly. A local wine from Naivasha is a good buy. Hairdressing, facials and massage are reasonable, of good quality, and usually available through hotels and such health lodges as Ol Pejeta near Mt. Kenya (hairdressing ranges from Kshs. 300 to Kshs. 500, facials are from Kshs. 200 to Kshs. 300, and massage is Kshs. 100 an hour). Baby-sitting is negotiable from Kshs. 30 an hour.

Air charters are fairly expensive, but this is true around the world. Taxi fares are very negotiable; bargaining is essential before you begin your trip, unless you take one of the big, black British cabs, which are metered and preferred. Car rental is a daily rate with the mileage rate on top of it, and it can be expensive for a long journey. Weekly rates are available and are reasonable, especially if several people share the cost. Always get car insurance. The train from Nairobi to Mombasa is a good value for the money at Kshs. 340 per person (first-class, one-way), with added charges for bedding and meals.

Sample Prices 1992 Cup of coffee, Kshs. 15; bottle of beer, Kshs. 25; Coca Cola, Kshs. 12; ham sandwich, Kshs. 80; taxi from airport to city center, Kshs. 350; shuttle bus to city center, Kshs. 150.

Passports and Visas

Americans U.S. citizens need a valid passport and a visa to enter Kenya. Visas can be obtained from the Kenyan Consulates in New York and Los Angeles, or the Embassy of Kenya (2249 R St., NW, Washington, D.C. 20008, tel. 202/387-6101). Visas are valid for six months. If you plan to travel to Uganda or Tanzania, you will need a visitor's pass to get back into Kenya; this can be obtained on arrival in Kenya if you have your visa. Anyone who has spent more than 90 days in the Republic of South Africa will need a visa, regardless of nationality. To renew your Kenya visa, go to Nyayo House on Posta Road in Nairobi.

To obtain a new passport, apply in person; renewals can be obtained in person or by mail. First-time applicants should apply to one of the 13 U.S. Passport Agency offices at least five weeks in advance of their departure date. In addition, local county courthouses, many state and probate courts, and some post offices accept passport applications. Necessary documents include: (1) a completed passport application (Form DSP-11); (2) proof of citizenship (certified birth certificate issued by the Hall of Records of your state of birth, or naturalization papers); (3) proof of identity (valid driver's license or state, military or student ID card with your photograph and signature); (4) two recent, identical, two-inch-square photographs (black-and-white or color head shot with white or off-white background); and (5) a $65 application fee for a 10-year passport (those under 18 pay $40 for a five-year passport). You may pay with a check, money order or exact cash amount; no change is given. Passports are mailed to you in about 10–15 working days. To renew your passport by mail, you'll need to send a completed Form DSP-82, two recent, identical passport photographs, your current passport (if less than 12 years old and issued after your 16th birthday), and a check or money order for $55.

Canadians All Canadian citizens need a valid passport to enter Kenya. No visa is necessary unless you have spent more than 90 days in

South Africa. To acquire a passport, send a completed application (available at any post office or passport office) to the Bureau of Passports (Suite 215, West Tower, Guy Favreau Complex, 200 René Lévesque Blvd. WI, Montreal, Quebec H2Z 1X4). Include $25, two photographs, a guarantor, and proof of Canadian citizenship. Applications can be made in person at regional passport offices in many locations, including Edmonton, Halifax, Montreal, Toronto, Vancouver, and Winnipeg. Passports are valid for five years and are nonrenewable.

Customs and Duties

On Arrival
Kenya
You can bring in any personal items for your stay, including cameras and any quantity of film, although videos and radios might create minor problems with customs officials. Anyone age 16 or older can also import up to 200 cigarettes or 50 cigars, one bottle of alcohol, and a half liter of perfume. However, do not bring ammunition or weapons—even imitation or toy guns—unless you have permits from the Firearms Bureau of the Kenya Police. Game hunting in Kenya is banned, except for limited bird-shooting with a license. Other items that are strictly forbidden include drugs, unless they're obviously prescription; pornography; pets; and agricultural or horticultural materials. Finally, don't tempt fate by bringing in too much jewelry or cash—use traveler's checks.

On Departure
U.S. Residents
You may bring home duty-free up to $400 of foreign goods, as long as you have been out of the country for at least 48 hours and you haven't made an international trip in past 30 days. Each member of the family is entitled to the same exemption, regardless of age, and exemptions may be pooled. For the next $1,000 worth of goods, a flat 10% rate is assessed; above $1,400, duties vary with the merchandise. Included in the allowances for travelers 21 or older are one liter of alcohol, 100 cigars (non-Cuban), and 200 cigarettes. Only one bottle of perfume trademarked in the United States may be imported. There is no duty on antiques or works of art over 100 years old. Anything exceeding these limits will be taxed at the port of entry and may be taxed additionally in the traveler's home state. Gifts valued at under $50 may be mailed duty-free to friends or relatives at home, but you may not send more than one package per day to a single addressee, and packages may not include perfumes costing more than $5, tobacco, or liquor.

Since Kenya is considered a "developing" country, it is listed under the U.S. Customs Service's GSP (Generalized System of Preferences) program. The program provides for the duty-free importation of a wide range of developing countries' products that would otherwise be subject to duties. Many items, including arts and handicrafts, are listed. You still will need to declare the items and state their value and use, but it won't count against your $400 limit. For a list of exempt items, contact your nearest Customs office, or write to the U.S. Customs Service, Box 7407, Washington, DC 20044. Articles and countries listed in the program are subject to change.

Canadian Residents
Exemptions for returning Canadian range from $20 to $300, depending on length of stay out of the country. For the $300 exemption, you must have been out of the country for one week. In any given year, you are only allowed one $300 exemption. You may bring in duty-free up to 50 cigars, 200 cigarettes, 2.2

pounds of tobacoo, and 40 ounces of liquor, provided these are declared in writing to customs on arrival and accompany you in hand or check-through baggage. Personal gifts should be mailed labeled "Unsolicited Gift—Value under $40." Obtain a copy of the Canadian Customs brochure *I Declare* for further details.

Kenya is a signatory to CITES (Convention on International Trade in Endangered Species of Wild Fauna and Flora), a treaty that prohibits trade in ivory, rhino horn, skins, and all other wildlife relics. The government spearheaded the drive to have the elephant declared a species in danger of extinction under CITES Appendix 1 and has strengthened its antipoaching efforts. If you get caught either buying or selling wildlife curios, it means almost certain prosecution in a country that recognizes wildlife as probably its greatest natural resource and is ultrasensitive about its reputation for protecting it. The export of live animals, birds, and reptiles, as well as diamonds, gold, and gemstones (such as the rubies found recently in Tsavo), is also banned, except where the dealer is a licensed professional.

An international departure airport tax of U.S. $20 per person is payable in foreign currency; the domestic departure tax is Kshs. 50.

Currency Regulations. Kenya has a strict Exchange Control Act: You cannot import or export Kenyan shillings, and you cannot deal outside the banks or major hotels and travel agents that are licensed to exchange foreign cash or traveler's checks. Shops are not authorized to exchange cash, and black-market dealings can get you in trouble. There is no limit to the amount of hard currency that can be brought into the country, but it has to be declared on arrival with evidence required on departure of how the money was changed. The customs and currency check on the way out is fairly rigorous. Officials often ask for proof of how you changed your dollars. Keep your receipts of all cash exchanges, and have your currency form stamped by the payor. Visitors are required to have in convertible foreign currency a sufficient sum for their own subsistence while in Kenya. The minimum in convertible foreign currency that must be shown to an immigration officer on request is the equivalent of U.S. $250. This rule does not apply to visitors on all-inclusive prepaid package tours. Note: All prices mentioned in this guide are in U.S. dollars unless indicated otherwise.

Traveling with Film

If your camera is new, shoot and develop a few rolls of film before leaving home to make sure you're using it correctly. Invest $10 in a skylight filter to protect your lens and reduce haze and glare. X-rays can spoil film, so never pack unprocessed film in check-in luggage. Instead, carry undeveloped film with you through security and have it inspected by hand. (Keeping it all together in a plastic bag helps expedite the process.) Inspectors at American airports are required by law to honor requests for hand inspection. Keeping your film in a lead-laminated bag is another way to protect it from low-dosage X-rays.

Bring an ample supply of film, as it is expensive in this part of the world. You will probably take more photos than anticipated, so allow yourself at least two rolls a day. Pack lens tissue to wipe off safari dust. Remember that the sun is more intense this close to the equator, so you need a faster exposure, especially on the coast or the plains of game reserves. Don't store film in the sun or in the glove compartment of the car or on the shelf under the rear window, because the heat will spoil it.

In East Africa you should not photograph people without their consent, not even villagers in remote areas. To gain permission, smile, wave your camera around, and offer a few shillings in payment for a photo. The Masai in particular are likely to demand considerable fees—$10 or more per picture. Offer them Kshs. 10 instead, or find someone less demanding. You are asking for trouble if you photograph airports, government buildings, military camps or vehicles or harbors.

Language

English and Swahili are Kenya's official languages. In addition, more than 40 other languages are spoken. Many Kenyans are multilingual, learning their local language as they grow up and picking up Swahili, English, and sometimes other European languages as they progress through school. English is spoken in the cities and national parks, but Swahili is prevalent in rural areas and at the coast, where it originated as an African language with Arabic influence. Swahili is relatively easy to pronounce, and verbs need not be conjugated for people to understand your meaning. A simple phrase book comes in handy, especially for negotiating prices. Throughout Kenya and Tanzania, locals greatly appreciate any efforts to communicate in Swahili or local languages (*see* Swahili Vocabulary).

Staying Healthy

Malaria is common throughout most of Kenya except at high altitudes. Begin taking daily antimalaria pills two weeks before your departure; continue throughout the trip and for two weeks after returning home. There is no consensus on the best medication, so ask your doctor for a recommendation. The favored dosage is two paludrine a day and one chloroquin a week (paludrine is available only in the United Kingdom). A new drug, Lariam, is said to be more effective against all strains of malaria, but it is difficult to find, and costs about $8 a tablet. Taking the pills does not eliminate all risk, however, since drug-resistant strains of malaria have spread in recent years. It is recommended that you carry a dose of antimalarial tablets with you at all times to take at the first sign of fever in case you can't reach medical care within 24 hours. Take plenty of insect repellent and a flying-insect spray containing pyrethrum. Burning mosquito coils at night also helps ward off mosquitoes; coils can be purchased all over the country. If you're camping or staying at lodges, find out if mosquito nets are provided. If not, take your own or buy a net in Nairobi.

Other diseases prevalent in Kenya include polio, cholera, typhoid fever, viral hepatitis, and meningitis, but the risk is not high unless you spend time off the beaten tourist track. The Kenyan Embassy in Washington recommends inoculation for yellow fever, meningitis, and cholera; vaccination certificates for these diseases are required of visitors entering Kenya from infected areas. (Local health departments in the United States maintain lists of these areas.) An antitetanus/typhoid shot also is not a bad idea. And if you plan to eat foods purchased from street vendors, be sure to get a gamma globulin shot as a precaution against hepatitis. Do not swim or wade in still waters or ponds, because many of these waters are infested with schistosomiasis, also called bilharzia, a disease carried by flukes that live in freshwater snails and burrow into animal or human skin to reproduce in the bloodstream.

There is also a high incidence of sexually transmitted diseases, including a penicillin-resistant form of gonorrhea. Central and East African countries are known to have an extremely high incidence of acquired immune deficiency syndrome (AIDS) among heterosexuals. The major modes of transmission are sexual intercourse, contaminated syringes, and blood transfusions, and heterosexuals are especially at risk in Africa. Women can pass the disease to men as well as men to women, and African women are dying of AIDS at the same rate as men. One report said that 60% of the prostitutes in the cities are infected. Western doctors, when consulted about safe sex in Kenya, always recommend abstinence. Casual sexual intercourse of any kind, even with precautions, will always put you at risk.

Regarding other modes of transmission, you should never allow yourself to be injected with an unsterilized needle. Avoid transfusions of blood. Nairobi Hospital does screen blood samples for the virus, but such screening facilities are rare in Africa. If you need or expect to need a transfusion, try to consult your embassy. Western embassies keep lists of recommended doctors, hospitals, and screened blood donors. However, there is no reason why AIDS should prevent you from visiting Africa.

Finally, take care in what you eat. As in any developing country, stay away from raw salads and fruit unless you can peel it yourself. Avoid unpasteurized milk and milk products and food that has been left out in the heat or exposed to flies.

Always protect yourself against the equatorial sun with sunscreens, hats, and sunglasses. It is generally hotter than you think it is.

Ask whether your tour operator subscribes to the **Flying Doctors' Society of Africa.** If not, buy a membership before leaving on safari. This charitable service will evacuate you by air in case of emergency and has ready access to safe blood. Contact the Flying Doctors (Box 30125, Nairobi, Kenya, tel. 2/336886 or 2/501301).

Africa Air Rescue (Box 41766, Nairobi, tel. 2/337030 or 337306) offers two types of coverage: air evacuation and basic hospital coverage within Kenya is Kshs. 4,380; if medical care cannot be provided in Kenya, overseas evacuation is Kshs. 4,745.

The **International Association for Medical Assistance to Travelers** (IAMAT) is a worldwide association offering a list of approved physicians and clinics whose training meets British and American standards. For a list of physicians and clinics in East Africa that are part of this network, contact IAMAT (417 Center St., Lewiston, NY 14092, tel. 716/754–4883; in Canada: 40 Regal Rd., Guelph, Ont. N1K 1B5; in Europe: 57 Voirets 1212 Grand-Lancy-Geneva, Switzerland). Membership is free.

Insurance

Travelers may seek insurance coverage in four areas: health and accident, loss of luggage, trip cancellation, and flight. Your first step is to review your existing health and homeowner policies. Some health-insurance plans cover health expenses incurred while traveling; some major medical plans cover emergency transportation; and some homeowner policies cover the theft of luggage.

Health and Accident
Several companies offer coverage designed to supplement existing health insurance for travelers:

Carefree Travel Insurance (Box 310, 120 Mineola Blvd., Mineola, NY 11501, tel. 516/294–0220 or 800/323–3149) provides coverage for emergency medical evacuation, accidental death, and dismemberment. It also offers 24-hour medical phone advice.
International SOS Assistance (Box 11568, Philadelphia, PA 19116, tel. 215/244–1500 or 800/523–8930), a medical assistance company, provides emergency evacuation services, worldwide medical referrals, and optional medical insurance.
Travel Guard International, underwritten by Transamerica Occidental Life Companies (1145 Clark St., Stevens Point, WI 54481, tel. 715/345–0505 or 800/782–5151), offers emergency evacuation services and reimbursement for medical expenses, with no deductibles or daily limits.
Wallach and Co., Inc., (Box 480, Middleburg, VA 22117–0480, tel. 703/687–3166 or 800/237–6615) offers comprehensive medical coverage, including emergency evacuation services worldwide.

Trip-Cancellation and Flight Insurance
Consider purchasing trip-cancellation insurance if you are traveling on a promotional or discounted ticket that does not allow changes or cancellations. You are then covered if an emergency causes you to cancel or postpone your trip. Trip-cancellation insurance is usually included in combination travel insurance packages available from most tour operators, travel agents, and insurance agents.

Flight insurance, which covers passengers in the case of death or dismemberment, is often included in the price of a ticket when paid for with American Express, MasterCard, or other major credit cards.

For information on insurance for lost luggage, *see* Airlines and Airports, below.

Car Rentals

You can rent cars in Mombasa or Nairobi, although each city can be managed on foot during the day or by taxi at night. If you are driving longer distances and decide to rent a car, it's best to make arrangements before leaving home. You won't save by waiting until you arrive in Kenya, and you may find that the type of car you want is not available at the last minute. Rental companies usually charge according to the exchange rate of the dollar at the time the car is returned or the credit card payment is processed. If you're flying into Nairobi and planning to spend a few days there, you can save money by picking up your car the day you leave the city. If you're arriving at and departing from different airports, ask for a one-way rental with no return fees. However, prices are usually higher for one-way rentals, and a number of companies don't allow them. Be prepared to pay more for cars with automatic transmission, since they are less available. Rental rates vary widely, depending on the car's size and model, number of days you are renting, insurance coverage, and special drop-off fees that are sometimes imposed. In most cases, rates quoted include unlimited free mileage and standard liability protection. The following costs are not included: personal accident insurance; collision damage waiver (CDW), which reduces your deductible payment if you have an accident; and gasoline. There are no local taxes on car rentals. You should get as comprehensive an insurance policy as possible. Make sure your rental car can be locked. Companies that serve Kenya include: **Avis** (tel. 800/331–1084 in the U.S., 800/879–2847 in Canada); **Hertz** (tel. 800/654–3001 in the U.S., 800/654–3131 in AK and HI, 800/263–0600 in Canada); and **National** (tel. 800/328–4567). Other car-rental firms are listed in the entertainment newspaper *What's On.*

Traveling with Children

Getting to Kenya with children, especially small ones, can be tiring, but it's worth the effort: Kenya is one of the best places for children. They are allowed almost everywhere, although there are certain lodges and tented camps that do not welcome children under 10 years old. Many restaurants even have children's menus. If you are traveling with very small children, bring along disposable diapers, formula, and baby bottles. Cleanliness can be maintained, even in the bush, and many lodges and tented camps can sterilize bottles. Malarial prophylactics are essential for children; check with your family doctor. Cots are available in hotels and lodges, but bring your own mosquito netting for small children, just in case it's not provided.

Publications *Family Travel Times* is an eight- to 12-page newsletter published 10 times a year by TWYCH (45 W. 18th St., 7th floor, New York, NY 10011). A subscription costs $35 and includes access to back issues and a weekly opportunity to call for specific advice.

Organizations **American Institute for Foreign Study** (AIFS, 102 Greenwich Ave., Greenwich, CT 06830, tel. 203/869–9090) offers a family vacation program in Kenya specifically designed for parents and children.

Rascals in Paradise Family Vacation (Adventure Express Travel, 650 Fifth St., Suite 505, San Francisco, CA 94107, tel. 800/U-RASCAL) organizes tours accompanied by a preschool teacher (depending on the age of the children) and emphasizes cultural exchanges with visits to schools and villages in Kenya.

Getting There On international flights, children under age two not occupying a seat pay 10% of adult fare. Various discounts apply to children age two to 12. Reserve a seat behind the bulkhead of the plane, which offers more legroom and can usually accommodate a bassinet (supplied by the airline). At the same time, inquire about special children's meals or snacks offered by most airlines. (See "TWYCH's Airline Guide" in the February 1990 and 1992 issues of *Family Travel Times* for a rundown on children's services offered by 46 airlines.) Ask the airline in advance if you can bring aboard your child's car seat. For the booklet "Child/Infant Safety Seats Acceptable for Use in Aircraft," write the

Federal Aviation Administration (APA–200, 800 Independence Ave. SW, Washington, DC 20591, tel. 202/267–3479).

Hints for Disabled Travelers

There are few facilities for handicapped travelers, although many lodges and tented camps are wheelchair-accessible, as are some minibuses. Toilets for the disabled and ramps, though, are rare. For further information, contact one of the following organizations or the Kenya tourist bureau on arrival:

The **Information Center for Individuals with Disabilities** (27–43 Wormwood St., First floor, Boston, MA 02210, tel. 617/727–5540) offers useful problem-solving assistance, including lists of travel agencies that specialize in tours for the disabled. The cost is $5 for anyone outside Massachusetts.

Moss Rehabilitation Hospital Travel Information Service (1200 W Tabor Rd., Philadelphia, PA 19141–3099, tel. 215/456–9600; TDD 215/456–9602) provides information on tourist sights, transportation, and accommodations in destinations around the world. The fee is $5 for up to three destinations. Allow one month for delivery.

Mobility International USA (Box 3551, Eugene, OR 97403, tel. 503/343–1284 voice and TDD [Telecommunications Device for the Deaf]) has information and referral services on accommodations, organized study, etc., for members. Annual membership is $20.

The **Society for the Advancement of Travel for the Handicapped** (SATH, 347 5th Ave., Suite 610, New York, NY 10016, tel. 212/447–7284) offers access information. Annual membership costs $45, or $25 for senior citizens and students. Send $2 and a self-addressed envelope for information on a specific destination.

The Itinerary (Box 2012, Bayonne, NJ 07002, tel. 201/858–3400) is a bimonthly travel magazine for the disabled. A subscription costs $10 a year.

Hints for Older Travelers

High altitude may affect the older traveler, bad headaches being the most frequent symptom. Diarrhea hits all ages, so pack a supply of Immodium capsules. Similarly, the dry heat and sun can be overpowering. Try to drink fluids constantly, and don't forget to wear a good sun hat wherever you go. When organizing your trip, be careful that it is not too hectic. It is best to contact companies in the United States and go with a package group. An East African safari appeals to recent retirees with ample energy and time, and many tour operators cater to the over-60 market (*see* Tour Groups, above). For more information, contact the following organizations:

The **American Association of Retired Persons** (AARP, 601 E St. NW, Washington, DC 20049, tel. 202/434–2277) offers discounts on hotels, airfare, car rentals, and sightseeing through the *Purchase Privilege Program*. The AARP also arranges group tours to Kenya through **RFD, Inc.** (4801 West 110th St., Overland Park, KS 66211, tel. 800/365–5358). AARP members must be age 50 or older. Annual dues are $5 per person or per couple.

When using an AARP or other identification card, ask for a reduced hotel rate when you call to make your reservation, not when you check out. At restaurants, show your card to the maître d' before you're seated, since discounts may be limited to certain menus, days, or hours. When renting a car, remember that economy cars, priced at promotional rates, may cost less than cars available with your ID card.

Travel Industry and Disabled Exchange (TIDE, 5435 Donna Ave., Tarzana, CA 91356, tel. 818/368–5648) is an industry-based organization with a $15 annual membership fee. Members receive a quarterly newsletter and information on travel agencies and tours.

National Council of Senior Citizens (1331 F St. NW, Washington, DC 20004, tel. 202/347–8800) is a nonprofit advocacy group with some 5,000 local clubs across the country. Annual membership is $12 per person or couple. Members receive a monthly newspaper with travel information and an ID card for reduced-rate hotels and car rentals.

Mature Outlook (6001 N. Clark St., Chicago, IL 60660, tel. 800/336–6330), a subsidiary of Sears, Roebuck & Co., is a travel club for people over age 50, with hotel and motel discounts, tours, a bimonthly magazine and newsletter, and access to a network of more than 11,000 travel clubs. Annual membership is $9.95 per couple. Instant membership is available at participating Holiday Inns.

Travel Tips for Senior Citizens (U.S. Department of State Publication 8970, revised Sept. 1987) is available for $1 from the Superintendent of Documents, U.S. Government Printing Office, Washington, DC 20402.

Further Reading

Literature | Many people admit that they visited Kenya because they were intrigued by Karen Blixen's *Out of Africa*. The best view of Africa aloft is Beryl Markham's *West with the Night*. Elspeth Huxley's *Flame Trees of Thika* also documents an era when East Africa was the new frontier for Europeans. You may find you enjoy reading Hemingway's short stories again while on safari, especially *The Green Hills of Africa*, *The Snows of Kilimanjaro*, or *The Short Happy Life of Francis MacComber*. Hemingway did some of his writing (and fishing) from Mahé island in Seychelles. The letters of Karen Blixen (alias Isak Dinesen) have also been published, as has a wonderful biography written by Judith Thurman.

Natural History | *Elephant Memories* by Cynthia Moss details her research at Amboseli National Park; somewhat more dated, but equally interesting, is Iain and Oria Douglas-Hamilton's *Among the Elephants*, which covers their research at Lake Manyara and their romance and life together on safari. *Run, Rhino, Run* by Chryssee and Esmond Bradley Martin is both a beautiful photo book and a serious, well-researched text on trade in rhino products. John G. Williams compiled an excellent *Guide to the Birds of East Africa*, now in paperback. Jonathan Kingdon's *Island Africa* is a richly illustrated reference for the evolutionary changes within the continent.

Human Origins and Archaeology | Louis Leakey wrote two autobiographies; *White African* is recommended. Mary Leakey's account of her life and discoveries in Tanzania, *Disclosing the Past,* is worthwhile. Robert Ardrey's *African Genesis* offers an interesting view of our ancestors; John Reader's *Missing Links* covers research in Europe, Asia, as well as Africa. *Lamu,* by Usam Ghaidan, a book on Swahili architecture and culture, is available locally. Delta Willis reports on discoveries in Kenya and Tanzania, with profiles of Richard Leakey and Stephen Jay Gould, in *The Hominid Gang.*

Explorations Peter Matthiessen has written two excellent books on the people and places of East Africa: *The Tree Where Man Was Born,* and *Sand Rivers. New Yorker* writer Alex Shoumatoff chronicles a common malady in *African Madness.* Charles Miller's *The Lunatic Express* is the best book on the building of the railroad from Mombasa to Lake Victoria, with a chilling account of the man-eating lions of Tsavo. Timothy Cornfield's book *The Wilderness Guardian,* published in Nairobi, offers detailed advice for independent travelers and is especially good for medical emergencies and bush smarts. The *Diaries of Richard Meinertzhagen* and *The Legendary Grogan,* by Leda Farrant, tell of a time before there were roads.

Photography Jonathan Scott's photographs and drawings dazzle in *The Marsh Lions,* with text by Brian Jackman, about a particular pride in the Masai Mara. Peter Beard's books *The End of the Game* and *Eyelids of Morning* are graphic displays of a contagious attachment to the endangered wildlife. The Sierra Club book *Isak Dinesen's Africa* is available in Nairobi, as are a series of coffee-table books on Africa by Camerapix.

Politics Jomo Kenyatta's *Facing Mt. Kenya* tells about the injustices that led to the "Mau Mau" movement for independence. *The Africans,* by *Los Angeles Times* reporter David Lamb, is a contemporary account of emerging Africa.

Choosing a Safari

By D. H. Doelker

D. H. Doelker is president of D. H. Doelker Inc., which publishes The Safari Rating Report, *an annual evaluation of East African safaris.*

The amount of time spent in preparation, cost involved, and expectations often makes a safari to Kenya or Tanzania the trip of a lifetime. Most visitors begin ordering brochures and talking with travel agents at least six months in advance. It is possible to plan your own itinerary or hire a Nairobi based guide, but most first-time visitors turn to a safari specialist. At present there are at least 50 United States–represented tour operators offering more than 300 regularly scheduled safaris to East Africa. The chart that follows lists some that book tours through travel agents and shows the type of tours they run. The cost of a safari, including international airfare, can range from $2,000 for a 10-day "spade and bush" or "no frills" lodge safari, in the nonpeak season, to $15,000 for a private two-week top-of-the-line mobile-tented excursion. Outlined below are many of the factors to consider when selecting a safari that best fits your budget and your expectations.

Type of Safari

The most popular type of safari is the non-escorted "lodge/ minivan" tour of major game parks and game reserves, with accommodations in lodges. The van holds up to nine passengers, it's driven by a local driver/guide, and access to a window or both window and roof hatch may not be guaranteed. The safari

Group Tour Operators Represented in the United States:

Scheduled Tours Bookable Through Travel Agents

Tour Operator		Lodge/Minivan	Deluxe Wing	Deluxe Mobile Tenting	Standard Mobile Tenting	Spade and Bush	Type of Activity/Interest
Abercrombie & Kent	800/323-7308	●	●	●	●		C,G,W
Adventure Center	800/227-8747	●	●		●	●	C,G,W
African Classics	800/828-8222	●	●	●			C,G,W
African Explorers	800/631-5650			●		●	G
African Travel	800/722-7755	●		●			G
Africatours	800/235-3692	●					G
Big Five Tours	800/445-7002; in NY 516/424-2036	●		●	●		C,G
Big Five Expeditions	800/445-7002; in NY 516/424-2036				●		G,W
Born Free Safaris	800/372-3274	●		●	●		C,G
Borton Overseas	800/843-0602	●	●	●		●	C,G,W
Brendan Tours	800/421-8446	●					G
Caravan Tours	800/621-8338	●					G
Collette Tours	800/832-4656	●					G
David Anderson's	800/733-1789	●	●				G
Encounter Overland	800/227-8747				●	●	C,G
Equitours Horseback	800/545-0019				●		R
Explore	800/227-8747					●	C,G,W
Foxglove Safaris	800/437-4807	●					G
GEO Expeditions	800/351-5041				●		G
Guerba Expeditions	800/227-8747					●	C,W
Global Safaris	800/548-3140	●					G
Harm safaris	800/541-0077	●		●			G

Company	Phone	Activities
International Expeditions	800/622-4734	C,G
Journey's	800/255-8735	C,G,W
Maupintours	800/225-4266	G
Micato Safaris	800/642-2861	G
Mountain Travel-Sobek	800/227-2384	C,W
Overseas Adventure Travel	800/221-0814	C,G,W
Olson Travelworld	800/421-2255	G
Park East	800/223-6078; in NY 212/765-4870	G
Questers Nature Tours	800/468-8668	G
Safaricentre	800/223-6046	C,G,W
Safari Trails	800/234-2585	G
Safaritravel	800/882-5537; in NY 212/888-7596	G,H
Safariworld	800/366-0505	G
Special Expeditions	800/762-0003	G
Sue's Safaris	800/541-2011	G
Tracks	800/225-2380	G,W
Travcoa	800/992-2003	G
Tusker Trail & Safari	213/399-1683	G,W
TWA Getaway	800/438-2929	G
United Touring (UTI)	800/223-6486	C,G,H,W
Unitours	800/621-0557	G
Wilderness Travel	800/247-6700	C,G,W
Wildland Adventures	800/345-4453	C,G,W
Wildlife Safaris	800/221-8118	G

C=Climbing Safari   G=General (Safari Vehicle/low activity)   H=Honeymoon   R=Horseback Safari   W= Walking Safari lodge is the closest thing to a hotel in the bush, and some lodges have the added advantage of overlooking salt licks or water holes for 24-hour game viewing. While less expensive, this type of safari may involve hours of driving over poorly maintained roads. Park East's Safari Adventure, Micato's Livingstone (some flights included), and Safariworld's Explorer are good-quality examples of this type.

The next most popular, but more expensive, type is the wing safari. (An example is Big Five Tours' On Golden Wings safari.) At least 70% of travel between the game parks is by light aircraft. They land on the strip next to such luxury permanent tented camps as Governor's/Little Governor's, Kichwa Tembo, Mara Intrepids, and Siana Springs in the Masai Mara and Larsen's or Samburu Intrepids in the Samburu reserve. En suite bathrooms with flush toilets and showers with hot running water are standard. Most game drives are in Land/Range Rovers, access to both a window and a roof hatch is often guaranteed, and you may have a tour escort or naturalist in addition to your driver/guide. Because these camps are in the more isolated areas animals often wander between the tents at night and fewer tourists are seen.

"Mobile tenting" safaris range from deluxe mobile to standard mobile to spade-and-bush. Usually you will see the fewest tourists on these types of safari.

The deluxe mobile safari (such as Abercrombie & Kent's Hemingway, Out of Africa programs, and Born Free's Classic Tented safari) generally provides large tents, 24 × 7 feet wide by 7 feet tall, with full-size spring beds, linen changed daily, en suite private "safari" bathrooms, four-wheel-drive Land Cruisers with guaranteed access to a roof hatch, a naturalist escort/guide, gourmet meals, a full bar, a staff/client ratio of at least two to one, and a group size of 12 or under.

The standard mobile safari (such as Wilderness Travel's East African Wildlife Safari)provides smaller two-person tents, cots that are close to the ground with a thin foam pad, linen, and a pillow, shared toilet/bath tents (up to six people), minivans or Rovers for game drives and for transport between most parks, and as many as 18 passengers per group.

The spade-and-bush safaris (such as some OAT, Guerba, and Tracks programs) use 16-passenger overland Bedford trucks; participants pitch their own tents and help cook; bring their own sleeping bags, linen, pillows, sheets, and personal-hygiene items; sponge-bathe from a basin, and find a favorite bush when nature calls.

Size of Group

Inquire about the number of participants and the ratio of participants to guides and staff. Generally the fewer people on the trip, the more personal attention you will get and the more you will pay.

Location

Some of the questions you should ask include, Which game parks or reserves does the tour cover? In what order? How much time is spent in each? What's the tourist density of each park? The season and migration patterns are factors in what animals you can expect to see in what parks and their densities (*see* Chapter 3: Kenya and Tanzania Parks and Game Reserves).

Accommodation

None of the lodges or hotels in East Africa can be considered the equivalent of a five star hotel, but you will be pampered in top camps like Kichwa Tembo in the Masai Mara. Meals, service, and amenities vary from lodge to lodge, but there are some constants you should investigate. Ask about sleeping arrangements. Very few lodges have double beds because most lodges cater to groups. The typical room has two twin beds (sometimes bolted to the wall to sabotage intimacy). Ask about the bathroom and shower facilities. Is there hot running water? Or does the shower consist of a bucket and a pull cord? Are bathrooms en suite or in a separate tent? The emphasis at most game lodges is on game drives, but ask if the property has a pool. At the Mt. Kenya Safari club and at some other non–game viewing locations there are golf courses, horseback riding and tennis. Air-conditioning is rare in game lodges but is often found in Nairobi and coastal hotels.

Meals

What meals are included? Is there an extra charge for bottled water and alcoholic drinks? Meals at the lodges or camps are served at a set time, the menu is usually standard British/Continental fare, and portions are bounteous. If you have any special dietary requirements, ask if special meals can be arranged.

Hospitality

Does the tour include a safari briefing? Will there be a tour escort in addition to a driver/guide? Welcome and farewell dinners or cocktails are sometimes part of the more expensive safaris.

Transportation

What kind of vehicle does the operator use? Game drives can take place in anything from a four-wheel custom Land Cruiser seating a maximum of five to large trucks that carry 18 people and their luggage, camping equipment, food, and water. Minivans almost always have a roof hatch from which you can photograph wildlife, but you will be guaranteed access to the hatch at all times only if there are six or fewer people in a nine-seater minivan. Access to the window is assured if the group is no larger than seven people. Some tours provide complimentary soft drinks and snacks in the van; others let you work up an appetite. A library and binoculars in the van can be immeasurably helpful for identifying wildlife.

Drivers/Guides

Who will be guiding the trip? What is the guide's background? Most tour companies use local drivers who double as guides. Special-interest tour operators or museum-sponsored tours provide their own guide/naturalist. In an effort to please their camera-toting clients, drivers will often leave the track to find game. This is an ecologically unsound practice and should not be encouraged. It is better to bring a long lens and plenty of patience.

Other Factors

If the tour includes flying, consider what percentage of time is spent flying versus driving. Is the tour operator a member of the Flying Doctors Society? The United States Tour Operators Association? Are park entrance fees or tips/service charges included? Are cities, museums, or other points of interest part of the itinerary? Does the tour include hot-air ballooning or other special sightseeing flights? Are the departures guaranteed? Are day rooms included when international flights connecting in Europe have a layover of more than four hours or when flights leave Nairobi late at night? Does the tour operator have inexpensive trip-cancellation insurance? What's the single-supplement cost? To pinpoint the safaris offering the best quality and value in your price range, you might want to order the Safari Ratings Report, which ranks these safaris according to some 30 criteria. It is published annually by D. H. Doelker, Inc. (tel. 212/888–7596 or 800/882–5537).

Arriving and Departing

From North America by Plane

Airlines and Airports KLM (tel. 800/777–5553) flies to Nairobi from New York Sunday, Wednesday and Friday, but you must change planes in Amsterdam. Kenya's two international airports are **Jomo Kenyatta,** about 10 miles southeast of Nairobi, and **Moi International,** ten miles from Mombasa. Most charter in-country flights leave from **Wilson Airport** in Nairobi.

Flying Time The trip to Nairobi lasts 16 hours (about eight hours from New York to Amsterdam, and about eight hours from Amsterdam to Nairobi). Actual travel time may be 19 hours, with a three-hour layover.

Discount Flights APEX tickets are certainly worth a thorough investigation for such a long trip. Flying to Kenya is still far more expensive from Canada or the United States than from the United Kingdom. Package deals that include hotel and some extras with the flight may be cheaper, but unless you like being part of a large group, they tend to be disappointing.

Enjoying the Flight The New York–Nairobi flight is a long one, and with a stop-off on the way, you are bound to be tired at the end. Most of the journey is at night, and the cabin staff makes special efforts to let passengers sleep. To avoid dehydration, drink one glass of water per hour in flight, and limit your intake of alcohol and caffeine.

Luggage Regulations You may check two bags at 70 lbs. (32 kilos) each on the New York to Nairobi flight. The maximum length plus width of the first bag is 62″ and on the second bag, 55″. You are also allowed one piece of carry-on luggage with maximum dimensions of 45″. Baggage allowances vary slightly among airlines, so check with the carrier or your travel agent before departure.

Lost Luggage and Luggage Insurance   Luggage can get lost on the way to Nairobi, so be on guard. All suitcases should be locked; carry any valuables with you. It's a good idea to put your home address and telephone number as well as the address and phone number of your hotel on all your luggage. Purchase travel insurance; it's worth it. Make sure you have a detailed list of all items in your bags in case you need to file a claim.

Airlines are responsible for lost or damaged property up to only $9.07 per pound (or $20 per kilo) for checked baggage on international flights. Coverage is up to $400 per passenger for unchecked baggage on international flights. If you're carrying valuables, either take them with you on the airplane or purchase additional insurance for lost luggage. Some airlines issue additional luggage insurance when you check in, but many do not. Hand luggage is not included. Insurance for lost, damaged, or stolen luggage is available through travel agents or directly through insurance companies. Two that issue luggage insurance at essentially the same rates are **Tele-Trip** (tel. 800/228–9792), a subsidiary of Mutual of Omaha, and **The Travelers Insurance Co.** Tele-Trip, operating with sales booths at airports, and through travel agents, insures checked luggage for up to 180 days, and for $500 to $3,000 valuation. For one to three days, the rate for a $500 valuation is $8.25; for 180 days, $100. The Travelers Insurance Co. insures checked or hand luggage for $500 to $2,000 valuation per person, also for a maximum of 180 days. Rates for one to five days for $500 valuation are $10; for 180 days, $85. For more information, write The Travelers Insurance Co. (Ticket and Travel Dept., 1 Tower Sq., Hartford, CT 06183). Both companies offer the same rates on domestic and international flights. Check the travel pages of your Sunday newspaper for the names of other companies that insure luggage. Before you go, itemize the contents of each bag in case you need to file an insurance claim. Be certain your home address is on each piece of luggage, including carry-on bags. If your luggage is stolen and later recovered, the airline must deliver the luggage to your home free of charge.

From the United Kingdom by Plane

Because Kenya was a British Protectorate until 1963, flights out of London are the most frequent and most reasonable of any European city. Both **British Airways** (tel. 071/897–5511) and **Kenya Airways** (tel. 071/409–0277) have nightly service to Nairobi, which takes 8½ hours. **Kenya Airways** has an office in New York (424 Madison Ave., tel. 212/832–8810 or 800/343–2506), where you can book a London to Nairobi flight, flights within Kenya, or from Nairobi to Tanzania and the Seychelles. The office is in the same building where you obtain your Kenya visa. The London weekly magazine **Time Out** has an extensive listing of discount flights to Kenya. Tickets are readily available on many airlines, and prices reflect the convenience of the flight (direct versus stopover, etc.). Several "bucket shops" offer cheap flights to Nairobi, among them **Trailfinders** (42–48 Earls Court Rd., tel. 071/937–5400) and **S.T.A. Travel** (74 and 86 Old Brompton Rd., tel. 071/937–9962). Many package deals that include airfare are available in the United Kingdom.

Staying in Kenya

Getting Around

By Plane   **Air Kenya** (Wilson Airport, Box 30357, Nairobi, tel. 2/501421/ 2/3, fax 2/500845), a domestic airline, operates daily scheduled flights from Nairobi to Mombasa and Malindi on the coast, as well as to the Masai Mara, Lake Turkana, Kiwayu and Lamu. About a dozen air charter firms operate out of Nairobi, Mombasa, and Malindi. Charter rates are calculated on a fairly stable per-mile rate plus a variable fuel charge, and there is a Kshs. 50 airport tax for all flights in Kenya.

Kenya Airways (Koinange St., Nairobi, tel. 29291/29271/ 332750) flies out of Jomo Kenyatta airport to Mombasa, Malindi, the Seychelles, Zanzibar, and Dar Es Salaam.

By Train   The long, slow overnight sleeper from Nairobi to Mombasa is a relaxing experience. All compartments convert to sleepers, and meals in the dining car are very reasonable. The train is not air-conditioned, but the high altitude keeps the Nairobi area cool, and the warm coastal region is not reached until early morning. Passengers generally spot wild animals before nightfall as the train crosses the Athi Plains.

The **Kenya Railways Corporation** also operates one daily train on the Nairobi-Kisumu route. It leaves Nairobi at 5:30 PM and arrives in Kisumu at 8:05 AM. It leaves Kisumu the next day at 6 PM and arrives in Nairobi at 7:30 AM.

By Taxi   Except for the black "London" cabs, few taxis in Kenya have working meters, so the price is negotiable at around 20¢ a mile. Nairobi's long-haul taxi service—**Rift Valley Province Peugeot Service**—packs as many passengers as possible into Peugeot station wagons for such destinations as Naivasha, Nakuru, Eldoret, Kitale, Kisumu, and Mombasa.

By Bus   Public bus and *matatus*—overloaded vans—serve African commuters and more adventurous tourists.

By Car   Driving in Kenya can be a hair-raising endeavor. Driving is on
Rules of the Road   the left side of the road, in the British tradition. Visiting drivers should follow the traffic laws that they know, not the example of the local daredevils. There are too few police to enforce the rules of the road, and many drivers are barely competent and drive without licenses or insurance. Vehicles are often overloaded or dilapidated. Other dangers are trailers whiplashing across the road and buses racing each other to the next passenger pickup—two abreast on a narrow road. Driving is most dangerous around Easter, when the Safari Rally is held and young drivers catch rally fever.

Road Conditions   The most serious hazard in Kenya is bad roads and bad drivers. Even poor roads can be negotiated as long as you have the appropriate vehicle for the terrain, but the thing to watch for on tarmac roads is passing on curves or hills and huge semis with several trailers that swerve and fishtail on the narrow roads. Since the roads are poorly marked for night driving, and for security reasons as well, you would be wise to avoid driving at night. You should carry food and water, extra fuel, and a flashlight. If you break down, other drivers will generally come to your aid.

Driver's Licenses A visitor between ages 23 and 70 who has held a valid driver's license for at least two years can drive in Kenya for up to 90 days. Licenses should be endorsed, however, at the nearest police station upon arrival.

For longer visits, a Kenya driver's license is issued if you present a valid driver's license, two photographs, and payment of a nominal fee. An international driver's license is also valid.

Insurance Third-party insurance is compulsory for motor vehicles in Kenya.

Fuel There are no restrictions on fuel, but it's imported and high priced—around Kshs. 12/50 a liter.

Safari Vehicles and Car Rental Numerous rental companies, including Hertz and Avis, operate in Nairobi, Mombasa, and Malindi. It's possible to shop around for deals, such as a monthly rate with unlimited mileage, among the smaller firms. You need a valid driver's license plus a hefty deposit unless you take out a collision damage waiver, which reduces your collision damage deductible. All major credit cards are accepted for car rentals. If you don't use a credit card, you'll have to pay a deposit based on estimated time and distance to be traveled.

Driving a rental car across the border between Kenya and Tanzania is illegal unless you have special permission. Drivers of private vehicles who want to cross the border need a permit from the Central Bank of Kenya for export of the fuel they have on board. There is no train or bus service between Kenya and Tanzania, although buses stop at a point near the border, where passengers can cross the border on foot and board a Tanzanian bus on the other side. There are restrictions on private flights between the two countries. It takes a week or more to obtain the necessary papers from the Ministry of Transport and Communications in Nairobi and the Directorate of Civil Aviation in Dar es Salaam.

Telephones

The country code for Kenya is 254.

Local Calls Local calls cost Kshs. 1 in Nairobi. Public telephones tend to be temperamental; it may take a few calls to complete your conversation. Make sure you have a pocketful of one shilling coins, because if you've found a phone that works, chances are there's a line of people waiting their turn to use it. Read the instructions on how to use the phone, since these tend to vary from phone to phone. To reach the local operator, dial 900. For directory information, dial 991.

International Calls International calls should be arranged through your hotel; consult a telephone directory to find out when rates are lowest. To place an international call through an operator, dial 0196 and give the name of the country and the number you want to reach. International operators speak English. Most hotels have fax and telex facilities.

Mail

Postal Rates Airmail letters cost Kshs. 11 for the first 10 grams; postcards cost Kshs. 5.

Receiving Mail You may have mail sent either to your hotel or to the American Express office on Standard Street. Check the telephone directory for the location of your post office.

Opening and Closing Times

Banks Hours are weekdays 9–2 and on the first and last Saturday of each month 9–11. Airport banks are open 24 hours.

Museums The Nairobi Museum in Nairobi is open daily 9:30–5.
The Fort Jesus Museum in Mombasa is open daily 8–6.
The Lamu Museum is open Monday–Saturday 9:30–6.

Shops Hours are from 8 or 9 until 6 (shops are usually closed from 12:30 to 2 for lunch).

Tipping

Many restaurants include a service charge on their bill. If you wish to tip the waiter, 10% of the bill should be adequate. Drivers on safari should be tipped well, especially if you have spent several days with them, and they have shown you all the animals you wanted to see. Tips for safari drivers could go as high as Kshs. 500. The recommended tip for lodge or tented-camp staff is Kshs. 20 per day per person. If you are a house guest, the same applies to private staff. You should tip fishermen who take you snorkeling at the coast; children who help push your car out of the mud; porters, maids, or bellhops at your hotel; and anyone else who has performed a small but appreciated service. Ten to 15 shillings is generally an acceptable tip.

Shopping

Clothes in Kenya tend to be expensive, and you'll find better quality at L.L. Bean or Banana Republic in the U.S. You may find you're not prepared for cold evenings in the bush, in which case you can visit **Spinner's Web**, on Kijabe Street (near the Norfolk) in Nairobi, which will have all the wool or cotton pullovers you need. **Bata,** just about the only shoe store in town, makes rugged safari boots for all ages, and they are a good bargain. If you're in the market for T-shirts, look for the Hardcore label: the shirts have Kenyan mottos across the front in brilliant colors, and they won't run when you wash them. There are several major shopping centers in Nairobi, the **Sarit Center** in Westlands, the **YaYa Center** in Lavington, and the **Karen Center,** featuring the **Siafu Gift Shop.** Beaded shoes and belts from **Kongoni** are beautiful (and not cheap), and the new **Utamadumi Craft Center** in Langata (East Bogani Rd., tel. 2/891–798) is the Bloomingdale's of the bush. Designer Yolande McIntyre's Bizaar, Bizaar (tel. 2/561–574) is the Kenya version of Victoria's Secret.

African Heritage is a world-famous emporium of African goods. **Gallery Watatu** on Standard Street displays the work of most local artists, while the **Antique's Gallery** on Kaunda Street offers heirlooms from the colonialists. If you're after good prices, browse first and return to negotiate.

Boutiques, curio shops, and *kanga* (lengths of cotton worn by African women) and *kikoi* (sarong) houses abound at the coast as well as in Nairobi. Be wary if you are hoping to buy authentic African relics such as head masks, tribal gear. These can be offered at exorbitant prices, and unless you have actually evaluated it, you may end up with an overpriced curio. Note: It is illegal to sell objects made from any part of a bird or an animal, such as elephant hair bracelets. If you are approached by anyone on the street offering such items, remember that buying them is also against the law and that you will be subject to strict fines if caught.

Bargaining Many shops have set prices, although if you are purchasing a large quantity, you will be entitled to a "discount." Vendors on the street and inside City Market curio stalls expect shoppers to bargain, so the first price they quote is anywhere from 70% to 100% more than their final price.

VAT At press time there is no VAT in Kenya, but a tax is being considered by the Kenyan Parliament. Contact the Kenya Tourist Office nearest you (*see* Government Tourist Offices, above) for the status of the VAT.

Sports and Outdoor Activities

Bird Hunting While hunting big game was banned in 1977, Kenya Wildlife officials encourage bird shooting because the birds are plentiful and the permit and license fees support conservation efforts. Seasons vary throughout the country; June through October for upland birds like guinea fowl and sand grouse; year-round for dove, pigeon, and quail; February through March for waterfowl. Bird-shooting can be organized alongside other safari activities in the Chyulu Hills, where the bird season is July-October. The cost for hunters can be as high as $400 per person per day (observers, $250 per day), and the fee includes license and area permits but not ammunition, the import license for guns, or gun rental.

Fishing
Big-Game Fishing The Kenya coast extends some 480 kilometers (298 mi), from Somalia to Tanzania. There are six principal known fishing grounds and other areas that are relatively virgin. There is no hard-and-fast season, but serious fishing begins in September and lasts until March or April. Months for billfish are October to April and also July or August, but the southeast monsoon tends to stir up the sea during this time. Some hotels close during the long rains around May and June, but this may vary from year to year. The principal game fish include barracuda, cananx cobia, dolphin (dorado), kingfish, marlin (black, Pacific blue, and striped), sailfish, shark (hammerhead, mako, and tiger), yellow-fin tuna, and wahoo.

Fishing is good all along the coast, but six resorts feature big-game-fishing hotels or clubs. These are, from north to south:

Lamu. The fishing is mainly light-tackle sport operated from Peponi's Hotel and Manda Island Lodge. Peponi's has its own private charter boat (Kshs. 7,000 per trip).

Malindi. Kenya's principal fishing competitions are organized by the Malindi Fishing Club at this developed resort in November and December. The area is noted mainly for sailfish.

Watamu. Four hotels serve this scenic area of coral cliffs, bays, and lagoons; two, including the recently renovated Hemingway's, are popular local fishing clubs.

Kilifi. The Mnarani Club, situated on the southern headland at the entrance to Kilifi Creek, is among the most luxurious and best-equipped hotel fishing clubs. The sport is good enough to keep the club open throughout the year.

Mombasa. Most hotels on the holiday beaches north of the island to Mtwapa Creek and south to Diani beach either operate fishing trips or cooperate with the largest Kenyan sports-fishing enterprise, **K-Boats,** whose rates for fully equipped and crewed trips are among the lowest in the world.

The Bahari Club, north of Mombasa island at **Kisauni** is another large specialist fishing operation. It hires out crewed boats and looks after a small fleet of craft belonging to local residents.

Shimoni. Spectacular marlin catches have been recorded here in the 500-fathom-deep Pemba Channel. The road to Shimoni has recently been tarred most of the way, and the Pemba Channel Fishing Club is becoming increasingly popular among serious local and visiting fishermen.

River Fishing Sport fishing in Kenya is largely for trout, which was introduced in the Gura River, high in the Aberdare Range, in 1905. Today, there are several good trout streams in Kenya, off the escarpments of the Great Rift Valley and in the area around Mt. Kenya, which is particularly well managed by the Fisheries Department. The rivers include the Sagana, Thego, Naro Moru, Burguret, Chania/Nyeri, and Gura, all in the Nyeri District; the Thiba, Kiringa, Rupingazi, and Nyamindi in the Kirinyaga and Embu districts; the Thiririka and Gatamaiyu in the Kiambu District; and the Chania/Murang'a, Thika, and North and South Mathioya, all in the Murang'a District. Parts of North and South Mathioya are private rivers for fly-fishing clubs. The Moruny River in the West Pokot district lies in the Cherang'ani Hills and has about 50 kilometers (31 mi) of water for rainbow and brown trout.

Before fishing on any private stream, obtain the landowner's permission. There is a bag limit of six fish a day.

There also are strict regulations on the use of live bait and artificial flies. Trout fishing has no closed season, but individual rivers may be closed for short periods at the discretion of the Fisheries Department, the department's Trout Hatchery at Kiganjo, or the Mountain National Parks' warden at Mweiga.

The Fisheries Department and local private associations operate a number of simple but attractive and inexpensive fishing camps at the most popular trout streams in the Mt. Kenya and Aberdares areas. These include Thiba, Thego, Kimakia, and Koiwa. It is not normally possible to book the camps in advance. The system is first come, first served. The camps are often full over weekends and public holidays, but at other times, visiting anglers are fairly sure to find accommodations. Visitors need to be fully equipped for camping, providing their own food, bedding, and so forth. Camp rates are nominal, at around the equivalent of $7.50 per person per day. The stay at any one camp is limited to 14 days.

A trout-fishing lodge is operated at Ngobit on Mt. Kenya. It has six doubles, each with separate bathroom, that rent for around $45 per double per day.

Most hotels in the vicinity of trout streams anywhere in the country will either organize fishing themselves or advise fully equipped visiting anglers on local conditions, locations, and regulations.

Lake Fishing   Four lakes in Kenya are well known and important for sport fishing: Naivasha, Victoria, Baringo, and Turkana. Apart from the famous black bass of Naivasha and the giant Nile perch at Turkana, numerous coarse fish abound in most of Kenya's lakes and in the more sluggish rivers. At all the large lakes, there is an established commercial-fishing industry. The most important of the coarse fish is the delicious tilapia. Now sold in Europe as a delicacy, tilapia are the most common of Kenya's freshwater fish. Other lake and river coarse fish include various species of barbus, lungfish, catfish, elephant snout fish, and eels, which may be taken in lakes such as Victoria, Turkana, and Baringo and in the lower reaches of nearly all the rivers.

Mountain Climbing   The prime attraction for rock climbers and mountaineers is Mt. Kenya, a long-extinct volcano straddling the equator and rising 5,199 meters (17,058 feet) above sea level. Weather conditions, a wide range of faces, and thin air make this mountain a challenge. Although the other mountain parks of Kenya lack the high standard of technical climbing afforded by Mt. Kenya, they do offer other attractions.

The Aberdare National Park has a well-developed road system for scenic high-altitude motoring, excellent trout fishing, game viewing, and high-altitude walking and scrambling trails in the northern sector. The Aberdares feature a number of spectacular waterfalls and two well-known game lodges.

Mt. Elgon offers trout fishing, game-viewing, and moorland motoring and walking. It also contains caves regularly visited by herds of elephants in search of salt.

The Marsabit National Park rises like a forested island from the surrounding arid plains. It supports a healthy population of elephants and has several hidden lakes.

Other mountains include the Mathews range, the Ndotos, Kulal, and Ololokwe, the Cherang'anis, the Chyulus, and the Taita Hills. They are generally undeveloped for tourism but offer interesting challenges to the more adventurous visitor.

The Mountain Club of Kenya has opened a number of areas for technical rock-climbing, including Lukenya Hell's Gate, Ndeyia, Nzaui, and Soitpus. Guidebooks are available from the club. Each of these crags offers a particular type of technical climbing, and all share a unique Kenya flavor.

The *Guidebook to Mount Kenya and Kilimanjaro* is published by the Mountain Club of Kenya, which is also the source of Peter Robson's *Mountains of Kenya*, an excellent and comprehensive guidebook. Contact The Warden, Mountain National Parks (Box 22, Nyeri), or The Secretary, The Mountain Club of Kenya (Box 45741, Nairobi).

Boating   If you don't care for snorkeling or windsurfing, a trip in a glass-bottom boat will let you see all the wonders of the coastal reef. Most coast lodges charter fishing boats and dhows, and Kiwayu features nighttime canoe trips. Hotels will arrange the trip for you or you can set up a time with one of the many fishermen along the coast. The price should be negotiated in advance and depends on the number in your group. Cruises are available on

Lakes Victoria, Baringo and Naivasha, and the *African Queen* travels on the Tana River Delta (Tana Delta Ltd., Box 24988, Nairobi, tel. 882 826; fax 882 939).

Car Racing The Safari Rally, which occurs each year at Easter, seems to take over the whole country for two or three weeks; everyone has rally fever. You can take a picnic lunch, pick any grassy spot with a good view, and watch some of the fastest and best rally drivers in the world pass in front of your nose. The best viewpoint is along Mombasa Road.

Horse Racing Nairobi's Ngong Racecourse is open almost every Sunday, and information about the race to be held will be in the newspapers that morning. You can place small bets of about Kshs. 40 each. The race course is very attractive, with a new restaurant called The Jockey Club.

Soccer "Football," as it is called in Kenya, is a national passion, and, if a match is scheduled, you can be sure that Nairobi's Nyayo Stadium will be packed. Kenya has some very skillful players, and soccer enthusiasts should not miss a chance to enjoy one of the weekly matches. Information is given in the newspapers on the day of the game.

Beaches

The reef off coastal Kenya creates exceptionally calm waters, which are not the best place for surfing. Windsurfers and sailing buffs enjoy winds that pick up in the afternoon and thanks to the reef, shark-free waters. Only at breaks in the reef, as at Kilifi Creek, is there any need to worry about sharks.

Mombasa's beaches are fairly narrow stretches of white sand, with palm trees separating sand from grass. Most of the coastline is devoted to tourism, except where mangrove swamps cling to the shoreline. Still, there is enough beach for privacy, especially in places like Kiwayu and the island of Lamu, where you can walk along the shore for hours.

There is a glut of restaurants, or "beach bars," along the Mombasa shore. Mattress and umbrella rentals are usually confined to hotel beaches. Most hotels also have pools just off the beach. Nudism, which offends the Muslims living in the area, is greatly discouraged. You can rent Windsurfers, sailboats, catamarans, and snorkel gear from almost every hotel along Diani and Nyali, the two main strips of beach as well as from Peponi's in Lamu and Kiwayu, and Hemingway's near Malindi.

Dining

African food is simple and cheap. Western visitors may find it plain, but it is certainly worth trying. The staple food is maize milled into flour and then boiled into *ugali*, a stiff maize porridge eaten as an accompaniment to beef or chicken stew. A hash with beans, potatoes and other vegetables is called *irio*, while the same dish with unmashed ingredients is *githeri*. A steamed banana porridge called *matoke*, home-grown rice, and a starchy pasta are also popular locally.

Asian cuisine in Nairobi includes Chinese, Indian, Korean, and Middle Eastern. Of these, Indian restaurants are generally best, occasionally rising to gourmet standards.

The final category, international—albeit with a pronounced English bias—is generally good. Ingredients are excellent, and a wide variety is available. Prices are low if the ingredients are not imported. Filet beef comes at around $2 a pound, as does venison—a haunch of impala or Thompson's gazelle—with everything else costing less. This includes a range of superb pork products and excellent lamb and mutton.

The best freshwater fish are the indigenous tilapia and farmed trout. Black bass and Nile perch are good with a curry or Portuguese sauce. Seafish are excellent, especially rock cod and parrot fish. Shellfish is usually available, though it is by no means abundant. Watch for jumbo prawns, small crabs—only occasionally available—and spiny lobster and langoustine, of which only the tail is edible. Try an explosive dish called *prawns pili pili*. This is best with tiger prawns—magnificent monsters weighing up to a quarter of a pound each. The pili pili butter, which gives them their name, is made with some or all of the following ingredients: butter, red chilies, garlic, lime juice, grated coconut, fresh coriander, paprika, and a little chili powder. For dedicated gourmets, the mini-oysters at Mia Creek above Mombasa are highly recommended.

Most varieties of fruit and vegetables are grown in Kenya, except for a few that are stubbornly temperate, such as cherries. But avocadoes, asparagus, artichokes, young green beans, and pineapple, mangoes, and *paw-paw* (papaya) abound.

The quality and cost of restaurant food vary enormously, but meals at the main hotels and city restaurants are not expensive by U.S. and European standards. Prices at a luxury hotel in Nairobi might run U.S. $7 per person for a Continental breakfast, $14 for lunch, and $20 for dinner without wine. A meal at an outstanding restaurant in Mombasa (the Tamarind, for example), might run $30 for a three-course dinner without wine. These are likely to be top-of-the-range prices. A three-course meal at a moderate restaurant can cost about $10 per person and an all-you-can-eat buffet, about $6.

Nairobi restaurants cover a wide range from superb nouvelle cuisine at the Ibis Grill in the historical Norfolk Hotel to genuine African cooking in the back streets of town (take a taxi). At the Kariokor Market try barbecued goat or chicken served with the ubiquitous *ugali* and delicious *sukuma wiki* (similar to Southern collard greens).

Most tourists on the coast eat at hotels, where the food ranges from adequate to first class. In international cuisine, restaurants along the coast are not always up to Nairobi standards, but they are good enough.

Mombasa and the coast—north and south—also feature scores of small hotel cafés, scruffy diners, shop-front delicatessens (African, Arab and Swahili), as well as stalls and individual enterprises that offer goat meat kebabs and corn or cassava roasted over *jikos* (charcoal stoves). The Indian *samosa*, a spicy envelope of papadum pastry and ground meat or vegetable filling, and *chapatis*, a thin skillet bread, are common throughout Kenya. The local beers—Tusker or White Cap—are good with any meal. Kenya also has a growing wine industry, with varieties produced from grapes grown at Lake Naivasha. Imported wine is expensive due to duties and taxes. One of Kenya's more than 30 exotic fruit juices may be the most refreshing drink.

For dessert there is a vast range of Indian sweetmeats, ice cream, and delicious halvah. To complete the meal, try a chew and a spit of betel leaves, a stimulant weed called *miraa*.

"Up-country" or northern restaurants tend to be basic African and Asian eateries, but small town hotels, game lodges, and tented camps often offer excellent, reasonably priced food. In the bush or on safari the meals include a full English breakfast, a large and varied cold table for lunch, and Continental cuisine in three courses for dinner. Indeed, the evening meal at the safari lodges is usually solid British fare a succulent roast, three vegetables, and a rich dessert.

Lodging

There are four main types of accommodation in Kenya: hotels, lodges, tented camps, and self-catering accommodations.

Hotels Hotels can be luxurious (the Mount Kenya Safari Club offers sunken bathtubs) or spartan. Many of the major hotel chains are represented in Nairobi and Mombasa: Inter-Continental, Hilton, and Serenas, with some elegant old establishments like the Norfolk and the New Stanley. There are a number of clean, perfectly adequate hotels for families or people on a tight budget. These offer special family rates, family mealtimes, and an army of baby-sitters on hand at all times. Then there are accommodations strictly for the adventurous, such as mosques and hotels frequented by trans-African truck drivers.

Most hotel prices cover the room only, with all food costing extra, but if you are on a package deal food will probably be included. Hotel prices can range from $250 per person to under $25. All luxury hotel rooms have their own bathroom. In moderate hotels, tourists should request private baths.

Lodges Usually away from the cities, these offer total accommodation, including breakfast, lunch, tea, and dinner, since you stay put once you are there. Again, they range in luxury and cost, and prices fluctuate with the season.

Tented Camps These may be permanent large tents with concrete floors and adjoining bathrooms or they may be a camping spot where you or your guide sets up a temporary camp. Prices vary widely, and it is advisable to consult with a tour operator or experienced camper, such as Tor Allan Safaris, beforehand. We list several campsites in Kenya, but you must have some bush smarts to camp without a guide.

Self-Catering In addition to the larger-than-life hotels lining the north and south coasts of Mombasa, there are beach houses, apartments, and maisonettes available for rent. These usually come with a cook and maid and offer the chance to feel at home in Kenya. Some of the complexes have pools, tennis courts, and Windsurfer and boat rentals. Tour agents in Nairobi have lists of houses and apartments with photographs. Houses can be rented for as little as Kshs. 500 a day. There are also *bandas*, or small cabins, for rent in many of the national parks and reserves, including the Shimba Hills Reserve, Tsavo West, Amboseli and Olorgesailie. These are very simple spaces, with simple costs and a wood-burning barbecue outside, but they cost less than $5 a day and feature spectacular views. Inquire at the park gate or contact the Kenya Wildlife Service (Box 40241, Nairobi, tel. 891–601/7).

Ratings	Category	Cost*
	Very Expensive	over $150
	Expensive	$100–$150
	Moderate	$50–$100
	Inexpensive	under $50

*per room, double occupancy, without taxes

Credit Cards

The following credit card abbreviations are used in this book: AE, American Express; DC, Diners Club; MC, MasterCard; V, Visa.

Security

In recent months there have been reports of street crime in Nairobi, ranging from money-changing scams by people pretending to be police or public officials to grab-and-run attacks with simple robbery the motive. Tourists are advised to exercise reasonable caution: not to walk alone, to take a cab rather than walk anywhere in the city at night, and to stay away from political rallies and gatherings.

There have also been instances of attacks on tourists in game parks, particularly the Masai Mara, which should be avoided until the Warning of May 1992 is lifted. You should not camp in small groups or travel in single-vehicle safaris, and it is a good idea to register with the American embassy in Nairobi (Moi Ave. and Haile Selassie Blvd., tel. 2/334141) or the consulate in Mombasa (Nyerere Ave., tel. 11/315101).

Safaris in East Africa are exciting for the same reason that they can also be dangerous: The creatures that you see are wild. A certain complacency may develop during your safari because most animals in the reserves seem "tame," scarcely bothered when you approach in a vehicle. This is because many wild animals have learned to disregard a vehicle that poses no threat to them. They often have quite a different reaction to the human form.

Visitors may unwittingly put themselves in danger by not knowing the rules of the bush. You can't expect to become an expert on wildlife behavior overnight, and even experts with decades of experience will tell you that an animal's behavior is not always predictable. So we urge you to regard the following carefully, even if you are on a guided tour, and especially if you are traveling independently.

Rules of the Bush In most of the national parks and reserves it is forbidden to travel with an open-top vehicle or to leave your vehicle and walk about where there might be wild animals. While Africa's big cats don't normally pursue a human meal, they may simply be surprised by your sudden appearance and react to human beings. This is why sun roofs for most vehicles are designed to allow you to peek out and photograph but still give you a cover overhead. If you rent a vehicle with a canvas top that you remove you can be fined or ousted from the park.

In parks like Amboseli and the Masai Mara, where the vegetation is extremely fragile, driving off the park road is forbidden. You usually receive a listing of the park rules when you pay your entrance fee. You should adhere to them carefully, as game wardens enforce them, and a new awareness of environmental problems has created a watchdog system among visitors.

Often tourist vehicles encircle a recent kill scene, to the annoyance of big cats. You should not encourage your driver to press closer; annoyed cats will often leave and return later to move the remaining carcass to another site. Do not extend yourself out of the roof or open the door to get a better shot; under no circumstances should you climb out of the vehicle and get on the hood.

Photographers often bang the side of the vehicle or whistle to get an animal to turn their way. It's not a good idea to carry it too far, and if you're going to make a clever bleating sound like a wildebeest calf, you'd better make certain your limbs and face are not exposed; you may also endanger other people in your group. Annoyed rhino and elephants have been known to charge vehicles.

Most guides and drivers refrain from harassing the wildlife, and you should discourage anyone in your group from this. You will find it much more rewarding to sit quietly and simply watch the animals for a few minutes. The longer you stay still and whisper, allowing the animals to ignore you, the more natural behavior you are likely to see, like cubs playing, or even lions mating.

Some tourist vehicles interrupt a chase or foil a kill by crowding cheetahs or lions as they stalk their prey. Do not try to race alongside or rush toward the "scene" (or what you figure to be prey); instead view it from a distance with binoculars or through your telephoto lens. Several years ago, the number of vehicles interrupting chases became so abusive in Nairobi National Park that cheetahs became dangerously lean during the tourist season. Not only is it considered a form of harassment, but there's no way to predict which way the chase will turn; you may accidentally hit and kill one of the animals, for which you can be banned for life from the park and fined, and your driver will lose his license and his job.

Patience pays for those who have come to Africa because they appreciate wildlife, and you are much more likely to enjoy long sequences of natural behavior if you maintain a certain distance and respect. It also allows you time to study the light and anticipate that really great photograph. Otherwise your safari could turn very ugly; animals may move away or react, and wildlife officials have become increasingly strict about harassment or interference. You may think you are alone, only to find your license plate being recorded by a game warden or another visitor, who watches with binoculars from a distance. Do not take your cue from others who choose to harass; tell them to back off, and if they persist, report them to the game wardens. They are spoiling your view of Africa!

Walking Tours In a few places, like Kenya's Mathews Range, the Chyulu Hills, Naivasha's Hell's Gate, as well as the Selous Game Reserve in Tanzania, there are organized walking tours, an opportunity for a different perspective. You often see lion or leopard spoor, and certainly you will hear many of the sounds of nature. Walking tours are usually led by an English-speaking naturalist who knows how to track game and to tell you about the plants and birds you see. It should also include a gun-bearer, for there is the odd chance of surprising a rhino or buffalo who may view you as an intruder or a threat. You may laugh at the instructions given beforehand: "If a buffalo charges, climb the nearest tree!" But if you are unable to climb a tree, you should think twice before going. You may not only put yourself in danger, but you may cause an "unnecessary" killing of an animal, which in the end would mar your memories of your safari.

Most tour operators ask you to sign an insurance disclaimer before taking such a walk, relieving them of responsibility. And though thousands have been conducted without incident, you should beware of assurances that animals are usually more frightened of you and are likely to run the other way. This is true most of the time. But animals are capable of a wide variety of behavior, and you can stumble across a new mother rhino who is nervous about her calf or an animal in a mood that we would describe as "having a bad day." You may also unwittingly make the animals feel cornered. You are likely to see much and return home unscathed, and most charges are "mock" charges, meant to warn you. But don't disregard the odds of an odd encounter.

Visitors are often disbelieving when warned of buffalo or hippo attacks. Buffalo appear to be very docile creatures when viewed from a Land Rover, but they should not be mistaken for just another sort of cow. A few tourists who have meandered from lodges or camps have been killed by buffalo, unwisely assuming that they can simply go for a stroll "in the woods" after lunch. One visitor, near Kenya's Governor's Camp, was fatally pinned to a tree by a buffalo a few years ago. Most camps issue warnings; do not dismiss them.

No matter how sophisticated your lunch or the setting, remember that wild animals are often right on the edge of the camps or lodges. Some, like baboons, may seem particularly friendly, and keen for a handout. But if you approach a baboon and push your telephoto lens in its face, you may find yourself confronted with its powerful canine teeth. According to many wildlife experts, the most dangerous creature in Africa is one that is half-tame, half-wild: accustomed to certain kinds of human behavior but thrown off by an approach it finds threatening. Baboons can do a lot of damage: the best defense is to yell and back off quickly. Keep your face to the animal and turn your camera away as you back off. With some animals (like elephants or lions), throwing up your hands and shouting scares them off. Ultimately, you must signal by body language that you do not intend to pursue them further. Never tease the animals with the opportunity of a chase.

Jogging Many visitors assume that they will be able to go on their daily jog while on safari, but beyond cities like Nairobi, jogging anywhere there may be wild animals is ill-advised. It should be remembered that lions, cheetahs, and leopards are big cats, and cats like to chase things.

It is possible to walk in areas along the river or lake at certain camps, but you must always ask before doing so. Problems sometimes occur when hippos are out of the water, feeding on land. Humans can unwittingly startle a hippo by blocking the animal's path to the water, where it wants to submerge out of fear of this strange, upright ape in safari shorts. Hippos on land are much faster afoot than you might imagine; they move with enormous force, and their tusks can cause serious damage.

Swimming When it's hot, the water looks wonderful. But you should never go for a quick swim where there are hippos in a small space, such as Kenya's Mzima Springs or its tributaries. While some have done so and lived to tell about it, there is always the odd chance that you may surprise the creatures, and if they feel cornered, they are likely to attack. There are some areas, such as Lake Baringo Island Camp and Lake Turkana, where you can swim with both hippos and crocodiles, largely because there is plenty of territory, and they are normally well fed. But you should consult with the leaders at your camp about the safe areas beforehand.

Snakes and Scorpions Fears about these creatures are generally overrated, because snakes generally avoid humans and tend to flee if given the chance. Snakes have poor hearing and poor eyesight but are keenly sensitive to ground vibrations. Cobras, it is said, can detect a barefooted approach at 40 yards. You are unlikely to encounter any problems; the only snakes you may see are at the snake parks in Nairobi Museum or at Lake Baringo, where they are milked. In the Northern Frontier District, sand vipers are small, insidious aggressors, and there is the rare chance of spitting cobra or puff adder. But make a lot of noise when you proceed, especially if you are walking at night to an outdoor "long drop" (toilet); carry a flashlight; and wear your desert boots and socks. Keep your tent door zipped, and if you are camping out in the middle of nowhere, always stuff your socks inside your shoes to prevent scorpions from nestling in them. If you are traveling independently in desert regions such as the Tana River or the Northern Frontier District, carry antivenin with you or the new snake-bite kits that work off a car battery. Forget the old stories about slicing open and sucking out the wound; it's ill-advised. If you have a lesion in your mouth, you will ingest the venom. Excellent instructions for treating snake bites can be found in Chapter 11 of Timothy Cornfield's book, *The Wilderness Guardian;* published by the David Sheldrick Wildlife Appeal (Box 48177, Nairobi). You should study the snake descriptions. Of 160 known species in Africa, only 10 are lethal and common. Learn to identify any snakes that you might see before you leave: Panic never helps and hysteria often causes more damage than the bite. Know the potential, take precautions and plan sensibly for solving any problem that might emerge.

Tent Tips Most tented camps have sophisticated tents, with tightly seamed floors and doors that zip closed. Always remember to zip your doors closed when setting out on game drives or going for a meal. If you are traveling independently, it is not wise to simply plop down a couple of sleeping bags, no matter how well-used the camp area looks. It's safer to sleep inside a simple enclosure even if it's a seemingly flimsy two-person tent. (The tent contains the human scent, and its shape appears "artificial.") In areas where there are elephants, you should position the tent close to your vehicle to give the herd a stronger reason for detouring around you. When in doubt, sleep in your vehicle;

private minibuses (called Combis in East Africa) are ideal for independent travel. Don't leave garbage or food supplies out at night; the smell may attract animals, especially baboons. Don't camp in a riverbed, even if the river is bone dry and it doesn't look like rain.

The rules of the bush are complex, but the best rule of thumb is to remember that in Africa, as in all wild terrain, you are an intruder and out of your element. The more respect you have for the nature you see in Africa, the more rewarding your safari. This respect involves a sensitivity not only to wild creatures whose behavior you may not understand, but to the local people, many of whom believe (not without reason) that their soul is stolen when a photograph is taken of them.

Great Itineraries

Reefer Madness

Highlights Dhow trip to Wasini Island

Snorkeling on the reef

Seafood picnic

The Main Route This day trip is so popular that it is hard to escape the crowds, but the exotic journey by *dhow* (Arab boat), the reef, the coastline, and the food make it memorable whether the tour is full or not. The dhow accommodates about 20 people and leaves the south-coast hotels in the early morning, traveling down to Wasini Island. Snorkeling equipment is provided, and the reef is a potpourri of corals and creatures (dragonfish, Imperial angelfish, and black-and-white damselfish, to name a few). Lunch, served on Wasini under a thatched awning known as a *mbati* roof, is a set menu of fresh seafood, fruits, and chilled drinks. After lunch there is a grace period when you may explore the island or lie under the mbati canopy. The dhows get everyone back to their hotels by teatime.

Length of Trip 1 day

Transportation From the south-coast hotels, transportation is by dhow or glass-bottom boat. Or drive on the Diani road from the Likoni ferry toward Tanzania about 65 kilometers (40 miles), until you reach the Shimoni turnoff. You will then have to negotiate a price with one of the fishermen, most of whom have snorkeling gear.

Information *See* Chapter 8.

Flocks of Gold

Highlights Lake Baringo and Lake Bogoria, where more than 400 species of birds have been recorded

Lake Nakuru, with large concentrations of greater and lesser flamingos

Meru National Park, a semiarid area renowned for good birdwatching.

The Main Route Traveling north from Nairobi and making the 3½-hour journey on good roads, you arrive at the beautiful Lake Baringo Island Camp. Birds are everywhere here, and local guides can escort you on walks. If you have a few nights, Lake Bogoria, a soda lake with spouting geysers, is another fine spot for birds, particularly flamingos.

Heading back down to Nakuru, about an hour and a half from Baringo on the same road, you can spend the day observing the greater and lesser flamingos that keep Lake Nakuru's shoreline pink.

The following day, a scenic route around the back of the Aberdares will bring you to Nanyuki and beyond into Meru. The next day, a trip around Meru National Park can bring some Western-world surprises, since many migratory birds from Europe favor the lush pockets of the park.

Length of Trip 3–5 days

Transportation The roads are good throughout this trip, and it is possible to do the whole thing in a rental car. Consult a travel agent in Nairobi.

Information *See* Chapters 5 and 7.

Arabic Heritage

Highlights Touring Lamu, Mombasa, and Zanzibar

Voyages by dhow

Beautiful beaches and coral reefs for snorkeling

The Main Route This tour of Kenya's coast covers the ancient Swahili culture—a combination of Arabic and African influences that resulted in the Swahili language—and traditional Islamic villages. It begins in Lamu, where the streets are narrow and women wear the traditional *boui-boui* black veils. Visit the Lamu Museum and the renovated Fort in the center of town, and the dhow-building village of Matadoni. There are beautiful beaches at Kipugani, Kiwayu island, and a short walk from Peponi's, where deep-sea fishing can also be arranged.

From Lamu, fly to Mombasa and sample the wonderful cuisine at the Tamarind, which has dhow cruises. Tour the renovated Fort Jesus Museum at Mombasa harbor, where you can see the big dhows in port.

From Mombasa, fly to Zanzibar, and explore historic Stonetown, where the streets are also narrow and a cathedral was built over the old slave market. Visit the outdoor market and the renovated City Hall. Take a van to the traditional fishing village of Bwejuu and stay at a bed and breakfast, like the Palm Beach Inn or the Mnemba Club, with beach cottages on a private tropical atoll just off the northeast coast.

Length of Trip 5 days

Transportation Lamu, Mombasa, and Zanzibar are best reached by air, but some cruise ships can stop at all three ports. Vans for the trip to the Zanzibar coast can be at the Africa Club. Any agent can arrange this tour for you.

Information *See* Chapters 8 and 9.

Walk on the Wild Side

Highlights The Yatta Plateau

Walk of about 96 kilometers (60 mi) along the Tsavo River

One night in a lodge in Amboseli

The Main Route Head southeast from Nairobi on the Mombasa road (a good tarmac road) for about 200 kilometers (120 mi). You turn off at Mtito Andei and follow a dirt track until you come to the river crossing that takes you to Tsavo Safari Camp. The Yatta Plateau looms above you, and one night at this tranquil tented camp gets you ready for nights under the stars.

The following morning you continue down the same road to the Tsavo gate entrance to Tsavo West National Park. The next six to seven days are spent walking along the river's edge at a rate of 16 kilometers (10 mi) a day. The spectacular colors of the flora, fauna, and birdlife contrast with the dry bush. Mt. Kilimanjaro is ahead of you. At Mzima Springs you stop for one night of rest in a lodge and then take a trip through Amboseli National Park on the way back to Nairobi.

Length of Trip 5–10 days

Transportation Safari operators use four-wheel-drive vehicles.

Information *See* Tsavo and Amboseli National Parks in Kenya and Tanzania Parks and Reserves, Chapter 3.

The Sky Is Not the Limit

Highlights Luxury tented camp

Game drives

Visit to a Masai village

Early morning ride in hot-air balloon

The Main Route It's not everyone's idea of a safari, but then again it's not in everyone's budget. A number of safari companies offer deluxe accommodation in the bush (Governor's Camp, Little Governor's, Kichwa Tembo, and Intrepid's are first-class permanent tented camps; Abercrombie & Kent and Ker and Downey offer old-style tented camping at their exclusive campsites). Good food, good wines, game drives through the rich grasslands of the Masai Mara, and an early morning hot-air balloon flight over the plains make up this memorable safari. Visits to nearby Masai *manyattas* (villages) are possible, where you can purchase beadwork done by the women.

Length of Trip 3–5 days

Transportation Roads to the Masai Mara are in poor condition, and it is advisable to fly. Transportation within the game park is in vehicles supplied by the camp.

Information *See* Masai Mara Game Reserve in Chapter 3. *Note:* At press time the Masai Mara was considered a security risk. Consult with tour operators or the Kenya Wildlife Service before making plans.

Hemingway Revisited

Highlights Ol Donyo Wuas with views of Mt. Kilimanjaro

Shimba Hills National Reserve adjacent to Diani Beach, Mombasa

Snorkeling on the reef off Diani Beach

Deep-sea fishing at Watamu

Shopping and browsing in Mombasa

The overnight train to Nairobi

The Main Route Hemingway made many safaris to Amboseli and immortalized it with such stories as "The Snows of Kilimanjaro." From Nairobi, you travel over beautiful flat grasslands enroute to Ol Donyo Wuas. Allow a couple of days here for horseback riding among herds of zebra and giraffe, and walking tours at sunset, before moving on to the Shimba Hills Reserve. The hills are famous for roan antelope, and the new lodge, which is built on stilts, is a good spot for night game-watching. The next two days are spent on the shores of Diani Beach, where there is access to the reef for snorkeling, glass-bottom boating, and windsurfing.

A few hours' drive on good roads up the coast brings you to Watamu, where deep-sea-fishing enthusiasts may cast their rods. Back to Nyali Beach, on Mombasa's north shore, muscle-sore fishermen may take in the sun or head into Mombasa town and visit the spice market. The overnight train to Nairobi takes 14 hours. Cool breezes fill the compartment while you enjoy an ample breakfast as you cross the Athi plains to Nairobi.

Length of Trip 5–10 days

Transportation Many Nairobi tour operators can arrange the trip, or you can drive yourself, since the roads are good. You can leave the car in Mombasa if you take the train, but arrange this with the rental agent ahead of time.

Information *See* Amboseli and Shimba Hills Game Reserve (Chapter 3) and Mombasa and the Kenya Coast (Chapters 8 and 9).

2 Portraits of East Africa

Aloft Over Africa

By Beryl Markham

Best known in Kenya as a professional horse trainer, aviatrix Beryl Markham was the first person to fly the Atlantic solo from east to west in 1936. This essay is excerpted from her West with the Night. *She died in 1986 at the age of 83 in virtual poverty.*

How is it possible to bring order out of memory? I should like to begin at the beginning, patiently, like a weaver at his loom. I should like to say, "This is the place to start; there can be no other."

But there are a hundred places to start for there are a hundred names—Mwanza, Serengeti, Nungwe, Molo, Nakuru. There are easily 100 names, and I can begin best by choosing one of them—not because it is first nor of any importance in a wildly adventurous sense, but because here it happens to be, turned uppermost in my logbook. After all, I am no weaver. Weavers create. This is remembrance—revisitation; and names are keys that open corridors no longer fresh in the mind, but nonetheless familiar in the heart.

So the name shall be Nungwe—as good as any other—entered like this in the log, lending reality, if not order, to memory:

Date—16/6/35
Type Aircraft—Avro Avian
Markings—VP—KAN
Journey—Nairobi to Nungwe
Time—3 hrs. 40 mins.

After that comes, Pilot: Self; and Remarks—of which there were none.

But there might have been.

Nungwe may be dead and forgotten now. It was barely alive when I went there in 1935. It lay west and south of Nairobi on the southernmost rim of Lake Victoria Nyanza, no more than a starveling outpost of grubby huts, and that only because a weary and discouraged prospector one day saw a speck of gold clinging to the mud on the heel of his boot. He lifted the speck with the tip of his hunting knife and stared at it until it grew in his imagination from a tiny, rusty grain to a nugget, and from a nugget to a fabulous stake.

His name eludes the memory, but he was not a secretive man. In a little while Nungwe, which had been no more than a word, was both a Mecca and a mirage, so that other adventurers like himself discounted the burning heat of the country, the malaria, the blackwater, the utter lack of communications except by foot through forest trails, and went there with shovels and picks and quinine and tinned food and high hopes, and began to dig.

I never knew what their digging got them, if it got them anything, because, when I set my small biplane down on the narrow runway they had hacked out of the bush, it was night and there were fires of oil-soaked rags burning in bent chunks of tin to guide my landing.

There's not much to be seen in light like that—some dark upturned faces impassive and patient, half-raised arms beckoning, the shadow of a dog slouching between the flares. I remember these things and the men who greeted me at Nungwe. But I took off again after dawn without learning anything about the success of their operations or the wealth of their mine.

It wasn't that they meant to keep those things concealed; it was just that they had other things to think about that night, and none of them had to do with gold.

I had been working out of Nairobi as a free-lance pilot with the Muthaiga Country Club as my headquarters. Even in 1935 it wasn't easy to get a plane in East Africa and it was almost impossible to get very far across country without one. There were roads, of course, leading in a dozen directions out of Nairobi. They started out boldly enough, but grew narrow and rough after a few miles and dwindled into the rock-studded hills, or lost themselves in a morass of red muram mud or black cotton soil, in the flat country and the valleys. On a map they look sturdy and incapable of deceit, but to have ventured from Nairobi south toward Machakos or Magadi in anything less formidable than a moderately powered John Deere tractor was optimistic to the point of sheer whimsy, and the road to the Anglo-Egyptian Sudan, north and west through Naivasha, called "practicable" in the dry season, had, when I last used it after a mild rain, an adhesive quality equal to that of the most prized black treacle.

This minor defect, coupled with the fact that thousands of miles of papyrus swamp and deep desert lie between Naivasha and Khartoum, had been almost flippantly overlooked by a Government road commission which had caused the erection, near Naivasha, of an impressive and beautiful signpost reading:

To JUBA—KHARTOUM—CAIRO—

I have never known whether this questionable encouragement to the casual traveller was only the result of well-meant wishful thinking or whether some official cursed with a depraved and sadistic humor had found an outlet for it after years of repression in a muggy Nairobi office. In any case, there the sign stood, like a beacon, daring all and sundry to proceed (not even with caution) toward what was almost sure to be neither Khartoum nor Cairo, but a Slough of Despond more tangible than, but at least as hopeless as, Mr. Bunyan's.

This was, of course, an exception. The more travelled roads were good and often paved for a short distance, but once the pavement ended, an airplane, if one were at hand, could save hours of weary toil behind the wheel of a lurching car—provided the driver were skillful enough to keep it lurching at all. My plane, though only a two-seater, was busy most of the time in spite of competition from the then barely budding East African—not to say the full-blown Wilson—Airways.

Nairobi itself was busy and growing—gateway to a still new country, a big country, an almost unknown country. In less than 30 years the town had sprung from a collection of corrugated iron shacks serving the spindly Uganda Railway to a sprawling welter of British, Boers, Indians, Somalis, Abyssinians, natives from all over Africa and a dozen other places.

Today its Indian Bazaar alone covers several acres; its hotels, its government offices, its racecourse, and its churches are imposing evidence that modern times and methods have at last caught up with East Africa. But the core of it is still raw and hardly softened at all by the weighty hand of British officialdom. Business goes on, banks flourish, automobiles purr importantly up and down Government Road, and shopgirls and clerks think, act, and live about as they do in any modern settlement of 30-odd thousand in any country anywhere.

The town lies snugly against the Athi Plains at the foot of the rolling Kikuyu Hills, looking north to Mount Kenya and south to Kilimanjaro in Tanganyika. It is a counting house in the wilderness—a place of shillings and pounds and land sales and trade, extraordinary successes and extraordinary failures. Its shops sell whatever you need to buy. Farms and coffee plantations surround it for more than a hundred miles and goods trains and lorries supply its markets with produce daily.

But what is a hundred miles in a country so big?

Beyond are villages still sleeping in the forests, on the great reservations—villages peopled with human beings only vaguely aware that the even course of their racial life may somehow be endangered by the persistent and irresistible pressure of the White man.

But white men's wars are fought on the edges of Africa—you can carry a machine gun 300 miles inland from the sea and you are still on the edge of it. Since Carthage, and before, men have hacked and scrabbled for permanent footholds along the coasts and in the deserts and on the mountains, and where these footholds have been secured, the right to hold them has been the cause of endless dispute and bloodshed.

Competitors in conquest have overlooked the vital soul of Africa herself, from which emanates the true resistance to conquest. The soul is not dead, but silent, the wisdom not lacking, but of such simplicity as to be counted nonexistent in the tinker's mind of modern civilization. Africa is of an ancient age, and the blood of many of her peoples is as venerable and as chaste as truth. What upstart race, sprung from some recent, callow century to arm itself with steel and boastfulness, can match in purity the blood of a single Masai Murani, whose heritage may have stemmed not far from Eden? It is not the weed that is corrupt; roots of the weed sucked first life from the genesis of earth and hold the essence of it still. Always the weed returns; the cultured plant retreats before it. Racial purity, true aristocracy, devolves not from edict, nor from rote, but from the preservation of kinship with the elemental forces and purposes of life, whose understanding is not farther beyond the mind of a native shepherd than beyond the cultured fumblings of a mortar-board intelligence.

Whatever happens, armies will continue to rumble, colonies may change masters, and in the face of it all Africa lies, and will lie, like a great, wisely somnolent giant unmolested by the noisy drum-rolling of bickering empires. It is not only a land; it is an entity born of one man's hope and another man's fancy.

So there are many Africas. There are as many Africas as there are books about Africa—and as many books about it as you could read in a leisurely lifetime. Whoever writes a new one can afford a certain complacency in the knowledge that his is a new picture agreeing with no one else's, but likely to be haughtily disagreed with by all those who believe in some other Africa. Doctor Livingstone's Africa was a pretty dark one. There have been a lot of Africas since that, some darker, some bright, most of them full of animals and pygmies, and a few mildly hysterical about the weather, the jungle, and the trials of safari.

All of these books, or at least as many of them as I have read, are accurate in their various portrayals of Africa—not my Africa, perhaps, nor that of an early settler, nor of a veteran of the Boer War, nor of an American millionaire who went there and shot zebra and lion, but of an Africa true to each writer of each book. Being thus all things to all authors, it follows, I suppose, that Africa must be all things to all readers.

Africa is mystic; it is wild; it is a sweltering inferno; it is a photographer's paradise, a hunter's Valhalla, an escapist's Utopia. It is what you will, and it withstands all interpretations. It is the last vestige of a dead world or the cradle of a shiny new one. To a lot of people, as to myself, it is just "home." It is all these things but one thing—it is never dull.

From the time I arrived in British East Africa at the indifferent age of four and went through the barefoot stage of early youth hunting wild pig with the Nandi, later training racehorses for a living, and still later scouting Tanganyika and the waterless bush country between the Tana and Athi rivers, by airplane, for elephant, I remained so happily provincial I was unable to discuss the boredom of being alive with any intelligence until I had gone to London and lived there a year. Boredom, like hookworm, is endemic.

I have lifted my plane from the Nairobi airport for perhaps a thousand flights and I have never felt her wheels glide from the earth into the air without knowing the uncertainty and the exhilaration of firstborn adventure.

The call that took me to Nungwe came about one o'clock in the morning relayed from Muthaiga Country Club to my small cottage in the eucalyptus grove nearby.

It was a brief message asking that a cylinder of oxygen be flown to the settlement at once for the treatment of a gold miner near death with a lung disease. The appeal was signed with a name I had never heard, and I remember thinking that there was a kind of pathetic optimism about its having been sent at all, because the only way it could have reached me was through the telegraph station at Mwanza—itself a hundred miles by native runner from Nungwe. During the two or three days the message had been on its way, a man in need of oxygen must either have died or shown a superhuman determination to live.

So far as I know I was the only professional woman pilot in Africa at that time. I had no free-lance competition in Kenya, man or woman, and such messages, or at least others not always so urgent or melancholy, were frequent enough to keep me occupied most days and far too many nights.

Night flying over charted country by the aid of instruments and radio guidance can still be a lonely business, but to fly in unbroken darkness without even the cold companionship of a pair of earphones or the knowledge that somewhere ahead are lights and life and a well-marked airport is something more than just lonely. It is at times unreal to the point where the existence of other people seems not even a reasonable probability. The hills, the forests, the rocks, and the plains are one with the darkness, and the darkness is infinite. The earth is no more your planet than is a distant star—if a star is shining; the plane is your planet and you are its sole inhabitant.

Before such a flight it was this anticipation of aloneness more than any thought of physical danger that used to haunt me a little and make me wonder sometimes if mine was the most wonderful job in the world after all. I always concluded that lonely or not it was still free from the curse of boredom.

Under ordinary circumstances I should have been at the aerodrome ready to take off for Nungwe in less than half an hour, but instead I found myself confronted with a problem much too difficult to solve while still half asleep and at one o'clock in the morning. It was one of those problems that seem incapable of solution—and are; but which, once they have fastened themselves upon you, can neither be escaped nor ignored.

A pilot, a man named Wood who flew for East African Airways, was down somewhere on the vast Serengeti Plains and had been missing for two days. To me and to all of his friends, he was just Woody—a good flier and a likable person. He was a familiar figure in Nairobi and, though word of his disappearance had been slow in finding attention, once it was realized that he was not simply overdue, but lost, there was a good deal of excitement. Some of this, I suppose, was no more than the usual public enjoyment of suspense and melodrama, though there was seldom a scarcity of either in Nairobi.

Where Woody's misfortune was most sincerely felt, of course, was among those of his own profession. I do not mean pilots alone. Few people realize the agony and anxiety a conscientious ground engineer can suffer if an airplane he has signed out fails to return. He will not always consider the probability of bad weather or a possible error of judgment on the part of the pilot, but instead will torture himself with unanswerable questions about proper wiring, fuel lines, carburization, valves, and all the hundred and one things he must think about. He will feel that on this occasion he must surely have overlooked something—some small but vital adjustment which, because of his neglect, has resulted in the crash of a plane or the death of a pilot.

All the members of a ground crew, no matter how poorly equipped or how small the aerodrome on which they work, will share equally the apprehension and the nervous strain that come with the first hint of mishap.

But whether storm, or engine trouble, or whatever the cause, Woody had disappeared, and for the past two days I had been droning my plane back and forth over the Northern Serengeti and half the Masai Reserve without having sighted so much as a plume of signal smoke or the glint of sunlight on a crumpled wing.

Anxiety was increasing, even changing to gloom, and I had expected to take off again at sunrise to continue the search; but here suddenly was the message from Nungwe.

For all professional pilots there exists a kind of guild, without charter and without bylaws. It demands no requirements for inclusion save an understanding of the wind, the compass, the rudder, and fair fellowship. It is a camaraderie *sans* sentiment, of the kind that men who once sailed uncharted seas in wooden ships must have known and lived by.

I was my own employer, my own pilot, and as often as not my own ground engineer as well. As such I might easily, perhaps even justifiably, have refused the flight to Nungwe, arguing that the rescue of the lost pilot was more important—as, to me, it was. But there was a tinge of personal sympathy about such reasoning that weakened conviction, and Woody, whom I knew so little and yet so well that I never bothered to remember his full name any more than most of his friends did, would have been quick to reject a decision that favored him at the expense of an unknown miner choking his lungs out in the soggy swamplands of Victoria Nyanza.

In the end I telephoned the Nairobi Hospital, made sure that the oxygen would be ready, and prepared to fly south.

Three hundred and fifty miles can be no distance in a plane, or it can be from where you are to the end of the earth. It depends on so many things. If it is night, it depends on the depth of the darkness and the height of the clouds, the speed of the wind, the stars, the fullness of the moon. It depends on you, if you fly alone—not only on your ability to steer your course or to keep your altitude, but upon the things that live in your mind while you swing suspended between the earth and the silent sky. Some of those things take root and are with you long after the flight itself is a memory, but, if your course was over any part of Africa, even the memory will remain strong.

When, much later than Nungwe or Tripoli or Zanzibar, or any of the remote and sometimes outlandish places I have flown to, I crossed the North Atlantic, east to west, there were headlines, fanfare, and, for me, many sleepless nights. A generous American press found that flight spectacular—and what is spectacular is news.

But to leave Nairobi and arrive at Nungwe is not spectacular. It is not news. It is only a little hop from here to there, and to one who does not know the plains of Africa, its swamps, its night sounds and its night silences, such a flight is not only unspectacular, but perhaps tedious as well. Only not to me, for Africa was the breath and life of my childhood.

It is still the host of all my darkest fears, the cradle of mysteries always intriguing, but never wholly solved. It is the remembrance of sunlight and green hills, cool water and the yellow warmth of bright mornings. It is as ruthless as any sea, more uncompromising than its own deserts. It is without temperance in its harshness or in its favors. It yields nothing, offering much to men of all races.

But the soul of Africa, its integrity, the slow inexorable pulse of its life, is its own and of such singular rhythm that no outsider, unless steeped from childhood in its endless, even beat, can ever hope to experience it, except only as a bystander might experience a Masai war dance knowing nothing of its music nor the meaning of its steps.

So I am off to Nungwe—a silly word, a silly place. A place of small hopes and small successes, buried like the inconsequential treasure of an imaginative miser, out of bounds and out of most men's wanting—below the Mau Escarpment, below the Speke Gulf, below the unsurveyed stretches of the Western Province.

Oxygen to a sick miner. But this flight is not heroic. It is not even romantic. It is a job of work, a job to be done at an uncomfortable hour with sleep in my eyes and half a grumble on my lips.

Arab Ruta calls contact and swings the propeller.

Arab Ruta is a Nandi, anthropologically a member of a Nilotic tribe, humanly a member of a smaller tribe, a more elect tribe, the tribe composed of those too few, precisely sensitive, but altogether indomitable individuals contributed sparingly by each race, exclusively by none.

He is of the tribe that observes with equal respect the soft voice and the hardened hand, the fullness of a flower, the quick finality of death. His is the laughter of a free man happy at his work, a strong man with lust for living. He is not black. His skin holds the sheen and warmth of used copper. His eyes are dark and wide-spaced, his nose full-boned and capable of arrogance.

He is arrogant now, swinging the propeller, laying his lean hands on the curved wood, feeling an exultant kinship in the coiled resistance to his thrust.

He swings hard. A splutter, a strangled cough from the engine like the premature stirring of a sleep-slugged laborer. In the cockpit I push gently on the throttle, easing it forward, rousing the motor, feeding it, soothing it.

Arab Ruta moves the wooden chocks from the wheels and steps backward away from the wing. Fitful splashes of crimson light from crude-oil torches set round the field stain the dark cloth of the African night and play upon his alert, high-boned face. He raises his hand and I nod as the propeller, whirring itself into invisibility, pulls the plane forward, past him.

I leave him no instructions, no orders. When I return he will be there. It is an understanding of many years—a wordless understanding from the days when Arab Ruta first came into my father's service on the farm at Njoro. He will be there, as a servant, as a friend—waiting.

I peer ahead along the narrow muram runway. I gather speed meeting the wind, using the wind.

A high wire fence surrounds the aerodrome—a wire fence and then a deep ditch. Where is there another aerodrome fenced against wild animals? Zebra, wildebeest, giraffe, eland—at night they lurk about the tall barrier staring with curious wild eyes into the flat field, feeling cheated.

They are well out of it, for themselves and for me. It would be a hard fate to go down in the memory of one's friends as having been tripped up by a wandering zebra. "Tried to take off and hit a zebra!" It lacks even the dignity of crashing into an anthill.

Watch the fence. Watch the flares. I watch both and take off into the night.

Ahead of me lies a land that is unknown to the rest of the world and only vaguely known to the African—a strange mixture of grasslands, scrub, desert sand like long waves of the southern ocean. Forest, still water, and age-old mountains, stark and grim like mountains of the moon. Salt lakes, and rivers that have no water. Swamps. Badlands. Land without life. Land teeming with life—all of the dusty past, all of the future.

The air takes me into its realm. Night envelops me entirely, leaving me out of touch with the earth, leaving me within this small moving world of my own, living in space with the stars.

My plane is a light one, a two-seater with her registration letters, VP-KAN, painted boldly on her turquoise-blue fuselage in silver.

In the daytime she is a small gay complement to the airy blue of the sky, like a bright fish under the surface of a clear sea. In darkness such as this she is no more than a passing murmur, a soft, incongruous murmur above the earth.

With such registration letters as hers, it requires of my friends no great imagination or humor to speak of her always as just "the Kan"—and the Kan she is, even to me. But this is not libel, for such nicknames are born out of love.

To me she is alive and to me she speaks. I feel through the soles of my feet on the rudder-bar the willing strain and flex of her muscles. The resonant, guttural voice of her exhausts has a timbre more articulate than wood and steel, more vibrant than wires and sparks and pounding pistons.

She speaks to me now, saying the wind is right, the night is fair, the effort asked of her well within her powers.

I fly swiftly. I fly high—south-southwest, over the Ngong Hills. I am relaxed. My right hand rests upon the stick in easy communication with the will and the way of the plane. I sit in the rear, the front cockpit filled with the heavy tank of oxygen strapped upright in the seat, its round stiff dome foolishly reminding me of the poised rigidity of a passenger on first flight.

The wind in the wires is like the tearing of soft silk under the blended drone of engine and propeller. Time and distance together slip smoothly past the tips of my wings without sound, without return, as I peer downward over the night-shadowed hollows of the Rift Valley and wonder if Woody, the lost pilot, could be there, a small human pinpoint of hope and of hopelessness listening to the low, unconcerned song of the Avian—flying elsewhere.

Cradle of Mankind

By Delta Willis

The Great Rift Valley is a 2,000-mile-long scar on the face of the Earth. It stretches from the southernmost tip of Turkey to Mozambique, and on a clear day, it is visible from the moon. Its geology is central to the search for human origins, and while most people come to Africa to see the wildlife, none of what you see on this terrain makes sense except in light of the past. As you photograph the creatures that appear on the surface of Africa's vast horizon, you might want to contemplate their ancestral forms, which surface in the Earth's strata.

This quest for roots begins as you approach Nairobi. Many flights from Europe arrive just after dawn, and if you request a window seat on the left side of the plane, you will have a good view of the lakes and volcanoes that are central to this story. (I like to sit with a map on my knees, so that I can identify the silver outlines of Lakes Turkana, Baringo, Nakuru, and Naivasha.) Evidence of our ancestors has been found along the shores of these lakes, in the valley floor, as well as in some arid basins, like Olorgesailie and Olduvai in Tanzania farther south.

The East African section of the Rift is known as the Cradle of Mankind because the oldest evidence of our ancestors was found here. The fossils from East Africa are 1 to 3 million years older than those found in Europe and Asia. In fact the oldest specimen of *Homo erectus* was discovered on the west side of Lake Turkana: The skeleton known as the Turkana Boy is 1.6 million years old. Two-million-year-old skulls of the first tool user, *Homo habilis*, were found on the east side of Lake Turkana and at Olduvai Gorge in Tanzania. And the earliest evidence of our ancestors' upright gait, over 3.5 million years old, was discovered just south of Olduvai, at a place called Laetoli. Thirteen skeletons of *Proconsul*, a small ape thought to be part of our ancestral stock, were discovered on islands in Lake Victoria.

More has been discovered in the last two decades than in the last two centuries, and new fossils appear after every rainy season. You don't have to be a scientist to appreciate what you see, and the discoveries are explained in many fine museums at the sites. And if you visit the Seychelles, you can explore the difference in wildlife and habitat between mainland East Africa and what's often called the Galapagos of the Indian Ocean, presenting the same sort of variety that inspired Charles Darwin to contemplate the causes for this infinite variety.

Although remains of ancient hominids have also been unearthed in Ethiopia, Zimbabwe, and South Africa, none of the sites is as accessible to the public as those in Kenya and

Tanzania. The Leakey family pioneered research in East Africa, finding many of these stones and bones themselves, and they also helped to establish small field museums at the sites so nonscientists could see the evidence.

With the reopening of the Kenya/Tanzania border, you can actually visit major excavation sites *and* see all the spectacular wildlife. Tanzania's Olduvai Gorge, for example, is between two of the world's most extraordinary game sanctuaries—Serengeti and Ngorongoro. And Kenya's Turkana basin, site of such famous discoveries as the fossil numbered 1470 (*Homo habilis*), is also the locale of the Jade Sea, with rich bird life and fishing for Nile perch. Stone tools made by *Homo erectus* can be seen within an hour's drive of downtown Nairobi. Coastal ruins of ancient Arab towns near Lamu and Mombasa are within a handaxe's throw of exquisite coral reefs.

Your first stop should be the Kenya National Museum in Nairobi, with excellent exhibits on human prehistory, including both fossil finds from Lake Turkana and a cast replica of the footprints at Laetoli, Tanzania. (Take a good look here, because the actual footprints in Laetoli are buried and overgrown with thorn scrub, to protect them until a museum can be built.) There's a huge display of a complete fossilized elephant, 17 million years old, and an extinct giant pig, which happened to be the first discovery of museum director Richard Leakey, at the age of six. (Richard's brothers Jonathan and Philip also made important discoveries.)

The legendary Louis Leakey, who died in 1972, was born in Kenya, the son of missionaries. At age 13 Leakey discovered stone tools around Kabete, just north of Nairobi. His parents were skeptical, because the tools weren't made of flint like those in Europe, but of a volcanic glass known as obsidian. But once the authenticity of the tools was established by a local expert, young Leakey's interest in prehistory was firmly established. As a student at Cambridge, he met artist Mary Nicol; today Dr. Mary Leakey is regarded by insiders as Louis's greatest find. Many discoveries credited to Louis were made by Mary, who only recently retired from field research in Tanzania. It was Mary Leakey's 1959 discovery of the Zinj skull that put East Africa on the map as the Cradle of Mankind.

One of the most famous finds from the Great Rift Valley is the partial skeleton known as Lucy, discovered by an American team in Ethiopia's Afar Triangle. The region is a geological hot spot; extraordinary volcanic activity followed a collision of three of the Earth's tectonic plates. A central feature of the Rift is volcanoes. Volcanic mountains are everywhere. Kilimanjaro has two craters; even the Ngong Hills near Nairobi are volcanic. Boulders, basalt, and ashes from more than 200 eruptions are used to date hominid bones and tools.

The Great Rift began around 14 million years ago when the Earth's crust began to pull apart from east to west, a result of tectonic plate shifts between "Africa" and "Eurasia." Faults along the Rift collided and uplifted to reveal ancient sediments; further exposure came with wind and rain. Consequently, paleontologists don't dig for fossils as in the classic portrait of excavation you might envision. As Richard Leakey allows, "Nature does most of the work."

The formation of fossils is enhanced by the geology of the Great Rift; alkaline volcanic ash helped fill the porous bones, and the rich sediments of deltas along the valley lakes helped bury them. Most bones are lost to erosion or scattered by predators. In a decade of searching the East Turkana terrain, only eight skulls were found, many of them by a team of Kenyans known as the Hominid Gang.

Their search for fossils is hardly confined to hominids—the upright primate that includes us (*Homo sapiens*) as well as our ancestors. Even delicate fossils of birds and insects are not ignored in this search, nor are microscopic samples of fossil pollen, which are used to discern the kind of vegetation that grew in the area 2 or 3 million years ago.

After a visit to the Nairobi Museum, the next logical stop is at Olorgesailie (Ol-**or**-ga-**sal**-lee), less than an hour's drive south of Nairobi. The modern, paved road to Olorgesailie curls around the Ngong Hills and descends into the eastern branch of the Great Rift Valley. The drive is spectacular, with Masai herding their goats en route and a vast arid horizon dotted with acacia scrub. As you descend into the valley, the volcanic mountains Suswa and Olorgesailie emerge.

The National Museums of Kenya have a small annex museum here as well as guides to take you around the various sites. Stone tools of the Acheulian industry lie scattered upon the sandy landscape, just as they were found in 1942 by the Leakeys. The distinctive style of the tools, including tear-shaped hand axes and choppers and flakes—aligns them with the work of *Homo erectus*. The same tool industry flourished at Olduvai Gorge well over a million years ago and, much later, in Europe.

After visiting Olorgesailie, you can set out from Nairobi in almost any direction and find more evidence of human ancestors. If you're on your own, obtain a museum brochure that lists Kenya's field museums. You can drive to Hyrax Hill, or Kariandusi, to see more recently discovered tools. You can fly directly to Koobi Fora, where there is a field museum and nearby excavation sites, or, if you drive to Lake Turkana, you might stay at the Ferguson's Gulf fishing lodge before crossing the lake to Koobi Fora. Tell the Nairobi Museum of your plans so they can make sure a guide is there—this most remote museum on an escarpment overlooking the lake doesn't have regular hours, and the only accommodations nearby are very basic *bandas*.

There are also field museums in Mombasa, including the beautifully renovated Fort Jesus, and 15th-century ruins in Gedi National Park. The Lamu Museum features ancient relics of the Swahili culture that originated here.

Olduvai Gorge is generally included on any tour of Tanzania's "Northern Circuit," but many groups rush through. It helps to read up on the subject before you arrive. The gorge is important because many hominid fossils were found here in association with stone tools. Beyond the anatomy of the fossil bones, stone tools are the central clue to how our ancestors might have behaved. Mary Leakey describes life at Olduvai in her autobiography, *Disclosing the Past*, now in paperback. Only when you know the careful work that went into these discoveries, and the long stretches when little was found, will you appreciate what you see at the gorge. Peter Jones, an archaeologist who worked as one of Mary Leakey's assistants, often serves as a tour guide, and he can give you a quick lesson in flaking tools and explain what you see at Olduvai. There are no accommodations at the gorge itself, so the best approach is to stay overnight at Ngorongoro, just to the south.

The archaeology of Olduvai is fascinating: There are several different types of tool here, indicating different industries or styles that prevailed during certain eras. The oldest is named Oldowan, after the gorge, but the style has since been found in other parts of Africa and there are also developed Oldowan and Acheulian styles.

Erosion in the gorge has left the strata easy to see; the gorge looks like the Grand Canyon. Layers of sediments can be seen in chronological order at certain spots, and volcanic tuffs are visible at some of the excavation sites. There is an excellent museum at Olduvai, but you must ask to see where Zinj was found.

The Zinj skull was an australopithecine with a very small brain and large teeth, so large that the press dubbed it the Nutcracker Man. Louis Leakey preferred to name it Zinj, the old Arabic name for the east coast of Africa. Geologists date Zinj at 1.75 million years old; until it was discovered, in 1959, no one thought human history went back that far. A few years later, in 1963, the Leakeys (assisted by their eldest son, Jonathan) came across fossil remains, which were named *Homo habilis*, or Handy Man. In contrast to the australopithecines, this was a large-brained hominid who is thought to be the first tool user.

Olduvai Museum has good displays of the different kinds of tools. It also has casts of giant antelope that lived at Olduvai. The recently renovated Natural History Museum in Arusha is in the center of town. Other archaeological treasures in Tanzania include the rock paintings of the Kondoa district, some distance south of Olduvai. Reproductions of these paintings appear in the Nairobi Museum.

3 Kenya and Tanzania Parks and Game Reserves

Introduction

By Daniel Stiles

Daniel Stiles is an American based in Nairobi. He first came to this country as a Berkeley graduate student in archeology, to do research at Richard Leakey's Koobi Fora camp on Lake Turkana, and then taught at the University of Nairobi. He serves as a consultant for the United Nations Environmental Program (UNEP), and is currently leading safaris and researching a book on the Swahili culture.

There are 50 national parks and reserves in Kenya, though only about two dozen are properly established in terms of their accessibility and facilities for tourists. A dozen more are difficult to get to, and usually one must go self-contained—that is, with food, water, and camping gear—but they are worth a visit for the more intrepid. Seven of these sites are marine parks and reserves, established to protect parts of Kenya's scenic coast and coral reefs. The remainder cover an area of more than 35,000 square kilometers (more than 13,500 sq. mi). Future parks and reserves to protect even more of Kenya's land are under consideration by the Kenya Wildlife Services.

Only national parks offer complete legal protection from uses other than wildlife conservation and tourism. National reserves and sanctuaries allow limited, controlled use by the local people. The difference is sometimes lost in practice, however, particularly when drought or need for more land causes people to encroach on park resources. Conservation in East Africa is a constant battle between the immediate needs of people for food and fuelwood and the ageless desire to conserve a spectacular and, in some ways, unique natural panorama.

The parks and reserves in the central and southern parts of Kenya tend to be the most accessible and, therefore, more crowded with other tourists. Masai Mara Game Reserve is justly celebrated for the splendor of its annual wildebeest migration. (The other half of the migration can be seen in the Serengeti National Park in Tanzania.) This is the best place in Kenya for sheer numbers of animals, and one of the best for variety of species. The Mara is also the place to go if lions and cheetahs are at the top of your must-see list. Amboseli National Park is a good choice if you want to see large numbers of elephants.

Tsavo West and Lake Nakuru national parks both have rhino sanctuaries and the population of rhino in Nairobi National Park has doubled in the last decade.

Tsavo West and East national parks are better known for their impressive landscape features—Mzima Springs, the Shetani lava flow, Mudanda Rock, Lugard's Falls, the Yatta Plateau— than for animals. Head to these areas to experience the timeless, atavistic expanses of Africa. Wildlife can be seen, however, particularly around the lodge water holes, but not in great variety.

The last of the major game-viewing sites in Kenya are Meru National Park and the triumvirate of the Samburu-Buffalo Springs–Shaba game reserves. They contain certain northern species not seen in the southern parks and reserves—the long-necked gerunuk, the thinly striped Grevy's zebra, the blue-shanked Somali ostrich, and the Beisa oryx.

Some of Kenya's secondary parks and reserves also deserve a visit, time permitting. Shimba Hills National Reserve offers some of the easiest-to-see wild sable and roan antelopes in the world, and its accessible location fits in well with a visit to Kenya's southern coast beaches. For those who are only passing through Kenya, or who are limited to a single free day, Nairobi National Park offers surprisingly good game-viewing just a few minutes from downtown Nairobi. Giraffes are a specialty

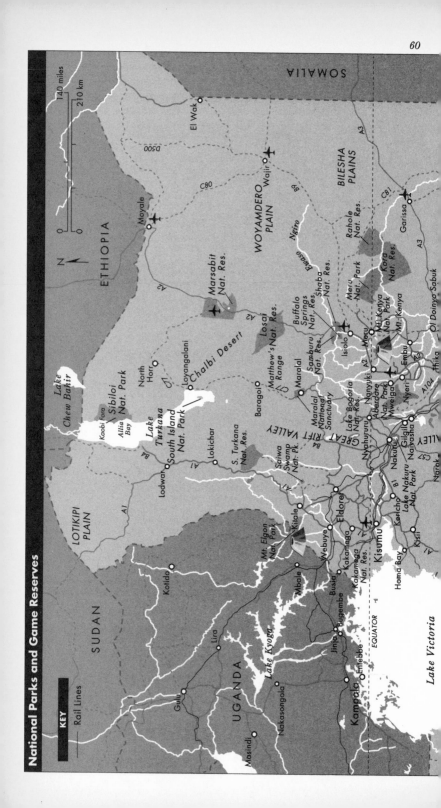

National Parks and Game Reserves

KEY
— Rail Lines

60

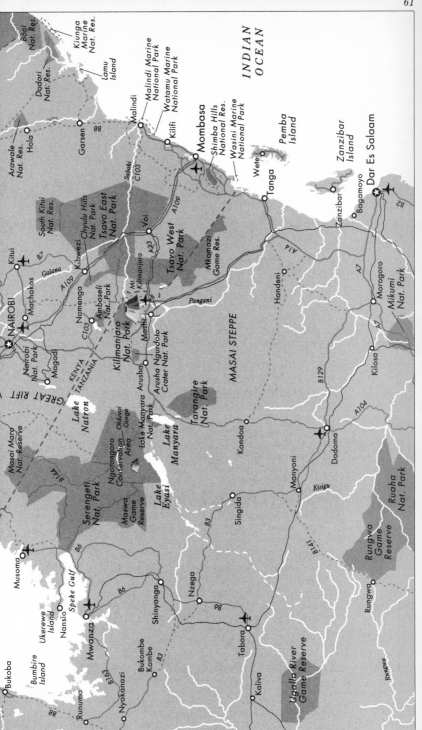

here, and the rhino population is steadily growing and now out-numbers that found in the Masai Mara or Amboseli.

The national reserves of Nakuru and Bogoria in the Great Rift Valley are among the best places anywhere to view massive numbers of greater and lesser flamingos, attracted to the shallow waters of the alkaline lakes by the presence of blue-green algae and diatoms upon which they feed. Farther north in the Rift Valley is the Jade Sea, Lake Turkana. On its northeastern shore lies the dry, eroded Sibiloi National Park, site of the thousands of human and animal fossils unearthed by Richard Leakey and his team. This park is most easily reached by chartered aircraft, as it would take a week to make the round trip from Nairobi in a four-wheel-drive vehicle. Some wildlife can be seen on the shores of the lake, particularly crocodiles and a local variety of topi, but the real attractions are the Koobi Fora Museum and the haunting lake itself.

In the same general vicinity as Sibiloi—which is to say, northern Kenya—are the welcoming cool air and green tropical mist forests of Marsabit National Reserve. Marsabit looms out of the searing lowland plains to a height of more than 1,600 meters (5,200 ft), offering a refreshing breather on the edge of a crater lake. The greatest of the highland parks, though, is Mt. Kenya National Park, which is crowned by Batian peak, the second highest spot in Africa at 5,199 meters (17,058 ft). Wildlife can be viewed from the comfort of a mountain lodge on its lower slopes, and the peak can be climbed relatively easily in two days. Aberdare National Park and the Maralal National Sanctuary are two other highland forest sites that offer comfortable game-viewing from the veranda of a lodge. Mt. Elgon National Park, on the border with Uganda, rounds out the highland attractions of Kenya.

The variety and geographical spread of the parks and reserves of Kenya make it necessary to choose discriminately before starting your safari—it would take months to see them all. A judicious choice of what you want to see in the way of country-side and wildlife will make your stay more enjoyable, and it is always best to try and combine a mix. There are mountains, deserts, lakes, beaches, and wildlife. It is also possible to combine a trip to Kenya with one to Tanzania, which is becoming more popular since the common border was reopened in 1985 and Tanzania has begun upgrading tourist services. It is considerably easier to reach Tanzania's Serengeti National Park, the Ngorongoro Crater, and Lake Manyara from Nairobi than to get to Marsabit or Lake Turkana.

Tanzania has set aside 247,535 square kilometers (95,575 sq. mi) of land for preservation of wildlife, consisting of 10 national parks, 10 game reserves, and the Ngorongoro Conservation Area. This is almost a quarter of the country and is the largest proportion of protected land of any country in the world. The most popular safari route—the Northern Circuit—is a round-trip starting in Arusha town, which goes to Lake Manyara National Park, the Ngorongoro (Crater) Conservation Area, and the Serengeti National Park. At least a week should be allowed for this, as you'll need a day to visit the archaeological sites at Olduvai Gorge, southeast of the Serengeti. The Northern Circuit can conveniently be combined with visits to Amboseli, the Masai Mara, and Nairobi in Kenya to make a two-week safari to East Africa that would offer the ultimate in game-viewing.

The Northern Circuit, including Mt. Kilimanjaro National Park, is the most accessible route for tourists. A visit to Mt. Kilimanjaro entails a five-day climb of Africa's highest mountain. Parks and reserves on the Southern Circuit, such as Selous and Mikumi, are more off the beaten track and take much longer to visit if overland travel is used. Chartering an aircraft is advised if time is limited; from Dar es Salaam to the northern edge of the Selous is less than an hour's flight, and there is also a train that runs south from Dar to the edge of the Selous, but its schedule is not dependable. To get to the Mahale Mountains you can fly Tanzania Airways or take the train from Dar to Kigoma, where you can take a boat to the park or connect with charter operator Roland Purcell (Greystoke Safaris, Ltd., Box 543, Arusha, tel. 255–57–7612).

The parks and reserves of Tanzania are less crowded than those of Kenya in general, though Ngorongoro, because of its small size, can be just as jammed as the Masai Mara at times. Neither is what one would call "crowded" in American or European terms, however. The tourist infrastructure in Tanzania is less developed than that in Kenya and, with fewer tourists and a larger portion of the land devoted to protected areas, visitors have more pristine land and wildlife all to themselves than farther north. It can become quite uncomfortable bumping around for several hours a day in a Land Rover or minibus, but the discomfort is usually offset by the enjoyment gained from seeing the dramatic countryside and beautiful animals. If comfort is a priority—and cost not a consideration—then flying is the answer.

The best parks for photographing wildlife are the Masai Mara in Kenya and Ngorongoro Crater and the Serengeti Plains in Tanzania. These sites do not contain all animal species or habitats, however, so to get variety a more northern area such as Samburu-Buffalo Springs reserves in Kenya would have to be added to your itinerary.

Unless otherwise stated, park and reserve entrance fees for nonresidents are Kshs. 220 for adults and Kshs. 25 for children 3-12. Vehicles cost Kshs. 30 in Kenya. In Tanzania, nonresident adults must pay at least $30 each day, and those age 16 or under $10 a day. The entrance fee for a Tanzanian-registered vehicle is Tshs. 200 and for a resident driver Tshs. 50. Since many things must be paid for with foreign currency in Tanzania, measured in U.S. dollars, visitors are advised to bring a good supply of dollar traveler's checks and cash.

Kenya

Lodging These price categories apply to lodging in and around all the Kenya parks and reserves that follow. Lodgings must be paid for in dollars (or other foreign currency) or by traveler's check.

Costs Highly recommended lodgings are indicated by a star ★.

Category	Cost*
Very Expensive	over Kshs. 3750 ($150)
Expensive	Kshs. 2500–3759 ($100–$150)

Moderate	Kshs. 1250–2500 ($50–$100)
Inexpensive	under Kshs. 1250 ($50)

All prices are for a standard double room; including hotel tax.

Aberdare National Park
Box 22, Nyeri, tel. Mweiga 24

Size 766 square kilometers (296 sq. mi)

Year Established 1950

Headquarters Nyeri

The park covers all of the Nyandarua (formerly Aberdare) range above 3,200 meters (10,500 ft), except for the salient, which stretches 20 kilometers (12.4 mi) down the eastern slope toward Nyeri. This used to be the annual elephant migration route between the Aberdares and Mt. Kenya before the Laikipia Plateau became so populated. The Nyandarua range of mountains starts near Nairobi in the south with Mt. Kinangop at 3,906 meters (12,816 ft) and ends 70 kilometers (43.4 mi) to the north. The range, on the eastern edge of the Rift Valley, maintains a height of almost 3,000 meters (9,144 ft) its entire length and is crowned by Oldonyo Lesatima at 4,001 meters (13,127 ft).

The national park consists primarily of the moorland plateau, but extends down to tropical forest in the salient, which is surrounded by farmland visible from the roof of Treetops mountain lodge. Treetop accommodations came into vogue when Princess Elizabeth—on vacation with her husband, Prince Philip—became queen upon the sudden death of her father King George VI. The park is an area of great scenic beauty, of rolling country covered in tussock grass, large areas of mixed giant heath, and forested patches of rosewood and Saint-John's-wort. Giant lobelias and groundsel are also found in sheltered valleys.

Streams of ice cold water thread their way across the moorland suddenly to disappear into valleys and ravines in a series of beautiful waterfalls. Most spectacular are the Gura and Karuru falls that lie on opposite sides of a deep valley, the Gura cascading more than 300 meters (1,000 ft) without interruption, and the Karuru falling in three steps. Easy access is afforded to the head of the Karuru Falls and there are breathtaking views of the Gura across the valley. Other impressive falls are the Chania Falls and the Cave waterfall.

The streams are stocked with rainbow, brown, and American brook trout, and fishing is permitted, provided a current trout-fishing license is held. There is a bag limit of six per rod per day from each stream, but only the rather difficult fly-fishing is permitted. The park's public campsites are closed, owing to problems with marauding lions. Now the only accommodations available in the moorlands are the bandas at the fishing lodge run by the Fisheries Department. There are also a few run-down houses that can be rented from the Forest Department. The BEWARE OF LION signs are not a joke!

Wildlife The park is endowed with a great variety and quantity of wild animals, despite the cold and periodic mist of the highlands.

Aberdare National Park

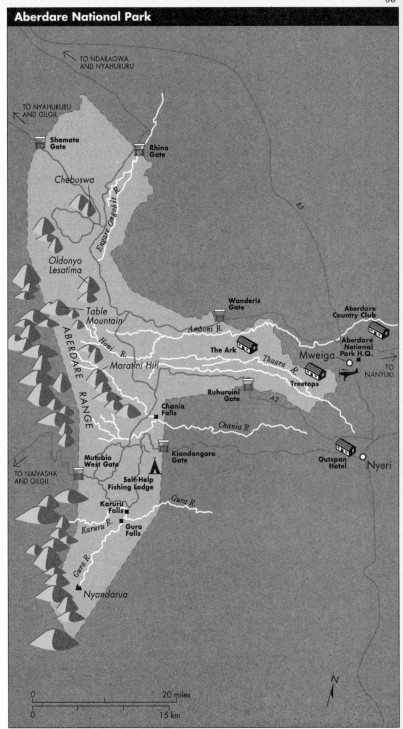

TO NDARAGWA
AND NYAHURURU

TO NYAHURURU
AND GILGIL

Shamata Gate

Rhino Gate

Chebuswa

Engare Ongobit R.

B5

Oldonyo Lesatima

Table Mountain

Wanderis Gate

Aberdare Country Club

Amboni R.

The Ark

Honi R.

Thaara R.

Mweiga

Aberdare National Park H.Q.

ABERDARE RANGE

Maratini Hill

Treetops

TO NANYUKI

Ruhuruini Gate

A2

Chania Falls

Chania R.

Kiandongoro Gate

Mutubio West Gate

Outspan Hotel

Nyeri

TO NAIVASHA
AND GILGIL

Self-Help Fishing Lodge

Karuru Falls

Gura R.

Karuru R.

Gura Falls

Gura R.

▲ *Nyandarua*

N

0		20 miles
0		15 km

Most of the game is found on the gentler eastern slopes of the chain. Elephant, buffalo, rhino, eland, waterbuck, bushbuck, reedbuck, several species of duikers, suni, bush pig, warthog, serval cat, leopard, colobus and Sykes' monkeys, hyena, and wild dog are all here. The park is also the best place in Kenya to see the rare giant forest hog and the most elusive of the antelopes, the bongo. The Aberdares also seems to have more of the black variety of leopard, serval, and genets than elsewhere. Black serval cats are often seen on the open moors, usually hunting duiker, francolin, or rodents. Melanism (dark pigmentation) is even seen here in the Augur buzzard.

Early morning or evening drives offer the best chance of seeing game, and a careful look at the various roadside salt licks, forest glades, and open valleys should prove rewarding. Be especially careful of buffalo, which are numerous in the park. If you spend a night at Treetops or the Ark you are likely to see resident spotted genets looking for handouts. Olive baboons are particularly troublesome at the lodges, as they will enter rooms through open windows to steal things and will even snatch your tea cakes off your dish.

Notable birdlife consists of the antelope-eating crowned eagle, the large, silvery-cheeked hornbill, and the flashing red Hartlaub's turaco. The red feather of this bird is very rare, as it has a true red pigment, rather than being simply a color reflection. The Jackson's francolin is found in the higher areas, while the scaly francolin replaces it lower down on the mountain.

The park has a good network of tracks, though not all circuits are marked with signs. A particularly enjoyable experience is to tour the salient after a night spent at the Ark or Treetops; you will almost certainly come within a few yards of elephant, rhino, and giant forest hog. Permission must be obtained and a four-wheel-drive vehicle is required, but several tour operators, such as Abercrombie & Kent or Ker and Downey, can set it up.

Getting There The park can be reached from the east through three gates. The most direct access is by the Ruhuruni gate, 4 kilometers (2.5 mi) past Nyeri on A2, and a second is through the Kiandongoro gate, 22 kilometers (14 mi) from Nyeri on the edge of the moorland plateau. The third gate, Wanderis, is reached via Mweiga just north of Nyeri.

From the west the park is approached from A104 leading from Nairobi to Naivasha, where just before reaching the Naivasha turnoff there is a sign on the right for Aberdare National Park and North Kinangop. After 14 kilometers (9 mi) the tarmac ends at the top of a steep hill; then you turn left at a signposted junction and go 24 kilometers (15 mi) to North Kinangop. The dirt road rises from here up the escarpment in a series of hairpin bends to the Mujubio west gate.

Lodging **The Ark.** The lodge, shaped like Noah's Ark, is located deep in *Very Expensive* the forest in the salient by a water hole. The rooms are small, but comfortable, and some have private baths (12 new rooms were recently added), but people don't spend much time in them, anyway, since they are in the observation lounge watching animals come up to drink at the water hole. Children under age 7 are not allowed. *Lonrho Hotels, Box 58581, Nairobi, tel. 2/723776. AE, DC, MC, V.*

Treetops. The oldest and most famous of the mountain lodges, it was originally situated in a tree. Today it is a massive wood affair on stout stilts in the salient. Elephants have destroyed the forest around the artificial water hole, leaving a large, open expanse, and nearby encroaching farms have reduced the number of animals that come to drink. Despite these drawbacks, it is still an enjoyable experience to spend a night here. No children under age 10. *Lonrho Hotels, Box 58581, Nairobi, tel. 2/723776. AE, DC, MC, V.*

Expensive **Outspan Hotel.** This large, colonial-style hotel on the edge of Nyeri has fabulous gardens and, on clear days, a spectacular view of Mt. Kenya jutting up between nursery-perfect trees. You can rent rods and a day license for fishing in the Chania River and pay a nominal fee to watch excellent tribal dancing by local Kikuyu in colobus-skin garb. The food is superb and a copious buffet lunch is served to those going for the night to Treetops. You may request to stay in Paxtu (Just Peace), the cottage in which Lord Baden-Powell, hero of the battle of Mafeking during the Boer War and founder of the Boy Scouts, ended his days. *Lonrho Hotels, Box 58581, Nairobi, tel. 2/723776. AE, DC.*

Moderate **Aberdare Country Club.** This remodeled former colonial farmhouse offers country-house charm and comfortable cottages, if an overnight stay is desired. Normally, people visiting the Ark for a night meet here to be taken up to the lodge in the early afternoon after a buffet lunch and stroll across the well-kept gardens. The club has its own golf course, tennis courts, and swimming pool. *Lonrho Hotels, Box 58581, Nairobi, tel. 2/723776; tel. 171/55017 or 55025. AE, DC, MC, V.*

Inexpensive **Green Hills Hotel.** Located in Nyeri, this modern hotel has a pool and underground disco. It is a favorite socializing spot for local people, which can add flavor to a stay, but also noise. *Box 313, Nyeri, tel. 171/2017 or 2687. AE, V.*

Amboseli National Park
Box 18, Namanga, tel. Amboseli 12

Size 392 square kilometers (150 sq. mi)

Year Established 1947, national reserve; 1977, national park

Headquarters Namanga

Amboseli is the Masai word for dust devils, which are common in this area and unfortunately have increased because off-road driving has turned much of the park into a desert. Please consult a reliable safari operator before going to Amboseli; it is over-crowded with tourists and the dust makes it very unpleasant. The park, with the glistening snows of Kilimanjaro overlooking it, is a spear's throw from the Tanzanian border, due south of Nairobi. It adjoins "Lake" Amboseli, actually a dry, flat, glaring white plain of evaporated salts some 1,190 meters (3,904 ft) above sea level. The lake is liable to flood during the rainy season, however, so beware of what might look like a solid surface after the rains—you could find yourself up to the axles in mud. Mt. Kilimanjaro, known as Kili to residents, dominates the southern horizon and looks as though it is in the park. It probably would be if England hadn't conceded the mountain to Germany as part of the 1886 Anglo-German Agreement. There is a widely believed legend that Queen Victoria gave the moun-

Amboseli National Park

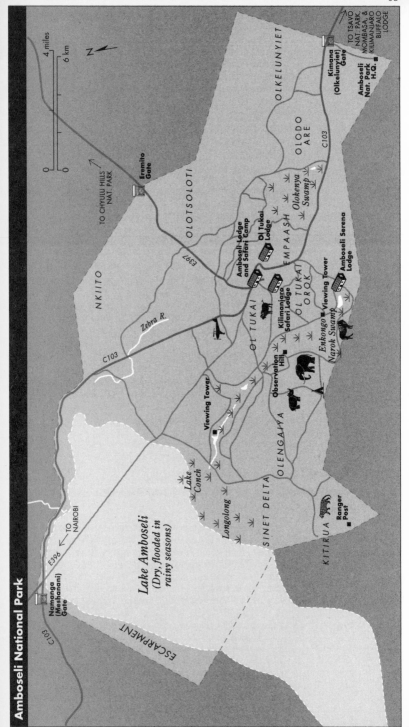

tain to her grandson, the German Kaiser Wilhelm, as a present—but it is only that, a legend.

Although it seems you could walk to Kili from Amboseli in a few minutes, it is actually in Tanzania, 40 kilometers (25 mi) away. The sheer size of its snow-capped Kibo (Uhuru Peak) at 5,894 meters (19,340 ft) can be overwhelming when the air is clear, and it offers the most spectacular backdrop to wildlife photography anywhere in Africa. Shutterbugs find the best time is just after sunrise, since clouds usually enshroud the mountain for most of the day.

Kibo, a symmetrical volcano, is the highest mountain in Africa and makes its neighbor, the sharply peaked Mawenzi, at 5,050 meters (16,900 ft), look insignificant, though it is still higher than any mountain in the United States except Alaska's Mt. McKinley. Aside from its aesthetic and photogenic qualities, the real importance of the mountain to Amboseli is the water that runs off its slopes through porous volcanic rock and collects in the Engongo Narok and Longinye swamps, attracting myriad birds and animals, as well as the Masai and their cattle.

The park once sheltered one of the biggest large-herbivore populations—rhinoceros, elephant, and hippopotamus—in Kenya. Because of this concentration, and the massive herds of wildebeests, buffalo, Burchell's zebras, impalas, and Grant's and Thomson's gazelles—which in turn provide supper to a wealth of lions, cheetahs, and a few leopards—the colonial government established a national reserve at Amboseli in 1947. But the swamp area was also an important watering and dry-season grazing area for the Masai. In an attempt to reconcile the needs of both wildlife and people for access to natural resources, the government in 1961 embarked on an experiment: The Masai Amboseli Game Reserve was put under the control of the Kajiado District Council, run by Masai elders. Rhino were still being poached and cattle were destroying the fragile ecosystem, however, so the New York Zoological Society devised a plan to create a core area for wildlife only, providing water to the Masai from boreholes and pumping it out of the swamps to outlying areas. In 1973 President Jomo Kenyatta decreed the 392 square kilometers (150 sq mi) around the swamps off-limits to the Masai and their cattle. Following the preparation of a detailed management plan and negotiations with the Masai, the area was designated a national park in 1977. This was hailed at the time as a great victory for wildlife conservation.

Unfortunately, boreholes and pumps break down, and sometimes grazing can become more important than water, as during the severe droughts of the late 1970s and early 1980s. Enormous herds of Masai cattle could be seen interspersed with even larger herds of wildebeest and zebra, which had all descended on the Amboseli swamps for water and sustenance. When the government tried to move the Masai out, some *moran* (warriors) waged an effective protest by spearing to death several rhino. The situation has greatly improved since 1984, but don't be surprised to see proud Masai warriors herding their cattle across dry flats in clouds of dust to water alongside the wildebeests at Engongo Narok.

The future is uncertain for Amboseli. The ecosystem is fragile, as demonstrated in the 1950s when the underground water level rose, bringing with it dissolved salts from the saline soil. The salt water killed hundreds of huge yellow-barked "fever trees," a species of acacia still gracing the wetter parts of Amboseli. Former forests became a barren waste. The crumbly white soil of the extensive flats is easily damaged by vehicles, and parts of Amboseli already resemble a California desert recreation area, crisscrossed and torn up by tire tracks. Off-road driving is illegal, but tour drivers often ignore the rules to get their clients close-up shots of animals. Paradoxically, Amboseli's future as a protected ecosystem depends on tourism, but it may be tourists who end up destroying this unique part of Kenya's wilderness. Urge your driver to stick to the designated tracks; you will still see plenty of game—and perhaps your grandchildren will, too.

Wildlife   Amboseli is divided into four basic areas, determined by vegetation and topography. Western Amboseli is made up mainly of dry lake flats and tufts of salt-tolerant grasses and shrubs. Game is sparse, but good photos of ostriches can be composed against a very realistic-looking mirage lake that develops in the shimmering heat. The Kori bustard finds this desert a good hunting ground for reptiles and insects, and *kongoni* (hartebeests) and eland frequent the area. The northern and eastern parts of the park are mainly acacia thornbush, with grasslands. These are good areas for the various antelope and gazelle species.

The southeastern part of the park is scrub, and not of much interest for game. The best area for viewing animals is the south-central part, which is logical, since here you find the green, well-vegetated swamps. From Observation Hill you can look down over the swamps and plains and spot the rare black rhinoceros, and sometimes see elephants down on their front knees in the thick swamp grass, munching away. Leopards can be found in the forested area in the far south around Kitirua.

The swamps also attract many of the more than 420 species of birds recorded in the park. Buffalo and giraffes go around with yellow- and red-billed oxpeckers stuck to them like darts, picking off ticks and other parasites. Around Ol Tukai Lodge, cattle egrets are often seen standing expectantly around the great, lumbering feet of elephants, waiting to pounce on insects stirred up by the heavy treading. Sometimes the Taveta golden weaver can be spotted, bright yellow gold with a green back, a bird seen only in this area. The comical marabou stork, strutting with derelict dignity, also congregates around Ol Tukai and the other lodges to look for garbage. The elegant crowned crane is common, and the sandgrouse congregate in flocks of hundreds in the dry season to invade the watering places. Migrant waders are found around the swamps between August and April.

Tours   The main lodges listed for the park all have vehicles on hand for those who fly in to Amboseli or for those who drive their own car and would prefer something a bit more sturdy. The drivers know the park well and will take the visitor to see all of the major attractions and main animal species. If a lodge vehicle is to be used, less driving would be involved if you stayed at one of the central lodges in the Ol Tukai area. A lodge vehicle in Amboseli will almost certainly be a minibus.

Getting There
By Car
There are three ways of approaching Amboseli, depending on where you are coming from, where you are going, and how much time you have. Amboseli can be seen as a day trip from Nairobi, but this is not recommended, since you probably won't see the snows of Mt. Kilimanjaro. You're more likely to see the clouds of Kilimanjaro, which are not very interesting. Ideally, you will be continuing on to Tsavo National Park. The most usual route from Nairobi takes you down A109 Mombasa road to the right-hand turnoff for Namanga and Tanzania, onto A104, just before the Kenyatta International Airport. You go by the grubby town of Athi (named after a legendary hunting-gathering people) and a cement factory, which is tearing up the land with quarrying, through the Athi-Kapiti plains. Almost treeless, these undulating plains can be dull brown and boring in the dry season or breathtakingly beautiful, transformed into a striking green during the rains, rolling away to Hemingway's *Green Hills of Africa* on all horizons. These plains were once wall-to-wall wildlife, but little is seen today. A good deal of this seemingly open land has been subdivided into group ranches or private holdings of the il-Kaputiei, the branch of the Masai who live here.

Passing through Isinya, with its Anglican mission, Masai handicrafts center, and French archaeological excavation of an Acheulian Stone Age site, you arrive at Kajiado, the district headquarters, 48 kilometers (30 mi) from Athi. Keep going. The gently undulating plains now begin to ripple a bit more. What you may take for a reddish brown boulder on the hillside is actually a Masai *enkang* (family settlement), its low oblong houses made from mud and dung slapped over a frame of bent saplings. The land flattens out a bit again, and when you see the giant rock face of Ol-Doinyo Orok (Black Mountain) and thicker bush with tall trees, you know you are approaching Namanga, 164 kilometers (102 mi) from Nairobi. A little farther down the road, past endless rows of beaded handicrafts and gourds, is the border with Tanzania.

Time Out
On the right, over a bridge built by Italian prisoners of war in the 1940s, is the rather dilapidated Namanga River Hotel. It is a cool, shaded spot, good for a drink before turning left off the main road onto the dusty track leading to the park.

Driving along the track to the park center at Ol Tukai, 80 kilometers (50 mi) away, can be misery if it hasn't been recently graded. A washboard surface develops that makes you feel as if you were on a bucking bronco while your vehicle speeds along in billowing dust. For this reason, many people fly to Amboseli. The road skirts the main "lake" flats and passes a tarmac landing strip before arriving at Ol Tukai, nestled between the swamps, where the Amboseli and Kilimanjaro safari lodges and the self-help *bandas* (simple huts) are located. The first structures at Ol Tukai were bandas set up by Paramount Pictures in 1948 while filming *The Snows of Kilimanjaro*. There is also a curio shop, a post office, and a service station, all open according to the whim of the attendants. Masai beadwork, T-shirts, postcards, and books are for sale at the curio shop.

An alternate route from Nairobi takes you straight down the Mombasa highway for 125 kilometers (78 mi) to Emali. Turn right on a dirt track just after crossing the overpass, and continue until you hit a road straight enough to be worthy of the Romans. (Well, it was built by Italian engineers.) This pipeline road will take you to Makutano ("meetings" in Swahili). From this road there's a good view of the Chyulu Hills on the left. Another right turn takes you through pristine bush to Ol Tukai through the Eremito gate.

Still another way of reaching Ol Tukai is from the Chyulu Gate of Tsavo West. It is about 105 kilometers (65 mi) from the gate past the Kimana Safari Lodge; through the Kimana gate to Ol Tukai over a good track.

By Plane **Air Kenya Aviation** (tel. 2/501421) has daily service from Nairobi's Wilson Airport to the tarmac strip near Ol Tukai in Amboseli. The flight takes a little more than 30 minutes and costs Kshs. 1,824.

Lodging **Amboseli Lodge and Safari Camp.** The oldest in the park, this
Expensive 60-unit lodge, constructed of Mt. Kenya cedar and local stone, has a large pool. It was recently enlarged and renovated, and game-drive vehicles are available for rent. It faces Mt. Kilimanjaro from near Ol Tukai. *Kilimanjaro Safari Club, Box 30139, Nairobi, tel. 2/338888. AE, DC, V.*

★ **Amboseli Serena Lodge.** A comfortable lodge with many attractive design features in the Masai style, Amboseli Serena has a good pool and excellent bird-watching in its gardens. In the southern area of the park, it faces the Engongo Narok swamp, which is often visited by elephants, and there is good viewing from many of the 96 rooms. *Serena Lodges and Hotels, Box 48690, Nairobi, tel. 2/338656. AE, MC, V.*

Kilimanjaro Safari Lodge. Originally a tented camp renovated into chalets, this lodge sits under acacia trees a short distance from Amboseli Lodge in the central area of the park, facing the mountain. It is said to be on the site of a Hemingway encampment. *Reservations:* see *Amboseli Lodge. AE, DC, V.*

Moderate **Kilimanjaro Buffalo Lodge.** This recently built lodge designed in traditional African style with luxurious *makuti* (dried palm leaves)-thatch rondavels is 15 kilometers (9 mi) east of the central park area through the Kimana gate. The lodge has a garden and a large pool, and the bar overlooks a water hole visited by game at night. A landing strip is within walking distance of the lodge. *Box 72630, Nairobi, tel. 2/336088. No credit cards.*

Kimana Safari Lodge. This attractive lodge has 24 rooms overlooking the Kimana River. A chance to fish in the river is an added feature of a stay. The lodge is 15 kilometers (9 mi) from the central park area through the Kimana gate, just off the Loitokitok/Emali Road, near the turnoff for the Chyulu gate in Tsavo West. *Box 43817, Nairobi, tel. 2/338888. AE, DC, V.*

Inexpensive **Ol Tukai Lodge.** These thatch self-help cottages have bath and toilet facilities. Crockery and cooking utensils are provided, and bedding can be rented, but you'll need to bring your own food. Cooking is done in a separate room on wood-fueled stoves. The cottages were originally built in the late 1940s as film-crew accommodations for Paramount Pictures, and the age shows. *Nomads Kenya Ltd., Box 24793, Nairobi, tel. 2/331826. No credit cards.*

Campsites Located at the edge of the woodland and outside the park, 3 kilometers (2 mi) south of Observation Hill, this site has no facilities. There is a booking office run by the Masai Group Ranch (no phone) on the southern boundary of the park, which is well marked.

Chyulu Hills National Park, *see* Tsavo National Park, *below.*

Kakamega National Reserve
Box 879, Kakamega

Size 50 square kilometers (19 sq. mi)

Year Established 1966

Headquarters Kakamega

Kakamega Forest is the only area of Central African-type rain forest—the classic "jungle" of Tarzan movies—in Kenya. Its existence is used to argue for the previous existence of continuous rain forest from the Atlantic coast in Zaire across to western Kenya. Of great biological interest, it is seriously threatened by the people who live around it, walk through it to reach farms, and poach firewood from it. The area is densely populated, and it has one of the highest population growth rates in the world, high even by Kenyan standards.

The forest is located in rolling farm country. Mornings, when butterflies can be numerous, hidden birds are singing, and the shrieks of the colobus monkeys reverberate through the trees, are the best time to visit.

Wildlife Almost 60 species of birds that cannot be seen elsewhere in Kenya are found here, including the magnificent great blue turaco, huge black-and-white casqued hornbills, bar-tailed trogons, metallic sunbirds, and many other colorful families such as barbets, wattle-eyes, and weavers.

A walk in the forest for the nonbirder is also a rewarding experience, as the huge trees, tangled vines, and dense undergrowth are a thousand shades of green. Blue, red-tailed, and black-and-white colobus monkeys can be seen feeding in the trees. If you are adventurous and lucky, a night walk with a guide from the forest station can turn up such nocturnal creatures as the potto ("bush baby") and flying squirrel.

Getting There The simplest way is to drive to Kisumu on Lake Victoria, 350 kilometers (215 mi) from Nairobi. From Kisumu take A1 north 41.5 kilometers (25.7 mi) and turn at a sign reading ARAP MOI SECONDARY GIRLS SCHOOL; continue for 11 kilometers (7 mi) to the Kakamega Forest station sign, which is 1 kilometer (.6 mi) down this track on the left. Park the car here and continue on foot into the forest.

Lodging **Kakamega Golf Hotel.** This large modern hotel in Kakamega
Inexpensive town has a swimming pool, disco, and a golf course. It is the cleanest and most comfortable lodging in the area. *Msafiri Inns, Box 42013, Nairobi, tel. 2/330820 or 29751. AE, V.*

Lake Bogaria National Reserve
Marigat, Nakuru, tel. Kabarnet 41

Size 107 square kilometers (41 sq. mi)

Year Established 1973

Headquarters Marigat

This small, narrow Rift Valley lake is located just south of Lake Baringo and north of Lake Nakuru in a cleft below a sheer fault scarp on the east that leads up to the Laikipia Plateau. About halfway down the lake on the western side is a series of hot springs and geysers that blast boiling water into the sky, the most impressive of their kind in East Africa. The lake is shallow, extremely alkaline, and impressive.

Wildlife The alkalinity of the lake water provides a perfect environment for the blue-green algae that lesser flamingos thrive on, and vast numbers—2 million—have been recorded here. The reserve was established to protect not the flamingos but the lesser kudu that come down from the Laikipia Plateau to take salt at the lake's edge in the evening on the eastern side.

Tours Vehicles and guides can be hired to go down the track on the western side of the lake from the Lake Baringo Country Club some 40 kilometers (25 mi) to the north.

Getting There Take A104 to Nakuru some 156 kilometers (97 mi) from Nairobi, then follow the signposts off to the right to go north on the tarmac B4 toward Lake Baringo. If you have four-wheel-drive you can turn off at Mogotio to travel through sisal plantations and over rocky hills to reach the southern end of the lake. The easiest way is to continue up to the signpost on the right leading to the lake via Loboi, an easy trip for any passenger car.

By Car

By Plane There is a landing strip near Lake Baringo Country Club, but ground transport would have to be prearranged.

Lodging Lake Bogoria has no lodging; there are two places to stay 40 kilometers (25 mi) north.

Expensive **Island Camp.** Located on an island in the middle of Lake Baringo, this tented camp is an oasis in the hot Rift Valley. The luxury tents, with running water, electricity, and attached bathrooms, are on a hillside at the narrow southern end of the island. There is a pool, water sports, lake boat tours (including an optional breakfast where guests boil their eggs in a natural hot spring on another island), and island walks to explore and watch the Njemps fishermen. *Abercrombie & Kent, tel. 800/ 323-7308. AE, DC, MC, V.*

Lake Baringo Country Club. A luxury hotel on the edge of Lake Baringo, this spot is a dream for bird-watchers—480 species have been counted. The property has a pool, and bird-watching foot safaris, camel rides, boat rides around the lake, and tours to Lake Bogoria are offered. *Block Hotels, Box 47557, Nairobi, tel. 2/22860 or 335807. AE, DC, MC, V.*

Lake Nakuru National Park
Box 539, Nakuru, tel. Nakuru 2470

Size 188 square kilometers (73 sq. mi)

Year Established Bird sanctuary, 1960; national park, 1967

Headquarters Just inside the Nakuru gate

Lake Nakuru, some 150 kilometers (93 mi) northwest of Nairobi, is one of a series of shallow alkaline lakes that formed on the floor of the Rift Valley, though it actually lies higher than Nairobi at an altitude of 1,758 meters (5,767 ft). Nakuru town is 3 kilometers (2 mi) north of the lake on the lower slopes of Mt. Menengai, an extinct volcano whose rim rises 514 meters (1,700 ft) above the lake and encloses one of the world's largest craters, some 11 kilometers (7 mi) across. Menengai means "place of the corpses" in Maa, the Masai language, and is said to derive from a battle in which the Naivasha Masai defeated the Laikipia Masai and forced a group of *moran* ("warriors") to plummet to their deaths from the rim of the crater.

The park is renowned for its birdlife, and the lake itself has been termed "the greatest bird spectacle on earth" by Roger Tory Peterson, one of the world's leading ornithologists, for its huge concentration of lesser flamingos, which at times forms a dense pink fringe around the blue waters of the lake. The park was originally established as a sanctuary for flamingos, even though they do not breed here. Flamingos are attracted by a microscopic blue-green algae called *Spirulina*, which when it comes into flower can produce a crop of up to 65,000 tons. When the algae is flourishing, more than a million lesser flamingos may be found on the edge of the lake feeding on it. The less numerous greater flamingos feed on diatoms, a microscopic organism that has a silica skeleton. Diatoms that aren't eaten eventually die and, the skeletons accumulate on the floor of the lake, leaving a white deposit exposed when the lake dries up.

Three seasonal rivers flow into Lake Nakuru, but there is no outlet, so thousands of years of evaporation have increased the mineral content of the water considerably. Most plant species are unable to survive this highly alkaline medium, but the algae thrive on it. Along with providing food for the lesser flamingos, the algae support a small alkaline-tolerant fish introduced as an antimosquito measure called *Tilapia grahami*. The abundant fish attract fish-eating birds such as pelicans, fish eagles, storks, herons, and cormorants, among others. Pelicans work in teams as they skim the surface of the water herding fish, then scoop them up with their pouched lower beaks.

The park's attractions are not limited to the flamingo population; there are more than 400 other bird species resident here, including large numbers of darters, ibises, plovers, and white pelicans. In addition there are 50 mammal species in the different habitats around the lake shore, including a relocated population of protected rhino.

An all-weather road completely encircles the lake, off which there are numerous tracks down to the lakeshore where parking areas are provided. Visitors should not drive too close to the lake's edge as the salt-encrusted shoreline conceals very soft mud. Instead leave your vehicle and walk along the shore, being careful not to startle the large flocks of birds.

The park's main gate reveals a road that follows the western shore of the lake, from which, off to the left, is the track to the mouth of the Njoro River, and after which are tracks leading to a wide, open shoreline. The dirt road going left from the main gate travels around the north shore, off to the right of which are tracks to Hippo Point, then a number of observation blinds.

Wildlife The lakeshore and surrounding grassland, bushland, and forest offer two contrasting habitats. Waders, avocets, and stilts feed in the shallows of the lakeshore and their numbers greatly increase in the winter when migrant species fly down from Europe. A variety of plovers resides at the lake and can be found nesting on the mud flats between June and August. Although neither flamingos nor pelicans breed at the lake, white-necked cormorants and African darters do. Large colonies are to be found at the mouth of the Njoro River, where birds breed actively most of the year. The pelicans use the Njoro for washing off the soda from the lake.

The fresh waters of the river and a series of springs along its north shore attract a large variety of birds, such as migrant waders and ducks, especially in the winter. The fresh water is much less turgid than the lake water, and herons and kingfishers prefer these areas for fishing. The resident hippos spend most of the day in the water by the fresh springs but come onshore to graze at night.

To the east the lake is bounded by rocky hills that are covered with a fascinating forest of strange *Candelabra euphorbia*, which is probably the best of its kind in Kenya. A rocky escarpment known as Baboon Rocks is to be found on the western shore and offers a superb view over the lake. Baboons are frequently seen in these areas, and the rock hyrax is common. Antelope found here include the sure-footed klipspringer and Chanler's reedbuck; the rocks are also the home of that elusive predator the leopard—which is increasing in number.

There are open grasslands running down to the lake on its northern and southern shores. The coarse spiky grass on the immediate shore and the lusher grass farther inland provide grazing for herds of Defassa waterbuck, impala, Thomson's gazelles and Bohor reedbuck. It is the only place in Kenya where these reedbuck can be seen in such large numbers.

Birds found in this habitat range from minute larks and ground-nesting plovers to the graceful crowned cranes, secretary birds, and magnificent ground hornbills. Rodents are common, especially in the dry seasons, and a variety of birds of prey frequent both this area and the bush and forest regions of the park. Away from the lake's edge the grassland merges into *Tarconanthus* scrub and this provides yet another habitat for the animals of the park. Birds found here include shrikes, rollers, and coucals; and among the mammals are Burchell's zebra, warthog, Grant's gazelles, and jackals.

Extensive tracts of yellow-barked fever trees (acacia) on the eastern shore and the south of the lake provide a habitat for vervet and colobus monkeys, and cover for the more secretive bush buck and Kirk's dik-dik. Between 300 and 400 buffalo inhabit the park—the most likely place to see them is in the forest areas at dawn or dusk. Colorful waxbills, sunbirds, hoopoes, and chats are well represented in the forest as well as larger birds of prey such as the magnificent long-crested hawk eagle and fish eagles. A rhinoceros sanctuary has been fenced off in the southwest portion of the park and populated with about 15 rhino relocated from Solio ranch on the Laikipia Plateau and others from a sanctuary located on Lewa Downs, a ranch just below the Laikipia.

Getting There   Take A104 northwest from Nairobi 156 kilometers (97 mi) to Nakuru town. Enter the town and follow the signs to the park gate which is 3 kilometers (2 mi) south of the town.

Lodging   **Lake Nakuru Lodge.** The lodge is an extensively remodeled for-
Expensive   mer farmhouse of Lord Delamere's Nderit Estate. It is on high ground on the edge of the park and offers a good view of the lake from its outdoor terrace, where excellent buffet lunches are served to both guests and visitors. Rooms are located in the main lodge or in cozy cottages on the grounds. There is a good

swimming pool. *Box 70559, Nairobi, tel. 2/20225; Box 561, Nakuru. AE, DC, V.*

Sarova Lion Hill. This former permanent tented camp has been completely renovated and now consists of bandas with all of the modern conveniences. It is located on the side of Lion Hill and visitors can sit on their shaded banda terraces and look down across the park and lake. There is a swimming pool and sauna for relaxing after a visit to the park. *Sarova Group, Box 30680, Nairobi, tel. 2/333233; Box 7094, Nakuru. No credit cards.*

Inexpensive **Midland Hotel.** Built in 1906, it is Nakuru town's oldest surviving building, located just off the A104. It offers second-rate lodging, but its back courtyard is a convenient place to stop and have a drink or simple lunch. *Box 908, Nakuru, tel. 37/41277. No credit cards.*

Maralal National Sanctuary
Box 53, Maralal, tel. Maralal 53

Size 553 square kilometers (214 sq. mi)

Year Established 1983

Entrance Fee Free

Headquarters Maralal

The Maralal sanctuary is a rather informally protected area for wildlife and forest around Maralal town. This highland forest area is under increasing pressure from Samburu cattle herders and wheat farmers, who claim more forest land each year. The word *maralal* means "glittering" in Samburu and was given by them to the first building put up there in 1934, which had a shining metal roof that could be seen from miles away.

There are no game-viewing tracks to follow in the sanctuary, and the only place to stay besides low-rent lodgings in town is the Maralal Safari Lodge. Maralal town is not worth a special visit but is a good place to overnight en route to somewhere else. Its main attraction is the Kenyatta House, where Kenya's first president was held prisoner by the British colonial government until 1961. It is an empty, tin-roofed bungalow and there is little to see.

Wildlife The sanctuary contains a full range of wildlife, though about the only place to view game is from the veranda of the Maralal Safari Lodge, where artificial pools and a salt lick attract zebra, waterbuck, warthog, buffalo, baboons, impala, and eland. The lodge also maintains a blind at Leopard Rock, a pleasant walk from the lodge, where leopard can be viewed at a flood-lit baiting spot.

Tours The Maralal Safari Lodge rents out four-wheel-drive vehicles and drivers, but there are no set tours.

Getting There Take A104 out of Nairobi past Naivasha and turn off into Gilgil town, then turn north and go 100 kilometers (62 mi) on tarmac road to Rumuruti, where the tarmac ends. Maralal is a further 112 kilometers (70 mi) on a dirt road that, depending on recent maintenance, can have some pretty rough spots.

Lodging **Maralal Safari Lodge.** The lodge is situated out of town and
Moderate higher up on a sparsely forested ridge. The rooms are luxury split-level A-frame cedar log cabins set in 19 acres of forest glade. Game can be viewed at close quarters from the terrace

and glassed-in lodge central room. An airstrip is located 2 kilometers (1.2 mi) away. *Thorn Tree Safaris, Box 42475, Nairobi, tel. 2/25641 or 25941. AE, V.*

Marsabit National Reserve
Box 42, Marsabit, tel. Marsabit 28

Size 2,088 square kilometers (806 sq. mi)

Year Established 1962

Headquarters Marsabit town

Marsabit is a large mountain that rises out of the burning arid plains surrounding it in the far north of Kenya. All the native peoples of the plains—Rendille to the south and west; Gabbra to the north and west; Boran, Sakuyu, and Somali to the east—are pastoralists. The good grazing of the mountain slopes and, more recently, the growth of Marsabit town, have attracted all of these pastoralists, making it a cosmopolitan hub. Many different peoples from farther south have come to set up shops and other businesses, and farmers and traders from Ethiopia have settled here as well, adding to the melting-pot nature of this mountain community.

The forest up to the reserve boundary has been completely cut down to make way for farms, but above in the national reserve is a thick tropical forest that forms a cap of drizzling mist every night, which slowly burns off in the morning. It is this 1,600-meter- (5,250-ft) high massif that provides the water catchment for the springs, wells, and water holes that permit life below in the plains. The mountain and its lower slopes are pitted with spectacular volcanic craters that sometimes fill to form seasonal lakes. The best-known is Lake Paradise, where the Americans Martin and Osa Johnson spent four years in the 1920s writing and filming what was then their private paradise. The lake is almost circular, about 2 kilometers (1.5 mi) in diameter, and ringed with a bright green marsh and grass where buffalo, baboons, and other wildlife are often seen. It also attracts varied birdlife, especially coots, for which a onetime hunter on Marsabit had an interesting recipe: Boil the coot together with a brick in a large pot for six hours, he wrote, then throw away the coot and eat the brick!

Below Lake Paradise is a rocky pool named Boculi, after the Johnsons' fine old gun-bearer. This pool is a popular watering place for elephants, buffalo, and greater kudu. There is also a swampy lake in front of the Marsabit Lodge named Sokorte Dika which attracts game and birds.

Not far from Marsabit town, reached by a small track to Ulanula, are the "singing wells." Dug by the pastoralists deep into the earth and rock of the mountain, the name derives from the chanting of the chain of men as they draw water from the well. Some extraordinary pictures can be taken here, but be sure to agree upon a price before photographing—the pastoralists carry spears!

There are dirt tracks that go through the reserve, and around it through inhabited areas, but the tracks are poorly maintained and signposted and it is advisable to take a local guide and to have a four-wheel-drive vehicle if explorations are to be made.

Wildlife Animals found in the park include buffalo, lion, leopard, caracal, striped hyena, reticulated giraffe, and aardwolf, but they are difficult to spot in the thick forest. The main wildlife attractions are the greater kudu, with their heavily spiraled horns, and the splendid elephants that have a reputation for large tusks. Two former "tuskers," Mohammed and Ahmed, had tusks approaching 45 kilograms (100 lbs) each. Ahmed was protected by presidential decree and was guarded by rangers until his natural death in 1974. A life-size model of him stands in the courtyard of the Kenya National Museum in Nairobi.

Ornithologist John Williams estimates that there are 52 species of raptors among the birds of the mountain, including the lammergeier on the cliffs of the largest crater, or "gof," Gof Bongole.

Tours No tours are available in Marsabit.

Getting There
By Car Four-wheel-drive is highly recommended, and if you are driving around in other parts of Marsabit District, it is advisable to have more than one vehicle in the party in case of breakdown. Take A2 to Isiolo, 255 kilometers (158 mi) on tarmac road from Nairobi (except for the stretch under repair before Nanyuki). At Isiolo all vehicles going farther north than the turnoff to Samburu-Buffalo Springs-Shaba National Reserves must go in convoy, accompanied by armed guards, for security reasons. Although extremely rare, attacks by *shifta* (bandits) have been known to occur on A2 in the north. The stony road is rippled and potholed, caused mainly by the speeding trucks in the convoys, and a rugged vehicle with high clearance is needed. Marsabit town is 273 kilometers (170 mi) away, about a five-hour drive from Isiolo.

By Plane There is a good, tarmac landing strip outside Marsabit town, but there is no ground transport or fuel. Planes can be chartered at Nairobi's Wilson Airport, but arrangements must be made for further ground transport with a tour operator.

Lodging
Moderate **Marsabit Lodge.** Located on the edge of a swampy lake in the reserve, this old lodge is the only one in Marsabit, so it can get away with being poorly managed and serving bad food. Its lovely location and peaceful, forested surroundings, however, make up for its defects. Elephants are often seen down on their front knees feeding in the swampy grass in front of the lodge. *Msafiri Inns, Box 42013, Nairobi, tel. 2/330820 or 29751. No credit cards.*

Campsites There are campsites just outside the Marsabit gate to the reserve and at Lake Paradise. The sites are reserved and paid for at the gate.

Masai Mara National Reserve
Box 72, Narok, tel. Narok 4

Size 1,800 square kilometers (695 sq. mi)

Year Established 1961

Headquarters Narok

Note: A May 1992 warning mentions incidents of robbery, sometimes with violence, usually involving single vehicles. Tourists are advised to avoid the Masai Mara but if they go, to travel only in multi-vehicle safaris with reputable tour companies.

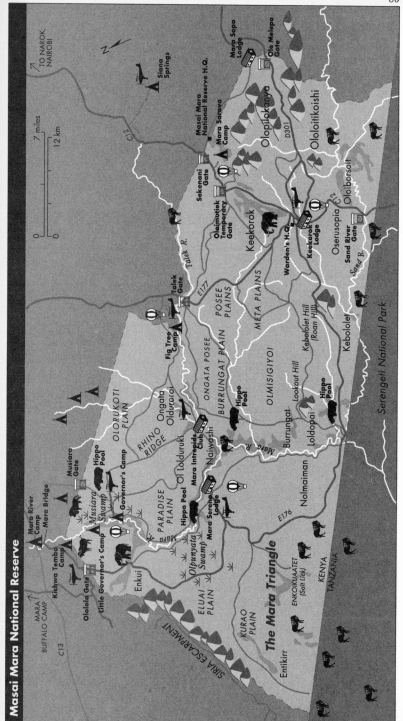

Masai Mara National Reserve

80

To Narok, Nairobi

7 miles
12 km

MARA BUFFALO CAMP
C13
Mara River Camp
Mara Bridge
Kichwa Tembo Camp
Ololola Gate
Little Governor's Camp
Musiara Gate
Hippo Pool
Governor's Camp
Musiara Swamp
Enkui
Oloolimutia
PARADISE PLAIN
Hippo Pool
Mara Serena Lodge
Mara R.
Olpunyata Swamp
ELUAI PLAIN
KURAO PLAIN
ENKOIKIUAATET (Salt Lick)
Entikirr

SIRIA ESCARPMENT
The Mara Triangle
KENYA
TANZANIA

OLORUKOTI PLAIN
RHINO RIDGE
Olduruki
Naiwoshi
Mara Intrepids Club
Ongata Oldururoi
Fig Tree Camp
Talek Gate
Talek R.
E177
ONGATA POSEE PLAIN
POSEE PLAINS
BURRUNGAT PLAIN
Hippo Pool
OLMISIGIYOI
Lookout Hill
Loldopai
Burrungat
Nolmaiman
E176
Mara R.

Masai Mara National Reserve H.Q.
Mara Sarova Camp
Sekenani Gate
Olaimutiek Temporary Gate
Warden's H.Q.
Keekorok
Keekorok Lodge
META PLAINS
Kebololet Hill (Roan Hill)
Kebololet

Mara Sopa Lodge
Ole Melepo Gate
Olopilokonya
Ololoitikoishi
D301
Oserusopia
Oloiborsoit
Sand River Gate
Sand R.
Siana Springs
C12

Serengeti National Park

The Mara, as it is called, represents most people's idea of East Africa. The landscape is one of rolling savanna, intersected by the dark green veins of acacia woodland on the banks of the Mara and Talek rivers and of their many seasonal tributaries. The word *mara* means "mottled" in Maa, the Masai language, and is only one of the many Maa adjectives describing the cow. The high rainfall—a result of Lake Victoria's humidity and a high altitude—makes the Mara greener and more temperate than other Kenyan parks.

The reserve, 249 kilometers (155 mi) west of Nairobi, is effectively an extension into Kenya of Tanzania's great Serengeti National Park, the two making up a single 24,860-square-kilometer (9,600-sq.-mi) ecosystem. Many consider it the best of Kenya's wildlife sanctuaries, where animals can still be seen in the vast numbers once common to much of the country, but it can be overcrowded with tourists. The greatest wildlife spectacle in the world takes place between July and October, when wildebeests and zebras move north from the Serengeti into the Mara, in a great migration in search of fresh grass after the long rains end in June. The wildebeest population is now at an all-time high (about 2.5 million), but not all are in the Mara.

The reserve is under the control of the Narok County Council, though the Kenya Game Department provides rangers. The park is divided in two: in one section the land can be used by the Masai, who graze their cattle alongside the wildlife; the other section is for wildlife only. In the area south of a line drawn between Little Governor's Camp and the Keekorok Lodge and east of the Mara River, the land is treated like a national park. This area measures about 500 square kilometers (193 sq. mi), and no settlement or cattle grazing is allowed.

If you are interested in the local culture, Masai *manyattas* (village communities) can be visited just outside the Musiara gate in the northwest part of the reserve. The manyattas are in typical Masai style, with low, oblong mud-and-dung houses strung around in a circle. This is a good place to pick up some of the brightly colored Masai beadwork, which is made into necklaces, bracelets, and earrings. To get a good price you must bargain extremely hard and get the seller alone in a corner somewhere. Depending on your skill, the same necklace could cost you 50 or 500 Kenyan shillings.

A visit to Tanzania's Serengeti National Park and even Ngorongoro Crater can be made by passing through the Sand River gate, but you will need a visa to enter Tanzania and small-denomination money for the U.S. dollar fees. You will also need a vehicle to pick you up on the Tanzania side if you are using a tour vehicle, since only private vehicles with Kenyan registration are allowed in. A three-month license costs $60.

Wildlife The eastern section of the reserve generally has heavier vegetation and is more hilly than the other parts. Much game can also be seen outside the reserve, but during the migration in this area the stupendous congregations of wildebeests and zebras cannot be seen, because the broken topography blocks long-range views.

A good game run would involve traversing the reserve from the Keekorok area, crossing the Talek River, and ending up in the Governor's Camp area in the Mara Triangle. There are many little tracks to take for exploring likely areas to find rhino and the big cats. Hippos can be found in the main hippo pools on the Talek and Mara rivers. A return could be made by heading south to Lookout Hill, then passing by Roan Hill and back to Keekorok. Drives along the rivers are also good for seeing game. If you are with a tour company or at a camp that has its own vehicles, as most do, the drivers usually are quite knowledgeable about where to go to find game.

Many species of plains animals reside in the rolling grasslands throughout the year, including buffalo, wildebeests, hartebeests, impalas, zebras, and gazelles. Common to Mara, but found in only a few other places in Kenya, are topi, which often stand on hillocks looking picture-perfect; they are actually on guard for predators. There is also a small colony of roan antelope in the western section of the reserve near the Siria escarpment—but not at the misleadingly named Roan Hill near Keekorok Lodge.

With all of this *nyama* (meat) around, it is not surprising that the Mara has Kenya's largest predator population. Lions are common, and prides of up to 20 or 30 animals can be seen, often under the baleful supervision of a large, black-maned patriarch. Cheetahs are also numerous, and the Mara is probably the best place for sighting leopards under natural conditions, though this predator is still rare.

The rhinoceros and elephant populations have been growing since the early 1980s, when antipoaching efforts were increased and poaching in Tanzania drove some north into the Mara. Latest counts, in 1987, show 20 rhino and more than 1,100 elephants. Elephants are commonly seen in the northern part of the reserve and around Governor's Camp and Keekorok. The rhino can be spotted by looking for a large congregation of minibuses and cars, though this also could indicate cheetahs. Off-road driving is *not* permitted in the Mara, because it destroys the habitat.

There are also many hyenas and silver-backed jackals, and packs of the rare hunting dogs are making their reappearance. Herds of up to 20 stately giraffes are seen in all parts of the reserve, and along the Mara River hippos gather in great profusion in pools. Large crocodiles frequent the banks and sandspits. In all, some 95 species of mammals, amphibians, and reptiles have been noted in the Mara.

The birdlife is equally diverse. A total of 485 species have been identified, 53 of them raptors. On the plains a variety of bustards can be seen strutting along with secretary birds, and the giant ground hornbill, over 3 feet tall, looks like a turkey mutant. The riverine forests have their own species, including the beautiful Ross's turaco, recognized by the flash of its scarlet wings through the trees.

Tours Every lodge and tented camp listed below has its own vehicles and drivers to take visitors on game drives. The drivers at Governor's and Little Governor's are particularly noted for their knowledge of the reserve, but the motley collection of Toyota Land Cruisers and Land Rovers are long in the tooth and are known to break down from time to time. The price for staying at Governor's includes two game runs a day, so it is wise to take advantage of the offer. Kichwa Tembo tends to have newer four-wheel-drive vehicles, and they can cover areas outside the reserve to the west of Mara River more easily. Keekorok has minibuses that are fine in dry weather, but if it has been raining they tend to get stuck in the mud.

Keekorok and Mara Serena lodges both offer an early morning hot-air-balloon ride to view game from about 50 meters (155 ft) above the animals. You wake before sunrise and climb into an open basket with a great big orange-and-white-striped balloon over it, somewhat like that seen in the movie of Jules Verne's *Around the World in 80 Days*. The aeronaut gives a blast from the gas jet into the balloon, and up you go. After about 45 minutes of floating silently, down you come to a champagne breakfast—for about $230 per person.

Getting There
By Car
From Nairobi, you can take the high or the low road. The high road is the smooth A104 through the highlands, where there are some wonderful views of the Rift Valley and Mt. Longonot below, and down a long sweeping drive through *shambas* (farms) to the Naivasha turnoff on the left, a distance of 84 kilometers (54 mi). The bad part is having to backtrack 35 kilometers (22 mi) on the old Nairobi-Naivasha Road to the Narok turnoff. The quicker, but more uncomfortable, route is 56 kilometers (35 mi) down the potholed and crumpled B3 to the Narok turnoff at the foot of the escarpment. A 90-kilometer (56-mi) drive across the Rift Valley floor, past the Longonot satellite station and the Suswa volcano, brings you to the escarpment on the other side and to Narok. After Narok the road is tarmac for 17 kilometers (10 mi) as far as Ewaso Ngiro, where three dirt roads fork left, right, and center. The left fork goes to Narosura and the Loita Hills, the center road goes past Siana Springs and through the Olemelepo gate to Keekorok Lodge, 90 kilometers (56 mi) away, and the right fork takes you through bush and wheat fields, the dumpy town of Lemek, and some pretty countryside to the Mara River, Mara Buffalo, Kichwa Tembo, and Governor's tented camps. It is about 110 kilometers (69 mi) of truly horrible road to the Olololo gate. If you are going to any of the northwestern camps and can afford it, fly.

By Plane
Air Kenya Aviation (tel. 2/501421) flies twice daily to any of the Masai Mara airfields, and **Executive Air Services** (tel. 2/500607 or 505122) flies once daily.

Lodging
Very Expensive
Governor's Camp and Little Governor's Camp. These two luxurious tented camps, near each other on opposite sides of the Mara River, represent the best that this type of lodging has to offer in Kenya. Situated in the riverine forest, Governor's looks out onto the river; Little Governor's has its own swamp, which attracts elephants, hippos, buffalo, and birds. There is an all-weather airstrip nearby, and vehicles are available for game runs. *Box 48217, Nairobi, tel. 2/331871 or 331041. AE, DC, MC, V.*

Mara Intrepids Club. This new, super-luxurious tented camp is situated on the Talek River. The decor is coastal Swahili, with Lamu chests, carpets, and canopied four-poster beds in the 22 double tents. The cuisine is excellent, but prices are high. *Mara Intrepids Club, Box 14040, Nairobi, tel. 2/335208. AE, DC, MC, V.*

Expensive
Keekorok Lodge. An institution in the Mara, the lodge itself, which offers both tents and rooms, is comfortable and well managed. There is a rather unsightly jumble of buildings leading up to it, however, and it has a disappointing view onto a nearby

rise. The lodge has a pool and its own tarmac airstrip. Balloon flights with champagne breakfast are available. *Block Hotels, Box 47557, Nairobi, tel. 2/22860 or 335807. AE, DC.*

Mara Sarova Camp. Conveniently located near the Olemelepo gate, this new luxury camp has 40 tents and a pool that is frequently visited by elephants. It is situated between two streams on the crest of a rise that offers an expansive view over the reserve. *Sarova Hotels, Box 30680, Nairobi, tel. 2/333233. AE, DC, MC, V.*

Mara Serena Lodge. Occupying a hilltop site with vast views over the Mara Triangle and Mara River, this lodge has pseudo-Masai architecture, and the interior decor makes effective use of Masai motifs. Traditional dancing is performed every evening after dinner. There is a decent pool, and the garden attracts countless species of birds. An all-weather airstrip is nearby. *Serena Lodges & Hotels, Box 48690, Nairobi, tel. 2/338656. AE, MC, V.*

Tented Camps Outside the Reserve

Expensive

Fig Tree Camp. This comfortable tented camp is outside the Talek gate, with the Talek River on three sides. It's more informal than many of the other camps, without sacrificing quality. *Box 67868, Nairobi, tel. 2/21439 or 20592. AE, MC, V.*

Kichwa Tembo Camp. This excellent tented camp is at the edge of a clump of forest on a gentle hill outside the northwest corner of the reserve, overlooking the Mara River, the plains, and the Governor's Camp area. It shares an airstrip with Governor's near the Olololo gate. Foot and vehicle safaris are available. The nature walk follows the riverine forest, where vervets, giraffes, and myriad birds are common. *Abercrombie & Kent, Box 20224, Nairobi, tel. 2/334955 or, in the U.S., tel. 800/323–7308. AE, DC, MC, V.*

Mara Buffalo Camp. This is another comfortable tented camp overlooking the Mara River, about 20 kilometers (12½ mi) from the Olololo gate. Walks can be taken up and down the river, but be careful of buffalo and predators. This camp is used exclusively by a Swiss tour company, but individuals can request prices and make reservations in writing. *Repotel, Box 46527, Nairobi, tel. 2/27828. AE, MC, V.*

Sekenani Camp features 8 double tents in a very private setting, *Utalii Tours and Safaris Ltd., Box 61542, Nairobi, tel. 2/333285 or 2/212370,1,2, fax 2/228875. No credit cards.*

Siana Springs. A new luxury tented camp with a central dining lodge has been built by Windsor Hotels at what was formerly known as Cottar's Camp. The 38 double tents spread under giant fig trees near a natural spring have large bathrooms en suite, electricity, and verandas. Siana Springs is about 15 kilometers (9 mi) from the Olemelepo gate. Walking safaris and night game drives are available in the hilly countryside. Take advantage of these, as they are not allowed inside the reserve. *Abercrombie & Kent, Box 20224, Nairobi, tel. 2/334995 or, in the U.S., tel. 800/323–7308. AE, DC, MC, V.*

Moderate

Mara River Camp. Downstream from the Mara Buffalo across the Mara bridge, about 30 minutes from the reserve, this camp also overlooks the river. The flat plains to the east offer good areas for cheetahs, which are after the numerous Thomson's gazelles. *Bookings Ltd., Box 20106, Nairobi, tel. 2/25255. AE, MC, V.*

Campsites There are several in the outer reserve, and some along the Talek River. The sites have no facilities, so campers must be self-sufficient. Bookings can be made at the gate. In high season, it is advisable to write to the reserve (Masai Mara National Reserve, Box 60, Narok, no phone).

Meru National Park
Park Warden, Box 162, Meru, tel. Radiocall Nairobi 3700

Size 870 square kilometers (336 sq. mi)

Year Established 1960, national reserve; 1966, national park

Headquarters 10 kilometers on track southeast of Meru Mulika Lodge

Meru National Park, 95 kilometers (60 mi) to the northeast of Mt. Kenya, is the least visited and the most unspoiled of Kenya's major parks and reserves—which is its primary attraction. Here Joy and George Adamson released the lioness Elsa, subject of the book and film *Born Free*. The park was once known for its protected, semitame group of white rhino—the only ones in Kenya—but the herd fell victim to poachers in 1988.

Although it straddles the equator in a hot, dry area, the park's northwestern perimeter lies in the foothills of the Nyambeni range, which receives a high volume of rainfall. The hills feed 19 rivers and streams, 15 of them permanent, that flow in or on the boundaries of the park. A number of swamps and springs also make the area a desirable one for wildlife. The park is bounded on the south by the Ura and Tana rivers and on the east by the Murera and Rojewero rivers, along whose banks stands a rich woodland of acacia, fig, and palm trees, alive with parrots and vervet monkeys.

The eastern flow of the Rojewero River from the Nyambeni Hills divides the park into two areas of contrasting topography. To the north are open grazing plains with light acacia woodland, cut through by numerous river courses running down from the hills and sprouting doum palms. The park's main concentrations of game are found in these areas, including many of the main species, and a number characteristic of the northern areas, such as the reticulated giraffe, Somali ostrich, Beisa oryx, and the occasional Grevy's zebra.

Due to the park's ecological variety and plenitude of water—and the low human population density outside its boundaries—it has the potential to be a wildlife paradise. Long-term poaching has taken its toll, but the creation of a park has brought back the decimated herds of buffalo and antelope. Many leopard have been reintroduced to the park, but there are virtually no remaining rhino.

A good network of tracks covers the park; a signpost system is used for identification in conjunction with the very good official park map available in almost any bookstore in Kenya. The tracks are generally well maintained and pose little problem for a sturdy passenger car in the dry season, but in the wet season—apart from the main tracks—a four-wheel-drive vehicle is recommended for negotiating the numerous river crossings and muddy drifts.

In the northwest of the park the tracks take the form of a series of long, thin loops parallel to the course of the many rivers and

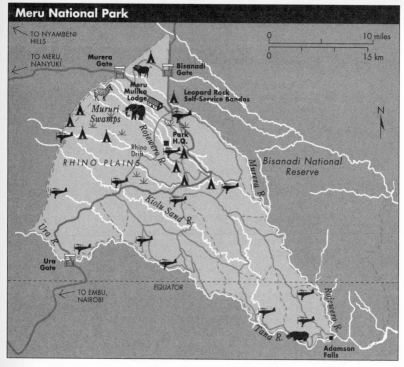

Meru National Park

TO NYAMBENI HILLS

TO MERU, NANYUKI

Murera Gate

Bisanadi Gate

Meru Mulika Lodge

Leopard Rock Self-Service Bandas

Mururi Swamps

Park H.Q.

Rhino Drift

RHINO PLAINS

Bisanadi National Reserve

Kiolu Sand R.

Rojewero R.

Murera R.

Ura R.

Ura Gate

TO EMBU, NAIROBI

EQUATOR

Tana R.

Rojewero R.

Adamson Falls

0 ——————— 10 miles
0 ——————— 15 km

N

main swamps of the plains. The plains surrounding the park headquarters are crisscrossed with a network of good tracks. South of the Rojewero a few tracks stretch out to the Ura and Tana rivers and, although it is a long dusty haul—24 kilometers (15 mi) each way—it is well worth the effort. The area here is completely different from the northern part of the park, being drier, covered in thick thornbush, and dissected by numerous sand *luggas* (ephemeral streams).

Wildlife In the area of the Meru Mulika Lodge and toward the Murera gate are a number of swamps harboring many of the park's 4,000 buffalo. They are also a favorite haunt of the elephants, which cross over the plain to cool off here and take mud baths. The southern thornbush territory is a good place to find the long-necked gerenuk standing on their hind legs, and the timid lesser kudu with its magnificent horns. The kudu can be more easily seen here than elsewhere in Kenya.

At the southeastern corner of the park near the confluence of the Rojewero and the Tana rivers are the Adamson Falls, where the Tana cascades through a surrealist confusion of quartzite and granite rocks weathered into strange shapes. The Tana is a particularly good place to see hippo and crocodile—and do not swim in the river! Cheetah also live in the thick bush, not their usual habitat, and zoologists speculate that they feed mainly on rodents and dik diks here.

More than 300 species of birds have been identified in Meru, with parrots in the forests, kingfishers and herons by the many rivers, and five hornbill species in the bush. The white-throated bee-eater is often seen perched on the very end of a branch of a thorn tree. Of special interest are the palm nut vulture and palm swift, both associated with doum palms. The vulture gnaws the sweet outer layer of the doum palm nut as well as scavenging meat. The palm swift builds a tiny nest on the underside of a palm frond, gluing feathers and twigs together with its saliva. The egg is glued inside to hold it in place. The nest is blown in the wind on the palm frond, and when the chick is hatched, it has to hold on upside down until it can fly. The rare tufted guinea fowl, along with the more common helmeted and vulturine guinea fowl, are all found in the park.

Getting There   There are two main access routes to the park from Nairobi. The first is via Meru town, 294 kilometers (183 mi), which is reached by A2 through Thika and Nanyuki. The C91 tarmac road leaves Meru and runs 48 kilometers (30 mi) into the Nyambeni range of hills to Maua, just before which a track to the left travels the remaining 25 kilometers (16 mi) to the Murera gate. A more direct route, and a better one until A2 to Nanyuki is rebuilt, is via Embu, some 138 kilometers (86 mi) from Nairobi. From Embu take B6 toward Meru, then fork right after 19 kilometers (12 mi) and go a further 80 kilometers (50 mi) before turning right for the well-signposted Ura gate 64 kilometers (40 mi) away. From this gate it is a further 48 kilometers (30 mi) to the Meru Mulika Lodge.

Lodging   **Meru Mulika Lodge.** This full-service lodge has comfortable
Moderate   thatched, round huts made of local materials. They have running hot and cold water and generator electricity. The lodge overlooks Mulika Swamp, and good concentrations of elephants, buffalo, and zebra can be seen from the terrace. *Msafiri Inns, Box 42013, Nairobi, tel. 2/29751 or 330820. AE, MC, V.*

Inexpensive   **Isaak Walton Inn.** This somewhat run-down hotel is located in Embu, and is known mainly as a jumping-off place for fishing the trout streams of the eastern side of Mt. Kenya. It has attractive gardens and rather standard, English-style food. *Box 1, Embu, tel. Embu 28. AE, V.*

Leopard Rock Self-Service Bandas. This lodge has 10 self-help bandas located under monkey-filled acacia trees overlooking a gurgling brook, just outside the park near the Bisanadi gate. All utensils and crockery are provided and there are private bathrooms; lighting is with kerosene lanterns. Bedding can be rented and there is a small shop, but it is recommended that you bring your own food. *Box 14982, Nairobi, tel. 2/339700. No credit cards.*

Bisanadi, Rahole   These reserves border on Meru National Park to the east and,
and Kora National   in the case of Kora, to the south of the Tana River. They are all
Reserves   thick acacia commiphora bush and are undeveloped for tourism. There are few tracks through them and signs are almost nonexistent. There are no public accommodations.

Mt. Elgon National Park
Box 753, Kitale, tel. Kitale 20329

Size   169 square kilometers (65 sq. mi)

Year Established   1968

Headquarters   Kitale

Straddling the Kenya-Uganda border, Mt. Elgon today is a remnant of what was once a huge mountain. Thousands of years of erosion have worn it down to an altitude of 4,321 meters (14,178 ft) at the crater peak of Koitoboss, which is in Uganda. The park contains a range of habitats from bamboo jungle, forest and green woodland, to alpine moor studded with giant heather, groundsels, lobelias, and everlasting flowers.

The park has a unique system of caves once inhabited by the Elgon Masai. They can be easily visited on foot, as some are near the park roads, and are worth visiting. At the entrance to Kitum Cave, for example, there is a pool that was used by elephants, which went to Kitum Cave for centuries in search of the salt contained in the rock walls of the cave. They mined great quantities of it with their tusks, going farther and farther into the dark cave. Unfortunately, the herds were destroyed by poachers. Thousands of bats roost in the rear of the cave, and it is an eerie and fascinating experience to explore the labyrinth with hundreds of eyes gleaming in the reflection from a flashlight. The caves inspired the setting for Rider Haggard's novel, *She*.

It is possible to climb to the summit of the mountain starting from the village of Laboot, which is located in the moorlands. Many visitors are content to walk in the Laboot area, but for those who wish to climb to the top it is an 8-kilometer (5-mi) walk to the base-camp mountain hut. The key to the hut is available from the warden in Laboot. The hut is at 3,650 meters (11,975 ft) and the crater rim is at 4,300 meters (14,110 ft), thus the climb is not arduous. After passing through fields of flowers and giant senecios, you follow a track that winds through towering cliffs and past a mountain lake before climbing abruptly to the summit of Lower Elgon. The true summit is 20 meters (65 ft) higher on the Uganda side of the mountain. From the crater rim there is an outstanding panorama (on clear days) of the Kadam, Cherangani, and Ruri hills to the north, east, and south respectively.

Visitors to the moorlands should be well equipped for harsh mountain weather, as snow and freezing rain storms are common.

Wildlife   There are many monkeys in the forest and bamboo, including blue monkeys and black-and-white colobus—one of the most exciting animals to see on the move as it jumps from tree to tree with its long cape of fur streaming out behind it.

Elephants are also relatively numerous in the forest, although they are difficult to spot. There has been some poaching in recent years of this animal, mainly from poachers walking in over mountain paths from Uganda. Buffalo, reedbuck, waterbuck, bushbuck, black-fronted duiker, bushpig, giant forest hog, genet cat, warthog, tree hyrax, rock hyrax, and leopard are all present in substantial numbers but can easily be missed in the Podocarpus forest and thick bamboo.

The birdlife is also very rich. There are many turacos, including the brilliant red and blue Ross's turaco, silvery-cheeked and red-billed hornbills, white-naped ravens, Kenya crested guineafowl, white-headed wood hoopoe, and red-fronted parrots.

Getting There   From Nairobi, take A104 to Eldoret, B2 to Kitale, and then continue on to Endebess township, where there is a signpost on the left to the park gate. A better access to the moorlands than the Endebess gate is along C43 southwest of Kitale for 42 kilometers (26 mi) to the right turn onto C42 to Kimilili. Shortly before Kimilili, another right turn leads to Kapsakwony, beyond which the road can be very wet: A four-wheel-drive vehicle is recommended. Passing through plantations, natural forest, and bamboo, the road finally emerges on the moorlands and the village of Laboot.

Lodging **Mount Elgon Lodge.** This converted farmhouse, just outside
Inexpensive the park boundary, has seen better days. Although poorly maintained and managed, one night here is tolerable because of its pleasant location and proximity to the park. *Msafiri Inns, Box 42013, Nairobi, tel. 2/330820 or 29751. AE, V.*

Mt. Kenya National Park
Box 69, Naro Moru, tel. Nyeri 2575

Size 715 square kilometers (276 sq. mi)

Year Established 1949

Headquarters Mweiga

Legend has it that Ngai, creator of all things, dwelt on the inaccessible summit of Kirinyaga. The name "Kenya" is a corruption of the Kamba pronunciation of Kirinyaga. When you enter the forests and highlands of Mt. Kenya you leave behind the intensely cultivated shambas of the farmers who live around its immense base—the Kikuyu, Meru, Tharaka, and Embu peoples. You enter a world of lush rain forest, giant bamboo, strange volcanic rocks, equatorial glaciers, and rolling moorlands, all dominated by the thrusting twin peaks of Batian and Nelion, the second and third highest in Africa. On a clear morning Mt. Kenya can be seen from Nairobi, a far-off and enticing spire, its glaciers glistening in the sun.

Mt. Kenya rises 3,048 meters (10,000 ft) above the surrounding highland plateau and extends some 80 kilometers (50 mi) in diameter. Although volcanic in origin, it does not retain the smooth contours of many other volcanic mountains, but is instead crowned by two snow-covered peaks: Batian at 5,199 meters (17,058 ft) and Nelion at 5,188 meters (17,022 ft), both named after respected Masai *laibons*, or spiritual leaders. These and the smaller peaks nearby are the remaining volcanic plugs of the now-eroded but once-massive volcanic crater.

The lower slopes of the mountain are heavily cultivated, particularly on the southern and eastern sides where high rainfall and rich volcanic soil support intensive farming. Higher up there are dense rain forests of cedar, olive, and podo that merge into a bamboo zone at around 2,440 meters (8,000 ft). This in turn gives way to a belt of rosewood trees and giant Saint-John's-wort before dying out at the heath zone at about 3,200 meters (10,500 ft).

The national park itself begins where the upper forest merges with the heath zone, with the exception of two salients at the Naro Moru and Sirimon approaches. At 3,500 meters (11,480 ft) the giant heather is replaced by open moorland covered in tussock grass and studded with many species of giant lobelia and groundsel growing to a height of 3 to 5 meters (10 to 17 ft). The ground is covered in a rich profusion of everlasting helichrysums and alchemillas and interspersed with gladioli, delphiniums, and "red-hot pokers."

Mt. Kenya National Park

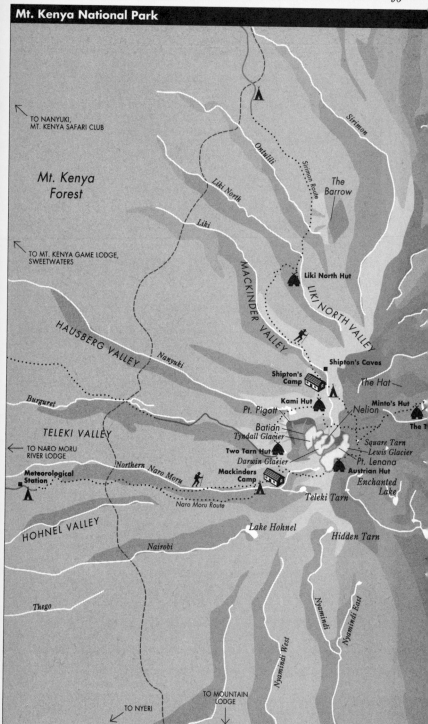

TO NANYUKI,
MT. KENYA SAFARI CLUB

Mt. Kenya
Forest

TO MT. KENYA GAME LODGE,
SWEETWATERS

Onthiliti

Sirimon

The
Barrow

Sirimon Route

Liki North

Liki

Liki North Hut

LIKI NORTH VALLEY

MACKINDER VALLEY

HAUSBERG VALLEY

Nanyuki

Burguret

TELEKI VALLEY

TO NARO MORU
RIVER LODGE

Meteorological
Station

Northern Naro Moru

Naro Moru Route

HOHNEL VALLEY

Nairobi

Thego

Shipton's Caves

Shipton's
Camp

Kami Hut

Pt. Pigott

Batian
Tyndall Glacier

Two Tarn Hut
Darwin Glacier

**Mackinders
Camp**

The Hat

Minto's Hut

Nelion

The T

Square Tarn
Lewis Glacier
Pt. Lenana
Austrian Hut

*Enchanted
Lake*

Teleki Tarn

Lake Hohnel

Hidden Tarn

Nyamindi West

Nyamindi

Nyamindi Easi

TO MOUNTAIN
LODGE

TO NYERI

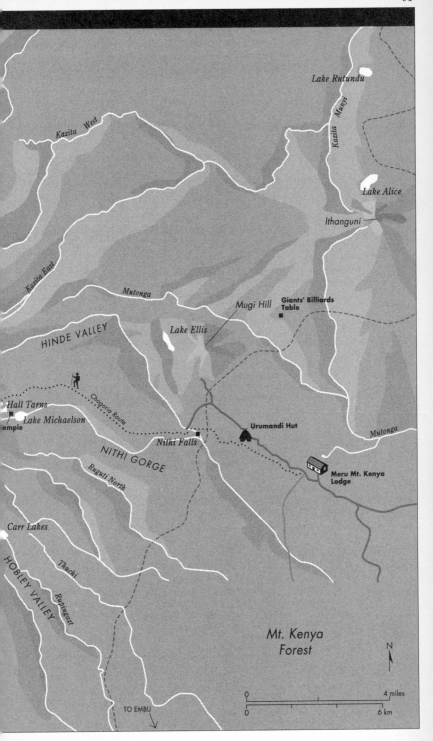

Lake Rutundu

Kazita West

Kazita Munyi

Lake Alice

Ithanguni

Kazita East

Mutonga

Mugi Hill

Giants' Billiards Table

HINDE VALLEY

Lake Ellis

Hall Tarns

Chogoria Route

Lake Michaelson

emple

Nithi Falls

Urumandi Hut

Mutonga

NITHI GORGE

Meru Mt. Kenya Lodge

Ruguti North

Carr Lakes

HOBLEY VALLEY

Thuchi

Rupingazt

Mt. Kenya Forest

N

TO EMBU

0   4 miles

0   6 km

Sir Halford Mackinder was the first person to climb the mountain in 1899, reaching the summit of Batian with his two Italian guides, Cesar Ollier and Joseph Brocherel, on September 13. Mackinder took a photograph of his two companions with his Kodak camera, and then they roped down into the Gates of the Mists, the icy col between the peaks. From that day until 1928 no one succeeded in climbing Batian again, while the summit of Nelion remained untrodden. In January 1929 Eric Shipton and Percy Wyn Harris climbed Nelion by what is now the Normal Route and crossed the Gates of the Mists to make the second ascent of Batian.

In 1943 three Italian prisoners of war who were in the prison camp at Nanyuki spent many hours behind the barbed wire looking up at the mountain. They hit upon an audacious idea: to escape, climb the mountain, and return to camp. How they made mountaineering equipment from bed springs and sacking, how they escaped, their gallant failure on Batian, and how they left the Italian flag on Point Lenana (another Masai laibon) are all superbly recounted in Felice Benuzzi's true-life adventure story *No Picnic on Mount Kenya*.

Climbing Mt. Kenya The central area of peaks, screes, valleys, and snowfields offers a great variety of climbing routes. Scaling Batian or Nelion calls for a high degree of mountaineering skill and experience of rock, ice, and snow techniques—and the necessary equipment. There are many enjoyable treks on the mountain that do not require real climbing, and for those who want to climb a summit, there is Point Lenana, which is suitable for those with no climbing experience.

Serious climbing is usually only attempted during Kenya's two dry seasons: late December to mid-March and July through September. Climbs can be made during the rainy seasons, but they are made more difficult by additional snow and ice, and the summits are more likely to be obscured by cloud if reached.

There are three main routes for climbing Mt. Kenya: the Naro Moru, the Sirimon, and the Chogoria. The vast majority of climbers aim for Point Lenana, at 4,986 meters (16,355 ft) a two-day climb that is within the capability of anyone who is moderately fit. Everyone from schoolchildren to retirees has scaled this summit. The main obstacle is the altitude, and a very fit athlete might fail where someone in poorer physical condition could succeed if he *goes slowly*. Do not rush even if you feel great. Your body needs to acclimatize to the increase in altitude to avoid pulmonary edema, an extremely serious illness.

Porters and guides can be hired for any of the three routes, though resident climbers make little or no use of them. You have three choices: Go alone, take porters and guides, or go with an upscale mountain-safari company. If you choose the latter, the following are recommended:

East African Mountain Guides (Box 44827, Nairobi, tel. 2/60728) and **Tropical Ice** (Box 57341, Nairobi, tel. 2/23649).

If you decide on taking the *Naro Moru Route*, contact the Naro Moru River Lodge (Box 18, Naro Moru, tel. Naro Moru 23). Here porters and guides can be hired for approximately Kshs. 65 per person per day. Warm clothing, gloves, and other gear can also be rented. To hire porters and guides for the *Sirimon*

Route contact the Bantu Utamaduni Lodge (Box 333, Nanyuki, no phone). Porters and guides are about Kshs. 90 per day. For the *Chogoria Route* contact Mt. Kenya Traversers (Box 449, Chogoria, no phone). Porters and guides are approximately Kshs. 100 per day.

The Naro Moru Route You leave your vehicle in the parking lot of the Meteorological Station on the west side of Mt. Kenya at 3,000 meters (9,750 ft). To help acclimatize, it is advisable to spend the night at the comfortable self-help cabins near the station in the forest. The ascent begins from the Met Station parking lot, up a winding dirt track through the rosewood forest to what is affectionately referred to as the "vertical bog," a sodden hill slope covered with tussocks. You will want to wear an old pair of athletic shoes, which can later be changed, or waterproof boots for this two-hour upward slog. The track is well marked with red and white poles every few hundred meters. When you crest the last ridge you are looking up the U-shape Teleki Valley.

The impressive peaks, projecting eerily above the rising fore-ground, their lower slopes still hidden, are now seen for the first time. With stops to take a breather and to appreciate the majestic countryside, giant lobelia, and groundsel, Mac-kinder's Camp is reached in another two hours up the valley. The entire trip takes about five hours and is as far as you should go the first day. Mackinder's Camp, at about 4,200 meters (13,650 ft), provides spartan accommodation in small pup tents on wood platforms. Be careful about leaving things outside, as hyraxes might run off with something. There is a large room where you can cook and eat, but the building is ugly and little has been done to improve it. If the sun has been out the walk up has been fairly warm, but at night it gets extremely cold.

The second day most people start early for Point Lenana, the third highest peak on Mt. Kenya. If you want to watch the sun-rise from the summit, you must start out at around 3 AM. The early morning cold makes it easier to walk over a boggy area at the head of the valley that will still be frozen solid. Your path crosses the ice tongue of a terminal moraine, and then you scram-ble up steep, sandy screes of the two steps forward, one step backward variety. At last the path reaches the ridge (by now you are feeling quite warm), and a short walk takes you to the Austri-an Hut, the highest large hut on the mountain, capable of sleeping about 30 people in three rooms. Two hundred meters (650 ft) away is the "Curling Pond," so named after an early explorer who amazed his guides by having a game of curling on its frozen sur-face. Some 200 meters (650 ft) of ascent remain to the summit across a snow field and up some rocks, about three hours in all from Mackinder's Camp. Point Lenana is a superlative location for viewing the surrounding countryside, including the eastern side of the mountain, the distant Nyandaruas (Aberdares), and, on a clear day, the far-off gleaming dome of Kilimanjaro. You can return to the Meteorological Station the same day.

The Sirimon Route This route starts from the northern side of the mountain at the end of a dirt track that turns off A2 to the right, not far before Timau. You leave your vehicle at a campsite beside a stream which crosses the track at 3,350 meters (10,900 ft) altitude. There is a path that leads toward a prominent hill called the Barrow, and you turn right on reaching a large stone cairn. The track contours around the Liki North Valley, then a steep climb goes up the west side of the valley to the ridge overlooking

Mackinder's Valley. You follow the valley side for 3 kilometers (2 mi), then cross up out of the valley to Kami Hut, by a little tarn (lake) located just north of Batian and Nelion.

This is the driest route and offers spectacular views northward to the arid lands and mountain ranges of the former Northern Frontier District.

The Chogoria Route This route is on the eastern side of the mountain opposite the Naro Moru. You can leave your car near the Meru County Council cabins, called the Meru Mt. Kenya Lodge, 500 meters (547 yds.) inside the park at 3,017 meters (9,898 ft), or at the end of the dirt road at Nithi Falls a further 8 kilometers (5 mi) away. The waterfall cascades some 20 meters (66 ft) into a dark pool.

A well-defined path follows the ridge westward from the Nithi Falls, and after about four hours of walking you reach Minto's Hut, set amid the five sparkling Hall Tarns. A bit of rock-scrambling is required to get this far, but nothing very difficult. A five-minute walk south of Minto's brings you to the Temple, from where you can look down to Lake Michaelson and into the Nithi Gorge, a classic U-shape glacial valley (formerly called Gorges Valley). Point Lenana is about a 2½-hour walk ahead up scree slopes past Square Tarn. You might want to spend the night in the small Minto's Hut.

If mountain climbing is not your goal, there are many interesting places to explore. If you are not with someone who knows the area, it is advisable to take the 1:50,000 map and a compass with you, and let someone at the cabins know you are going out, just in case. The lovely countryside is forest and rolling moorlands with streams and lakes.

A little north of the roadhead is Lake Ellis, and there is a fine view from the summit of nearby Mugi Hill. East of Mugi lies the Giants' Billiards Table, easily recognizable from the Meru County Council cabins. Lake Alice and Ithanguni at 3,894 meters (12,775 ft) make a good three-day excursion, and beyond this is Lake Rutundu. Lake Alice was discovered only in the 1930s. The Mountain Club of Kenya proposed that the lake, with the permission of Her Royal Highness Alice, the Duchess of Gloucester, be named after her. Buckingham Palace replied that "Her Royal Highness is greatly touched by their kind thought and has much pleasure in giving her approval." And so the lake under Ithanguni officially became Lake Alice in 1938.

Wildlife The forests below the moorlands contain an abundance of game animals, including elephants, rhino, buffalo, bushbuck, several species of duiker, giant forest hog, warthog, leopard, spotted hyena, suni—the smallest of the antelopes—and the rare bongo. Black and white colobus monkeys and Sykes' monkeys are common in the forests. Elephants are rarely seen, but buffalo are numerous and the walker should be very alert to stay out of the path of these dangerous beasts, especially in the bamboo zone.

Lions inhabit the moorlands, although they are not common. Eland are often seen on the northern and drier parts of the moorlands and zebra migrate up from the lower plains when grazing is scarce there. Two endemic rodents, the giant Mt. Kenya mole rat and the mole shrew, live where the bamboo merges into the moorlands. They burrow, leaving large molehills and tunnels running beneath the earth. The tracks of the rare leopard and wild-dog pack have been found in the peaks zone in snow above 4,575 meters (15,010 ft), where they find easy prey among the varieties of rodents and rock hyraxes.

More than 150 species of birds have been recorded in the park. Among the most distinctive species are the crowned eagle, mountain buzzard, and Mackinder's eagle owl in Teleki Valley; Cape grass owl, long-eared owl, and Jackson's francolin all in the moorlands; giant kingfisher and mountain wagtail along mountain streams; green ibises in clearings bordering streams and near Met Station; white-starred bush robin especially in the bamboo zone; and Verreaux's eagles, soaring over the camps where they feed on the plentiful rock hyraxes. Scarlet-tufted malachite sunbirds can be seen feeding on the flowers of the giant lobelias and mountain chats (thrushes) resting on tussocks in the moorland zone.

Tours Nanyuki-based Chrissie Aldrich offers private luxury tours in the area, including trout fishing, horseback riding, and walking safaris. *Flame Tree Safaris, Box 82, Nanyuki, tel. 0176/22053.*

Getting There Take A2 north out of Nairobi past Thika, where the four-lane
By Car highway narrows to two. A two-hour drive from Nairobi brings you to Karatina, a bustling town growing quickly with the cash produced by healthy tea and coffee crops. The rich Central Highlands are home to the Kikuyu people, and the peaceful, bucolic scene in this green, steeply sloped hill region is a stark contrast to Nairobi's slums.

Naro Moru Route: Before reaching Nyeri there is a right turn toward Nanyuki, still following A2. The land turns drier on the Laikipia Plateau. The road is being rebuilt at present, and much of the trip will be made on dirt bypasses. A 40-minute drive brings you to the small trading center of Naro Moru. The Naro Moru River Lodge is a few kilometers to the left, and opposite on the right is the track leading to the national park gates 17 kilometers (10.5 mi) away. Here you sign in and give your schedule to the ranger on duty. A further 8 kilometers (5 mi) brings you to the Meteorological Station.

Sirimon Route: From Nanyuki, 13 kilometers (8 mi) on A2 toward Timau, and just before the road winds down to the Sirimon River, a signposted dirt track turns off to the right southeast and leads 10 kilometers (6 mi) to the national park gates at 2,440 meters (8,000 ft). Three kilometers (2 mi) past the gate a series of steep gradients begins. A four-wheel-drive vehicle is recommended for this trip. The end of the road is a further 5 kilometers (3.2 mi), at 3,350 meters (10,900 ft), when you reach the stream and campsite.

Chogoria Route: There are two possibilities. You can take A2 through Nanyuki to Timau and continue on east around the northern end of Mt. Kenya to the town of Meru, where the road becomes B6. Continue south on a good tarmac road 64 kilometers (40 mi) to the turnoff to the right up a dirt road to the small village of Chogoria. Follow the signs to the Meru Mount Kenya Lodge, though they are not easy to see and you might have to ask for directions. The national park gates are 30 kilometers (18.6 mi) farther through deep forest and up steep gradients. If it has been raining, you will need a four-wheel-drive vehicle to reach the gates and the lodge cabins. The second possibility is the most practical if you are starting from Nairobi. Take A2 north, but turn right onto B6 signposted for Embu some 45 kilometers (28 mi) from Thika. From Embu the Chogoria turnoff to the left is about 54 kilometers (33 mi) north.

By Plane It is possible to charter a light aircraft to fly to either Nyeri or Nanyuki. Air Kenya has daily scheduled flights to these towns from Nairobi's Wilson Airport for Kshs. 2,600 round-trip. You must arrange ground transport in advance.

Lodging **Mount Kenya Safari Club.** Located up a small road to the right
Very Expensive just before entering Nanyuki from the south, this is one of the most luxurious hotels in Kenya. You can stay in one of the elegant rooms in the large, white, colonial-style main building or choose—for an extra charge—one of the cottages located on the extensive, landscaped grounds. There are spectacular views of Mt. Kenya, and grounds are stocked with many exotic birds. There is a heated swimming pool and a golf course. The lunch buffets and à la carte dinners are excellent. *Lonhro Hotels, Box 58581, Nairobi, tel. 2/723776. AE, DC, MC, V.*

Expensive–Very **Mountain Lodge.** Just beyond Karatina a marked dirt track
Expensive leads off to the right upward and into the forest on the lower slopes of Mt. Kenya. The rustic-looking lodge, built on stilts and made entirely of wood, is in a deep forest setting. Game is viewed around a pool and salt lick from a common room or from various other points from within the building, including a ground-level hide for close-up photography. *African Tours and Hotels, Box 30471, Nairobi, tel. 2/336858. AE, DC, V.*
Lewa Downs. A 40,000-acre private ranch north of Nanyuki is run by the Craig family, with horseback riding safaris. With only 3 cottages, the number of guests is limited to 12. *Flame Tree Safaris, Box 82, Nanyuki, tel. 176/22053.*

Expensive **Ol Pejeta Lodge** is located near Nanyuki on the 110,000-acre ranch formerly owned by the Saudi entrepreneur Adnan Khashoggi. The private game ranch has elephant, giraffe, zebra, and rare Petas monkeys, with Mt. Kenya as a backdrop. The facilities include two swimming pools, floodlit tennis courts, a sauna, a steam room, a Jacuzzi, and a well-equipped gymnasium. A maximum of 28 guests are accommodated in the main wood-beamed house and comfortable cottages. Horse riding is also available. *Lonhro Hotels, Box 58581, Nairobi, tel. 2/723776. AE, DC, MC, V.*
Sweetwaters. This camp has 25 superbly appointed en suite tents overlooking a waterhole and salt lick that are floodlit at night. It is located on the Ol Pejeta ranch within an hour's drive of the Ol Pejeta Lodge. Sweetwater's offers game drives at night, as well as walking and camel safaris. There are a 25,000-acre rhino sanctuary and a resident naturalist. An excellent restaurant and outdoor bar overlook the salt lick, and there's a small swimming pool. *Lonhro Hotels, Box 58581, Nairobi, tel. 2/723776, fax 723 738. Lonhro in London (Metropole Hotel, Edgeware Rd., London W2 1JU, tel. 071/402–4141) can make bookings for Ol Pejeta or Sweetwaters. AE, DC, MC, V.*

Moderate **Naro Moru River Lodge.** This lodge is located in 40 acres of forest on the Laikipia Plateau just west of Naro Moru village. A river runs by the lodge, and rods can be rented for trout fishing. The lodge offers accommodations in rooms and chalets, and a bunkhouse or campsite is available for the budget-minded. The food is simple, English-style cuisine. From here climbers can hire porters and rent equipment and mountain huts. *Alliance Hotels, Box 49839, Nairobi, tel. 2/337501 or 29961; tel. 176/62023. AE, DC.*

Inexpensive **Meru Mount Kenya Lodge.** There are five large, self-help cabins and one large cottage located just inside the park boundaries for the Chogoria Route. They are situated on a grassy slope overlooking the forest and offer views of Mt. Kenya. They have electricity, running water, and a fireplace, and bedding and all utensils are supplied. *Box 60342, Nairobi, tel. 2/29539. No credit cards.*

Sportsman & Arms Hotel. This is a rustic set of cottages just outside Nanyuki town, good for families and independent travellers. With its outdoor garden, it's a nice place to stop for a cold beer. *Box 3, Nanyuki, tel. 0176/22598. No credit cards.*

Campsites **Mackinder's Camp.** Located in the beautiful Teleki Valley, this is the main place to stay when climbing the mountain using the Naro Moru route. Lodging is in small pup tents and there is a large communal room for cooking and eating. There are water and toilet facilities. *Let's Go Travel, Box 60342, Nairobi, tel. 2/29539 or 340331. No credit cards.*

There are campsites at Naro Moru River Lodge and at Meru Mount Kenya Lodge. Camping is also possible near any of the mountain huts, but caution should be advised because of the extremely low (below freezing) night temperatures year-round.

Nairobi National Park
Box 42076, Nairobi, tel. 2/891613

Size 114 square kilometers (44 sq. mi)

Year Established 1945

Headquarters Near main gate off Langata Road; Kenya Wildlife Services and an educational center are based here.

The most striking feature of Nairobi National Park is not an unusual geological formation, nor a group of rare animals, but that it is here at all. It is a wedge of wild Africa thrusting into the southern suburbs of this bustling capital of more than 1 million people, whose city center is only 8 kilometers (5 mi) north. For visitors staying in Nairobi it is only a few minutes down the road and it should not be missed. Where else can you get a photo of wildlife in its natural habitat with city skyscrapers as a background?

A bronze monument by local sculptor Terry Matthews commemorates the burning of 12 tons of ivory in 1989.

The park is fenced on its western edge, which abuts the suburbs of Langata and Karen, and on its northeastern boundary, which fronts the Mombasa highway; the fence does not prevent the wandering of the occasional leopard or lion, however, which have been known to attack livestock or dogs in the suburbs. There is an open corridor to the south which allows game to migrate to and from the Kitengela plain and the Ngong Conservation Area, but it becomes more congested every year as new farms and fences spring up. When the corridor is finally closed, the park will become an open-air zoo.

The landscape is principally open plains that slope gently from west to east and are broken into ridges and valleys by numerous seasonal streams running southeast into the Mbagathi-

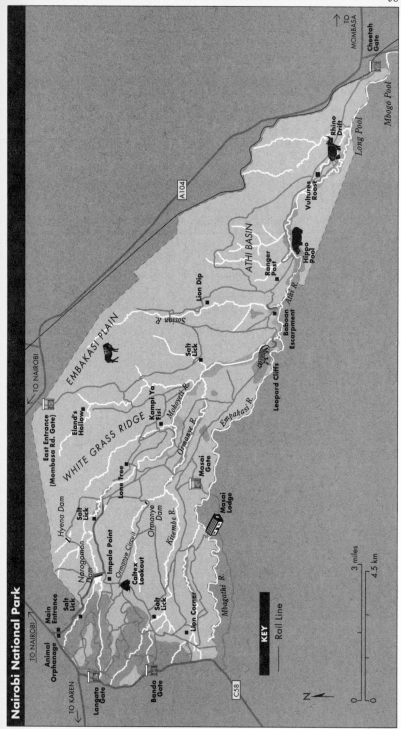

Nairobi National Park

98

Athi River. These ridges are often steep and rocky with richer vegetation than the surrounding plain, including stands of acacia woodland. The permanent Mbagathi-Athi River is lined with a rich forest of yellow fever trees and other thorn trees as it winds its way through the park. In the west it runs through a deep gorge where rocky outcrops are reputed to be a favorite haunt of leopards.

At various places in the park the seasonal stream courses have been dammed to create marshy reservoirs. Besides providing well-spaced permanent water for wildlife, they form a watery habitat that attracts migrant waders and other water birds not previously seen in the park.

The park's comprehensive network of paved and all-weather dirt roads is suitable for passenger cars, and the junctions are generally signposted and clearly marked on the official map of the park. Visitors should not expect such colorful place names as "lion corner" or "leopard cliff" to be necessarily indicative of current residents—wild animals are never predictable.

Warning. Open roof hatches are not permitted in the park, and visitors should not leave their vehicles, except where permitted by signposts. Nairobi Park has a history of maulings.

Wildlife Despite its urban location and small area, the park contains a good selection of the main species of game found throughout Kenya, with the exception of elephants, which avoid the corridor. Plains game—zebras, wildebeests, Coke's hartebeests, eland, impala, and both Grant's and Thomson's gazelles—are particularly well represented. Scampering warthogs and arrogantly strutting ostriches are also common on the open plains.

Larger game includes the Masai giraffe, which browse in much of the woodland, and a population of 64 black rhino—the largest in any Kenyan park—sometimes found in the light bush around the forest area. Predators are one of the park's main attractions, with about 30 resident lions present; cheetahs are also to be found stalking game on the plains. The rangers keep a careful note of their movements and so it is worth asking advice on the best area to try. Crocodiles and hippos are present in the larger pools of the Mbagathi-Athi River and can be viewed on foot from a nature trail in the eastern section of the park around the appropriately named Hippo Pool.

In the extreme west a low ridge is covered by a highland forest of hardwoods, home to herds of bushbucks and impala as well as some of the park's olive baboons. Impala Point, at the edge of the ridge, makes a good vantage point from which to view the park and to scan the plains with binoculars for concentrations of game or vehicles grouped around an important find. To find a cheetah or rhino undisturbed you need to enter the park when it opens at 6 AM.

Birdlife is varied, and around the dams you will find Egyptian geese, crowned cranes, yellow- and saddle-billed storks, herons, African spoonbills, sacred ibises, hammerkop, Kittlitz's sand plover, and marabou storks. In the plains look for ostriches, cattle egrets, secretary birds, vultures, helmeted guinea fowl, bustards, yellow-throated sand grouse, larks, pipits, and Jackson's widowbird, which "displays" (to attract a female) during the long rains (May–June). The forests hold cuckoo shrikes, tits, sunbirds, waxbills, flycatchers, and warblers.

Adjacent to the park's main entrance on Langata Road is the Animal Orphanage, which opened in 1963 and shelters stray, orphaned or sick animals until they can be reintroduced to their natural habitat. It does not like being called a zoo, yet it offers an opportunity to photograph cheetah, leopard, pygmy hippo, and other animals more difficult to capture on film in the wild.

Tours There are dozens of tour operators in Nairobi that conduct day trips to the park at a modest price. Many are to be found along Kenyatta Avenue, Kimathi Street, Standard Street, and Moi Avenue (*see also* Guided Tours, Chapter 4).

Getting There From downtown Nairobi, take Uhuru Highway in the direction of Mombasa and the international airport. Turn right at Langata Road and pass by Wilson Airport; the main gate is located on the left side 3 kilometers (2 mi) farther on.

Ol Doinyo Sabuk National Park and Fourteen Falls
Box 1514, Thika, tel. Doinyo Sabuk 16Y4

Size 18 square kilometers (7 sq. mi)

Year Established 1967

Headquarters Thika

This small national park, located 80 kilometers (50 mi) from Nairobi, is a single forested hill rising to a 2,148-meter (7,040 ft) altitude. A stony track leads to the summit with extensive views over the surrounding heavily populated countryside. Coffee fields and small farms are spreading into the area. In clear weather Mt. Kenya is prominent to the north, and the Nyandaruas (Aberdares) line the western skyline. The graves of early Kenya settlers Sir Northrup and Lady McMillan, and their servant Louise Decker, are just off the track about halfway up the mountain. The McMillan Library near the Jamai Mosque in Nairobi is named for them.

Nearby, the Athi River flows over a horseshoe-shaped net of waterfalls, it is spectacular in the rainy season. Fourteen Falls has a parking area, from which a vantage point can be reached on foot.

Unfortunately, both Ol Doinya Sabuk and Fourteen Falls have serious security problems and robberies are common. Do not venture there except in large groups.

Wildlife Bushbuck, impala, buffalo, and Thomson's gazelles live in the area, but they are shy and it is unlikely that you will see any.

Tours Several tour operators in Nairobi offer a visit and picnic lunch which is an easy half-day trip.

Getting There From Nairobi, take A2 north to Thika on a dual-lane highway. After 44 kilometers (27 mi) there is an exit and flyover marked for Thika town. The name is familiar from the book *The Flame Trees of Thika* by Elspeth Huxley and the television miniseries of the same name. From Thika take the paved A3 route to the east signposted for Garissa. After 23 kilometers (14 mi) follow the signpost to the right to Ol Doinyo Sabuk, which is clearly visible as the only hill. After 1 kilometer take the dirt road left at a T-junction, and 2 kilometers (1.2 mi) farther on the track crosses the Athi River. Immediately after the bridges is a small market and a right turn signposted to the Ol Doinyo Sabuk National Park.

To go to Fourteen Falls, look for the parking area just before reaching Athi River bridges. From there a footpath leads downstream to the falls.

Lodging It is not necessary to spend the night away from Nairobi to visit these attractions, but if for some reason you wish to you can try the inexpensive **New Blue Posts Hotel** (Box 42, Thika, tel. 22241). This old colonial-style bed-and-breakfast is located next to the Athi River and Thika Falls, which can be viewed from the lovely lawn garden furnished with tables. It is now a watering hole for the locals of Thika and the bar is busy, but families and handholding couples are also frequent guests. It is a good place to meet Kenyans. The rooms are not of international standards, but will do in a pinch.

Saiwa Swamp National Park
Box 753, Kitale, tel. Kitale 20329

Size 2 square kilometers (.77 sq. mi)

Year Established 1974

Headquarters Kitale

This tiny park, near Mt. Elgon National Park in the Rift Valley, was created to protect a herd of sitatunga, a large, beautiful antelope that spends most of its time partly submerged in the swamp waters. Vehicles cannot enter the park, though a series of footpaths, wood bridges, and tree-high viewing platforms provide observation opportunities over much of the area.

Wildlife The sitatunga, which has long hooves, moves slowly through the dense reedbeds while feeding. A small population of De Brazza's monkeys are resident in the thickly wooded areas along the valley sides. There are also marsh mongoose, white-tailed mongoose, Bohor reedbuck, and bush duiker in the area. Birds are plentiful, including several very localized species such as the gray-winged ground robin, and one of East Africa's most beautiful songsters, the snowy-headed robin chat.

Getting There From Nairobi, take A104 via Nakuru to Eldoret some 310 kilometers (192 mi) on good tarmac road, then turn off north onto B2 and continue on to Kitale for 70 kilometers (43 mi). Take A1 from Kitale north for 18 kilometers (11 mi) on tarmac, then turn right at the sign to Saiwa Swamp and go 6 kilometers (4 mi) on a dirt road to the park gate.

Lodging **Lokitela Farm.** This working farm has accommodations for up
Moderate to 10 guests. Hosts Tony and Adrianne Mills can talk at length about a wide variety of excursions, and they offer a guided trip of the farm and day trips to Mt. Elgon. The farm is reached via a rough road that starts from Marshall's garage in Kitale. The Lokitela signpost is obvious on the left after 18 kilometers (11 mi). *Box 122, Kitale. No phone or credit cards.*

Sirikwa Safari's Guest House and Campsite. This small establishment, operated by the Barnley family, is no longer run as a farm, but the house has much of the character and homeyness offered by this type of accommodation. There are two double rooms within the house (without private bathrooms), and three double furnished tents erected in the garden. Wholesome home-style cooking is served in the house with the family. Guides are available for excursions, including to Saiwa Swamp. It is located 24 kilometers (15 mi) north of Kitale on A1 to

Kapenguria, 6 kilometers (4 mi) past the turnoff to the swamp. *Box 332, Kitale. No phone or credit cards.*

Inexpensive **Kitale Hotel.** The hotel is a bit run-down, but it is the most comfortable place to stay in Kitale town. It is located 1.5 kilometers (1 mi) south of town at an altitude of about 1,900 meters (6,230 ft), thus the nights are cool. There is an airport with scheduled flights to Nairobi. The club offers golf, tennis, squash, and snooker. *Box 41, Kitale, tel. 325/20041. No credit cards.*

Samburu-Buffalo Springs-Shaba National Reserves
Park Warden, Box 29, Isiolo radio tel. 21Y2

Size Samburu, 225 square kilometers (87 sq. mi)
Buffalo Springs, 339 square kilometers (131 sq. mi)
Shaba, 239 square kilometers (92 sq. mi)

Year Established Samburu, 1962
Buffalo Springs, 1962
Shaba, 1974

Headquarters Isiolo

These three national reserves are grouped around the Uaso Nyiro River ("brown water" in Maa), where the foothills of Mt. Kenya peter out into the hot, arid lands of northern Kenya. You may hear the region referred to as the Northern Frontier District or NFD. Samburu and Buffalo Springs reserves lie to the west of the Great North Road (A2); Samburu lies north of the Uaso Nyiro, and Buffalo Springs is south of it. Shaba reserve is south of the river, but east of the road opposite Buffalo Springs. The Samburu-Buffalo Springs reserves are connected by a bridge across the river, located just upstream from the Samburu Lodge.

The country is mostly semiarid plains covered in thornbush, with a few open grazing areas, but contrasting sharply is the thick band of rich woodland along the river through the reserve. There are also some rocky hills in the northern part of the reserve, and farther north is the rugged granite outcrop of Mt. Ololokwe, gleaming in the sun.

All three reserves were created with help from the Adamson family—Joy, George, and George's brother, Terence—and funds from the Elsa Trust, set up with proceeds from the books and films based on *Born Free* and the Adamsons' subsequent work with big cats. Joy Adamson was murdered in Shaba in 1980 while working to rehabilitate leopards to the wild. George was killed by *shifta* (bandits) in August 1989. The Munitalp Foundation, whose chairman Sir Malin Sorsbie used to hunt in the area, also helped finance the establishment of the reserves.

Both Samburu and Buffalo Springs have a well-established and signposted set of tracks for game runs. In the dry season, most game are seen along the riverbank tracks, though lions and cheetahs are most often spotted away from the river. In Samburu, downriver from the bridge, there is good access to the riverbank. To the south, the "Lower River Circuit" and "Upper River Circuit" are well marked and cover a variety of habitat from thornbush to doum palm. In the southeast Buffalo Springs, the river lookout, the swamplands, and the grazing lands can all be taken in during a run of a few miles, and this is probably the best area for viewing reticulated giraffe and Beisa oryx.

Samburu and Buffalo Springs Reserves

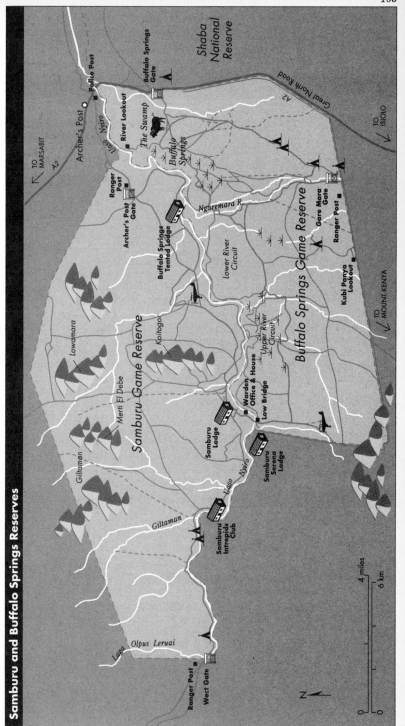

Shaba reserve does not have a good set of tracks, and poaching has been a serious problem. The reserve takes its name from the copper color of the lava rock that the visitor has to cross to reach this remote and isolated wilderness. Beyond the lava lie open savanna and acacia woodland around Mt. Shaba, whose summit is 1,622 meters (5,322 ft) high. Joy Adamson's camp was located in a grassy plain beyond the mountain, and a 12-meter (40-ft) waterfall to the northeast on the Uaso Nyiro River is called "Penny's Drop," after the leopard named Penny that she was working with at the time of her death. The reserve has a poor reputation for game-viewing, but it is particularly beautiful after the rains, when the bouldered hillsides blossom with wildflowers and the plains are filled with tall green grass.

Wildlife For such a small area the reserves sustain a surprising number and variety of game year-round, made possible by the long stretch of permanent river waters. In the acacia–doum palm riverine zone are to be found elephants, buffalo, impala, waterbuck, and many baboon troops, the latter munching away on palm nuts. Numerous hippo and crocodile can be seen in the river, and the best place for viewing crocs is from the terrace bar at Samburu Lodge. This overlooks a wide stretch of river whose shallows and banks are home to dozens of crocodiles that often leave the river to bask alongside the terrace. The sign DON'T FEED THE CROCODILES means for patrons to stay on the terrace side of the low stone wall.

The reserves are one of the best places in East Africa to view and photograph the typical northern species of Grevy's zebra, Beisa oryx, reticulated giraffe, and Somali ostrich. These will be found in the plains away from the river. The reserves also abound with gerenuk, and the elusive leopard can be spotted at either Samburu Lodge or Samburu River Lodge, where baits are set out under spotlights at night.

Another likely area to find wildlife is at the Buffalo Springs, a group of clear pools which forms from the underground runoff from Mt. Kenya. Besides attracting visitors who want to cool off, the springs draw game and a constant stream of birds to the lush vegetation and welcome shade. The swamp area between the springs and the nearby river is also a good area for viewing wildlife.

More than 300 species of birds inhabit the reserves, among them the dik-dik-eating martial eagle and the insect-eating pygmy falcon. There are also many varieties of bustards, and the red-rumped buffalo weaver and the red-billed hornbill.

Tours Samburu Lodge, Samburu River Lodge, Larsen's Camp, and Sarova Luxury Lodge all offer vehicles and drivers for hire to make game drives.

Getting There From Nairobi take A2 north to Nanyuki, then continue on past Timau to the fork to the left, which heads down off Mt. Kenya to Isiolo, a distance of 255 kilometers (158 mi). At Isiolo you pass through a police barrier, then leave the tarmac to go 26 kilometers (16 mi) on a washboard dirt road north to the Ngare Mara gate to the Samburu-Buffalo Springs reserves on the left. A few kilometers farther north is the Buffalo Springs gate on the left and the gate to Shaba on the right.

Lodging **Larsen's Camp.** A new luxury tented camp that is set in the
Very Expensive trees on the northern bank of the river in Samburu reserve,

this highly priced camp offers excellent food and service. No children under age 10 are allowed. *Block Hotels, Box 47557, Nairobi, tel. 2/335807. AE, DC, MC, V.*

Samburu Intrepids Club. Run by the same people who manage the Mara Intrepids Club, this new tented lodge on the banks of the Uaso Nyiro accommodates 50 people in spacious tents with mahogany furniture and marble bathrooms en suite, plus private decks. The tents are covered by makuti roofs, and an overhead fan makes you feel as cool as Sydney Greenstreet in a white linen suit. The complex has a dining room, lounge, bar, gift shop, and pool. Transfers from the Samburu airstrip, camel rides and game drives are extra. *Prestige Hotels Ltd., Box 74888, Nairobi, tel. 2/338 084 or 2/335 208, fax 2/728 503, telex 22043. AE, DC, MC, V.*

Expensive **Samburu Lodge.** This well-established lodge is built of local stone and mountain cedar and has an international reputation for comfort, cuisine, and good management. It overlooks the river in Samburu reserve and has a very pleasant bar-terrace. There are a swimming pool, gas pump, and souvenir shops. Nearby is an airstrip. *Block Hotels, Box 47557, Nairobi, tel. 2/335807. AE, DC, MC, V.*

Samburu Serena Lodge. Recently taken over by new management, this peaceful lodge is located on the south bank of the river just outside the Buffalo Springs reserve. It has the best swimming pool in the three reserves and is known as a good bird-watching area. Hot-air balloons that travel over the park depart from here. *Serena Lodges and Hotels, Box 48690, Nairobi, tel. 2/338656. AE, MC, V.*

Sarova Shaba Lodge. A brand-new five-star lodge with 70 luxury cottages, eight luxury suites, and one presidential suite, this establishment offers comfort and leisure in Shaba reserve. There is a swimming pool and sauna and a nearby landing strip. *Sarova Hotels, Box 30680, Nairobi, tel. 2/333233. AE, DC, MC, V.*

Moderate **Buffalo Springs Tented Lodge.** This permanent tented camp is situated on the south bank of the Uaso Nyiro River near the Buffalo Springs. It is not at the same level of most luxury tented camps, but it has a pool and is in a good area for gameviewing. *African Tours and Hotels, Box 30471, Nairobi, tel. 2/336858. AE, DC, V.*

Campsites There are several campsites that can be booked at reserve headquarters in Archer's Post. Check with tour operators in Nairobi about nonpermanent luxury tented camps. Be careful with personal effects: Many robberies have been reported in camps in these reserves.

Shimba Hills National Reserve
Box 30, Kwale, tel. Kwale 36

Size 1,922 square kilometers (742 sq. mi)

Year Established 1968

Headquarters Kwale

The reserve lies 55 kilometers (34 mi) from Mombasa and only 45 kilometers (28 mi) from Diani Beach, making it an easy excursion out of the humid coastal belt to the fresher, cooler, 450-meter (1,460-ft) range of hills. Though small, the reserve is unique in Kenya for having the country's only herd of sable antelope and an almost equally rare population of roan antelope, transferred from the Ithanga Ranch near Thika in the 1960s. The landscape consists of green rolling hills patched with areas of ancient forest.

If you stay at the Shimba Hills Lodge, the resident host will take you on arrival for a short nature walk through the thick forest of the Mkomba Valley, pointing out interesting botanical facts. The trail has several wood blinds to jump into in case elephants or buffalo also decide to use the path. For guests who stay more than one night, it is possible to hike to Sheldrick's Falls, where you can swim in the clear pool at the bottom of the 23-meter (75-ft) cascade.

Wildlife The reserve is small and the circuits are well marked and easy to follow. You are most likely to see sable and roan antelope between the Longo-Magandi Forest and Giriama Hill, the latter having a splendid view down to the coast. There are a few elephants in the reserve, but they are timid and best seen at night at the Shimba Hills Lodge. Lions and leopards are rare and seldom seen. Your best chance to spot leopards is also at the lodge, where bait is set out at night. Other animals include buffalo, bushbuck, Bohor reedbuck, and colobus monkeys.

Birdlife is profuse and includes occasional clouds of carmine bee-eaters, palm-nut vultures, Fischer's turacos, silvery-cheeked hornbills, and, of course, spurfowl—*kwale* in Swahili and the name of the district itself. Butterflies are a particular attraction, as are ground orchids, gladioli, and other wildflowers decorating the meadowland.

Tours The Shimba Hills Safari Lodge offers tours with its own four-wheel-drive vehicles, and the resident host will accompany your party if he is not too busy with other duties. The tour here is more personalized than at the other, larger park lodges because of the lower volume of tourists passing through.

Getting There From Mombasa, cross the entrance of the Kilindini Harbor via the Likoni ferry to the south coast and drive 24 kilometers (15 mi) to the marked turnoff to Kwale. Turn right and go on the well-paved road that winds up into the hills, through Kwale town, and onto a dirt road. After a short distance, you will see the reserve entrance at the Kidongo gate on the left. If you are going to the Shimba Hills Lodge, continue on for another kilometer to the sign on the right.

Lodging **Shimba Hills Lodge.** Kenya's newest "treetop" lodge is by far
Expensive the most pleasant and attractive. It is surrounded by deep forest, and the restaurant and bar are outdoors, looking directly down on the water hole. A central tropical garden in the lodge and a wood walkway 60 meters (200 ft) long, which offers several vantage points for gazing down on game around the water hole and its approach, take you outside the usual stuffy lodge atmosphere and closer to nature. Game drives are offered in the mornings for an extra charge. *Block Hotels, Box 47557, Nairobi, tel. 2/22860 or 335807. AE, DC, MC, V.*

Inexpensive Ten bandas (cabins) were built in 1990 to accommodate independent travelers. Cooking utensils are provided, and bedding can be rented. Book with park officials at the gate or via *Kenya Wildlife Services in Langata, Box 40241, Nairobi, tel. 2/891601 or 2/891607. No credit cards.*

Sibiloi National Park
Box 98, Marsabit, tel. Marsabit 28

Size 1,554 square kilometers (600 sq. mi)

Year Established 1973

Headquarters Marsabit

The park is unlike any other in Kenya in that it has no established set of tracks or formal public accommodations such as a lodge or tented camp. The park was established at the urging of Richard Leakey, formerly chief executive of the National Museums and now director of Kenya Wildlife Services to protect the famous fossil-bearing deposits on the northeastern shores of Lake Turkana. In the starkly eroded badlands around Koobi Fora and Ileret, teams of researchers and scientists from Kenya, the United States, and Britain uncovered thousands of fossils, including those of hominids (human ancestors). These fossils have provided the oldest clues of early human evolution found anywhere on earth. Hence the area is often called the Cradle of Mankind.

The Sibiloi is hot, dry, and wind-blasted, and due to its remoteness, it receives very few visitors. The vegetation is sparse thorn scrub, with an occasional volcanic hill (*koobi* in the Oromo language). The area is sparsely inhabited by Gabbra camel pastoralists and, along the lakeshore, Dassenech fishermen, who occasionally travel to the lake from Ethiopia. In places associated with former or present water are found stone cairns and rings. These are graves of prehistoric pastoralists who lived in the area between 4,000 and about 100 years ago. The Gabbra and Rendille pastoralists still bury their dead under smaller stone cairns, carrying on millennia-old traditions.

At Koobi Fora a long sandspit pokes out into Lake Turkana, the "Jade Sea." Richard Leakey's base camp for the scientific work is located here, but most research has now shifted to the western side of the lake, and the base has been converted to a summer school for university students. Visitors can stay in the simple thatched bandas where the researchers used to lodge within sight of the lake. There is a good beach here, and swimming in the slightly greasy alkaline lake is a great delight. There are many small lake crocs that bask along the spit, but no one has ever been attacked by one. A small museum, on a ridge overlooking the lake not far from the base camp, contains replicas of some of the area's more famous fossils and explanations of the geological and biological history that led to what one sees today.

Sibiloi hill is located to the right of the track at the signposted (but unmanned) entrance to the park. Strewn around its base are chunks of petrified wood dated to 7 million years ago, which show that there was once a juniper forest here, indicating much greater volume of rainfall in the past.

Although fossil fragments litter the ground in many places, nothing may be picked up and taken home as a souvenir—the maximum fine for doing so is Kshs. 10,000 and/or six months in jail.

The Koobi Fora International School of Paleontology offers hands-on training in fossil-finding, identification and geology.

The six-week sessions, conducted in association with Harvard, are good for college credit. *Kenya National Museums, Box 40658, Nairobi, tel. 2/742121, or Dept. of Anthropology, Harvard University, Cambridge, MA 02138.*

South Island and **Central Island national parks,** both in Lake Turkana, were established in 1983. They are important breeding grounds for crocodiles and water birds. The parks consist of dry, practically barren piles of rock.

Wildlife For such a hostile environment, the area supports a surprising variety of wildlife. There are sizable herds of the northern game species of oryx, topi, and smaller antelope, and large crocodile and hippo populations at the lakeshore. The first Europeans to visit the lake, the Austrians Count Teleki and Lieutenant Von Hoehnel, reported many elephants and rhino in 1888, but they have been completely poached out. The shoreline near Koobi Fora is a good place to see game.

Sibiloi is also remote enough for discerning and sometimes distinguished royal bird-watchers to relax and enjoy their hobby in a totally unspoiled multicolor seascape. There are sometimes many thousands of flamingos on Lake Turkana, as well as pelicans, gulls, waders, ducks and geese, and rarities such as the black-tailed godwit and spotted redshank. Between March and early May the lake is invaded by vast numbers of European migrant birds, especially wagtails and marsh sandpipers.

Tours The Koobi Fora base camp maintains a Land Rover and guide: They can be hired through the National Museum in Nairobi. The tour includes a visit to the Koobi Fora museum and two excavation sites away from Koobi Fora, one of a fossil elephant and another of a giant fossil tortoise. A boat tour to South Island National Park can be arranged through Oasis Lodge in Loyangalani.

Getting There There are two approaches. If you have come to Marsabit, you
By Car take the rough track off the mountain 95 kilometers (50 mi) to the small settlement of Maikona at the southeast corner of the Chalbi Desert. From here you cross the Chalbi (in the dry season) to North Horr, about 90 kilometers (56 mi) away to the northwest. If it has been raining, there is a very bad, rocky track to North Horr along the plateau above the Chalbi, which should be taken, as the Chalbi is a playa lake. From North Horr it is a little over 100 kilometers (62 mi) to Allia Bay (watch for the pile of stones and signpost on a barren plain where the road forks to Loyangalani on the left and to Allia Bay on the right) and a further 80 kilometers (50 mi) to Koobi Fora. Marsabit to Koobi Fora is an all-day drive.

Coming directly from Nairobi, it is best to go the 724 kilometers (450 mi) to Allia Bay via Nyahururu, Maralal, and Loyangalani on C77. After Loyangalani and the El Molo villages the track turns east to the north of Mt. Kulal and precariously climbs a rocky escarpment to a plateau. The track heads for North Horr, but take the fork to the left (north) at the signposted pile of stones for Alia Bay about 45 kilometers (28 mi) before North Horr.

The trip by road should be made with four-wheel-drive vehicles, spare tires and tire-patching kits, and plenty of food, water, and fuel. A broken-down vehicle cannot count on a passer-by—except for a pastoralist with a camel. The last places for fuel are Isiolo on A2 and Nyahururu on C77. There is usually—but not always—fuel for sale at Marsabit and Maralal.

By Plane There are three landing strips near Koobi Fora, but only the farthest one from the camp, on a hard plain, is recommended. The other two are in sand and are short. Planes can be chartered at Wilson Airport, but reservations for the bandas and notification to the camp for pickup should be made through the National Museum office in Nairobi before leaving.

Lodging **Oasis Lodge.** This expensive lodge on the edge of Loyangalani is
Expensive the only place to get a cold drink on the eastern side of Lake Turkana. The 25 rooms are adequate, with all of the amenities, and food is flown in from Nairobi. There is a swimming pool, boat rentals, fishing, and a good tarmac airstrip next to the lodge. *Muthaiga Connexions, Box 34464, Nairobi, tel. 2/ 750036. No credit cards.*

Inexpensive **Koobi Fora Bandas.** These simple thatched huts have sand floors, open-air windows, no running water, kerosene lantern lighting, and outhouse toilet facilities—but they are wonderful! Bedding is provided. The camp staff are very hospitable and will cook and serve for visitors and, if you are lucky, will present freshly caught fish from the lake on the table in the central banda. To be on the safe side, bring all your own food and drink. The bandas are located just a few meters from the lake. *National Museum, Box 40658, Nairobi, tel. 2/742121. No credit cards.*

Campsites For Sibiloi, there are designated campsites with no facilities, except toilets, near Alia Bay and Koobi Fora. Book at the Alia Bay office or Koobi Fora base camp. For South Island, there is a large campsite with many facilities and a security fence around it outside Loyangalani.

Tsavo National Park and Chyulu Hills National Park
Tsavo West, Box 71, Mtito Andei, tel. Mtito Andei 39
Tsavo East, Box 14, Voi, tel. Voi 285

Size 20,808 square kilometers (8,034 sq. mi)

Year Established 1948

Headquarters **West:** Through Mtito Andei gate; follow signs

East: Through Voi Gate; follow signs

Tsavo is by far the largest park in Kenya, covering an impressive 20,808 square kilometers (8,034 sq mi), the size of Israel. It stretches 241 kilometers (150 mi) from the Tanzanian border in the south to well north of the Galana River, called the Athi River upstream and the Sabaki River downstream at the coast.

The park's two sections, Tsavo West and Tsavo East, are separated by the unambiguous Mombasa highway. The first gates to both are at Mtito Andei, 250 kilometers (155 mi) from Nairobi, halfway to Mombasa. In theory they are one park, but with separate headquarters, wardens, field staff, and entrance fees, they operate autonomously. Tsavo was the first national park established in Kenya, and its sheer size lets you separate yourself from other tourists if you wish. Both parks have an excellent signboard system at road junctions.

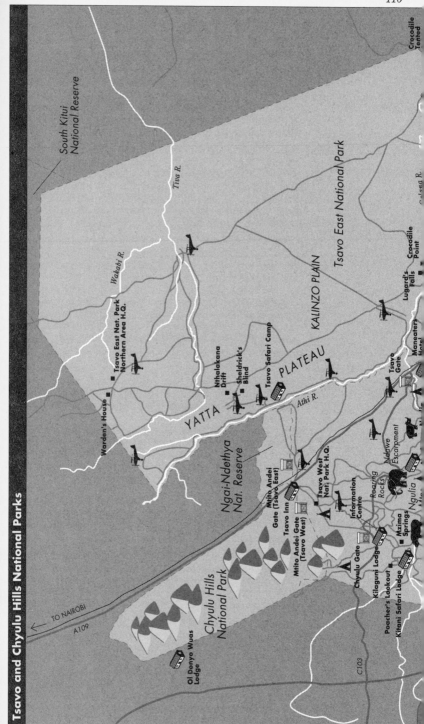

Tsavo and Chyulu Hills National Parks

South Kitui National Reserve

Tiva R.

Wakabi R.

■ Tsavo East Nat. Park Northern Area H.Q.

Nthalakana Drift

Sheldrick's Blind

Tsavo Safari Camp

Warden's House

YATTA PLATEAU

KALINZO PLAIN

Tsavo East National Park

Athi R.

Lugard's Falls

Crocodile Point

Galana R.

Crocodile Tented

Maneaters Hotel

Tsavo Gate

Ngai-Ndethya Nat. Reserve

Mtito Andei Gate (Tsavo East)

Tsavo Inn

Tsavo West Nai. Park H.Q.

Information Centre

Mtito Andei Gate (Tsavo West)

Ndawe Escarpment

Roaring Rocks

Ngulia Lodge

Chyulu Gate

Mzima Springs

Kilaguni Lodge

Kilaguni Lodge

Poacher's Lookout

Kitani Safari Lodge

Chyulu Hills National Park

Ol Donyo Wuas Lodge

TO NAIROBI

A109

C103

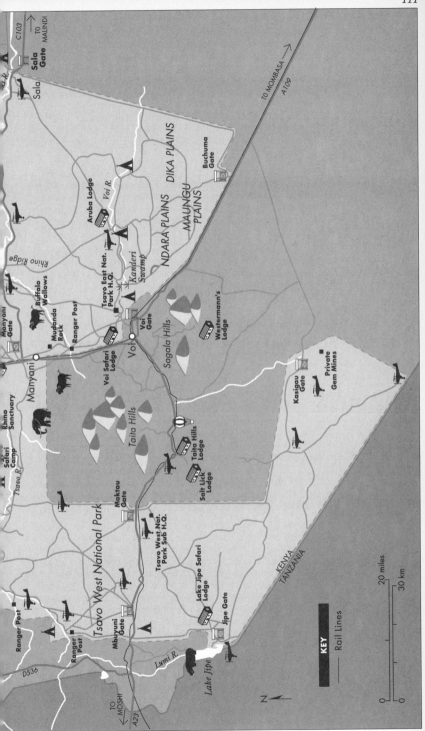

KEY

Rail Lines

Tsavo East is mainly dry thornbush country, sparsely vegetated, and cut by ephemeral streams. The vegetation was once much thicker, but a large elephant population in the early 1970s drought devastated the *Acacia commiphora* bush. The elephants pushed over the trees to get at the leaves and branches and gouged the trunks for edible bark, leaving a blitzed, battle-scarred plain in their wake. The vegetation is beginning to recover, and after the rains the tall green grass and flowering shrubs and trees are all that one could desire from an African landscape. Tsavo West has denser vegetation than Tsavo East and a more varied landscape, punctuated by isolated hills and hill ranges.

Jutting out from Tsavo West, north of the Tsavo River, is the newly established **Chyulu Hills National Park** (*see below*), which is essentially the volcanic mountain range of that name, formerly a Game Conservation Area. Kenya Wildlife Service planned to install an admission gate and ranger headquarters in 1992.

The Chyulus were virtually unexplored until 1938, when botanist Peter Bally (of the Swiss shoe family) and his wife, Joy, surveyed this region for the Nairobi Museum. (Joy Bally later married game warden George Adamson and is better remembered today as the subject of the book and movie *Born Free*. She was also a talented artist, whose water colors of wildflowers in the Chyulus are in the Nairobi Museum collection.)

The range is 80 kilometers (50 mi) long, with a rough road cut along the top, which requires four-wheel-drive. You must bring along your own camping gear, extra gasoline, and water. The rains that fall here do not collect but filter down deep through the porous volcanic soil, to form underground rivers that emerge at Mzima Springs. Water from the Chyulus is piped to Mombasa.

The trend toward off-the-beaten-track safaris has created new interest in the Chyulus because of their dreamy, unspoiled panaromas, with a view of Kilimanjaro, 45 miles to the southeast. There are no accommodations within the park, but Ol Donyo Wuas, a small, exclusive lodge, is just outside the park on a Masal group ranch, and temporary campsites can be arranged by operators like Let's Go Travel.

Because the Chyulus are largely uninhabited, there is a Garden of Eden quality to this landscape, where clouds hug the peaks until noon. The range reaches a maximum height of 2,170 meters (7,130 ft), and the cones range in age from about a thousand years to the youngest, Shaitani (Swahili for "devil"), which is about 200 years old. A trip across the top of these hills from the oldest peak to the young Shaitani is like a journey in time: you see deep and verdant greens changing to lighter greens, then to blond grasses, and eventually you come to the black barren lava flows. You see in microcosm the way vegetation succeeds in a barren landscape.

The oldest crater has a dense cedar forest, carpeted in orchids and ferns. The middle range has younger tree stands, wildflowers, succulents, and beautiful grasses. The youngest cones are black magma, with just a few plants taking hold. Windblown seeds take root in the crevices of magma where soil collects, and slowly these roots break the volcanic rock into manageable bits. As you gaze across the grassland of the Kibiwezi plains, dotted with whistling thorn acacias, you can see that the plant species that take root in the volcanic rock are completely different from those on the plains. This change in habitat may also explain the curious mix of animals you find here: there are zebra, lion, and giraffe, but also herds of oryx, which are normally found in a semiarid or desert landscape.

If you have a bit of extra time, consider a trip to Lake Jipe, 405 kilometers (250 mi) from Nairobi. The lake is tucked away in the southwest reaches of the park and can be reached from the Maktau gate off the tarmac road from Voi that passes by the Taita Hills. You might want to stop on the way at either the Salt Lick or the Taita Hills lodge, both Hilton properties and both outside the park. Lake Jipe is a small, shallow lake sitting astride the Tanzania border, with excellent views of both Mt. Kilimanjaro and the Pare Mountains in Tanzania. A stay at the Lake Jipe Safari Lodge, with its authentic Swahili dhow (having the unauthentic name of *African Queen*), is much more enjoyable than it used to be when only self-help bandas were available. The birdlife around the heavily reeded lake is rich, and hippos are common. A sail on the lake in the dhow is recommended, and the more daring can even go swimming with the hippos.

Wildlife   A wide variety of wildlife is represented in Tsavo, but most dominant is the elephant. In the 1960s it had tens of thousands, but drought and poaching—in recent years mainly the latter— have taken their toll. Today there are only a few thousand elephants. Most of the game species are present, including large herds of buffalo. In Tsavo East the dry-country animals such as the fringe-eared oryxes, gerenuks, and magnificent lesser kudus can be seen. Lions and cheetahs are numerous but difficult to spot because of the high grass. The best places to see game are around the water holes of the lodges, particularly in the dry season. A rhino sanctuary has been set up in Tsavo West near Ngulia Lodge. You will see wildlife on a game drive, but not in such profusion as in Amboseli or the Masai Mara. Tsavo's asset is the almost limitless space, its wildness, and its variegated landscapes.

Birdlife is profuse, especially around the rivers and dams, with more than 400 different species regularly noted. Tsavo is also on a migration corridor from the coast, and Palaeartic migrants from the north fly over the park in November and December; some 40 species have been recorded. Ornithologists have tracked birds from as far north as Leningrad. Several species of starlings and weaverbirds abound, along with hornbills, which are always ready to take tea with guests at the Kilaguni Lodge. European and lilac-breasted rollers are common, and there is a good variety of raptors, including the snake-eating secretary bird. Water birds such as herons and yellow-billed and saddle-billed storks are common sights.

The two outstanding geological features in Tsavo East are the Yatta Plateau and Mudanda Rock. The plateau, varying in width from a few hundred meters to 3 kilometers, is one of the world's longest lava flows, starting from near Nairobi and ending 322 kilometers (200 mi) to the southeast. It forms an impressive escarpment under which the Galana River flows. Mudanda Rock is a mile-long outcrop of stratified rock 24 kilometers (15 mi) north of Voi Safari Lodge, just off the track leading between the Manyani and Voi gates. A natural water hole forms from the runoff of the rock, around which hundreds of elephants, buffalo, and other game congregate during the dry season. The spectacle of dense game can be viewed from a terrace ledge halfway up the rock, reached by steps leading up the side opposite from the water hole.

There are two main circuits in Tsavo East, centering on the park headquarters and lodge at Voi. The first takes you directly north to Mudanda Rock, then right for 27 kilometers (17 mi) to the Galana River. Turn right and drive along the Galana, where in the dry season much game can be seen, until you reach the turnoff to Lugard's Falls. Here you can walk down to the river to view broad rapids skidding over the giant flat rocks. A short walk downstream brings you to the falls themselves, a violent gush of white water squeezed within a narrow fissure in solid rock. Below the falls are the calmer pools of Crocodile Point, where crocs are sometimes spotted. The return track takes you via Rhino Ridge, now a misnomer. The second route follows the seasonal Voi River woodland and marsh eastward to the Aruba Lodge (where there is a permanent reservoir of about 200 acres) before returning through light bush. Aruba is a good spot for birding.

Central to the track network in Tsavo West is Kilaguni Lodge, Kenya's oldest park lodge (recently remodeled). Eastward from the lodge, tracks with many interesting diversions wind through the hills and escarpments to Ngulia Lodge and make a good circuit for viewing elephants. A stop at Roaring Rocks is worthwhile for the view from the top of the 300-foot cliff. Klipspringers as well can be spotted on the rock outcrops of the Ngulia Mountains along the way, sometimes bouncing around like mountain goats, but mostly just standing like silent sentries. South from Kilaguni, tracks lead to the famous Mzima Springs and Poacher's Lookout, where, from the top of a grassy volcanic hill, there are excellent views over the park toward Mt. Kilimanjaro.

At Mzima Springs lush vegetation surrounds large pools of clear spring water that surfaces at the rate of 50 million gallons a day, having traveled south 48 kilometers (30 mi) along lava tunnels from the Chyulu Hills catchment area. Much of the water is piped to Mombasa, where at one time it was the principal supply. From an underwater observation chamber sunk into the upper pool, hippos can be seen prancing as if through murky air, along with barbel fish and crocodiles. The surrounding forest is full of birds, vervet monkeys, and baboons. A well-worn nature trail encircles the springs area.

Tours In Tsavo East, vehicles with drivers can be hired from the Voi Safari Lodge and in Tsavo West from either Kilaguni or Ngulia lodges. In each park, it would take a full day to visit all of the important sites, and another day is needed to see Lake Jipe.

Chyulu Hills National Park

Getting There There are several entrances to the park off A109 Mombasa
By Car highway. The first are at Mtito Andei, for both East and West. Forty-nine kilometers (30 mi) down the highway you can enter Tsavo East at Manyani, 289 kilometers (179 mi) from Nairobi; at Voi, 331 kilometers (206 mi) from Nairobi; or at the Buchuma gate, another 48 kilometers (30 mi) farther, at the southern

corner of the park. If you are driving from the coast, the Voi gate is 157 kilometers (98 mi) from Mombasa. Entrances to Tsavo West are at Mtito Andei and Tsavo, 250 kilometers (156 mi) and 290 kilometers (181 mi) respectively, from Nairobi.

Another frequent approach to Tsavo West is from Amboseli, where a good murram (dirt) road leads past the velvety green Chyulu Hills on your left. You enter the park at the Chyulu gate, only 25 kilometers (16 mi) from Kilaguni Lodge. Tsavo East can be reached through the Sala gate from Malindi on the coast via an almost straight dirt road 121 kilometers (75 mi) long. This road is not recommended in wet weather unless you have a four-wheel-drive vehicle (preferably two, for safety's sake).

By Plane There are no scheduled flights to Tsavo, but light planes can be chartered at **Safari Air Services** (tel. 2/501211), **Executive Air Services** (tel. 2/500607, or 505122), or **Air Kenya Aviation** (tel. 2/501421) to any of the many airstrips in the park.

Lodging **Ol Donyo Wuas.** This magnificent retreat, with only six
Very Expensive thatched cottages, is not really a lodge, but a secluded semiprivate accommodation on the edge of the Chyulu range. Each spacious cottage has a fireplace, a private bath and a veranda, and some have views of Mt. Kilimanjaro. The main dining area also has a spectacular view. Because Ol Donyo Wuas (whose name means "the spotted hills") is outside the park, guests are treated to nature walks in the area, as well as game drives, and horseback riding is available. *Richard Bonham Safaris, Box 24133, Nairobi, tel. 2/882521; fax 2/882728. USA: A.K. Taylor International, 2724 Arvin Rd., Billings, MT 59102; tel. 406/ 656–0706, fax 406/252–6353. No credit cards.*

Expensive **Kilaguni Lodge.** Big, busy, and full to bursting in season, this well-sited lodge has its own water hole and salt lick for attracting game, as well as good views of the Chyulu Hills and Mt. Kilimanjaro. There are 50 rooms, a pool, conference room, gas station, and the lodge's own airstrip. Game runs are available with lodge vehicles. *African Tours and Hotels, Box 30471, Nairobi, tel. 2/336858. AE, DC, V.*

Lake Jipe Safari Lodge. Located on the shores of Lake Jipe, with spectacular views of Kilimanjaro and the Pare Mountains, this lodge has spacious rondavels en suite with a main complex featuring a sunken lounge, grill room, dining area, shop, and three bars. It's quiet and a good place to relax in peaceful surroundings. *Box 31097, Nairobi, tel. 2/27623. AE, MC, V.*

Salt Lick Lodge. A Hilton phantasmagorical creation that recalls the glories of Hollywood spectaculars of days gone by, this lodge is outside the park, south of the Voi-Taveta Road, in a private game reserve 11,340 hectares (28,000 acres) in size. The rooms resemble African huts; they sit on stilts overlooking a large water hole and salt lick that attract animals in the evenings. *Hilton Hotels International, Box 30624, Nairobi, tel. 2/ 334000 or 800/445–8667. AE, CB, DC, MC, V.*

Taita Hills Lodge. Another Hilton creation, this lodge is located near Salt Lick Lodge and is styled after a World War I fort, though the British soldiers never lived in such luxury. It also has its own water hole and salt lick, hot-air ballooning and an airstrip. *Reservations: see Salt Lick Lodge. AE, DC, MC, V.*

Tsavo Safari Camp. Situated on the far side of the Athi River, this luxury tented camp has a pool and its own airstrip, reached by camp boat. Walks or game drives can be arranged from the camp, and tours of the farther reaches of Tsavo East are available, even an overnighter to the top of the Yatta Plateau to visit a viewing blind built by David Sheldrick, the first warden of the park. The camp is 30 kilometers (19 mi) east of Mtito Andei on a dirt road. *Kilimanjaro Safari Club, Box 30139, Nairobi, tel. 2/338888. AE, DC, MC, V.*

Voi Safari Lodge. This large full-service lodge, brilliantly situated high on the Woressa Hill, overlooks the park plains and three water holes. The water holes can also be viewed from the rooms, but the latter do not have terraces. The lodge has a pool and a gas station. It is close to the Voi gate and the park headquarters. *African Tours and Hotels, Box 30471, Nairobi, tel. 2/336858. AE, MC, V.*

Moderate **Ngulia Safari Lodge.** This full-service lodge sits on a rise at the head of a valley overlooking a water hole and plain on one side. A vista of the park from the edge of the Ndawe escarpment as far as the Yatta Plateau to the north is on the other side. The lodge has a small pool, gas pump, and its own airstrip nearby. At sundown the veranda is a great spot to watch the animals amble over the plains up to the water hole. *Reservations:* see *Kilaguni Lodge. AE, DC, MC, V.*

Tsavo Inn. Located halfway between Nairobi and Mombasa, this is the only tourist-class hotel in Mtito Andei. It is closed indefinitely but could reopen anytime. The hotel is good for lunch, and a quick dip in its pool on the way to or from the coast is refreshing. It is in Mtito Andei. *Kilimanjaro Safari Club, Box 30139, Nairobi, tel. 2/338888. MC, V.*

Inexpensive **Aruba Lodge.** These six self-help bandas face the Aruba reservoir, a favorite watering place for elephants. All have bathrooms and kitchen facilities, and bedding can be rented. There is no restaurant, but simple food and drinks can be bought from the shop. *A. A. Travel Ltd., Box 14982, Nairobi, tel. 2/742926. No credit cards.*

Crocodile Tented Camp. This is a luxury tented camp with pool 5 kilometers (3 mi) outside the Sala gate on the banks of the Galana/Sabaki River just off the road to Malindi. It is certainly worthy of its name as there are crocs on banks of the Galana River. *Inside Africa Safaris, Box 59767, Nairobi, tel. 2/21760 or 339680. AE, DC, MC, V.*

Hunter's Lodge. The lodge is outside the park at Kiboko on the main highway, 155 kilometers (96 mi) from Nairobi. Situated next to a pond containing black bass and tilapia, it is shaded by tall acacia fever trees. Not luxurious, it is nevertheless a good place to stop and rest and watch the Kamba woodcarvers. *Box 30471, Nairobi, tel. 2/23285. DC.*

Kitani Safari Lodge. These six self-help bandas, located close to the Tsavo River, all have bathroom and kitchen facilities. The bandas face onto well-manicured lawns with spreading acacia trees; after a few meters a wall of thornbush takes over. Bedding is for rent, and there is a shop for nonperishable food and soft drinks. *A. A. Travel Ltd., Box 14982, Nairobi, tel. 2/742926. No credit cards.*

Ndara Ranch. This private ranch provides safari cottages, where game can be plentiful. It is 15 kilometers (9 mi) south of Voi on the main Mombasa-Nairobi road, then 2 kilometers west to the ranch on a dirt road. It has a bar, pool, and camp cookouts with steaks and seafood. *Box 3, Voi, tel. 155, or United Touring Company, Box 42196, Nairobi, tel. 2/331960. No credit cards.*

Ngulia Safari Camp. These six large self-help bandas built on a rocky hillside overlook a water hole on a game trail. All bandas have a bathroom and equipped kitchen, but there is no restaurant (meals can be taken at the lodge), shops, or bedding. *Reservations: see Kitani Lodge. No credit cards.*

Westermann's Safari Camp, about 29 kilometers (16 mi) south of Voi and 10 kilometers (6 mi) west of the A109 Mombasa-Nairobi highway, is a beautifully situated set of 16 simple cottages with a main dining room and shared toilet facilities. *Box 5, Voi, or book via Abercrombie & Kent, Box 90747, Mombasa, tel. 11/ 316539. No credit cards.*

Campsites There are campsites in Tsavo West at the Mtito Andei, Chyulu, and Mbuyuni gates, and in Tsavo East at the Voi Gate and Aruba. All sites have water and toilets.

Tanzania

The headquarters for Tanzania National Parks is Box 3134, 6th floor, Kilimanjaro Wing, International Conference Centre, Arusha, tel. 3471.

Lodging Costs These price categories apply to lodgings in and around all the Tanzania parks and reserves that follow. Lodging must be paid for in dollars (or other foreign currency) or by credit card. Highly recommended lodgings are indicated by a star. Reservations are essential at the game park lodges and a 50% deposit must be made in advance, in U.S. dollars or British pounds.

Category	Cost*
Expensive	over $75
Moderate	$45–$75
Inexpensive	under $45

*All prices are for a standard double room; excluding service charge.

Arusha Ngurdoto Crater National Park
Box 3134, Arusha, tel. Arusha 3471

Size 137 square kilometers (58 sq. mi)

Year Established 1960

Headquarters Arusha

Located 32 kilometers (20 mi) northeast of Arusha, this small park is an easy day trip. There are three distinct areas in the park: Ngurdoto Crater, the Momela Lakes, and Mt. Meru, which is 4,566 meters (14,976 ft) high.

After entering the park at Ngurdoto gate, you drive through the Ngurdoto Forest toward the crater, passing wild mango, African olive, and wild fig trees. Visitors are not allowed to descend into the crater, but a drive around the rim offers views of wild date palms, ferns, orchids, and lichens, plus vistas of Mt. Kilimanjaro to the northeast and surrounding countryside and lakes. The area and crater floor abound with wildlife.

From the crater, follow the signs to Momela Lakes. There are numerous observation points and picnic areas along the way to stop and leave the vehicle. The lakes form a watery chain that attracts animals and birds from miles around.

From the lakes, the track leads on toward Mt. Meru into forest and a profusion of wildflowers. There is a pretty waterfall by the road. Walks are allowed, if you are accompanied by a park warden, and they lead up to the rim of Meru Crater, which offers a breathtaking view of a sheer cliff rising to the summit. It is also possible to climb Mt. Meru, but it takes three days and two nights to make the ascent and descent. There are mountain huts along the way that sleep 24 to 48 people. The cost is $125 per person including fees, guide, porter, and accommodations. Bookings should be made through the warden of Arusha National Park.

Wildlife Many baboons and other monkeys, including colobus, are seen in the Ngurdoto Forest. On the crater floor are buffalo, rhinoceros, waterbuck, hartebeest, and elephants. On the road to the Momela Lakes reedbuck and waterbuck are common, and close to the lakes you may see elephants, giraffes, hyenas, and, if you are lucky, a leopard. There are no lions in this park.

The lakes abound with birds, including geese, flamingos, pelicans, herons, egrets, storks, spoonbills, ducks, plovers, and raptors. Hippos are also common in this area.

In the forest around the base of Mt. Meru watch out for buffalo; there are dik-dik, warthogs, monkeys, and red forest duikers as well. Higher up you may spot klipspringers atop the cliff walls.

Tours There are tours with game drives operating out of Arusha or from the newly renovated Momela Lodge. *Lion's Safari International, Box 999, Arusha, tel. 3181 or 6422; or Park East Tours, 1841 Broadway, New York, NY 10023, tel. 212/765–4870.*

Getting There From Arusha, take A23 some 23 kilometers (14 mi) east toward Moshi, then turn north (left) to reach the park gate after about 5 kilometers (3 mi).

Lodging **Momela Lodge.** This comfortable lodge, just outside the north-
Expensive west edge of the park, has 9 spacious cabins and 37 thatched-roof rondavels. Formerly a hunting lodge, it was originally built for the filming of *Hatari!* The lounge has a beautiful fireplace, and there is a vast dining room with an indoor barbecue. *Lion's Safari Int., Box 999, Arusha, tel. 057/3181, or 6422; telex 42119. MC, V.*

Campsites There are four campsites in the park with water, toilet facilities, and firewood. The cost is $15 per night. Bookings should be made in advance with the park warden in Arusha.

Gombe Stream National Park

Size 52 square kilometers

Year Established 1968

Getting There This small park is well known because of Jane Goodall's study of the chimpanzees here and the popular films of her work produced by the National Geographic Society. The park is north of Kigoma near the Burundi border and can be reached on the MV *Liemba* as well as in water taxis, which leave from Kilalangabo (north of Kigoma) between 9 and 10 AM daily except Sunday. The park entrance fee per person per day is $50.

Lodging   **The Railway Hotel** in Kigoma overlooks the lake and has doubles for $15 a night.

Camping and Hostels   There are campsites at the park but permission must be obtained in advance from park headquarters (*see above*). The youth hostel huts sleep six; a single bed costs $10 a night, and you must bring your own food. Because the park has become very popular and somewhat crowded, baboons can be a problem around campsites and the hostel.

Kilimanjaro National Park
Box 96, Marangu, tel. Arusha 50

Size   1,665 square kilometers (643 sq. mi)

Year Established   Game reserve, 1960; national park, 1973

Headquarters   Marangu

When John Rebman reported back to Great Britain in 1848 that he had discovered a mountain that was snow-capped all year, yet lay only 3° below the equator, he was thought to be mad. Some years later, Ernest Hemingway immortalized the mountain in his book *The Snows of Kilimanjaro*. He described it "as wide as all the world, great, high, and unbelievably white in the sun, was the square top of Kilimanjaro." It is the highest mountain in Africa and one of the world's highest free-standing mountains. Much of the time it's hidden in the clouds and can be seen only at dawn.

Sixty-four kilometers (40 mi) wide at its base, Kilimanjaro is composed of three extinct volcanoes: Kibo, Mawenzi, and Shira. The highest peak, Uhuru, is 5,895 meters (19,340 ft) high and is at the top of Kibo. Any normally fit person can make the five-day trek up Uhuru with no mountain-climbing experience, with the assistance of a guide and porters, via the gentle Marangu Route. This route requires staying four nights in mountain huts. Other routes are more rugged and require some ice-climbing experience. Kilimanjaro lies entirely within Tanzania near the Kenya border. At one time it was possible to start the climb from the Kenya side, but this is no longer allowed.

Moshi is the largest town in the area, and is 56 kilometers (35 mi) east of Kilimanjaro Airport. You can stay there before your climb or continue to Marangu, 39 kilometers (24 mi) to the northeast, which is only 7 kilometers (4 mi) from the park entrance.

Kilimanjaro can be climbed year-round, although the best months are January, February, and September, followed by July, August, November, and December. At other times there is snow on the top and rain at the base, and visibility is poor. December through February are the warmest months, although it is never below freezing at the top.

The Marangu climb starts at the Kilimanjaro National Park Gate at 2,000 meters (6,560 ft). After registration, which takes one to two hours, it is a three- to four-hour walk through the rain forest to the Mandara Hut at 3,000 meters (9,840 ft), where you spend the first night. Coffee, banana, and corn grow

Kilimanjaro National Park

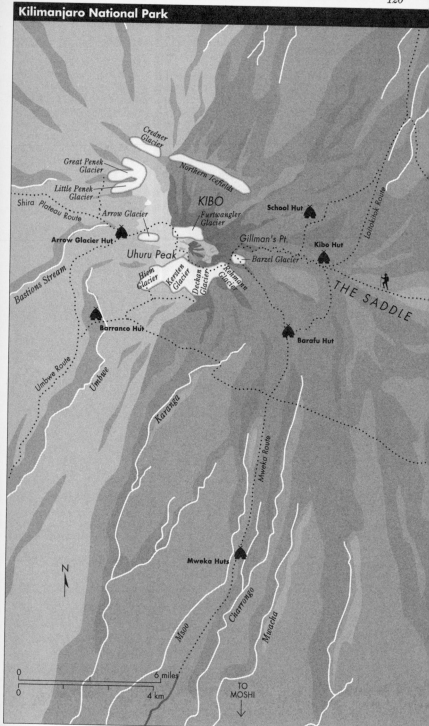

Credner Glacier

Great Penek Glacier

Little Penek Glacier

Shira Plateau Route

Arrow Glacier

Arrow Glacier Hut

Northern Icefields

KIBO

Furtwangler Glacier

School Hut

Lonokilok Route

Gillman's Pt.

Kibo Hut

Uhuru Peak

Barzel Glacier

Hiem Glacier

Kersten Glacier

Deckan Glacier

Rehmann Glacier

THE SADDLE

Bastions Stream

Barranco Hut

Barafu Hut

Umbwe Route

Umbwe

Karanga

Mweka Route

Mweka Huts

N

Charrongo

Mwacha

Msoo

0 — 6 miles
0 — 4 km

TO MOSHI

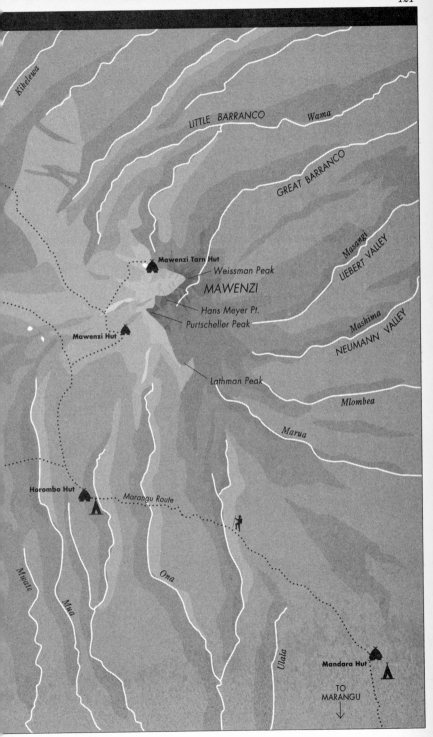

Kibelewa

LITTLE BARRANCO

Wama

GREAT BARRANCO

Masongi

LIEBERT VALLEY

Mawenzi Tarn Hut

Weissman Peak

MAWENZI

Hans Meyer Pt.

Purtscheller Peak

Mawenzi Hut

Mashima

NEUMANN VALLEY

Lathman Peak

Mlombea

Marua

Horombo Hut

Marangu Route

Ona

Mwate

Mwa

Ulala

Mandara Hut

TO
MARANGU

in this area, and you will see monkeys, birds, antelope, elephants, buffalo, rhino, and an occasional leopard.

The next day you leave the last glades of the forest and follow a gently ascending path through open alpine meadow and giant lobelia. The altitude now asserts its presence, cautioning one to tread slowly and pause just enough to enjoy the flora and the view. The Horombo Hut at 4,100 meters (13,450 ft) is reached in about five to seven hours, and you spend the second night here.

The next day you continue past cactus-like giant groundsel and the last water hole and move on to the lunar landscape of the saddle between Kibo and Mawenzi peaks. Surprisingly, you may even see herds of eland at this height. The Kibo Hut, at 4,635 meters (15,200 ft), where you spend the third night, is reached in five to six hours.

Climbers are awakened at 2 AM the next day so they can see the sunrise before the clouds encircle the peak. The loose stone is frozen at this altitude, making it easier to climb. For five to six hours you climb the steepest, most demanding part of the route to Gillman's Point at 5,592 meters (18,345 ft) on the crater rim. The remaining 45 minutes to two hours to the summit are easier. If you feel up to it, you can descend into the crater, which has sulfurous gas and warm sand.

The descent is far less tiring, and one night is spent at the Horombo Hut. The next day, you stop for lunch at the Mandara Hut; you should be at the park gate by midafternoon.

The Mandara Hut is a group of A-frame huts with dormitory rooms and bunk beds, a dining area, and outdoor toilets. The total capacity is 60 persons. The Horombo Hut is similar but larger, with a capacity of 120 persons, outhouses, and outdoor flush toilets. The Kibo Hut is a stone building with dormitory rooms that hold 60 people, and it has a dining area and outhouses. Water at Kibo is carried from Horombo.

There are several park regulations for climbing Kilimanjaro. Before you start, you must check in at park headquarters and give details of your planned route and schedule. This is essential in case you need to be rescued. It is mandatory to hire a guide to the summit. No children under age 10 are allowed above the upper limit of the forest at 3,000 meters (9,840 ft). You should also never go above this point if you have a cold, sore throat, cough, or fever. Rescue fees must be paid in advance even if you do not need to be rescued; they are not refundable.

The entrance fee to climb Kilimanjaro is $200 per person, and it includes the hut accommodations, rescue fee, and a guide. The fee for a porter is Tshs. 1,200 for the five days; you will need one porter for each person. To that you must add the cost of food for yourself, the guide, and porters; equipment; and clothing if you need to rent it. You can rent clothing and equipment for Tshs. 1,220 per person and must leave your passport as a deposit. If you book through one of the hotels or a travel agent, the price range is $450–$750 per person, so it pays to shop around. At the end of the trip you should tip the guide $10 per person and the porters $5 per person.

You should bring your own shoes to wear on the easier part of the climb and around the hut and sturdy hiking boots for the summit. If you bring your own clothes, which is preferable—although clothing can be rented—pack a sweater, water- and windproof jacket, long underwear, a hat, gloves, and socks. You must take one or two changes of clothing, as you must change if your clothes get wet, because of the danger of hypothermia. Other essentials include sunglasses, sunblock, toilet paper, a first-aid kit, medicine, sweets, nuts, fruit, money to buy water at the Mandara Hut, a water bottle, and a flashlight.

You have to be in good physical condition to make it to the top. If you can jog or run for half an hour without getting short of breath, you're okay. But even the physically fit can be overcome by altitude sickness, which causes shortness of breath, increased heart rate, slow thinking, headache, nausea, fatigue, insomnia, swelling of hands and feet, lack of coordination, and, in severe cases, hallucination. Acclimatize yourself by ascending slowly, breathing deeply, and drinking a gallon of water each day. Though you will not feel hungry at high altitudes, you should consume 4,000 calories each day, so bring high-carbohydrate foods. Citrus fruit and bananas reduce the effects of altitude sickness. Avoid fats, rich food, cigarettes, and alcohol.

If you get sick and cannot continue, you must descend immediately; you will not get better with time. There is a rescue team on the mountain, and one of Tanzania's best hospitals, the Kilimanjaro Christian Medical Center (tel. 2741), is in Moshi.

You can make your own arrangements to climb Kilimanjaro, but this involves hiring porters, cooks, and guides; obtaining permission and making hut reservations with the warden at Kilimanjaro National Park (Box 96, Marangu, tel. 50); and obtaining your own food, wood, cooking equipment, clothing, and lamps.

Tours The Kibo and Marangu hotels, both in Marangu, can make all arrangements for you to climb the mountain and will provide you with everything you need. These are expensive tours and should be booked well in advance. Somewhat cheaper climbs can be arranged through the Kilimanjaro Mountain Club (Box 66, Moshi) or the YMCA (Box 865, Moshi, tel. 2362).

Getting There The village of Marangu is the starting point for the Marangu
By Car Route up Mt. Kilimanjaro. From Arusha, take the good tarmac A23 east 88 kilometers (55 mi) to Moshi. From here continue east 27 kilometers (17 mi) to Himo, and turn left to Marangu for 8 kilometers (5 mi). If you do not have your own vehicle, it is possible to take a bus or group taxi from Arusha to Moshi for Tshs. 100 per person, a trip of about two hours. From there, onward travel must be negotiated with a taxi driver.

By Plane Kilimanjaro International Airport is located 56 kilometers (35 mi) east of Moshi. Visitors can fly in directly from Europe or by chartered aircraft from elsewhere. There are buses and taxis to Moshi, and a taxi can be rented to go all the way to Marangu.

Lodging **Kibo Hotel.** This is the largest (75 rooms) and best hotel in
Expensive Marangu, and each room has a private bath. *Box 102, Marangu, tel. 4. No credit cards.*

Moderate **Marangu Hotel.** This small hotel (29 rooms) in Marangu has no private baths, but it is reasonably comfortable and has good food. *Box 40, Moshi, tel. Marangu 11. No credit cards.*
Moshi Hotel. This hotel has 62 rooms, a restaurant, bar, and gift shop. *Box 501, Moshi, tel. 55/55211 or 54160 3071. No credit cards.*

Osirwa Safari Cottages. Located 80 kilometers (50 mi) north-west of Moshi, these comfortable cottages are situated on a beautiful wheat farm on the slopes of Mt. Kilimanjaro at 1,950 meters (6,400 ft), with spectacular views of Masailand, Amboseli National Park in Kenya, and the mountain. *Box, West Kilimanjaro, tel. West Kilimanjaro 542; or contact Osirwa Safari Cottages, 9 Upper Grosvenor St., London W1, tel. 071/499–4850. No credit cards.*

Inexpensive **YMCA.** This is a large, clean hotel with a gym, restaurant, and coffee shop, but no private baths. Women are accepted. *Box 865, Moshi, tel. 55/52362. No credit cards.*

Youth Hostels. There are two youth hostels at the Marangu park entrance. Both have dormitory sleeping areas with bunk beds and a dining room. If you bring your own food, the cook will prepare it for a small fee. *Reservations can be made through the Warden, Kilimanjaro National Park, Box 96, Marangu, tel. 50. No credit cards.*

Campsites There is a campsite next to the youth hostel at the park gate and next to Kibo Hotel. Rates are $8 per person per night.

Lake Manyara National Park
Tanzania National Parks, Box 3134, Arusha, tel. Arusha 3471

Size 330 square kilometers (127 sq. mi)

Year Established 1960

Headquarters Mto wa Mbu

The park lies at the foot of the escarpment of the eastern branch of the Great Rift Valley, 945 meters (3,100 ft) above sea level. The road leading to it coming from Arusha continues on up to the Ngorongoro Crater; thus a visit here can easily be combined with a safari to Ngorongoro and Serengeti National Park.

The park is small—more than two-thirds of it is lake—but it is one of the most popular and attractive wildlife sanctuaries in East Africa. Its charm lies in the variety of habitats and therefore the diversity of animals and birds that can exist in such a small area. Manyara is set in a semiarid region where the average annual rainfall is less than 760 millimeters (30 in) and the maximum daytime temperature is 30° Celsius (86° F). There are several vegetation zones, including groundwater forest with giant fig and mahogany trees, marshland and reedbeds, stretches of open grassland, acacia woodland, and, on the escarpment slopes, thornbush and baobabs. The southern end of the park has sulfur hot springs.

At the park entrance near the village of Mto wa Mbu (Mosquito River) there is a lush forest, interspersed with swampy glades, where towering figs, date palms, tamarind, and mahogany trees grow. The air is cool in the forest but, as the town name implies, mosquitoes can be bothersome. Lake Manyara also has its share of tsetse flies—though they do not carry sleeping sickness—so cover up and use insect repellent.

The park headquarters near the entrance feature a small exhibit, a picnic area, and rest rooms. Prepared lunches can be obtained from your hotel or from the Mto wa Mbu market.

Wildlife Blue monkeys and chattering vervets swing among the forest treetops, and guinea fowl scurry along the forest floor. Ba-

boons are everywhere. Where the forest becomes acacia woodland, lions can be seen; often they are draped sleepily over the
branches of trees—apparently to escape the tsetse flies and
heat. Impala stay close to the acacia zone, as they browse on the
leaves. They can be seen either in large breeding herds of fe-
males—a "harem"—with one dominant male, or in a "bache-
lors' club" of males. Many elephants can also be seen in the
acacia zone.

The open grassland supports huge herds of buffalo, as well as
zebra, giraffes, wildebeests, bushbuck, and waterbuck. At the
edge of the grassland is a large hippo pool, where marabou and
other storks gather. There are a few rhino, but their number
has unfortunately been decreased by poachers. In the marshland, watch out for large, tree-climbing monitor lizards.

In addition to the rich wildlife, there is a stunning array of
birds, especially along the lakeshore where pelicans perch in
the trees. Flamingos are sometimes found along the water's
edge in the slightly alkaline lake, along with ducks, geese, waders, herons, and kingfishers. The level of the lake varies from
year to year, and how close you can get to it on the road depends
on how much rain fell during the last rainy season. In the
woods, larks, hornbills, swallows, and doves are abundant.
Three hundred eighty bird species have been identified in the
park.

Tours The Lake Manyara Hotel can arrange cars and drivers.

Getting There From Arusha, take the tarmac A104 west out of town for 82 ki-
By Car lometers (51 mi) to Makuyuni. Turn right here to reach the
park gate at Mto wa Mbu after another 38 kilometers (24 mi).

By Plane There is a landing strip for light aircraft near the Lake
Manyara Hotel.

Lodging **Lake Manyara Hotel.** Perched on the escarpment, the hotel has
Expensive a beautiful garden as well as a magnificent view of the park 305
meters (1,000 ft) below. There are 100 comfortable rooms, two
suites, a swimming pool, and a gift shop. A landing strip is
nearby. *Tanzania Tourist Corporation, Box 2485, Dar es Salaam; Box 3100, Arusha, tel. 057/3842. No credit cards.*

Inexpensive **Bandas.** There are 10 self-help bandas located just before the
entrance to the park in Mto wa Mbu. There is a central kitchen
and dining banda. ($10 per person.) *Tanzania National Parks,
Box 3134, Arusha, tel. 057/3471. No credit cards.*
Starehe Bar & Grill. This African-style hotel is located on the
escarpment near the Lake Manyara Hotel and is suitable only
for those on a budget. It is clean but has no electricity or hot
water. There is a restaurant that serves very basic food. *No
phone. No credit cards.*

Campsites There are two campsites just before the entrance to the park.
Both have water, firewood, toilet, and shower facilities, and,
unfortunately, many mosquitoes. The rate is $15 per person
per day. There is a campsite in the park—with toilet facilities.
Campsites can be booked with the game warden at the park entrance.

Mahale Mountains National Park

Size 622 square miles

Year Established 1985

Headquarters This tropical rain forest on the eastern edge of Lake Tanganyika harbors one of the largest wild populations of chimpanzees. The chimps have been studied by a Japanese team at the Kasoge Research Camp since 1965, and some of them, accustomed to human presence, can be approached within a few feet.

Wildlife While not as famous a park as Jane Goodall's Gombe River Stream Park (*see above*), it is much more exciting terrain, and ecologically stunning. Lake Tanganyika is enormously deep (1,435 meters/4,710 feet) and renowned for its unusual fish, which are as colorful and varied in form as coral-reef fish. The bird life is rich, with many West African species. The vast lake, frequented by majestic fish eagles, forms the border with Zaire. The best time to visit is May–October; the entrance fee is $45 per person per day. Independent travelers must be fully self-sufficient, with camping gear and food supplies.

Getting There There are no roads to the park or within it; it is accessible only
By Boat by boat or air. In the village of Lagosa, just north of the park, small fishing boats can be chartered. Lagosa is one of the ports of call for the MV *Liemba*, a World War I steamer that calls at Kigoma and Bumjumbura (in Burundi) weekly. You can get to Kigoma on regular flights from Dar (for $245 round-trip) or on the TAZARA railway from Dar (about Tshs. 5,000 one way first class.

By Plane The *Liemba* can be crowded, hot, or delayed; a first class-cabin costs around $60 and is worth every dime of it. The vessel has a fascinating history, including being pickled and sunk to hide it from the enemy, later raised by the British and subsequently revived to continue her runs. She was built by the Germans in 1914, two years after the sinking of the *Titanic*, and has outlived the *Graf Zeppelins*, the Pan Am Clipper, and the *Queen Elizabeth*, not to mention Freddie Laker Airways and the Eastern Shuttle. If you're steeped in Paul Theroux and S. J. Perelman, go for it. Meals on board are basic and inexpensive.

There is a small airstrip at the northern border of the Mahale park, which can be reached by single- or twin-engine charter planes.

Lodging **Mahale Mountain Camp.** Roland Purcell, a self-described ape
Very Expensive fanatic and a director of the Mountain Gorilla Project in Rwanda after Dian Fossey's death, has a small inspired camp of Ottoman-style tents on the sandy lakeshore. His four-day itinerary, the Great Ape Escape, includes sunset cruises on a dhow, fishing and snorkeling, in addition to treks into the forest to see the chimps. He also conducts bird-watching cruises by dugout canoe. The white canvas and mahogany tents are mosquito-proof and each has a private shower and toilet under nearby palms; there is a large dining tent with a bar, where fresh sushi is a specialty, and a smaller library/museum tent. Visitors need good walking boots and must be in reasonable shape, although hiking over the forest terrain is much easier than gorilla trekking. Purcell collects visitors in his six-seater plane from Kigoma, Mukimi, or the Beho Beho airstrip in the Selous. Package prices for the Great Ape Escape tend toward $250 per person per day (depending on the number of people in a group), which includes the park entrance fee. *Greystoke Safaris, Box*

1373, Kigoma. In Nairobi, Ulf Aschan, Box 44715, tel. 2/
337312, fax 2/503391. In Arusha, Ngare Sero, Box 425, tel. 57/
3629, fax 57/2123. No credit cards.

Camping Sites within the park cost $10 per person plus the park en-
trance fee, but you must pack in your own equipment and food.

Mikumi National Park

Size 1,300 square kilometers

Year Established 1970

Headquarters Mikomi, Box 62, Morogoro

Once a part of the Selous Game Reserve, the park is now separated from it by the TAZARA rail line. It can be reached by rail, by
the A7 west of Dar (300 km) and there is a small airstrip. The most
accessible big game park from the capital city, Mukimi is rich in
lion, wildebeest, zebra and vast herds of buffalo. The Makata
flood plain attracts elephant throughout the year, and hippo gather at the pool just 5 kilometers from the park gate.

Lodging   **Mikumi Wildlife Lodge.** Built around a watering hole, this
Moderate   lodge has a swimming pool, gift shop and gas station/garage.
Rooms are moderately priced, about $60 for a double, with
breakfast; lunch costs about $12, dinner about $14. *Book
through TTC, Box 2485, I.P.S. Bldg., Dar, tel. 51/2485. No
credit cards.*
Mikumi Tented Camp. Comprising 10 luxury tents with toilets,
hot water and decent food, the Mikumi Camp is managed by the
same people who run the Oyster Bay Hotel in Dar (tel. 516–
8631). *No credit cards.*
Morogoro Hotel. This one-story lodge at the foot of the Ulu-
guru Mountains has 50 double rooms, a restaurant, bar and pool.
Morogoro is 10 kilometers east of the Mukimi entrance gate
on the A7. *Busktrekker Safaris, Box 3173, New Arusha Hotel,
tel. 513727, and Box 5350, Dar, tel. 31957. No credit cards.*

Camping There are campsites for about $10 per person per night, 4 ki-
lometers (2½ mi) from the park entrance gate. Contact the
Park Warden (see above).

Mkomazi Game Reserve
Box 3134, Arusha, tel. 3471

Size 1,350 square miles

This newly created game reserve is just south of the Kenya border, where it forms a natural extension of Tsavo West National
Park; it is east of Mt. Kilimanjaro National Park. The area has
spectacular views of Kilimanjaro, as well as the Pare and
Usambara mountains, which define its southern border. Taita
Hills and Ndea Hill can be seen from the Vitewini escarpment,
and the Dindira Valley is pristine. The Mkomazi area is the focus of efforts to preserve cheetah and wild dog by the George
Adamson Conservation Trust, headed by Tony Fitzjohn. The
area is rich in birds. There are no lodges in Mkomazi, but camping and walking safaris can be arranged by Abercrombie &
Kent in Arusha.

Off the   In his book *Island Africa*, Jonathan Kingdon describes the
Beaten Track **Usambara Mountains** as "the focal center for biological abundance" on the entire coast of East Africa. The species are rare

and spectacular, including many birds and the exotic frogfoot moon moth. This area is for the intrepid nature lover, but it is worth the trip if you like to get away from the crowds. There are several good paths, one of the most popular leading to an area known as the Viewpoint, which overlooks the Masai plain and the Mombo/Tanga Road. Driving that road will give you a vertigo as well as views, with hairpin curves and sheer drops. To get there, take the A14 north from Dar, then bear left at the fork to Lushoto rather than Tanga.

Lodging　　**The Lawns Hotel,** a colonial-style lodge with a lofty view of the Usambaras, offers double and triple rooms for under $15. On the edge of The Lawns green is the **Kilimani Guest House,** whose clean, simple rooms surround a courtyard with a bar. There is no running water, but the food is good. Contact Coastal Travels in Dar (Box 1192, tel. 51/28485, 35638, or 26500).

Ngorongoro Conservation Area
Box 776, Arusha, tel. Arusha 3339

Size　　259 square kilometers (102 sq. mi)

Year Established　　1959

Headquarters　　Crater Village

The Ngorongoro Crater is about 12 miles across, the largest undamaged caldera (collapsed volcano) in the world. The rim is at an altitude of 2,285 meters (7,500 ft), so those who stay in the hotels here enjoy cool nights. From the rim, the vast floor of the crater spreads out 610 meters (2,001 ft) below. From the rim, down a couple of hundred meters around the outside of the crater, is tropical forest. This forest used to extend much farther down the volcanic mountain, but farms are slowly working their way upward as the area's population expands. The conservation area was created to protect this extraordinary natural wonder.

There is only one rather narrow, rocky track down into the crater, and another one up. Both were built by hand by prisoners in the 1950s. Those with their own four-wheel-drive vehicles, which are picked up (and paid for) at the headquarters in Crater Village, must take a ranger with them. If you hire a vehicle from one of the hotels ($60 half-day and $95 full day), the driver is all you need.

The descent to the crater floor takes about 30 minutes because of the steepness and condition of the road. The vegetation on the way down is dense and lush, but there are undesignated viewpoints where you can stop and take photos from the car windows. There is a picnic area in the crater with water and toilets, and it is a good idea to bring a box lunch so that the whole day can be spent in the crater.

Wildlife　　It is estimated that on average more than 30,000 animals live in the crater. Because the crater floor is mostly flat grassland, with patches of acacia woodland here and there, game-viewing is excellent. A set of tracks covers almost all parts of the crater floor, including approaching the central soda lake, called Magadi, which means salt.

The crater is home to abundant numbers of wildebeests, zebras, hartebeests, Thomson's and Grant's gazelles, lions, hyenas, and buffalo, but no giraffes because the inside walls are too steep for them. There are also no cheetahs, because the aggressive hyenas chased them out. It was in Ngorongoro that Dr. Hans Kruuk discovered that spotted hyenas are proficient hunters. Elephants migrate in and out of the crater, and on occasion some big tuskers can be found.

The Ngorongoro Crater is one of the best places to view a lion or hyena hunt. Early in the morning is the most likely time, but even if you miss the actual hunt, it is not uncommon to find a sated lion pride, presided over by a majestic black-maned patriarch, lying in the sun licking their chops around a half-eaten buffalo carcass.

Hippos live in Magadi Lake, and there are several black rhino, which can be approached fairly closely for good photos. The alkaline lake attracts flamingos and these are sometimes to be found in great numbers, along with other waders. Because the lake has no fish, many water birds are absent, though it attracts ostriches, egrets, secretary birds, and crested cranes.

Masai with their herds of cattle are a common sight in the crater. They are allowed to bring cattle in to take mineral salts around the lake, necessary for their health. No one group is supposed to remain longer than necessary in the crater, but this is not always easy to control.

Tours　Vehicles with drivers can be hired from the Ngorongoro Crater Lodge and the Ngorongoro Wildlife Lodge.

Getting There　From Arusha, drive southwest 82 kilometers (51 mi) to Makuyuni, then turn right, off the paved road, toward Lake Manyara. Continue on the same road, which is dirt and steep in parts, some 70 kilometers (43 mi) to the gate to Ngorongoro Conservation Area.

Lodging　**Gibb's Farm.** This private farm and coffee plantation is now a
Expensive　lodge consisting of 15 cottages. It is located in green country-
★　side near Karatu halfway up the crater from Lake Manyara. There is a lovely garden and nature walk to a water hole frequented by wildlife. Lunch is a huge buffet and dinner a three-course meal. *Box 1501, Karatu, tel. Karatu 25. No credit cards.*
Ngorongoro Crater Lodge. The lodge is set up along the rim with individual buildings containing 50 double rooms, some with views down into the crater. It was renovated in 1990, with all new facilities and new landscaping, and a central dining lodge and gift shop. *Abercrombie & Kent, 1420 Kensington Rd., Oak Brook, IL 60521, tel. 800/323-7308; or A & K, Arusha, tel. 3303; fax 057/7003. V.*

Inexpensive　**Ngorongoro Rhino Lodge.** Located away from the rim of the crater, this former youth hostel is small and spartan and all rooms share a bath. *Box 1, Ngorongoro, no phone. AE, V.*
Ngorongoro Wildlife Lodge. This Tanzania Tourist Corporation property resembles a Colorado ski lodge. The lounge and restaurant are glass-enclosed for an uninterrupted view of the crater below. All rooms are centrally heated and there is a gift shop. *Box 3100, Arusha, tel. 3842. AE, V.*

Campsites　Camping is no longer permitted on the crater floor. The Simba campsite at the top of the crater has toilets, hot showers, water, and firewood at $12 a day per person. Arrangements should be made in advance with the Conservator (Box 1, Ngorongoro, tel. 6/7).

Off the Beaten Track You can drive to the soda **Lake Natron** (20 km/12 mi from the park), as well as to **Ol Doinyo Legai** (the volcanic Mountain of God), or you can arrange to see them through **Peter Byrne** (fax 337 703) or **Chris Marshall** (fax 338 193) in Nairobi, on camping safaris with vehicles, gear, food and guides provided (expensive).

Ruaha National Park

Size 1,300 square kilometers

Established 1964

Park headquarters Msembe

Wildlife This park, 130 kilometers (80 mi) west of Iringa, is one of the least explored in East Africa, although it's nearly as large as the Serengeti. It was divided from Rungwa Game Reserve in 1964 and made a separate park. The landscape features gargantuan baobab trees and is rich in bird life; there are photography blinds you can use to capture close-ups. The Ruaha River, full of hippo and crocodiles, attracts elephant and lion, and you are likely also to see greater and lesser kudu, as well as sable and roan antelope.

Getting There You can fly by charter plane to the Msembe strip near park headquarters on the eastern boundary, or come by car from Iringa, after taking the A7 from Dar. The roads are impassable during the rains, and it's best to visit between June and December.

Lodging **The Ruaha River Camp.** Built around a large kopje formation, *Moderate* this camp has a good restaurant and bar and bandas, or cabins, that overlook the Ruaha River. Meals are included in the rates, but game drives cost extra, and you should reserve a vehicle when you book if you are not bringing your own. *Note:* Extra fuel for visitors' vehicles is not always available for sale. *Foxtreks Ltd., Box 84, Mufindi, or Coastal Travels Ltd., Dar es Salaam, tel. 051/37479 or 051/37480, fax 051/36585.*

Selous Game Reserve

Size 54,600 square kilometers

Year Established 1905

This is the largest game reserve in Africa, located 360 kilometer (223 mi) south of the Kenya border, characterized by its many rivers; the Great Ruaha and Kilombero rivers deliver to the Rufiji, which in its turn creates a delta. The reserve was named after Frederick Selous, a British soldier, elephant hunter, and naturalist, whose grave is near the Beho Beho River. The rapids around Stiegler's Gorge are good for white water just after the rains. During the dry season, many lower streams become rivers of sand that you can traverse on foot or with a four-wheel drive.

Wildlife The principal attraction of the Selous is space, and its specialty is walking safaris where you are likely to encounter no other humans. The area south of the Rufiji is divided into hunting blocks, and various hunting guides have concessions here, for shooting buffalo and impala. There were once great herds of elephant, some 300,000 strong, and the Selous was the home of the big tuskers. But they have been mowed down by poachers, and, sadly, what you will see is small herds with small tusks. There's no shortage of hippo, and you will see hundreds on the Rufiji.

Tours The only part of the Selous developed for tourists is north of the Rufiji, although walking safaris can be arranged down the Mbarangandu River, the focus of Peter Matthiessen's book *Sand Rivers*. Walks cover 10 kilometers a day in hot, sultry weather. Such safaris are not for everyone, but if you want an off-the-beaten-path trek, this is the place. The best time is from July through October.

Getting There Air charters fly into the Selous from Dar and may cost $300–$400 round-trip, depending on how many passengers there are. You can also take the TAZARA train from Dar to the Fuga Railway Station, but you must arrange in advance to be met there, and the charge for this is about $50.

Lodging **Richard Bonham** has a well-managed base camp on the Beho
Very Expensive Beho River and arranges temporary, lightweight camps reached on foot or by boat on the sand rivers at Lake Tagalala and at Stiegler's Gorge. With Bonham, who limits his groups to eight and prefers to cover a lot of wild terrain, you might take a dip in natural hot springs or fish for your lunch. His cook and staff are exceptionally well organized, and guests are often surprised to arrive at a pretty spot at midday and again at sundown to discover their camp waiting, along with a cold beer. *Box 24133, Nairobi, tel. 2/882 521, fax 2/882 728. USA: A. K. Taylor, 2724 Arvin Rd., Billings, MT 59102, tel. 406/656–0706, fax 406/252–6353. No credit cards.*

Expensive **Mbuyu Safari Camp.** This luxury tented camp on the banks of the Ru fi ji is 300 kilometers (186 mi) from Dar and best reached by air charter. Each tent has a bathroom en suite, electric lights, and wooden frame beds rather than cots. Most tents have a good view of the river and are spaced away from the dining and bar area. Each game drive and boat trip costs about $20 per person extra. The camp is closed from mid-March to late May. *Selous Safari Co. Ltd., Box 1192, Dar, tel. 28485/35638, fax 28486. Coastal Travels Ltd., Box 3052, Dar, tel. 37479/37480, fax 36585. No credit cards.*

Moderate **Rufiji River Camp.** This camp, also on the banks of the Rufiji, is a dozen years strong, with 10 double tents with toilets and showers outside, plus Land Rovers and boats for hire. It is the closest camp to Dar (80 miles by air), and can be reached by four-wheel-drive vehicle, but no fuel is sold at the camp, so you must bring enough for your return. All meals are included in the rates, but walking safaris, boat trips and game drives are extra. *Owned by Tanzania Safari Ltd., Box 2005, Dar, tel. 63546; offices on Puga Rd., across from the TAZARA railway station. Book also through Coastal Travels in Dar, Upanga Rd. at Ohio St., tel. as above. No credit cards.*

Camping **Beho Beho Camp.** This primitive place is now being renovated and is under new management. It has lovely views and an airstrip, but it's best to obtain details on accommodations from the management. *Oyster Bay Hotel, Dar, tel. 68631.*

Serengeti National Park
Box 3134, Arusha, tel. Arusha 3471

Size 14,763 square kilometers (5,700 sq. mi)

Year Established 1951

Headquarters Seronera

From Ngorongoro Crater, most visitors proceed to the most spectacular gathering of wildlife in the world—the Serengeti Plains. Serengeti National Park contains millions of animals and birds in four habitats: open plains in the south; savanna with scattered acacia trees in the center; hilly, wooded grasslands in the north; and extensive woodlands and black clay plains in the west. Small lakes, rivers, and swamps are scattered throughout the park, particularly in the north and west.

The altitude varies between 920 and 1,850 meters (3,000 to 6,000 ft) and temperatures rarely exceed 32° Celsius (90° F), with the average being 25° Celsius (78° F). The Masai use the southern part of the park to graze their cattle, and the pastoralist-wildlife interaction is being studied by conservationists and ecologists. Long-term studies of various aspects of the ecosystem have been going on for 30 years, based at the Serengeti Research Institute.

The annual migration takes place at the end of the rainy season, about June, led by 2 million wildebeests. The Serengeti is dry from June to December. In April, animals are spread out horizon to horizon over the plains in the south. In May they begin moving northward and westward, forming long weaving lines of several thousand wildebeests each. By June many race north into the Masai Mara in Kenya in search of the pasture they know, after thousands of years of experience, is awaiting them. Tens of thousands of zebras, gazelles, and antelopes accompany them, along with migratory lions. Not all lions are migratory; many remain in the Serengeti.

There are a good number of tracks in the park, and it is best to go with a guide who knows the area. If you have a private vehicle—not an organized-tour vehicle—it is possible to cross into the Masai Mara National Reserve in Kenya at the Sand River gate. It is 40 kilometers (25 mi) from the Lobo Lodge in the Serengeti and Keekorok Lodge in the Masai Mara.

Wildlife The southern grass plains contain large numbers of grazers: wildebeest, gazelle, topi, zebra, and buffalo. Ostriches and secretary birds skirt through the grass, and warthog families can be seen down on their front knees grubbing for roots—when they see you they take off with their tails sticking straight in the air.

Throughout the Serengeti are granite outcrops called *kopjes*, Dutch for "little heads," a reference to what they look like from a distance. These rock islands attract numerous wildlife, particularly baboons, hyraxes, hyenas, and klipspringers. If none of these animals is about, there might be a leopard lair in one of the crevices.

In the central, more wooded area one finds more of the browsers, such as giraffes, impalas, elephants, but also the shy grazer, the eland, and more buffalo. Lions are more likely to be found here as they have places to hide when stalking their prey.

Watch for vultures circling in the sky to lead you to a fresh kill. You may also spot one of the park's rare rhino in this area.

In the hilly northern part of the Serengeti, wildebeest, zebra, and buffalo herds will be seen on the grassy slopes. In the west there is not as much game, but large areas of flat swampland attract thousands of water birds such as the crowned crane, sacred and other ibises, plovers, egrets, and others. Tracks tend to disappear under water in the far west, and this part of the park should be avoided during the rainy season.

The Serengeti has some of the world's best bird-watching, with more than 500 species identified.

Tours Both the Seronera and Lobo lodges have vehicles with drivers for hire. If you're interested in conservation and scientific research, request a visit to the Serengeti Research Institute, which must be arranged in advance.

Getting There The Naabi Hill gate of the park is a 130-kilometer (81-mi) drive northwest on a good dirt road from Ngorongoro. A drive directly to the park will take about four hours, but most people allow an extra couple of hours for a side visit to **Olduvai Gorge** (*see* Tanzania, Chapter 9), the famous canyon gouged in the plains where Louis and Mary Leakey worked for many decades, uncovering fossils and archaeological remains of humankind's evolution.

Lodging **Grumeti River Camp** is a luxury tented camp for 12 guests that
Very Expensive offers private game drives. *Archer's Tours, Box 40097, Nairobi, tel. 2/223 131, fax 2/340 182. No credit cards.*

Expensive **Lobo Wildlife Lodge.** The lodge is built around a massive kopje rock that fills a large portion of the restaurant/lounge. The swimming pool is also fashioned around a rock and looks out over the vastness of the plains. There are 75 comfortable rooms and a suite with night-time electricity and hot water. Lobo is in the northern section of the park, 75 kilometers (45 mi) from Seronera Lodge. *Tanzania Tourist Corp., Box 3100, Arusha, tel. Arusha 3842. AE, V.*

★ **Seronera Wildlife Lodge.** Containing 75 rooms, the lodge is built on and around a kopje, and parts of the natural rock must be trod to reach various areas of the establishment. It is located in the center of the park—strategic for witnessing the migration or simply for heading out in different directions for exploration. The lodge suffers periodic water shortages. *Tanzania Tourist Corp., Box 3100, Arusha, tel. Arusha 3842. AE, V.*

Moderate **Ndutu Safari Lodge,** near the southern border of the Serengeti
★ National Park, overlooks Lake Ndutu. There are 30 double rooms, plus new cottages built in 1990, and an excellent restaurant. It's a popular place for seeing the wildebeest migration and visiting Olduvai Gorge. *Box 1501, Karatu, or telex 42041, Arusha. U.S. agent: Jackie Allen, 7765 91st St., Plaza del Rey, CA 90293, tel. and fax 213/823-2643.*

Campsites There are nine campsites in the park, four at Seroners and one each at Lobo, Moru Kopjes, Naabi Hill gate, and Kirawira. Most have toilets and water. Those with facilities charge $15 per person per night, those without are $8. Arrangements can be made with the Tanzania National Parks, Box 3134, Arusha, tel. 3471, or at the Naabi Hill gate.

Serengeti National Park and Ngorongoro Conservation Area

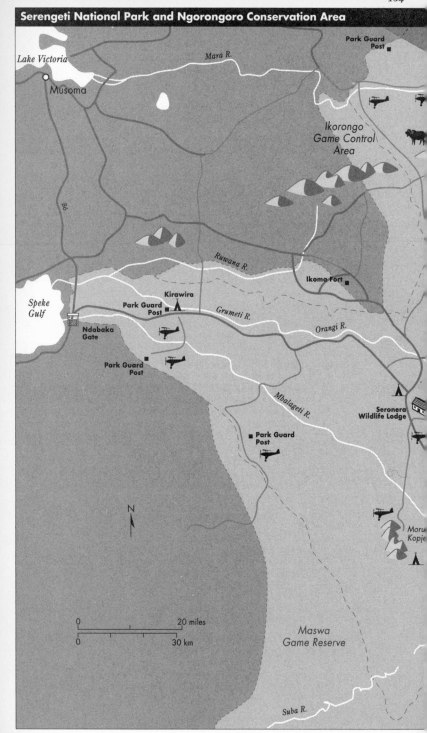

Lake Victoria

Musoma

Mara R.

Park Guard Post

Ikorongo Game Control Area

Bó

Ruwana R.

Ikoma Fort

Kirawira

Park Guard Post

Grumeti R.

Speke Gulf

Orangi R.

Ndabaka Gate

Park Guard Post

Mbalageti R.

Park Guard Post

Seronera Wildlife Lodge

N

Moru Kopje

0   20 miles

0   30 km

Maswa Game Reserve

Suba R.

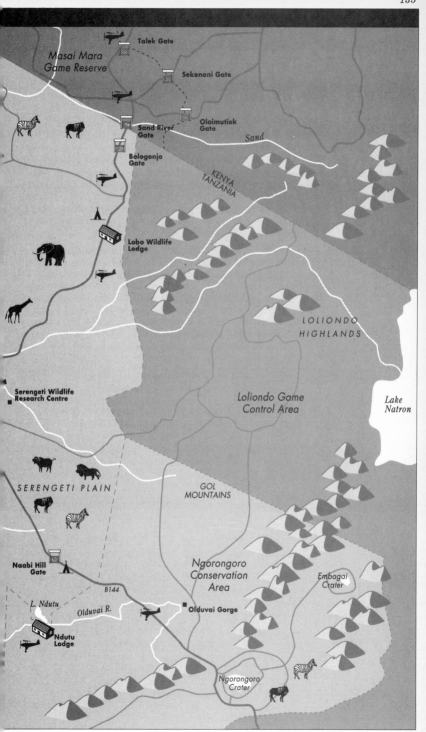

Tarangire National Park
Box 3134, Arusha, tel. 3471

Size
2,600 square kilometers (1,560 sq. mi)

Headquarters
Tarangire Main gate

Tarangire National Park is 115 kilometers (69 mi.) southwest of Arusha, just east of the new Dodoma Road. During the dry season this small park is second only to Ngorongoro crater in concentration of wildlife, which depend on the Tarangire River.

Wildlife
There are more than 300 species of birds, including Martial and Bateleur eagle; large herds of eland, oryx, wildebeest, and zebra; and a good population of elephant from June to September. The park is rich in baobab trees and has a variety of habitats, with doum palms, acacia woodland, and a shallow soda lake, Burungi, that attracts flamingos and pelicans in the rainy season. Pythons can often be seen in trees near the swamps. Many people visit Tarangire on their way to or from Lake Manyara. For some reason, this lovely park is a well-kept secret.

Lodging
Moderate
Tarangire Safari Lodge. This luxury tented camp 10 kilometers from the park gate has tents overlooking the Tarangire River, a restaurant, and a small pool. The 35 double tents each accommodate two and have bathrooms en suite. There are also five bungalows that accommodate small families. *Box 1182, Arusha, tel. 057/3090, telex 42038. In the U.S. Kjell Bergh, Borton Overseas, Ltd., 5516 Lyndale Ave. S, Minneapolis, MN 55419, tel. 800/843-0602.*

4 Nairobi and Excursions

Introduction

By Leslie Duckworth

An artist and graphic designer, Leslie Duckworth was born in Zimbabwe and has lived in Nairobi for more than 10 years. She has contributed to numerous guidebooks on Kenya.

The sight of the Nairobi skyline often surprises first-time visitors, whose vision of this country may have been shaped by films such as *Out of Africa* and the television series "Flame Trees of Thika." Some early architecture—such as the classic Norfolk Hotel—survives, but downtown Nairobi is dominated by the Kenyatta Conference Center, along with several modern skyscrapers housing international hotel chains, corporate headquarters, and government offices.

Located 140 kilometers (87 mi) south of the equator, this city with a population of more than a million people has a rich architectural and ethnic heritage. In addition to the many tribal peoples of East African origin who reside in Nairobi, there is a large Indian community, a Muslim enclave, and refugees from Somalia and Uganda. Most residents wear Western clothes and speak English, but occasionally you will see someone in traditional dress, especially at the marketplace or in the shantytowns that separate the business center from the elegant suburbs.

The largest city between Cairo and Johannesburg, Nairobi is the communications and financial center of East Africa, and with its urban advantages come disadvantages: Pickpockets are rampant, luggage and cameras are likely to be stolen from even the locked trunk of your rental car, and the streets are thick with beggars and aggressive hawkers selling "elephant hair" bracelets, usually made of plastic.

As the capital of the fastest-growing nation in the world, Nairobi is a study in contrasts and rapid change. Less than a century ago the best form of transportation on the muddy city streets was an ox-drawn cart—or, as one doctor preferred, a domesticated zebra. Today the traffic jams rival those of Rome, and exhaust fumes cloud thoroughfares such as the Uhuru Highway—renamed following Kenya's Independence (*Uhuru* is Swahili for independence). From this concrete jungle, a visit to the suburbs reveals private estates as plush as those of Beverly Hills: elaborate wrought-iron gates, tennis courts, stables, and swimming pools abound. You can study such contrasts when venturing to the Karen Blixen Museum, in the suburb named after her, Karen. (Karen Blixen wrote *Out of Africa* under the pen name Isak Dinesen.)

Essential Information

Arriving and Departing by Plane

Airports and Airlines **Jomo Kenyatta International Airport** (tel. 2/822111), named after the country's first president, lies 13 kilometers (8 mi) southeast of Nairobi. More than 30 international carriers fly into the airport, including **Kenya Airways** (tel. 2/29291), which has good service from London and Rome, as well as domestic service and flights to Seychelles and Tanzania. Customs and immigration facilities are also at **Wilson Airport** (Langata Rd.), but international flights from the small domestic port are rare and usually come from nearby Tanzania, Uganda, or Zaire. Wilson is a likely departure point for chartered flights within Kenya, say to the Masai Mara Game Reserve or the island of Lamu. The following companies operate charters out of Wilson Airport: **Air Kenya Aviation** (Box 30357, Nairobi, tel. 2/501601 and 501421), **Boskovic Air Charters** (Box 45646, Nairobi, tel. 2/501210 and 501219), and **Safari Air Services Ltd.** (Box 41951, Nairobi, tel. 2/501211).

If your visit has been arranged by a tour operator, you will be met by a driver and perhaps your safari guide at the airport. They usually stand in the arrival area just outside immigration, holding a placard with the name of the tour company or your own name.

If you are traveling independently, it is best to obtain Kenya shillings at the airport; there are banks both inside the baggage/customs area and outside in the arrivals area. Otherwise you can obtain local currency at your hotel.

Between Jomo Kenyatta Airport and City Center
By Rental Car
If you have reserved a rental car, you can arrange to have your vehicle waiting for you at the airport, delivered there by a driver, whom you should tip. The modern four-lane highway into downtown Nairobi, its median planted with bougainvillea, is an excellent place to practice driving on the left.

By Train
There is no train service from the airport into downtown Nairobi, although from Nairobi there is an excellent overnight train to Mombasa.

By Taxi and Bus
Both buses and taxis are very cheap by Western standards. After leaving customs you will be approached by taxi drivers. Try and check your taxi and be sure to agree on a price before getting in. Many are up for hire at twice the going rate, but have no horn or brakes! The fare into the city center should be around Kshs. 250. **Kenatco** (2/25123) is a reliable taxi firm, with airport offices and official fixed rates.

Kenya Airways runs an hourly shuttle bus with drop-offs at its Koinange Street terminal or any centrally located hotel for Kshs. 40.

Getting Around

The easiest, and often the fastest, way of traveling around Nairobi city center is on foot. It is certainly the mode used by the majority of the city's inhabitants and the best way of appreciating the international atmosphere. While walking about and enjoying all the sights, be careful to keep a tight hold on your purse; don't wear any jewelry that might attract unwanted attention. Gold chains and handbags are favored by Nairobi's fast-fingered street thieves.

By Taxi
Taxis are found outside cinemas, theaters, restaurants, large hotels, the train station, and at official parking stands. They cannot be hailed on the street. They are sometimes metered, but often the meter is broken, so always negotiate a fare before getting in. The rate is around Kshs. 50 for a trip within the city center and Kshs. 250 for airport trips. Always take a taxi, rather than walking, after dark.

By Matatu
These vans are easily identified by their speed, the overflow of passengers, and, often, the poor state of the vehicle. Their name is a derivation of *Senti tatu*, Swahili for 3 pennies, which was the original fare. Unless you are looking for high risk, Matatus are not recommended.

By Bus The municipal bus service (KBS) is jammed during the morning (7:30–8:30) and evening (5–6) rush hours and has a very unreliable timetable. The main city bus terminal is at the bottom of River Road. Other principal bus and matatu stops include the Ambassadeur/Hilton Hotel (Moi Ave.), Nation House (top of Tom Mboya St.) and the General Post Office (Kenyatta Ave.).

By Car Both self-drive and chauffeured rental cars are available at competitive prices. **Hertz** (Box 42196, Nairobi, tel. 2/331960), **Avis Rent-a-Car** (Box 49795, Nairobi, tel. 2/336794), and **Europe Car** (Box 49420, Nairobi, tel. 2/332744) are widely represented and you can drop off the vehicle in Nairobi, Malindi, or Mombasa at the end of your trip. Local firms offering similar vehicles at lower rates include **Kesana Car Hire, Ltd.,** in the Muthaiga Shopping Center (tel. 2/749062 or 2/749363; fax 2/741636), **Let's Go Travel** (Box 60342, Nairobi, tel. 2/29539), **Wheels Car Hire** (Box 47173, Nairobi, tel. 2/336038), and **Concorde Car Hire** (Box 25053, Nairobi, tel. 2/743011). During high season, it's best to reserve a vehicle far in advance.

For a typical small car expect to pay Kshs. 1500–Kshs. 2000 per day at the major firms, plus Kshs. 3/60–Kshs. 4/50 per kilometer; a collision damage waiver is Kshs. 100–Kshs. 170 per day. Unless you have a major credit card, a cash deposit of at least Kshs. 5000 will be necessary. A driver's license from home is valid for six months in Kenya, provided it has not been endorsed over the past two years. Driving is on the left. Look out for traffic light jumping, and potholes.

Finding a parking space in the center of Nairobi is very difficult. Due to shortages, parking in Nairobi has fallen under the jurisdiction of parking men—an assortment of youths, many of them handicapped, and silver-haired old hands. They will find you a spot whether you want one or not, claim that a space you found was theirs, and offer to "look after" your car—all this for a small fee. Even if they were not there when you parked, they will be there when you return and will be very expectant of tips. There is a secure parking lot across from the Norfolk Hotel, run by the Cultural Center. The daily fee is Kshs. 20.

Important Addresses And Numbers

Tourist Information The best way to get current and accurate information is through a tour operator (*see* Guided Tours, below) or through your hotel. Nairobi's **Tourist Information Office** on Mama Ngina Street, opposite the Hilton, is now a booking office for Kenya Airways/African Tours and Hotels. The staff will give you information, but usually only on their services. Additional information on Nairobi can be found in newspapers, the telephone directory, or through embassies or travel agents. The free tourist magazines *What's On,* a monthly, and *Tourist's Kenya,* a bimonthly, are also useful.

Embassies **U.S. Embassy,** U.S.A. Embassy Building, Moi Avenue, tel. 2/334141.

Canadian Embassy, Comcraft House, Haile Selassie Avenue, tel. 2/334033.

British Embassy, Bruce House, Standard Street, tel. 2/335944.

Emergencies **Police and Ambulance** (tel. 2/999).

Hospitals Two good private hospitals, the **Aga Khan** (Box 30270, Side Parklands Ave., tel. 2/742531) and **Nairobi Hospital** (Box 30270, Kodhek Agwin Rd., tel. 2/722160), have intensive-care facilities and screen blood for transfusions. **Gertrude's Garden** (Box 50305, tel. 2/65305) specializes in children's illnesses. For an up-to-date list of doctors and dentists ask at your embassy or hotel.

Late-Night Pharmacies Pharmaceuticals are available but expensive, so any visitor requiring long-term medication should come supplied. The major pharmacies run a late-night *rota* (timetable), which is posted on their door and in the national daily papers. Pharmacies at the major hospitals are open 24 hours.

English-language Bookstores The **Nation** (Kenyatta Ave., next to the entrance of the New Stanley Hotel, tel. 2/333507) is one of the busiest with a good selection of local maps. **Select** (Kimathi St., opposite the New Stanley Hotel, tel. 2/21546) is a larger, slightly run-down shop with a small antique Africana section. **Prestige** (tel. 2/23515) and **Book Corner** (tel. 2/28820), both on Mama Ngina Street, stock up-to-date Africana titles. **Text Book Centre** (Kijabe St. and Sarit Centre, tel. 2/330340) has a wide selection of textbooks and equipment, plus Africana and popular fiction.

There are several street bookstalls on Tom Mboya Street and a secondhand shop on Banda Street where you may come across the occasional bargain. Antique Africana can be found at the **Antique Gallery** (Kaunda St., tel. 2/27759) and also at the **Antique Auction** (Moktar Daddah St., tel. 2/336383) rooms.

Travel Agencies **Let's Go Travel** (Caxton House, Standard St., tel. 2/29539, 29540, and 340331) has comprehensive travel information and efficient service. Current listings of hotel and car-rental rates are available free, as is information on new or off-the-beaten-track itineraries. The American Express representative in Nairobi is **Express Kenya Co.** (Standard St., Box 40433, tel. 2/334722). Other reliable travel agencies include **Bunson Travel Service Ltd.** (Standard St., Box 45456, tel. 2/21992), **AA Travel** (Hurlingham Shopping Centre, Box 14982, tel. 2/339700), and **United Touring International** (Muindi Mbingu St., Box 42196, tel. 2/331960).

Guided Tours

Orientation Most tour operators offer an orientation **city tour** in a small minibus. Usually it consists of a three-hour introduction to the streets and avenues, parks and gardens, monuments, noted buildings and varied peoples of Nairobi. As a rule it includes visits to the City Market, Parliament buildings, National Museum, and Snake Park. Both Bunson Travel and Let's Go Travel (*see* Travel Agencies, above) can arrange city tours.

Abercrombie & Kent (tel. 2/334955/6/7), an international company that opened in Nairobi 25 years ago, offers a wide range of services, from expensive, private-camping safaris to lower-priced group tours via minibus. It can also make lodge reservations, should you prefer a self-drive vacation. Its centrally located office is on the sixth floor of Bruce House on Standard Street, just around the corner from the New Stanley Hotel.

Personal Guides Many individuals associated with tour companies occasionally offer personalized guide service around Nairobi. There are also personal guides who will organize your entire safari in Kenya, from meeting you at the airport to seeing you off on your departure. In addition to those listed in Chapter 1, there are **Robin Hurt Safaris, Ltd.** (Box 24988, Nairobi, tel. 2/882 826; fax 2/882 939) which offers tented camping, both luxury and simple, and **Brian Nicholson** (Richard Bonham Safaris, Ltd., Box 24133, Nairobi, tel. 2/882 521; fax 2/882 728), a former game warden who was profiled in Peter Matthiessen's book *Sand Rivers*.

Exploring Nairobi

Orientation

Visitors can usually explore the city center on foot, but your time in Nairobi is likely to be brief, and most people venture to the highlights by car or minibus. Several priority stops are not within walking distance of most hotels: the Nairobi Museum, for example, is 2 kilometers (1.2 mi) from city center, and it is best to take a taxi for security reasons. Even farther are the Carnivore Restaurant, Karen Blixen Museum, the AFEW Giraffe Center, and Nairobi National Park. Also, because the city is at 5,500 feet, it's best to acclimatize slowly.

Highlights for First-time Visitors

AFEW Giraffe Center (*see* Excursions from Nairobi, below)

African Heritage Shop and Restaurant (*see* Shopping, below)

Carnivore Restaurant (*see* Dining, below)

City Market (*see* Exploring Nairobi, below)

Karen Blixen Museum (*see* Excursions from Nairobi, below)

Kenya National Museum (*see* Exploring Nairobi, below)

Kenyatta International Conference Center (*see* Exploring Nairobi, below)

Nairobi National Park (*see* Kenya and Tanzania Game Parks, Chapter 3)

Norfolk Hotel (*see* Exploring Nairobi; Lodging, below)

Railway Museum (*see* Exploring Nairobi, below)

Nairobi City Center

Numbers in the margin correspond to points of interest on the Nairobi map.

The triangle of central Nairobi, approximately 4½ square kilometers (2.8 sq. mi), is bordered by the Nairobi River, the six-lane Uhuru Highway, and the railway. Kenyatta Avenue and Moi Avenue bisect this triangle into three main districts: Northwest, Southwest, and East. Southwest Nairobi contains government buildings, banks, offices, monuments, excellent shops, and luxury hotels. It is the most imposing sector of town, dominated by Nairobi's tallest landmark, the 28-story Kenyatta International Conference Center. The Northwest district constitutes a more modest and denser area of shops, restaurants, and hotels, while the Eastern area encompasses the poor, inner city. This is where you find the capital's cheap restaurants and hotels; bus stations and matatu terminals;

large cloth, vegetable, and art markets; and much of Nairobi's real character.

1 **Kenyatta Avenue** is a good starting point for exploring Southwest Nairobi. Originally designed so a cart drawn by a team of 16 oxen could turn with ease, the avenue now contains six lanes of heavy traffic. On the northeast corner of the Uhuru Highway/Kenyatta Avenue traffic circle stands the one-story former **Provincial Commissioner's Office** (1916). Now boarded up, dwarfed, and replaced by **Nyayo House,** which towers behind, it is a prime example of the scale, style, and speed of Nairobi's development. Kipande House (1913), farther along the avenue on the left, where *kipandes* (identification cards) were issued during the colonial era, is now a bank.

2 Along on the right is the **General Post Office** (GPO), one of the city's busiest places as many people have their post box there. It provides free *poste restante* facilities (for those without permanent addresses); you can also send cables and telexes here. After the GPO is **Koinange Street,** named after an important preindependence politician. Here also is the carved block of the **Galton-Fenzi memorial** to the first man to drive from Nairobi to Mombasa in 1926, thus starting the Kenyan Automobile Association. Farther along Kenyatta Avenue, on the left side, past **3** **African Heritage,** Nairobi's largest curio shop, stands the **ICEA Building** (1982). From its vertigo-inducing glass paneled elevators you have a good overview of the streets, trees, people, shops, traffic, and hustle of central Nairobi.

One block north Wabera Street stands the imposing neoclassi- **4** cal **McMillan Library** (1928), with stone steps flanked by huge lions. It is open for borrowing books, at a low price, weekdays during business hours and on Saturday mornings. **Grindley's Building** (1923), on the Kenyatta Avenue/Kimathi Street junc- **5** tion, is the earliest example of Nairobi brickwork. The **New Stanley Hotel** opposite is one of the oldest hotels in town. One of the New Stanley's most famous guests was Ernest Hemingway, and many a safari began at the notorious Long Bar. The bar has since been renovated, but it's still a popular place to meet in the center of the city for a Pimm's Cup.

Time Out The **Thorn Tree Cafe** in the New Stanley Hotel is a well-known meeting place. Here you can sit for hours, as service is notoriously slow, watching Nairobi walk past. The fare includes decent hamburgers and Kenya's excellent Tusker beer. A huge acacia thorn tree in its central courtyard was Kenya's first post office. Before Kenya had a postal system, travelers to and from the bush pinned messages there to one another. Today the tree is a message board covered with personal notes, vehicle-sharing or -selling deals, and offers for unused air tickets.

Follow **Kimathi Street**—named after Dedan Kimathi, a leader of the "Mau Mau" movement in the 1950s that led to Kenya's independence—southeast from the New Stanley Hotel to the **6** tall circular columns of the **Hilton Hotel,** built in 1964 with American money as a gesture of confidence in the new Kenyan government. Many tourist shops and offices are clustered around its base. Around the corner on **Moi Avenue,** stands the **7** colonnaded, yellow stone **National Archives,** originally the Bank of India building, now a museum/art gallery. *Admission free. Open 8–4:30.*

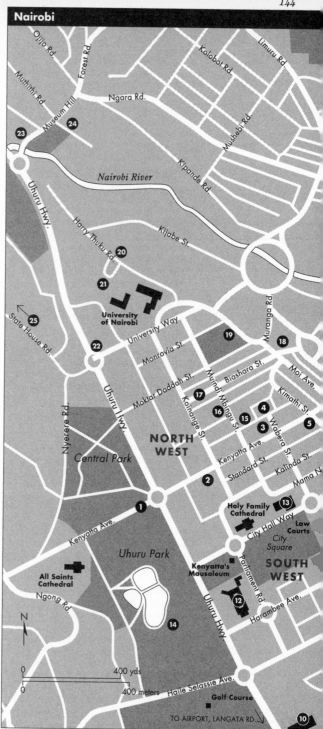

Nairobi

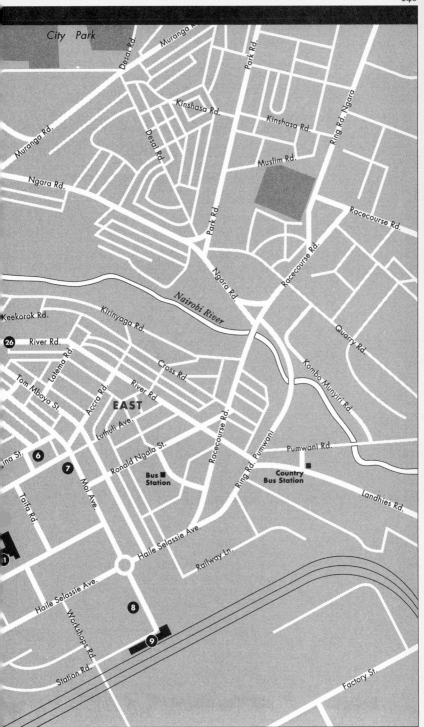

The only other permanent art gallery worth visiting, beyond those at the National Museum, is the **Gallery Watatu** (Standard St.), which holds exhibitions and work by various artists, usually with an African theme. The **Goethe Institute,** the **French Cultural Centre** (Monrovia St.), and the **British Consulate** (ICEA Buildings, Kenyatta Ave.) also hold occasional exhibitions.

From here walk south along Moi Avenue toward the dignified colonial edifice of the **Railway Headquarters** (1929), which conceals an inner courtyard and stands near Nairobi's origin—the **Railway Station.** The station has one of the best restaurants in Nairobi—if you like meat and potatoes and good value. It is rarely, if ever, visited by tour groups, so you are likely to be surrounded by Kenyans. The dining room is very plain but has a view of the railway platform. The prices are exceptionally reasonable. *No reservations.*

A 10-minute signposted walk southwest from the station is the **Railway Museum.** It features artifacts from the famous Lunatic Express line, including the wooden rhino-catcher (as opposed to cow-catcher) on which Teddy Roosevelt sat astride during his 1908 safari. There is also beautiful silverware from the dining car and amusing color posters of the era. *Admission: Kshs. 5. Open Sun.–Fri. 8:30–4:30, Sat. 8:30–3:30.*

Walk back past the colorful fruit and *chai* (tea) stalls fringing the approach to the station, turn north, cross Haile Selassie Avenue, until you reach Harambee Avenue (Swahili for "pull together"). Turn left and, ahead on the right, in **City Square,** stands the 28-story **Kenyatta International Conference Center** built in 1974. Nairobi's tallest building is a symbol of its status as an international center. The building is said to resemble a Masai hut, a juncture between traditional Africa and the modern world. The view of Nairobi and its surrounds from the building's occasionally revolving rooftop restaurant is unbeatable, particularly on a clear day when you can see both Mt. Kenya and Mt. Kilimanjaro. A large statue of Jomo Kenyatta sits in stately stone at the center of the wide, flagstone courtyard, fronted by the Conference Center and the law courts. During conferences when the flags are flying, the fountains are playing, and the tribal dancers are performing, this is one of Nairobi's most impressive views.

Close by are the **Parliament buildings** (open Tues. 9:30–12:30, Wed. and Thurs. 2:30–6:30). Along Parliament Road, past **Kenyatta's Mausoleum** and the Inter-Continental Hotel, is the **Holy Family Cathedral,** hub of Roman Catholic Nairobi. Beyond, on City Hall Way, rises **City Hall,** designed in the early 1950s during the declaration of a State of Emergency, the so-called Mau-Mau uprising, which eventually resulted in Kenyatta's election as Kenya's first president.

Across Uhuru Highway from the Inter-Continental lies **Uhuru Park,** with a small lake where you can rent a rowboat. Stay out of the park after dark as it has frequent muggings.

Northwest Nairobi can best be approached from the **Jamia Mosque** (behind McMillan Library). Its decorative facade, painted white and green with cupolas and minarets, contrasts with its simple and spacious interior. On holy days the outside courtyard fills with Muslims, all facing the holy city of Mecca. Across Muindi Mbingu Street from the mosque is **City Market.**

Designed in 1930 as an aircraft hangar, this huge brick hall, with its balcony viewpoint of fruit, vegetable and flower stalls, and curio and basket shops, is a jumble of color, noise, and action. The market is surrounded by fish and meat stalls, frequented by Nairobi's hostesses and restaurant chefs. The market is an excellent place to buy souvenirs and gifts for friends; you must bargain. Especially good value are the carved Kiisi stones, carved wood utensils, and colorful baskets, some flat enough to pack.

17 **Biashara Street,** near the market, is *the* main street for fabric, tailors, haberdashers, seamstresses, mosquito nets, *kikois*, and *kangas*. The last two items are wonderful sarongs, good for wearing over a bathing suit or throwing over a picnic table as a cloth. Priced at $40 at Banana Republic stores in the United States, on Biashara Street they cost $6, two for $10. Keep your eyes raised as you explore this quarter as there are many quaint and original colonial facades, often engraved with a house title and date.

18 At the far end of Biashara Street is the **Khoja Mosque,** the center of Kenya's Ismailia, the Aga Khan's Muslim followers. Far-
19 ther along Moi Avenue lie **Jeevanjee Gardens,** under the stern gaze of Queen Victoria, a good spot to eat a lunchtime sandwich, entertained by fanatical preachers or agile acrobats.

Farther along Moi Avenue starts the **University of Nairobi,** and
20 along Harry Thuku Road is the landmark **Norfolk Hotel,** founded in 1904 by a Major Ringer.

Time Out The **Norfolk terrace** (Harry Thuku Rd., tel. 2/335442) is a shady place to sit and rest while watching the people pass by and the safari trips come and go. The terrace is in three sections, each with its own habitués: The area to the left of the lobby, as you enter, is for tea and pastries; the area to the right is for lunch or "sundowners," the Kenyan version of happy hour at 6 PM; past that is a standing bar that is impossible to see on a Friday evening for all the young, trendy Nairobi crowd toasting the weekend.

21 Opposite the Norfolk is Kenya's **National Theatre,** built in 1952. The stone in its foyer and the rosemary bush outside its door are both from Shakespeare's birthplace, Stratford-upon-Avon.

The junction of University Way and Uhuru Highway is known
22 as **God's Corner,** owing to the profusion of religious buildings on this roundabout. From here travel north to the Museum Hill
23 roundabout, pass the **International Casino,** and take the next
24 junction right to the Kenya **National Museum,** Nairobi's major sightseeing attraction, with extensive collections of ornithology, paleontology, and ethnography. The museum, headquarters of the National Museums of Kenya (largely developed by the Leakey family), features excellent exhibits of paintings by Joy Adamson, and one of the best displays on human evolution anywhere. The main building has a columned facade, and within a courtyard you can see a life-size cast of the famous big tusker, Ahmed. Modern buildings in back house the Louis Leakey Memorial Center and a lecture hall and auditorium. Many international experts give public lectures here, and there are often film screenings. Check the schedule posted for evening events. *Museum Hill Rd., tel. 2/742161. Admission: Kshs. 10 residents, Kshs. 30 nonresidents. Open daily 9:30–6. Guides available on request.*

Back at God's Corner head down State House Road until you
25 meet Arboretum Road, which leads to the **Nairobi Arboretum.**
Although somewhat shabby and overgrown, it is a lovely spot
for a stroll among the 300 labeled species of trees. *Admission
free. Open daily during daylight hours.*

26 **River Road** of **East Nairobi** is made up of an extraordinary collection of colonial, Arab, Asian, and African influences, all run-
down and run into each other. The atmosphere is vibrant with
local music pouring out of overflowing day and night bars.
Drivers, handcarts, and pedestrians all jostle with one another
for sidewalk and road space. River Road is home to one of the
city's best Indian restaurants, the Supreme Hotel, which also
features meals for takeout and a spectacular variety of desserts.

What to See and Do with Children

Drive out to the **Animal Orphanage,** on Langata Road (at the
entrance to Nairobi N.P.) and see the big cats in their cages
and the baby elephants. Stop at the **Carnivore Restaurant,** also
on Langata Road, on the way back for a slice of crocodile, impala, or specialty of the day. It has a good playground. Visit the
Railway Museum, off Station Road, and sit at the controls of retired steam locomotives. The **National Museum,** on Museum
Hill, has some exhibits of interest to children, but more time
can be spent on the living exhibits in the adjacent **Aquarium**
and **Snake Park,** with a tortoise pit and crocodile pool (there's a
sign saying that if you drop litter in, you will have to retrieve it
yourself!). Children will also enjoy the **AFEW Langata Giraffe
Center** (Go Go Falls La., Langata, tel. 2/891658/078), where
they can feed Africa's tallest mammals from an elevated platform (*see* Langata in Excursions, *below*). The terrace at the
Norfolk Hotel serves a children's menu.

Off the Beaten Track

The **Uhuru National Monument** is a 33-meter-tall, three-sided
obelisk flanked by sculptures that reflect the Nyayo philosophy
of *harambee* and patriotism through love, peace, and unity. Unfortunately, the spire was putting aircraft landing at Wilson
Airport at serious risk and had to be shortened. The monument
was constructed to commemorate the 25th anniversary of
Uhuru (Independence) in 1988. A major reason for this excursion will be a drink at the Carnivore Restaurant across the way.
The house drink, *dawa* (Swahili for "medicine"), a mixture of
honey, lime juice, and vodka, is strongly recommended.
Langata Rd., past Wilson Airport.

The **Community Development Education Tour** is a 4- to 5-hour
tour organized by the Undugu Society, which rehabilitates underprivileged youths. It is renowned for its excellent boys'
band, which can be hired out for social occasions. The tour visits the Undugu head offices and workshops, a screen-printing
workshop, a community school, wood-carvers, and the Undugu
shop at Westlands. *Tours leave Wed. from the city center; tel.
2/540187 and 552211; Kshs. 120 per person.*

Shopping

Department stores are useful for those who are traveling independently; there is a big Uchumi store downtown near the New Stanley Hotel and another in Westlands. Opening hours of major shops is 8 to 6, sometimes with a break for lunch. Bargaining is acceptable in all places where prices are not marked, and some where they are. Prices can often be negotiated down to less than half the original price.

Recommended buys include **woven baskets** (*kiondo/vyondo*), which are widely available and come in many different varieties. Most are made from sisal, using natural or artificial dyes, but they are also made from bright plastic, wool mixes and, more expensively, from a cord made from baobab tree bark.

Carved wood salad utensils are ideal gifts. They are both inexpensive and practically flat, so they pack easily. They usually feature giraffe or rhino on the handles. Carvings, along with the little *kisi* (soapstone), can be found at the City Market.

Shops

A new craft center featuring works of local artists is called *Utamaduni*, which means legacy. It is an easy stop en route to the Giraffe Manor or the Blixen Museum and has a small restaurant (East Bogani Rd., Langata, tel. 891 798).

Woven Baskets **City market,** Muindi Mbingu Street, and its environs are basket havens. You can also purchase from any of the many street stands around the city, but the best place is undoubtedly **Kariakor Market** (Ring Rd., Ngara).

Batik and Paintings Although widely sold on the street, quality batik and painting can be found at the **African Heritage/Pan African Gallery** (Kenyatta Ave.), **Gallery Watatu** (Standard St.), and **Roland Ward** (Standard St.). At these three shops you will find quality ethnic jewelry and genuine tribal crafts, including spears, masks, *makonde* (intricate ebony) carvings, and domestic ware.

Carvings Wood and soapstone carvings make excellent gifts, and they come in a wide range of quality, from street renditions to sophisticated works of art. **African Heritage** (Kenyatta Ave.), **Kumbu Kumbu** (at the Hilton), and the **African Cultural Gallery** (Mama Ngina St.) are recommended for high-quality merchandise at top prices. The **City Market** has a good selection of lower-priced work.

Kitenge, Kangas, and Kikoys These cloth squares are found on Biashara Street, where **Lucky Wear** has an excellent selection. **Maridadi Fabrics** started in 1966 as an income-generating community project for underprivileged women. A large workshop produces the wide range of prints available in the store. *Landies Rd., tel. 2/554288. Open weekdays 8–5, Sat. 8–12:30.*

Semiprecious Stones Two reliable jewelry shops are **Treasures and Crafts** (Kaunda St.) and **Al-Safa Jewellers** (New Stanley Hotel). **Rock Hound** (Westlands) has some carved ornaments, ashtrays, and solitaire boards in local marble and rock.

Woven Cottons **Spinners Webb** (Kijabe St., near Norfolk Hotel) is a consignment handmade-craft shop stocking woven cotton materials; hand-knitted sweaters from hand-spun and natural-dyed local

Nairobi Shopping

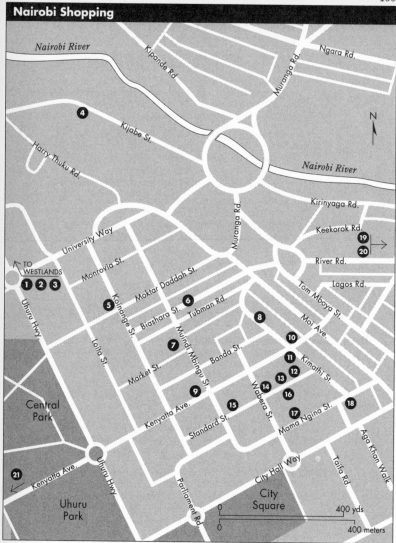

African Cultural Gallery, **17**

African Heritage/Pan African Gallery, **9**

Al-Safa Jewellers, **11**

Celebrity, **5**

City Market, **7**

Colpro, **8**

Gallery Watatu, **16**

Jisaidsie Cottage Industries Craft Shop, **15**

Kariakor Market, **19**

Kumbu Kumbu, **18**

Laid Bare, **3**

Lavington Church, **2**

Lucky Wear, **6**

Maridadi Fabrics, **20**

Rock Hound, **1**

Roland Ward, **14**

Spinners Webb, **4**

Treasures and Crafts, **12**

Uchumi, **10**

Utamaduni, **21**

Zawadi, **13**

wools; multicolored sisal hats; place mats; and other original and well-finished crafts. **Lavington Church** (Lavington Green) stocks similar merchandise, as does **Jisaidsie Cottage Industries Craft Shop** (Phoenix House, Standard St.), which also coordinates sales for specific workshop projects.

Safari Clothes Generally speaking, clothes in Nairobi are overpriced, and savvy shoppers buy khakis and safari shirts from L. L. Bean or Banana Republic before their trip. Some of the lodges (Keekorok, Mount Kenya Safari Club) and permanent tented camps (Kichwa Tembo) offer good quality T-shirts, cotton sweaters, and hats.

Boutiques selling safari outfits and souvenir T-shirts abound. **Colpro** (Kimathi St.) is a good-quality safari-style outfitter while **Celebrity** (Koinange La.), **Zawadi** (Standard St.), and **Laid Bare** (Apic Centre, Westlands) cater to the designer-clothes market.

Sports and Fitness

Participant Sports

Fitness Centers Before you exercise remember that Nairobi is 5,500 feet high, an altitude at which it is more difficult to exercise than at sea level. The sun is bright and the weather is pleasant year-round.

Hilton International Nairobi (Mama Ngina St. and Moi Ave., tel. 2/334000), located near Uhuru Park, has a large outdoor pool, a squash court, and a gym with modern fitness equipment, free weights, sauna, steam bath, and massage.

Inter-Continental Nairobi (City Hall Way, Box 30353, tel. 2/335550) has tennis courts, an outdoor heated pool with a sun deck, and golf nearby.

Nairobi Safari Club (Koinange St. and University Way, Box 43564, tel. 2/330621) also has a large outdoor pool with a terrace, a small gym, and steam and sauna rooms.

Golf Nairobi has many immaculate courses, including **Karen Country Club** (Karen Rd., tel. 2/882801), **Limuru Country Club** (Limuru, tel. Karuri 40033), **Muthaiga Golf Club** (Muthaiga Rd., tel. 2/27333), **Railway Golf Club** (Ngong Rd., tel. 2/22116), **Royal Nairobi Golf Club** (Ngong Rd., tel. 2/27333), **Sigona Golf Club** (Kikuyu, tel. 2/32152), and the **Windsor Golf & Country Club** (tel. 2/726 702).

Horseback Riding Safaris from the **Arifa Riding School** can be arranged through **Bookings Ltd.** (Standard St., Nairobi, tel. 2/25255, 21845 and 20365). Also at Windsor (*see above*).

Jogging There is a university track north of **Central Park** and in **Uhuru Park**, and, if you have transport, **City Park**. However, do not jog after dark or wear flashy jewelry and keep in mind the city's altitude of 5,500 feet.

Mountaineering and Cave Exploration Both these activities have a large resident following. Contact **Mountain Club of Kenya** (Box 45741, Nairobi, tel. 2/501747) or **Cave Exploration Group of East Africa** (Box 45741, Nairobi, tel. 2/501747). Both clubs meet every Tuesday at 7:30 PM at the Mountain Club, Wilson Airport.

Tennis and Squash Courts are available at main clubs and some hotels, including **Goan Gymkana** (Ngong Rd., tel. 2/74369), **Impala Club** (Ngong Rd., tel. 2/568573), **Karen Club** (Karen Rd., tel. 2/88280), **Limuru Club** (Limuru, tel. Karuri 40033), **Mount Kenya Safari Club** (University Way, tel. 2/330621), **Nairobi Club** (Ngong Rd., tel. 2/23603), **Parklands Sports Club** (Ojijo Rd., tel. 2/742829), **Boulevard Hotel** (Harry Thuku Rd., tel. 2/27567), **Utalii Hotel** (Thika Rd., tel. 2/802540), and **Jacaranda Hotel** (Westlands, tel. 2/742272).

Water Sports Sailing takes place on and in Nairobi Dam, off Langata Road. Contact **Nairobi Sailing Club** (Langata Rd., tel. 2/501250).

Spectator Sports

Auto Racing The three-day **Safari Rally** is an annual Easter event. The 4,117-kilometer (2,552-mi) circuit starts outside the Kenyatta International Conference Center in City Square. Nairobi comes down with severe Safari fever—a sudden rash of brightly resprayed look-alike rally cars complete with sawn-off exhausts zooming around at terrifying speeds.

Horse Racing Regular Sunday (except the second Sunday of each month) meetings are held in the perfect setting of **Ngong Racecourse,** on Ngong Road. They are well worth a visit if only to watch the different echelons of Nairobi's society. The season lasts from January to June, with highlights in January, **Kenya Guineas** and **Fillies' Guineas;** April, **Kenya Derby** and **Building Security Stakes;** May, **Kenya Oaks;** and in June, with the **Champagne Stakes** and the **Kenya St. Leger.**

Polo This fast-paced sport is played year-round (unless the ground is too hard or too soft), every Saturday at 3 PM and Sunday at 10 AM at **Jamhuri Park.**

Soccer Nairobi's most popular sport draws huge crowds that root for the national team, **Harambee Stars,** who play international and national matches at the **Nyayo** and **City Stadiums.**

Dining

By Kathy Eldon

A freelance journalist, Kathy Eldon is the author of seven books on East Africa, including Tastes of Kenya *and* Specialties of the House. *Her* Guide to Eating Out in Kenya *covers over 385 restaurants nationwide and has earned her the name Iron Stomach.*

Kenya's multitude of cultures and superb natural ingredients make its cuisine generally interesting and full of flavor. Don't expect one continuous gourmet delight on the tourist beat, but do expect well-prepared, tasty fare. Kenya's lodges are famous for their massive buffet lunches and candle-lit, four-course dinners. Traditional safari clients, too, will enjoy their meals, served in a mess tent set up under acacia trees. Safari cooks, or *mpishis,* spurn the marvels of modern civilization and bake light rolls and cakes in a tin box set on charcoal. Hearty English breakfasts with all the trimmings are de rigueur, offering a rare treat for those normally accustomed to cornflakes and who find the sight of buffalo grazing on the plains enhances hot plates of sausage, egg, and grilled tomato. Pots of steaming tea accompany the traditional early morning call in Kenya, and on safari comforting brandies or hot drinks are usually served before bedtime.

Nairobi is a modern city that offers sophisticated dining, if that's what you want, in elegant restaurants where the menus are in French. The Hilton and Inter-Continental hotel restaurants are fair, though the famous old Norfolk Hotel has a fine restaurant featuring superb nouvelle cuisine.

Indian food is outstanding in Kenya, often better than that found in India, owing to the high quality of the ingredients in Kenya. There is a staggering variety of other ethnic restaurants, from Yugoslav and Korean to Japanese and Thai. Visitors can also sample street food, such as *mkati mayai*, a square pancake filled with ground beef and spices and cooked over a charcoal fire, or spicy shish kebab, chunks of (sometimes) tender meat marinated in yogurt and spices before being grilled. There are few experiences that will linger longer in your mind than a wander through the back streets of the coastal towns at dusk, when the streets come alive with black-veiled women, and glorious smells waft through the sticky air.

Swahili food, available at the coast, is a delectable blend of African and Arab cooking that was brought to the region by Arabs. Dishes are slightly sweet and often flavored with coconut milk, cardamom, cinnamon, and exotic *masalas* (thick, spicy sauces). Fish and rice are food staples in the towns by the Indian Ocean.

Farther inland, locals exist on a diet of *ugali*, a stiff cornmeal porridge often served with *sukuma wiki*, a delicious concoction of kale or other greens flavored with onions, tomatoes, and anything else the cook has handy. Meat is too expensive for most Kenyans but seems very cheap to foreigners, who find tender lamb chops, beef fillets, and succulent pork chops on restaurant menus. Game is not found on most restaurant menus, though wildebeest, impala, and, occasionally, loin of giraffe are featured at the Carnivore Restaurant. Hunting has been banned since 1978 in Kenya, and game for consumption is carefully monitored. Freshwater fish is recommended, especially tilapia and Nile perch, huge fish hauled in from Lake Victoria.

A ban on imported foods has meant the development of such local delicacies as smoked trout and smoked sailfish; interesting cheeses, including excellent Brie and caraway; as well as wonderful homemade preserves, chutneys, and other condiments for fresh-baked bread. Local wines still have to make it into the big time, although there are some fairly decent labels produced from grapes grown near the shores of Lake Naivasha. Due to high taxes and import duties, imported wines and spirits are very expensive. The best drink in Kenya is locally produced beer: Tusker, Whitecap, or "high octane" Premium, which Kenyans prefer warm or at room temperature. Ask for it *baridi*, and it should arrive ice cold.

Tap water is safe to drink in Nairobi and Mombasa; lodges provide filtered or purified water. Avoid fresh salads and mayonnaise in questionable establishments, but you can eat without anxiety in hotels and decent restaurants, for the standard of hygiene is usually quite high in Kenya. With the exception of the Mount Kenya Safari Club, the Nairobi Safari Club, and the Windsor Golf & Country Club—which still insist on jackets and ties—dress is fairly casual, although shorts are frowned on in Nairobi's elegant establishments. Tips are often included in the bill, so ask the waiter before adding 10% to 12%. Credit cards are accepted in most establishments. Lunch hours are generally from 12:30 to 2:30, dinner from 7 to 10:30. Unless noted, dress is casual and reservations are not necessary.

Highly recommended restaurants are indicated by a star ★.

Category	Cost*
Expensive	over Kshs. 406
Moderate	Kshs. 162–Kshs. 406
Inexpensive	under Kshs. 162

per person, excluding drinks and service

Expensive **Alan Bobbe's Bistro.** During the filming of *Out of Africa*, Robert Redford was a regular at Alan Bobbe's tiny, mirror-lined bistro. Alan can be difficult if you arrive casually dressed, but he is an old charmer if you show the proper respect for his cuisine. Seafood is a specialty, with crab claws and grilled lobster particularly popular. Try the garish chilled beetroot soup for a visual and taste treat, and finish with the wickedly delicious liqueur-laced chocolate mousse. *Caltex House, Koinange St., tel. 2/21152 or 2/26027. Reservations recommended. Dress: neat but casual. AE, DC, V.*

Foresta Magnetica. A glitzy, polished restaurant and piano bar, frequented by Nairobi's version of beautiful people, the Foresta is also the only cafeteria in town. The cafeteria operates at lunch only, serving an impressive array of dishes from inexpensive chicken and meat pies to lavish displays of Italian salads and pastas. In the evening the atmosphere is cool and sophisticated, with a good pianist and average food. *Corner House, Mama Ngina St., tel. 2/23662. Reservations recommended for dinner. Dress: casual. AE, DC.*

★ **Horseman.** The suburb of Karen is the site of this cozy Tudor-style restaurant, with a blazing fire in the bar, a handwritten (nearly illegible) menu, and a larger-than-life Austrian owner, Rolf Schmid. Outside, there is an open-air pizza garden and snack area, with a veranda for barbecue, and a salad bar. *Corner of Ngong Rd. and Langata Rd. Roundabout, tel. 2/882782 or 2/882033. Reservations recommended on weekends. AE, DC.*

★ **Ibis Grill.** This Norfolk Hotel restaurant features excellent nouvelle cuisine created by Eamon Mullan, one of the country's finest chefs. His recipes have been published in *The Tastes of Kenya* and reflect his talent for producing chic cuisine with a Kenyan twist. Specialties change daily, but there is always an excellent selection of hors d'oeuvres, a roast trolley (cart with variety of roast meats), and catch of the day. The atmosphere is cool and sophisticated, with a lovely view of the Norfolk's gardens. *Harry Thuku Rd., tel. 2/335422. Reservations required. Jacket required. AE, DC, MC, V.*

Red Bull. One of Nairobi's most popular restaurants, the Red Bull is a lively, atmospheric little place packed with business and professional people, as well as a healthy mix of tourists and travelers. The food is hearty and filling, based on the Germanic tastes of the original owner. Try the impala; Zanzibar fish, gently flavored with coconut; and any of the delicious desserts. *Silopark House, Mama Ngina St., tel. 2/335717 or 2/28045. Reservations required. AE, DC, MC, V.*

★ **Tamarind.** Known as one of the best seafood restaurants in town, this is great fun for a romantic dinner for two or an expense account lunch. The lights are kept low. Try *prawns piri piri* (spicy, buttery prawns grilled over charcoal), deep-fried crab claws, ginger crab, or any lobster dish. Kenyan oysters are delicious: tiny but very flavorful and served either raw or as classic oysters Rockefeller. The food is excellent, the service attentive, and the experience memorable. *National Bank of Kenya Bldg., Harambee Ave., tel. 2/338959. Reservations required. AE, DC, V.*

Moderate

★ **Carnivore.** A meat lover's paradise, this restaurant is a 20-minute drive out of Nairobi toward the suburb of Karen. Hundreds of pounds of meat, including giraffe, wildebeest, and impala, are grilled daily over a vast charcoal fire, creating a tantalizing aroma that would tempt any vegetarian. There is even a vegetarian menu, plus a big salad bar. Waiters carry long skewers of meat through the restaurant and will carve what you wish on to the hot steel platters that serve as plates. The experience is unforgettable. Several times a week there's a live band or disco dancing. *Langata Rd., tel. 2/501775. Reservations recommended. AE, DC, V.*

★ **China Plate.** Szechuan cooking in downtown Nairobi? Why not? The specialty here is spicy Hunan and Szechuan delicacies prepared with the finest ingredients in Kenya. The atmosphere is bustling in this large, well-decorated restaurant, which features intricately carved Chinese furniture and real Chinese plates and bowls. Try the chicken wings flavored with aniseed and other exotic spices; sweet corn soup; ginger crab (messy but delicious); and braised prawns, Szechuan style, tossed with chopped spring onions, garlic, and chilies. *Accra/Taveta Rd., tel. 2/25225. Reservations recommended. AE, DC.*

La Galleria and the Toona Tree. These two restaurants are in the International Casino. They offer contrasting experiences in good eating. La Galleria is very chic, serving hearty Italian fare in a large, airy room filled with a changing collection of paintings. The seafood is particularly good, as are the pastas. Upstairs, the gaming tables provide a lure for those who don't mind losing money. The Toona Tree is a delightful open-air restaurant that offers a change of scenery for a leisurely, less expensive meal, snack, or drink. The restaurant encloses a vast toona tree, which gives the facility a remarkably rustic feeling. *International Casion, tel. 2/742600. Reservations recommended for La Galleria. AE, DC.*

★ **Minar.** Excellent Mughlai food is the attraction of this slightly faded, but very popular, restaurant. Try the tender chicken kebabs, which are marinated in yogurt and spices before being baked in a traditional tandoor oven; the subtly flavored curries; puffy *nan* (Indian bread); and delicious *kulfi*, an Indian ice cream spiced with saffron. A second Minar is located in the Sarit Centre, in Westlands, a 10-minute drive from town. *Banda St., tel. 2/29999, and Sarit Centre, tel. 2/748340. Reservations advised for both. AE, DC, V.*

Rasoi. Excellent Indian food is served in this barn-like, candlelit room opposite Nairobi's only professional theater. The atmosphere is intimate, thanks to dim lighting and lots of candles. Ask for help on the menu, but include chicken kebabs and a *kerai* dish, prepared and served in a copper bowl. *Parliament Rd., tel. 2/25082 and 26049. AE, DC, MC, V.*

Trattoria. Although chaotic and noisy, this is one of the town's most popular people-watching venues, ideal for a quick cappuccino, pizza, pasta, or homemade ice cream, as well as for a major

Dining

African Heritage Cafe, **14**

Alan Bobbe's Bistro, **13**

Carnivore, **29**

China Plate, **21**

Durga Restaurant, **6**

Foresta Magnetica, **22**

Horseman, **30**

Ibis Grill, **5**

Jax, **20**

La Galleria and the Toona Tree, **3**

Minar, **15**

Rasoi, **28**

Red Bull, **24**

Tamarind, **27**

Trattoria, **19**

Twigs, **26**

Lodging

Fairview, **12**

Hilton International, **25**

Hotel Boulevard, **4**

Hotel Inter-Continental, **23**

Hurlingham Hotel, **10**

Iqbal Hotel, **17**

Jacaranda Hotel, **1**

Nairobi Safari Club, **7**

Nairobi Serena Hotel, **8**

Nairobi Youth Hostel, **9**

New Stanley Hotel, **16**

Norfolk Hotel, **5**

Panafric Hotel, **11**

Safari Park Hotel, **31**

Six Eighty Hotel, **18**

Utalii Hotel, **2**

Windsor Golf & Country Club, **32**

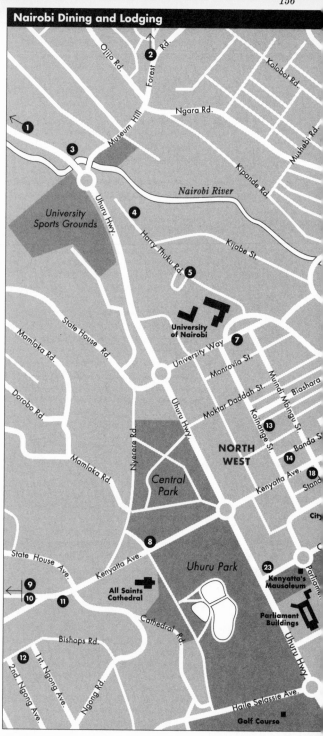

Nairobi Dining and Lodging

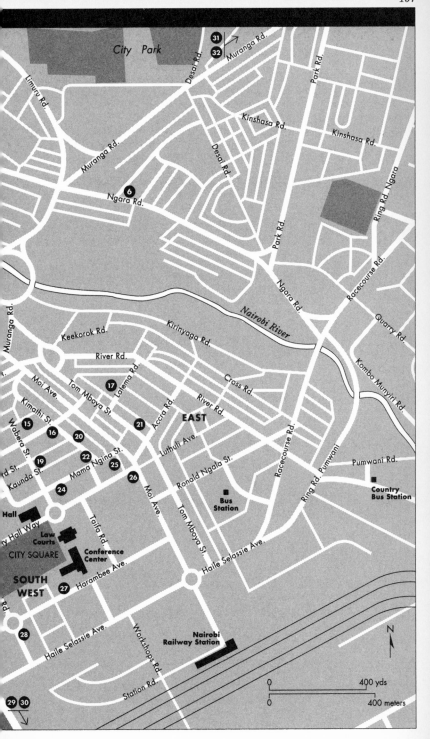

Italian meal. Service is indifferent at best, but the lively atmosphere makes up for any shortcomings. There are four sought-after tables outside for a really good view. *Wabera St., tel. 2/340855. Reservations recommended. No credit cards.*

Twigs. This is a cozy place with seafood and Italian and French dishes, located above an Italian ice-cream parlor of the same name. The lobster and banana flambé are highly recommended, as is the excellent service. *Tumaini House, Nkrumah Rd., tel. 2/335864, 2/336308, or 2/335243.*

Inexpensive   **African Heritage Cafe.** Nearly every tourist drops into the café for a plate of almost genuine African food, including *sukuma wiki*, fried plantains (a form of banana), *matoke* (steamed bananas), fish curries, and meat stews. There is an outside garden with variable service and overpriced food, but the pleasant atmosphere and chance to meet the movers and shakers in Nairobi's arty crowd make it all worthwhile. *Banda St., tel. 2/22010. No credit cards.*

Durga Restaurant. Cheap and cheerful, the Durga attracts vegetarians and others who enjoy Indian savories and sweets, including gently spiced *samosas* (triangular pastry stuffed with vegetables and spices, then deep fried), crispy fried vegetables dipped in batter *(bhajias)*, and a lavish array of colorful Indian desserts. *Chai masala* (sweet spiced tea) is a specialty of the house, which is nothing more than a plain room filled with well-used tables and unmatched chairs set on a busy market street. *Ngara Rd., tel. 2/742781. No credit cards.*

Jax. For well-prepared, inexpensive, and interesting food in the center of town, try Jax, a self-service restaurant that is frequented by a professional crowd for quick lunches, coffees, or substantial teas. The atmosphere is bustling, the interior decor simple, but the food, which includes Indian dishes from Goa, really is delicious. *Old Mutual Bldg., Kimathi St., tel. 2/23427. AE, DC.*

Lodging

The most expensive hotels are found nearest the city center. These cater to tourists who wish to shop and executives who need to be downtown. Hotels outside the city center tend to have larger gardens, tennis courts, and better parking facilities, more suited to longer stays or family groups.

Highly recommended lodgings are indicated by a star ★.

Category	Cost*
Very Expensive	over $150 (Kshs. 3,750)
Expensive	$100–$150 (Kshs. 2,500–3,750)
Moderate	$50–$100 (Kshs. 1,250–2,500)
Inexpensive	under $50 (Kshs. 1,250)

*All prices are for a standard double room; excluding hotel tax.

Very Expensive   **Hilton International.** The international character of this property has been mellowed slightly by local artist Joni Waites's large wildlife mural in the foyer. The Hilton tower is a Nairobi landmark and dominates the entire block of shops and agencies on which it is built. Opened in the early '60s, the hotel was refurbished in 1982. *Watali St., off Mama Ngina St., Box 30624, tel. 2/334000, 800/HILTONS. 328 rooms. Facilities: outdoor pool, shopping arcade, communications center, meeting rooms, health club. AE, DC, MC, V.*

Inter-Continental Nairobi. Nairobi's largest hotel boasts a fine rooftop restaurant, Le Château, which is popular for its dinner/dance evenings and as a venue for fashion shows. Also popular, particularly with parents of young children, is the heated pool. *City Hall Way/Uhuru Hwy., Box 30353, tel. 2/335550 or 800/332–4246. 440 rooms. Facilities: heated pool with terrace bar, shopping arcade, casino. AE, DC, MC, V.*

★ **Nairobi Safari Club.** This prestigious place functions as a hotel but requires membership, so you cannot walk in off the street to use the bar or restaurants. Completed in 1984, it was originally known as the Mount Kenya Safari Club. The S-shaped building, known as Lilian Towers, is 11-stories tall and is clad in white on a base of local brown marble. The interior is designed with attractive fountains and foliage. Suites in Lilian Towers feature a sitting room with desk and a small balcony. Views from the suites are excellent; however, there are no windows in the main restaurant on the first floor. The restaurant on the top floor, Kirinyiga, is first class. Children under age 12 are not welcome. *Koinange St. and University Way, Box 43564, tel. 2/330621, or 800/332–4246. 146 suites. Facilities: small outdoor pool, sauna, health center, hairdressers/barbers, meeting rooms. AE, DC, MC, V.*

★ **Norfolk Hotel.** Mementos of this landmark's past, including the rickshaw that has become the Norfolk insignia, are parked in the interior courtyard of the "aviary" gardens. The Norfolk first opened its doors to the public on Christmas Day, 1904, and has had a reputation as one of Nairobi's foremost meeting places ever since. It was extensively renovated in 1991. *Harry Thuku Rd., Box 40064, tel. 2/335422. 120 rooms, including 20 luxury cottages. Facilities: shops, outside pool, 2 restaurants, bars, ballroom, meeting rooms, aviary. AE, DC, MC, V.*

Safari Park Hotel. A virtual village of its own, the new Safari Park complex, completed in 1990, is north of Nairobi on Thika Road. *Box 45038, Nairobi, tel. 2/802 561; fax 802 477. Facilities: 125 rooms with bath, 3 restaurants, 2 bars, pool, conference rooms, tennis and squash courts. AE, MC, V.*

Windsor Golf & Country Club. This Victorian-style complex 15 minutes north of downtown Nairobi on Garden Estate Road, was completed in 1991. There are 15 cottages, 100 double rooms and suites. *Windsor Hotels, tel. 2/726702, 2/726505; fax 2/726328. US: book with Utell Int'nl through your travel agent. Facilities: 2 restaurants, health club, conference room, 2 tennis courts, 2 squash courts, 18-hole golf course, horseback riding. AE, MC, V.*

Expensive **Nairobi Serena Hotel.** An extra-large parking lot and minibus service into town make this West Nairobi hotel popular with business travelers and tourists. The atmosphere of the terrace café, bordered with ornamental pools and tall reeds, is resonant with the croaking chorus of resident bullfrogs. *Nyene Rd./Kenyatta Ave., Box 46302, tel. 2/725111. 192 air-cond. rooms with baths. Facilities: shop, pool, health club, meeting rooms. AE, DC, MC, V.*

★ **New Stanley Hotel.** This property has the distinction of being Nairobi's oldest, although it has not always stood on its present site. The Thorn Tree Cafe has a long-standing reputation as a meeting place, with a fine, but often overlooked, mural by Michael Adams on the wall of its inside section. (Adams now lives in Seychelles; *see* Chapter 10.) *Kenyatta Ave./Kimathi St., Box 30680, tel. 2/333233. 220 rooms and 10 suites. Facilities: meeting rooms, restaurant, shops. AE, DC, MC, V.*

Panafric Hotel. This functional West Nairobi hotel with a large pool and pool-side service from its Flamingo Garden café is within easy reach of the city center. The Simba Grill and Bar has a resident band (Monday–Saturday). *Kenyatta Ave., Box 30486, tel. 2/720822. 162 rooms, 6 suites and 42 apartments. Facilities: pool, shop, hairdressing salon, meeting rooms. AE, DC, V.*

Moderate **Jacaranda Hotel.** Though it is 5 kilometers (3.1 mi) out of the city center, this family hotel has excellent access to the expanding amenities in the Westlands Mall, including the Sarit Centre and the Apic Centre. The former Agip Motel underwent modernization in 1987 and now has a clean and efficient image. *Chiromo Rd., Westlands, Box 14287, tel. 2/742272. 130 rooms. Facilities: pool with café, tennis, volleyball, playground, pizza garden. AE, DC, V.*

Six Eighty Hotel. Peace Corps volunteers, who get special rates at this economical hotel, can often be found at the ground-floor terrace bar. The bar and Japanese restaurant draw residents for lunch. *Muindi Mbingu St. and Kenyatta Ave., Box 43436, tel. 2/332680. 388 double rooms. Facilities: Japanese restaurant, shopping arcade, pub. AE, DC, MC, V.*

Inexpensive **Fairview.** Colonial styling and an attractively landscaped garden add to this hotel's relaxed and casual atmosphere. Many of its clientele are up-country residents, often with their families. *Bishops Rd., Box 40842, West Nairobi, tel. 2/723211. 110 rooms, 16 family suites. Facilities: playground, garden. No credit cards.*

★ **Hotel Boulevard.** Just down the road from the illustrious Norfolk, this hotel offers excellent value for its location—close to the city center and virtually on top of the Nairobi Museum. Built in 1971, it has been recently refurbished. *Harry Thuku Rd., Box 42831, tel. 2/27567/8/9 and 337221. 70 rooms. Facilities: tennis court, pool, several shops. AE, DC, V.*

Hurlingham Hotel. With its tin roof and small garden café decorated with bright assorted kanga tablecloths, this hotel has a colonial charm. It is a small family hotel popular with local residents. *Argwings Kodhek Rd., West Nairobi, Box 43158, tel. 2/721920 and 723001. 14 rooms. No credit cards.*

Utalii Hotel. This square, redbrick building, 7 kilometers (4.3 mi) north of town on the Thika Road, is the government's hotel training school. The service at this facility is unbeatable. It is particularly popular with airline crews, who can be seen around the pool. (*Utalii* is Swahili for tourism.) *Thika Rd., Box 31067, tel. 2/802540. 50 rooms. Facilities: restaurant, gardens, pool, tennis courts. AE, DC, V.*

Very Inexpensive **Iqbal Hotel.** For many years the top choice of trans-Africa travelers on a budget, the Iqbal is reasonably secure and clean. It provides hot water and a choice of single, dormitory, or double-room accommodation for well under Kshs. 100. The restaurant serves good, cheap, basic fare. *Latema Rd., Box 11256, tel. 2/20914. No credit cards.*

Nairobi Youth Hostel. Though it is clean, safe, and cheap (Kshs.

25 per night), this hostel is about 2 kilometers (1.2 mi) from the General Post Office. There are lockers available for which you must supply a lock. You must be a member of the Youth Hostels Association to stay here. *Ralph Bunche Rd., Box 48661, tel. 2/ 723012. No credit cards.*

The Arts and Nightlife

For information on events, theater, and cinema, see the local papers and *What's On,* a free monthly publication available at hotels and some travel agencies. *Tourist's Kenya,* a free fortnightly publication, also has some information. Also check the events schedule at the **Nairobi National Museum.** Internationally renowned scientists frequently lecture at the Louis Leakey Memorial Auditorium, and naturalists/filmmakers often introduce their films. Local experts on wildlife conservation and archaeological research also lecture. A well-kept secret: The evening programs at the museum are exceptional, and are often standing room only.

The Arts

Theater There are two main public theaters, the **Kenya National Theatre** (opposite the Norfolk Hotel) and the **Professional Centre** (Parliament Rd.). The latter is the more active, with a small resident company in a small theater (seating 110) producing a large range of drama which changes every three weeks. The National Theatre puts on plays, musicals, and, from time to time, concerts. The **French Cultural Centre** and the **British Council** also organize special films, performances, concerts, and talks.

Film There are 12 cinemas in Nairobi showing American, English, and Indian films. These include two drive-ins—**Fox** and **Belle-Vue**—plus three modern cinemas—**Kenya, Nairobi** and **Twentieth Century**—which show recent releases. (Note: Always stand up for the Kenyan national anthem.)

Concerts Visiting artists perform about once a month at the National Theatre—usually classical, sometimes jazz. The **Nairobi Music Society** presents choral concerts in All Saints' Cathedral, plus a variety of lunchtime recitals every other month, usually at the British Council. The **Nairobi Orchestra** puts on a classical concert three times a year.

Dance The **Bomas of Kenya,** out at Langata, has tribal-dance performances. *Admission: Kshs. 60. Performances are weekdays at 2:30, weekends at 3:30.*

Nightlife

Although there are a few theaters and cinemas, dining, drinking, and dancing are the main evening activities in the city.

Bars and Nightclubs Nairobi has many in all price brackets. In the city center the **New Florida** (Koinange St.), and its sister, the **Florida 2000** (Moi Ave.), both have good sound systems, fancy lights, and a floor show. **Visions** (Kimathi St.) offers a smaller, similar scene, with more mirrors, multiple video screens, and occasionally bubbles. **Hallian's Night Club** (Tom Mboya St.) has a band most nights, lots of local clientele, and a relaxed atmosphere. Other nightclubs, all along similar lines, include the

Hollywood Night Club (Moktar Daddah St.), the Milano Club (Ronald Ngala Rd.), and the Beat House (Kimathi St.).

Slightly out of town, the JK Resort (Mombasa Rd.) provides excellent *nyama choma* (spicy meat) and an open-air dance floor. The best place for a sophisticated evening of Western-style dinner and dance is Le Château at the Inter-Continental Hotel.

Discos   Dancing and drinking take precedence over much else in many of the clubs already mentioned. Bubbles (International Casino, Museum Hill) is a popular spot with teenyboppers. The Carnivore Restaurant (Langata Rd.), just behind Wilson Airport, has a good Saturday-night disco, with a live band on Wednesday, Friday, and Sunday.

Casinos   The International Casino (Museum Hill), the major gambling joint in town, offers roulette, pontoon, blackjack, and one-armed bandits. The Casino de Paradise (Safari Park Hotel, Thika Rd.) was completely remodeled and reopened in 1988, but it is 11 kilometers (6.8 mi) out of town. The RKL Casino at the Inter-Continental is very small.

Singles   Every Friday night Nairobi's young people congregate on the Norfolk Terrace. Bubbles and the Carnivore are also hot spots for singles.

Excursions from Nairobi

Many of the prime sights that can be seen as side trips from Nairobi are national parks and reserves, which are described in Chapter 3. The excursions that follow consist of the other major attractions often visited from Nairobi.

Lake Magadi and Olorgesailie Prehistoric Site

Of all the Rift Valley lakes only Lake Turkana (Lake Rudolf) is lower than Lake Magadi, whose altitude of 580 meters (1,903 ft) produces an arid climate radically different from Nairobi's. The arid conditions mean much evaporation, which creates rich supplies of soda. Striking scenery, abundant waterbirds, Masai herdsmen, and the Olorgesailie Prehistoric Site make the 110-kilometer (68-mi) drive from Nairobi to Magadi more than worthwhile. The road is in good condition, so any car can make the trip.

Exit from the city via Langata Road past Wilson Airport and Nairobi National Park. One kilometer after the park entrance, Magadi Road forks to the left. The tarmac ends after 5 kilometers (3 mi), and there is a bumpy section for 11 kilometers (7 mi) to Kiserian Village, where the new road begins and provides smooth traveling. Both Magadi and Olorgesailie are basins of the eastern branch of the Great Rift Valley.

After Kiserian the route climbs over the southern end of the Ngong Hills for fine views of the spacious ranching landscape. Volcanic hills rise out of the plain as the road drops into hot, dry country where the Masai graze their herds. At the village of Olepolos, the track off to the right leads to the Ngong circular tour.

Sixty-five kilometers (40 mi) from Nairobi, the Olorgesailie Prehistoric Site is well marked, 2 kilometers off the road to the left. A small field museum, with exhibits of hand axes and ani-

Nairobi Environs

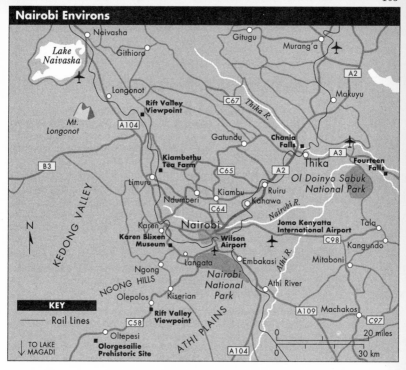

mal bones in situ, gives a clear impression of the Stone Age culture that existed about 700,000 years ago. Discovered in 1919 by geologist J. W. Gregory, the site was excavated by Louis and Mary Leakey in the 1940s (*see* Cradle of Mankind, Chapter 2) and made a national park in 1947. It is now administered by the National Museums of Kenya, which provides tour guides of the site. To check the availability of *bandas* (huts) at Olorgesailie, contact the Nairobi Museum (tel. 2/742161).

Magadi is 45 kilometers (28 mi) past Olorgesailie. Flanked by hills, the road follows the valley of the Olkeju Ngiro River where Masai water their cattle in an impressive gorge close to the road. The terrain drops steadily toward the lake with views of the Nguruman Escarpment framing the waters of the lake, rich in diatoms upon which flamingos feed.

The *trona* (soda) is exploited by the Magadi Soda Company, but the factory and drying pans only intrude into the lake landscape at its midsection, where the company's causeway permits access to the western shore. Even close to the factory, waterbirds are plentiful: African spoonbills, wood and sacred ibis, and pelicans are all common, but the lesser flamingos are the most prolific.

A road south along the east side of the lake goes past company houses, golf course, and airstrip to a scenic rise overlooking the southern end of the lake. There are hot springs and usually large numbers of flamingos here.

It is possible to reach the Nguruman Escarpment and eventually Narok via the causeway; this route is across remote and difficult-to-traverse country, and only four-wheel-drive vehicles can travel here with ease, but it is full of game and a wildly beautiful setting. Most car-rental firms in Nairobi rent four-wheel-drives, but bear in mind that this is a full-day tour for the adventurous and independent traveler.

Ngong Hills and the Karen Blixen Museum

The Ngong Hills stand 25 kilometers (15 mi) southwest of Nairobi, on the very edge of the Great Rift Valley. Rising to 2,460 meters (8,071 ft), they form a scenic backdrop to Nairobi National Park and create a natural divide between small-scale farming developments on the Nairobi side and the arid floor of the Rift Valley. The Ngongs are volcanic in origin.

A walk along the grassy crest of the hills gives views of both the city to the east—and sometimes Mt. Kenya beyond—and the hot dry country, studded with distant volcanic hills, to the west. The summit is accessible to cars along a rough, steep track from Ngong Village, and it is easy walking along the ridge where buffalo are sometimes seen.

Warning: Unfortunately robberies have become common, despite police patrols. Visitors are warned not to take valuables with them and to travel in *large* parties.

The 100-kilometer (62-mi) Ngong circle begins at Ngong Village, easily reached from Nairobi by Ngong Road, past the racecourse, Ngong Forest, and the Karen Shopping Center. The circuit is marked right from the main street and winds across the northern shoulder of the hills, bearing left at the junction, into the dry thornbush and acacia country of the Rift Valley floor. The track skirts the foot of the hills, which climb 1,000 meters (3,280 ft) to the left before gradually rising to meet Magadi Road, at Olepelos, 26 kilometers (16 mi) from Ngong. Here Masai, wearing traditional dress, sell bead ornaments. A left turn at the village leads back to Nairobi via Langata Road, past Nairobi National Park and Wilson Airport, a distance of 40 kilometers (25 mi).

Karen Blixen Museum is the restored former house and estate of Danish author Karen Blixen, aka Isak Dinesen. The farmhouse is well designed, with square, wood-paneled rooms furnished with a few original and period pieces. Readers of *Out of Africa* will recognize the veranda and appreciate the mounted clock above it, with the hands stopped. Mementos of Karen Blixen's life and work are also on exhibit, along with agricultural implements. *Karen Rd., next to Karen College, tel. 2/ 882779. Admission: Kshs. 50. Open daily 9–6.*

Horseback rides are available in the Karen/Ngong area. An experienced guide accompanies a small group on a morning ride to Broughton House, Ololua Forest, and the Ngong Foothills. Refreshments and a visit to Karen Blixen Museum are included. The trip is only for accomplished riders. *Contact Bookings Ltd., tel. 2/25255. Cost: Kshs. 550 inclusive of transport from city center.*

Langata

Set in a pocket of indigenous forest only 18 kilometers (11 mi) from the center of Nairobi, the **AFEW (African Fund for En-**

dangered Wildlife) **Langata Giraffe Center** provides an opportunity to come face to face with Africa's tallest mammal. The
15-acre preserve is dedicated to educating schoolchildren on
the need for wildlife preservation, but adults are also
enchanted by the chance to observe and feed giraffes. More
than 160 species of birds have been identified on the grounds, in
addition to warthog, bushbuck, and dik-dik. The center has a
teahouse and a gift shop stocked entirely with giraffe mementos. *Go Go Falls La., near Hardy Estate Shopping Center,
Langata, tel. 2/891658. Admission: adults Kshs. 50 minimum
donation. Open school days 4–5:30, weekends 10–5:30, school
holidays 9:30–5:30.*

Within sight of the Giraffe Center is the **Giraffe Manor,** a distinguished two-story Scottish mansion featured in the movie
White Mischief. The elegant manor house was built in 1932 for
coffee king David Duncan and was later the home of Jock and
Betty Leslie-Melville, founders of AFEW. It is now available
as a lodging for small groups or couples. Because there are only
three double bedrooms with private baths, reservations must
be made well in advance. Staying here does not come cheap.
Double accommodations, including three meals, wine, and
laundry service is $400 per night (singles are charged less), but
this includes a $300 partially tax-deductible donation to
AFEW. *In the United States, call 301/346–6146.*

The **Langata Bird Sanctuary** is a private preserve where
birdwatchers are accompanied by an ornithologist. Blinds are
positioned near feed trays and water troughs for photographing the birds. There is also an area of dense bush. Take your
binoculars and telephoto lenses. The sanctuary is open by reservation only. *Contact Bookings Ltd., tel. 2/25255. Admission:
Kshs. 350.*

Markets and Kiambethu Tea Farm

Nairobi has many out-of-town markets frequented by locals
which tourists never see. **Wakulima Market** (Wakulima Rd., off
Haile Selassie Ave.) is the city's major wholesale produce market. (*Wakulima* is Swahili for "farmer.") It is worth visiting
early in the morning when the produce arrives from the country.

Nairobi's largest market, **Gikomba Market/Lhandies Mawe**
(Sakwa Rd.), stretches across the Nairobi River by way of a
precarious bridge. Here a sea of people garbed in brightly colored kangas leads into a huge scrap-metal recycling area. The
Gikomba Market is full of hustle and bustle; here you can buy
copper telephone-line bracelets and see old fuel drums being
fashioned into woks. The market is off the beaten track: Walking among the stalls is risky, and the surrounding neighborhood is dangerous for the unescorted.

In the heart of Kenya's tea-growing region 35 kilometers (22
mi) northeast of Nairobi, Mrs. Mitchell lives on **Kiambethu Tea
Farm.** She will brew a fresh pot for you, take you on a short
walk around the indigenous forest to see colobus monkeys, and
provide you with a brief history of tea in Kenya. Mrs. Mitchell
knows whereof she speaks: Her father in 1910 was the first person to grow tea commercially in Kenya. *Tigoni, tel. 0154/40756.
Visits are Kshs. 250. By reservation only.*

5 Mount Kenya and the Aberdares

Introduction

By Terry Burke and Delta Willis

Avid mountaineer Terry Burke is Assistant Chief Security Officer for the United Nation's Environment Program in Nairobi.

"The northern horizon was filled by a gigantic cone of misty purple, capped by a band of cloud. Over this, apparently floating high above a still sleeping world of tropical color, was a graceful spire of rock and ice, hard and clear against the light of blue sky. The sun, not yet risen to my view, had already touched the peak, throwing ridge and corrie into sharp relief, sparkling here and there on a gem of ice."

This was explorer Eric Shipton's view of Mt. Kenya, as written in his 1947 book *Upon that Mountain*. The people of Africa had their own view of the volcanic mountain. Legend has it that Ngai, the creator of all things, lived on the inaccessible summit of Kirinyaga (in Kikuyu, "the mountain of brightness"). The brightness was, of course, the snow; the darker peaks, volcanic rock. Such contrast led to the name K'enya, or cock ostrich, for the peaks resembled these tall, flightless African birds. (Kenya is pronounced with a short *e*, as in "kin" or the name of its first president, Jomo Kenyatta, rather than with a long *e*, as was the preference of the colonials. This is an important distinction, as many Africans consider the former pronunciation of "Keenya" derogatory.)

Before you enter the forest and highlands of Mt. Kenya and the Aberdares, you pass through the cultivated *shambas* (small holdings) of the Kikuyu farmers. From here you ascend to a world of moorlands, lush rain forest, giant bamboo, and dramatic volcanic flows dominated by equatorial glaciers near the twin peaks of Batian and Nelion, the 17,000-foot-plus summits separated by the icy Gates of the Mists.

Mt. Kenya is one of the first things many visitors see of this land, for pilots often point out its alpenglow when making their approach from Rome and London into Nairobi. Like Mt. Kilimanjaro in Tanzania, Mt. Kenya's slopes are easily accessible to most people in good physical condition. You don't have to be a mountain climber to enjoy a trek up one of its 14 marked paths. Above 10,500 feet, Mt. Kenya is a National Park.

Essential Information

Important Addresses and Numbers

Guided Tours **Tropical Ice** (Muthaiga Shopping Center, tel. 2/740811) is headed by Iain Allen, an expert guide in mountain climbing. Allen also arranges camel safaris, mostly in the Tana River region of Tsavo East.

Mountain Club of Kenya, headquartered at Nairobi's Wilson Airport (Box 45741, tel. 2/501747), publishes *A Guide to Mt. Kenya and Mt. Kilimanjaro*, which is available in Nairobi bookstores.

Arriving and Departing

By Plane **Air Kenya** (tel. 2/501421, 501422, or 501423) has daily flights to nearby Nanyuki and Nyeri from Wilson Airport. Round-trip fare is Kshs. 2,600, or about U.S. $110.

By Bus The bus from Nairobi to the base of Mt. Kenya, a distance of 177 kilometers (110 mi), costs about Kshs. 150. (Use the "luxury" buses from Nairobi; matatus are not recommended.) The cost of the last leg, from the mountain base to the trailhead, is exorbitant, nearly Kshs. 1,000.

By Car There are good roads to Mt. Kenya, and good maps of this region are available from the **Mountain Club of Kenya** (*see* Important Addresses and Numbers, above). This is the recommended form of transport because it frees you to alter your itinerary and gives you more time to appreciate the unfolding scenery.

Lodging Unlike in the great savannas, where you drive in search of wildlife, at the forest lodges, salt licks and water holes entice creatures to come to you. It's a great pleasure to sit in the dark and anticipate what might appear in the shadows; when the animals come closer, they are illuminated. Visitors who sit quietly in the dark are able to observe them closely. Ground-level bunkers allow you to photograph them, but be sure to bring along fast film, as flashes are not permitted.

Many insiders recommend for your first view of wildlife the Ark and the Mountain Lodge. Often safaris begin here before venturing onto the savannas. Most guests prefer to spend most of the night sitting on the veranda, but you can leave a wake-up call. The staff will alert you in your bedroom by buzzer when one of these creatures appears, so you won't miss seeing them. Some of the rooms face the salt licks, so you may not even have to dress.

The lodges and accommodations in Mt. Kenya and the Aberdares are described in Chapter 3.

Exploring

Numbers in the margin correspond to points of interest on the Mt. Kenya and the Aberdares map.

From Nairobi take the excellent four-lane highway (A2) north **❶** from Muthaiga, which passes **Thika**, immortalized in Elspeth Huxley's classic *The Flame Trees of Thika*. There's not much to see in this provincial town, though you can drop your cards and letters off here to be postmarked "Thika." The **Blue Posts Hotel** at the northern entrance to Thika is a pleasant stop for refreshments and a view of the broad Chinia Falls. A short excursion from Thika along the Garissa Road takes you to the Athi River Falls and Ol Doinyo Sabuk National Park (*see* Chapter 3), mainly an outlook and picnic spot. (Be careful of buffalo along the path: They may seem as docile as cattle, but they charge when startled by humans.) It is possible to drive to the summit of Sabuk when the road is dry.

The highway bypasses Thika by 6.5 kilometers (4 mi), then narrows as it runs through shambas, terraced gardens on the slopes of hills. The *murram* (red soil) is in vivid contrast to the lush green, reminiscent of Australia's Red Center. A two-hour **❷** drive from Nairobi brings you to **Karatina,** a typical African town where Kikuyu women in bright kangas attend the market. The colorful straw baskets for sale for $30 in the United States can be found in Karatina for the equivalent of less than $3. Pass cautiously through town, picking your way among the crush of country buses and overloaded matutus. Dubious-look-

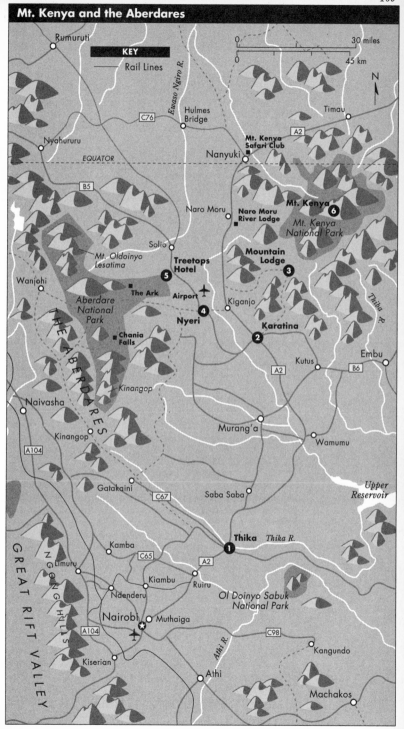

Mt. Kenya and the Aberdares

ing lodging places abound, such as the Three in One Hotel. Just beyond Karatina, a dirt road on the right takes you into the forest to the **Mountain Lodge,** a first-class treetop lodge set in the foothills (*see* Lodging, below). A salt lick and water hole bring the game to the lodge, where elephants, buffalo, rhino, and even leopard can be seen.

About 20 kilometers (12 mi) beyond Karatina, a left turn from A2 at Kiganjo leads to **Nyeri,** the principal town of the Kikuyu. It lies at the base of the Aberdares' eastern slopes and is the center for this farmland plateau. Robert, Lord Baden-Powell, founder of the Boy Scout movement, who once wrote, "The nearer to Nyeri the nearer to bliss," is buried along with his wife in the town cemetery. Baden-Powell distinguished himself in the Boer War as the hero of the siege of Mafeking. At 45 he was then the youngest general in the British Army. However, it is as the founder of the scout movement that Baden-Powell is justly remembered. In the grounds of the Outspan Hotel in Nyeri is **Paxtu** (Just Peace), a cottage built from money collected by scouts and guides all over the world. Lord Baden-Powell died in 1941, and his obituary summed up his place in history: "No chief, no prince, no king, no saint was ever mourned by so great a company of boys and girls, of men and women in every land."

Time Out   If you leave Nairobi in the morning, the **Outspan Hotel** makes a good lunch stop. Before your meal, enjoy a drink on the lawn outside the dining room. It is difficult to think of another hotel in Kenya whose gardens match those of the Outspan, and if the clouds do not encircle Mt. Kenya, it will be framed between the trees at the foot of the sloping lawn. The Outspan and its gardens exude an atmosphere of calm and serenity. You can sit in the dining room or on the terrace by the lawn for lunch. Prices vary according to your choice but should be around Kshs. 250.

The Aberdares

Most of the Aberdare range, at 9,000 feet for around 70 kilometers (43 mi), is a national park. There are no alpine peaks here such as the spire of Mt. Kenya, standing in splendid solitude some 80 kilometers (50 mi) away, but a superb scene of rolling moorlands, sudden deep valleys where bubbling streams cascade down in a series of waterfalls. Coming out of the lush rain forests toward the moorlands you pass through a surrealistic forest of giant lobelia and yellow-flowered groundsel. Redwing starlings are plentiful, and the sun glints off the luminescent sunbirds as they hover around the giant plants.

The western slopes of the range constitute part of the Rift Valley wall and drop sharply to the Kinangop Plateau. The eastern slopes are less steep and fall to the highland farming country escarpment between the Aberdares and Mt. Kenya. The slopes of the range are covered with a thick forest of hardwoods.

The park covers an area of 590 square kilometers (366 sq. mi), consisting primarily of the moorland plateau, but extending down through the rain forest in the northeast in the area of the Treetops salient.

Among the most spectacular of the many waterfalls are the Gura and Karuru falls, which lie on opposite sides of a deep valley. The Gura cascades almost 1,000 meters (3,280 ft) without interruption and the Karuru falls in three steps.

Toward the north of the Aberdares stands 3,999-meter (13,120-ft) Ol Doinyo Lesatima, the highest point in the range. Jagged volcanic cones near Lesatima are aptly named the Dragon's Teeth. Turning toward the south you can see 3,906-meter (12,815-ft) Kinangop, the most impressive summit in the Aberdares. The big ridges of Kinangop are in marked contrast to the rolling moorlands of the northern Aberdares, and the summit is reached by scrambling up a volcanic outcrop.

The Aberdares have a great variety and quantity of wildlife, but because of the dense forest you may see very little. The western slopes of the range are relatively steep; most of the animals are found on the gentler eastern slopes. Elephants, buffalo, eland, bongo, the giant forest hog, lion, and leopard are in the forests, and among the many monkeys is the black-and-white colobus—one of the most exciting animals to see on the move as it jumps from tree to tree with its long fur streaming out behind it. This beautiful fur was what made the colobus endangered; once spread throughout Kenya, colobus are now found only in rare patches.

❺ Built high in cape chestnut trees, **Treetops Hotel** was where young Princess Elizabeth, on vacation with Prince Philip in 1952, learned of her father's death and became Queen of England.

Visitors usually arrive at the Outspan for lunch, then continue the 16 kilometers (10 mi) to Treetops in hotel transport. From the vehicle, guests are escorted to the mountain lodge by armed escort. Treetops' balcony overlooks a water hole and is illuminated by floodlights at night, so guests can watch the changing pageant of forest wildlife at any hour. The myriad night noises in the lush tropical forest are unforgettable, and on the balcony at night, visitors are frequently visited by galagos, or bush babies, which climb up and sit on the railing, and elephants, rhino, and buffalo often wallow in the salt lick.

Those heading to **The Ark,** another mountain lodge 40 minutes by hotel transport in the Aberdare National Park, generally have lunch at the Aberdare Country Club, a colonial-era building set in acres of gardens, with its own golf course, swimming pool, and tennis courts. The Ark, as its name suggests, is built of cedar and brown olive in the shape of a boat. You descend from the transport and walk about 100 yards along a curved wood catwalk—raised some 15 feet off the ground—to the Ark. The salt lick and water hole are on the other side of the Ark, and two balconies and an indoor viewing area give a superlative position to watch the animals. During the night you can leave a "bongo call" or a "rhino call," in case one of these creatures appears.

Mt. Kenya

From Nyeri take A2 north toward Nanyuki. The road is rough while repairs are being carried out, but any car can manage it. You jolt north onto a plain, open grasslands, and sandy soil, after the vivid red murram. A 40-minute drive brings you to a collection of simple houses—Naro Moru Village. Turn off onto a dirt track at the sign for the **Naro Moru River Lodge,** which is hidden in 40 acres of woods, through which meanders the icy Naro Moru River, fed by the glaciers high above the moorland. The mildly dilapidated lodge offers accommodations consisting of rooms, bunkhouses, and wood chalets, and warm and friendly service. A path takes you for a mile or two along the river bank, and in the evenings, when you return, an attendant will prepare a log fire in the grate in your chalet.

Although the mountain is in front of you, in the afternoon it is often hidden by a curtain of clouds which parts in the evening to reveal moonlit glaciers.

❻ Mt. Kenya, the country's highest mountain, rises 3,048 meters (10,000 ft) above the surrounding highland plateau and is some 80 kilometers (50 mi) in diameter. It is crowned with two jagged, snow-covered peaks: Batian, 5,199 meters (17,057 ft), and Nelion, 5,189 meters (17,024 ft). These and the smaller peaks nearby are the remaining volcanic plugs of the now-eroded, but once-massive, volcanic craters (*see* Chapter 3).

From the central peaks area of Mt. Kenya, continue on A2 and then southward on B6 until you complete the circle around Mt. Kenya and rejoin A2 and drive back to Nairobi.

Off the Beaten Track

Few people reach the moorlands north and northeast of the Chogoria roadhead at the Nithi Falls, on the eastern slopes of Mt. Kenya, as the central peaks are their principal destination. But with a good map and a compass you can explore to your heart's content. Just north of the roadhead is **Lake Ellis,** and a fine view is obtained from the summit of nearby Mugi Hill. East of Mugi is the **Giants' Billiards Table,** which can be easily spotted from the Meru Mt. Kenya Bandas. Lake Alice and Ithanguni, 3,894 meters (13,070 ft), make a good three-day excursion. Beyond this is Lake Rutundu.

A really satisfying excursion is a walk around the central peaks, which can be comfortably done in two days. Around the central peak area lie some 32 beautiful tarns and spectacular scenery.

There are the Carr Lakes at the head of Hobley Valley, Enchanted Lake, Hidden Tarn, Emerald Tarn, Hausberg Tarn, among the more than 30 small lakes—most of which are hidden—at the head of narrow rocky valleys. (*See also* Chapter 3.)

To the north and west of Mt. Kenya are little explored moorlands, with hidden lakes that make great two-day camping trips. On the western side are alpine gorges and the Vivienne Falls, named after Vivienne de Watville, who camped up here in 1920s and wrote much about Mt. Kenya in *Speak to the Earth*.

6 North Central Kenya and Lake Turkana

Introduction

By Phoebe
Vreeland and
Delta Willis

Writer/researcher
Phoebe Vreeland
spent three years
in Kenya traveling
and contributing
to a variety of
tourist
publications.

With the exception of Samburu National Park and the lush oasis at Loyangalani, north central Kenya remains relatively unvisited. This is hardly surprising, considering the rugged nature of the territory. North of the Ewaso Nyiro River there are few permanent rivers, though seasonal rivers, known as *luggas*, cut serpentine paths through hundreds of miles of desert scrub punctuated by hot-spring oases and forested mountain glades. The area remains a destination for the adventurous traveler; its harsh climate and limited number of lodges combine to make the trip north challenging, although there are comfortable tour packages to such places as the Mathews Range, Samburu Lodge, and Koobi Fora.

The terrain still called the Northern Frontier District (NFD) offers solitude and vast unspoiled vistas, as well as a glimpse of the hardy peoples of Kenya who maintain their traditional lifestyle. Samburu, Rendille, Turkana, Gabbra, Boran, and Somali tribes survive virtually untouched by modern civilization, eking out their nomadic existence as they have for centuries.

The ultimate destination for a tour of Northern Kenya is Lake Turkana. Air charters and some organized tours go to Koobi Fora and Loyangalani on the east shore, and you can fly across to Ferguson's Gulf on the west, but should you venture to the lake by road, it is best to travel in convoy.

The camel tracks of Rendille nomads and Samburu have been consolidated into a road, which can be negotiated by a regular rental car in the dry season. However, there is soft sand in the *luggas*, treacherous crossings of basalt, and plenty of thorn scrub to give you a flat tire. Four-wheel-drive vehicles are strongly recommended, and you should be well-equipped with food, extra gas, spare tires, and gallons of drinking water. Road conditions should be checked en route with police and game department officials.

One of the best ways to get a feel for the area is by camel safari, which allows time to appreciate the landscape. Such safaris are for those with leisure time, however, and many travelers opt for scheduled flights to Loyangalani or charter flights to Kalakel, Koobi Fora, Marsabit, Maralal, and the Mathews Range. Most of the region is off the beaten track, ensuring an authentic safari in the tradition of Hemingway.

Two itineraries are possible. The most popular takes you from Nyahururu through Maralal, Baragoi, and South Horr. The second begins just north of Samburu National Park at Archer's Post (Isiolo) and traces the Mathews Range north to Marsabit, North Horr, and south to Loyangalani. While the tours and excursions discussed here are geared to the independent traveler, details are provided for those who choose to arrange their visit through a tour operator.

Essential Information

Important Addresses and Numbers

Emergencies Membership in an emergency air-rescue service such as the **Flying Doctors' Society** or **Africa Air Rescue** (*see* Staying

Healthy in Chapter 1) in case of accident or illness in remote areas of Northwest Kenya is highly recommended.

Arriving and Departing

By Plane The following airlines have scheduled flights three times a week to Loyangalani. Many private pilots operating out of Nairobi's Wilson Airport charter small aircraft to Koobi Fora as well.

Air Kenya (Nairobi, tel. 2/501421, 501422, or 501423) departs from Nairobi every Wednesday and Sunday at 12:30 PM. The flight takes approximately two hours and costs Kshs. 6,620 round-trip.

Executive Air Services (Box 42304, Nairobi, tel. 2/500607 or 501897). Five-, eight-, and 10-seater twin-engine Cessnas can be chartered to any northern destination—landing strip and weather permitting. The cost to charter a five-seater Cessna to Loyangalani is approximately Kshs. 18,725 one way. Passengers returning the same day are charged a waiting fee. Round-trip flights departing at a later date costs Kshs. 37,450.

Safari Air Services (Box 41951, Nairobi, tel. 2/501211). Twin-engine Cessnas for five, seven, and 12 passengers can be chartered at rates comparable to those above.

Africair/Z. Boskovic Air Charters, Ltd. (Box 45646, Nairobi, tel. 2/501210 or 501219). "Bosky" has a wide range of aircraft, including smaller planes that can be chartered for three passengers.

Note: Those arriving at a northern destination by plane should prearrange transportation to their lodge and overland exploration. Otherwise they may be limited to excursions available from the lodge.

Getting Around

By Four-Wheel Drive Rough road conditions demand a four-wheel-drive vehicle. While portions of some roads are new two-lane blacktop, most of the northern routes range from well-maintained all-weather murram to bone-shaking, corrugated tracks, or washboard, and there are river crossings in the Mathews Range.

By Car If you rent a car from Nairobi, make sure to inform the firm of your destination and consider hiring a driver who has experience in this part of the country. Travelers who decide to make the drive alone should have adequate water, extra fuel, tools, spare parts, and mechanical know-how. Several spare tires are necessary. Ideally, vehicles heading north should travel in tandem. Also, when you travel through the NFD, check with the police upon your arrival in a central town.

Seasonal factors must also be considered when planning to travel by land. During six months of the year the average midday temperature is 104° F; the other six months, the roads are virtually impassable due to flooding. Torrential rains are not uncommon. Of the two rainy seasons, the long rains, between March and June, have a more pronounced effect on the NFD. The short rains, from October to December, may also affect travel conditions but are not as dramatic.

By Truck Safari A popular alternative to renting your own vehicle is an overland truck safari, which has become synonymous with Turkana expeditions. In almost all cases, Loyangalani is the final destination, with overnight camping stops in the Samburu park areas or Lake Baringo, Maralal, and South Horr. This option is ideal for those who have plenty of time, not much money, lots of team spirit, and a sense of humor. The vehicles, usually converted Bedford trucks with seats in the beds, allow you to appreciate every one of the 570 kilometers (353 mi) between Nairobi and Loyangalani.

Safari Camp Services, Ltd. (Box 44801, Nairobi, tel. 2/330130). The "Turkana Bus," the best-known and oldest of the overland truck-safari operations, is run by Dick Hedges, who boasts of having transported more than 2,000 visitors in the last decade. His pride is the Turkana bus, a specially adapted 911 Mercedes truck that can defy even the harshest road and weather conditions. It can transport 18–22 intrepid passengers and departs every other Saturday throughout the year. The week-long expedition includes a driver/guide, all meals, and basic camping equipment. Overnight stops are at established campsites in Maralal, South Horr, Loyangalani, and Samburu (Cost: Kshs. 3,400).

Tour Operators **Bushbuck Adventures** (Box 67449, Nairobi, tel. 2/728737). Somewhat more upmarket than a truck safari, Bushbuck offers a 12-day northeastern Kenya safari 10 times a year. Stops include Mt. Kenya, Shaba National Park, the Mathews Range, the Ndoto Mountains, South Horr, Mount Porr, Maralal, and Lake Bogoria. Travel is by four-wheel-drive Land Rover with five passengers per vehicle, and all safaris are accompanied by a professional safari guide. Luxuries include shower and toilet tents.

Flame Tree Safaris, run by Chrissie Aldrich (Box 82, Nanyuki, tel. 176/22053. U.S. Agent, Members Afield, 217 E. 85th St., New York, NY 10028, tel. 717/477–5983) has three Range Rovers and three Toyota Land Cruisers, for taking small private groups around on luxury "off the beaten track" safaris in Northern Kenya and walking safaris around the NFD.

Game Trackers (Box 62042, Nairobi, tel. 2/338927). Travel in four-wheel-drive trucks with a 17- to 19-passenger capacity, accompanied by a driver/guide and a cook. Game Trackers' trips are longer than those of other operators, and they include some unusual stops. In addition to offering an eight-day trip along the Lake Baringo–Loyangalani–Samburu route (Cost: Kshs. 3,600), it is one of the few companies to offer an eight-day excursion following the Marsabit–North Horr–Chalbi Desert route (Cost: Kshs. 4,500). A 10-day truck excursion with stops at Naro Moru, Marsabit, the Ndoto Mountains, Kaisut Desert, and Loyangalani includes the opportunity to walk through some of the terrain. Trips leave Nairobi every Friday during the high season (or dry season), every other Friday during the low season (the light rains).

Special Camping Safaris (Box 51512, Nairobi, tel. 2/338325). Ten-day excursions to Loyangalani leave Nairobi every other Sunday (except in November and May). The first night is spent at Lake Baringo and the last at Bantu Lodge (Mt. Kenya). A driver, cook, and guide accompany each expedition. Groups are of 12–18 passengers per Bedford truck.

Yare Safaris (Box 63006, Nairobi, tel. 2/725610). Yare's campground and hostel in Maralal serves as a learning center and base camp for students and other low-budget travelers interested in exploring the Samburu area. Yare organizes five-day truck safaris to Loyangalani from Maralal. Transport to the camp leaves twice a week from Nairobi and the Kshs. 160 fare can be used as a deposit on any of its safaris.

By Country Bus While local transport—"country buses"—operate regular services to most northern centers, they are undependable, slow, overcrowded, and generally not recommended.

By Camel **Ewaso River Camel Hikes** (Box 243, Gilgil, or book through Just the Ticket, Box 14845, Nairobi, tel. 2/741755). Camel-assisted walking/camping safaris along the Ewaso Nyiro River guarantee true adventure and appreciation of the rugged scenic beauty. Standard trips last from five to seven days but can be arranged for up to three weeks. Camel hikes to the Mathews Range or the Ndoto Mountains can also be arranged. (Cost: Kshs. 1,200 per person per day, excluding tips and transport to base camp. Trips are made September–February and April–June.)

Mountain Club of Kenya (Box 45741, Nairobi, tel. 2/501747). The club can supply valuable background information to those planning to explore or climb some of the mountain ranges in the north.

Yare Safaris (*see* By Truck Safari, above). Basic camel safaris from Yare's Maralal base camp allow even the most budget-conscious traveler a chance to walk or ride through the wild. A five-day safari costs Kshs. 4,500.

Exploring

North to the Lake *Numbers in the margin correspond to points of interest on the North Central Kenya and Lake Turkana map.*

❶ Nyahururu (or **Thomson's Falls**) is a regular stop on northbound journeys. The town is the hub for farmers and traders in the region. The attraction for tourists is the country's third-highest waterfall at 73 meters (240 ft), named after the Scottish explorer Joseph Thomson of the Royal Geographical Society, who trekked from Mombasa to Lake Victoria in 1883. In the 1970s, during Africanization, the falls was renamed Nyahururu.

Nyahururu is the highest town in Kenya. At 2,360 meters (7,743 ft) above sea level, the air is crisp and clear, in marked contrast to the intense heat farther north. Drive straight through the town to Thomson's Falls Lodge for a look at the falls.

The road north to Maralal passes the southern fringes of the Marmanet Forest and on to Rumuruti. During the colonial era **❷ Rumuruti** was a thriving center of the ranching district. Today it is merely an avenue lined with *dukas* (small shops), with a post office and police station, and is best known as the spot where the tarmac peters out into murram. From here the route continues up through ranch land, running parallel to the eastern edge of the Rift Valley through the Lerochi Plateau and the Karisia Hills to the east. At Kisima, the road meets a junction,

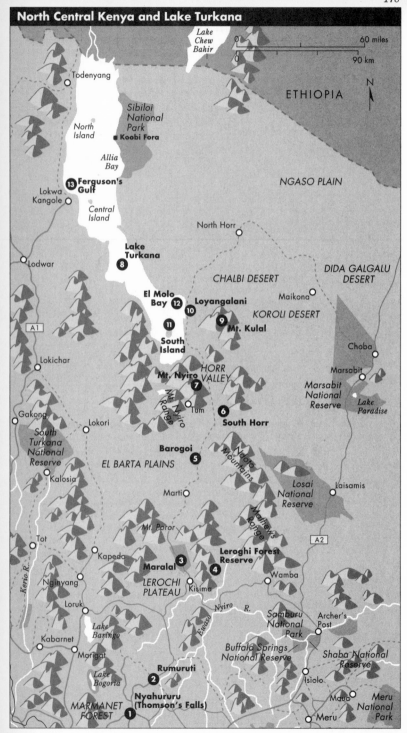

North Central Kenya and Lake Turkana

ETHIOPIA

Lake Chew Bahir

Todenyang

North Island

Sibiloi National Park

Koobi Fora

Allia Bay

NGASO PLAIN

13 Ferguson's Gulf

Lokwa Kangole

Central Island

North Horr

Lodwar

8 Lake Turkana

CHALBI DESERT

DIDA GALGALU DESERT

Maikona

El Molo Bay 12

10 Loyangalani

KOROLI DESERT

A1

11

9 Mt. Kulal

Lokichar

South Island

Choba

Gakong

Mt. Nyiro

HORR VALLEY

Marsabit

Lokori

Mt. Nyiro 7

Mt. Nyiro Range

Tum

6 South Horr

Marsabit National Reserve

Lake Paradise

South Turkana National Reserve

Ndoto Mountains

Barogoi 5

EL BARTA PLAINS

Kalosia

Marti

Losai National Reserve

Laisamis

Tot

Mt. Poror

Mathews Range

A2

Kapeda

Leroghi Forest Reserve

Nginyang

Maralal 3

4

Wamba

Loruk

LEROCHI PLATEAU

Kisima

Nyiro R.

Ewaso

Samburu National Park

Archer's Post

Kabarnet

Lake Baringo

Morigat

Buffalo Springs National Reserve

Shaba National Reserve

Lake Bogorta

Rumuruti 2

Isiolo

Maua

Meru National Park

MARMANET FOREST

Nyahururu (Thomson's Falls) 1

Meru

Kerio R.

0   60 miles

0   90 km

N

and Maralal lies an additional 19-kilometer (12-mi) drive on a well-graded murram road.

3 An attractive trading center set in conifer-forested hills, **Maralal** is a welcome relief after the flat and arid ranch lands. The area was a Samburu spiritual center before it became the district administrative headquarters for the Samburu Council. Maralal provides the first close look at the colorful Samburu, a Maa-speaking tribe closely related to the Masai, from whom they probably divided 200 years ago; they still share similar customs. The Samburu are pastoralists whose diet consists primarily of milk, often mixed with blood let from their cattle, and occasionally meat. Samburu communities are divided into age-set groupings. At puberty the boys are circumcised and initiated into the warrior, or *morani*, class. The proud young warriors tend the herds and defend the community. Many hours are spent on physical adornment. Their hair is plaited and colored with ocher and their earlobes and chests are draped in colorful beadwork. At about age 30, after a warrior has passed from junior to senior warrior distinction, he becomes a junior elder and takes his first wife. The girls, sometimes circumcised at puberty, marry immediately after the circumcision.

Maralal's small dusty street, lined with quaint inns, *hotelis* (small hotels), and dukas, offers a charm characteristic of the North. **Kenyatta House** a tin-roof bungalow where the late Mzee Jomo Kenyatta was detained in 1961, is a national monument and of historic interest. *Admission free. Open daily 9–5.*

Maralal is within a national sanctuary (*see* Chapter 3), the habitat of zebra, baboon, impala, eland, warthog, buffalo, and hyena. The best way to view the animals is from the terrace of the Maralal Safari Lodge. Maralal is the last town on the northern route where you can change money and be assured of buying gas or finding a mechanic. This is also the last chance for a cold beer before Loyangalani, approximately a seven-hour drive north. The road climbs past a wheat-growing project and **4** through the **Leroghi Forest Reserve,** a mix of cedars either dripping with moss, described as "Old Man's Beard," or eerie skeletons of trees, with barren, twisted limbs, that have succumbed to the parasitic moss.

The spectacular Suguta Valley can be seen from the Lesiolo Escarpment. At 825 feet below sea level, it is Kenya's Death Valley and 3 million years ago may have been part of Lake Turkana, before Teleki's volcanos created a barrier for the lake. Ask for directions to the turnoff at the lodge in Maralal.

The road continues along the escarpment past Mt. Poror and winds down into El Barta Plains and eventually to the township **5** of **Barogoi,** little more than a one-horse street lined with brightly colored dukas. There is a mission, an airstrip, and extremely expensive gas. If you are thirsty, you are limited to local hotelis. While often dingy and flyblown, these establishments are friendly and good spots to people-watch.

Time Out At the first tea shop on your right as you approach the town, tea is served weak, sweet, and milky with a slightly smoky flavor from the gourds used to store the fresh milk. If you prefer it black, order a *strungi*. Try the *anjera* or *mkate mayai*—both sweet crepes that taste like pancakes.

From Baragoi the road continues north through **El Barta Plains.** The distant mountains seem distorted as you view them from various angles along the curving road. The dry, flat, scrub plains are enlivened by the occasional glimpse of a lone nomad or herds of grazing camels.

❻ The approach to **South Horr** is welcoming. The road becomes smooth, white, and sandy, and the Horr Valley, which is set between Ol Doinyo Mara and Mt. Nyiro ranges, is inviting, cool, and green. South Horr is a forest oasis of thick vegetation that still supports some elusive game. The area is rich in birdlife and butterflies.

The town has expanded from a mission settlement and now includes a police depot, a few dukas, and a campsite. When visitors arrive, Samburu women appear magically on the roadside and cluster around, eager to sell their wares.

From South Horr, Loyangalani is still several hours' drive away, approximately 130 kilometers (80 mi). While there is no lodge in South Horr, it is an ideal place to camp. If you are there in the morning, at least stop for a walk and refreshment.

❼ Nearby, **Mt. Nyiro** makes a worthwhile detour, for four-wheel-drive only, along a track south of Mt. Nyiro to Tum, a small village and forest-department camp set in a lovely watered valley. It is possible to trek across the Nyiro massif, avoiding the 2,831-meter (9,288-ft) peaks, a scenic excursion through glades and ridges that affords a splendid view of Lake Turkana. The area contains buffalo and possibly greater kudu. A local guide is essential. The road continues on through the Horr Valley, gateway to Lake Turkana, and the terrain becomes increasingly rough and barren.

Around Lake Turkana No matter how much you have read or heard about **Lake Turkana,** you will still not be prepared for the spectacle. The **❽** lake appears suddenly on the horizon, a mercurial shimmer contrasting with the harsh, desolate landscape. The water is constantly changing color, from silver-gray to luminous blue and occasionally the curious shade of green mentioned by John Hillaby in *Journey to the Jade Sea.* The lake takes its color from algae, the changes occurring as the wind stirs the particles.

Named Lake Rudolf in 1888 by explorer Count Teleki von Szek, after Crown Prince Rudolf of Austria, in 1975 the lake was renamed in honor of the main tribe indigenous to the area. Largest of the Great Rift Valley lakes—250 kilometers (155 mi) in length—Turkana was created when the lowering of the Rift Valley floor cut it off from the Nile. It contains several islands, of which Central and South are a national park and national reserve, is fed by only the Omo River from Ethiopia, and has no outlet. The region's high temperatures and relatively little rainfall (an average of 10 inches a year), are causing the lake to evaporate and the shoreline to recede at a rate of 3 meters (10 ft) a year. Since the publication of *Journey to the Jade Sea* in 1973, more adventurous travelers have come to this "jewel in the desert." Many tourists ventured to East Turkana as a result of *National Geographic* articles on research at Koobi Fora (*see* Sibiloi National Park in Chapter 3). Now the search for ancient fossils has shifted to the west side of the lake, with sites stretching from near Ferguson's Gulf to Nariokotome, where the oldest *Homo erectus* was found in 1986.

The lake is known for its enormous freshwater fish and is a popular spot for sportfishing as well as commercial ventures. Nile perch, evidence of the lake's former link with the Nile, grow to 400 pounds, and a 200-pound catch is not uncommon. The more palatable tilapia are fished commercially. Tigerfish, named for their toothy jaws, can be caught from the shore. Lake Turkana produces even a small puffer fish, usually found near coral reefs and thought to be evidence of a onetime link with the Mediterranean. The lake is home to reptiles—10,000–22,000 Nile crocodiles—as well as snakes. Nevertheless, swimming in populated areas is relatively safe, but choose your spot carefully and seek local advice.

The surrounding area has an unusual beauty with its volcanic hills, craters, cones, and islands. Most striking is **Nyambutom** ("elephant stomach"), a caldera in the lake's southernmost extremity. The southern shoreline is marked by large, black lava flows, dropping as steep cliffs into the green water, rich in algae. To the north of the Kerio delta the landscape is more peaceful: gentle sandy beaches fringed with doum palms and acacia scrub.

❾ To the east, **Mt. Kulal** stands sentinel, source of the scorching winds so characteristic of the lakeshore. The cool mountain winds are quickly heated as they cross the desert floor toward the lake. Area tribes believe that the mountain has mystical properties, and it is strewn with jasper, blue agate, quartz, and amethyst, which can be found if you search carefully, or, more easily, purchased from the locals who display their finds for sale at the lodge entrances. Climbs, always worthwhile, should be attempted by only the enthusiastic and hardy. The views of the lake below from the forested peak of Kulal are breathtaking. Trips can be arranged through the lodges, and day visits by vehicle to the settled side of the mountain are another option.

Despite the dramatic scenery, the arid conditions make the Turkana area difficult to explore. At midday temperatures average 40°C (104°F), and the strong easterly winds can reach up to 80 kilometers per hour (50 mph). Lake tempests with deadly waves are not uncommon. More locals die on the lake from the unpredictable weather conditions than from crocodiles.

The hot equatorial sun can be very hard on visitors who are unaccustomed to the climate. Don't overdo it, no matter how short your visit. Plan excursions for the early morning and cool late afternoons, and spend the hot midday hours at the oasis springs. Drink plenty of water.

The nomadic Turkana, who populate the lake's western and southern shores, can be frequently seen around Loyangalani. They tend cattle, camels, goats, sheep, and donkeys, and weave beautiful large baskets from the leaves of the doum palm. Their adaptability has allowed them to survive in the country's harshest terrain.

Because of their limited contact with the outside world, they remain the country's most independent tribe and are well-known for their proud attitude. Despite their photogenic appeal, they are especially sensitive, and care and respect should be taken when pointing your camera. You'll need to work out an agreement with your subject before taking a picture. *Note:* The

Turkana hold the reputation of being the country's hardest bargainers.

⑩ **Loyangalani,** a hot-spring oasis of doum palms on the lake's southeastern shore, is a perfect rest spot after the demanding journey and an ideal base for travelers who wish to explore the area further. The town is a small community that has grown around the mission, school, and fishing lodge. As a trading center for the area, Loyangalani attracts an interesting cultural mix, including Samburu cattle herdsmen, Italian nuns, Rendille camel nomads, and local Turkana fishermen from the lake's western shores.

One of the best places to people-watch unobtrusively is in the town's hotelis, where the locals sit and sip sweet milky tea. The walls of the tea shops are usually adorned with amusing notices and murals. Samburu or Turkana dances are often staged on the lakeshore. Loyangalani has a tarmac airstrip located virtually on the doorstep of the two lodges.

⑪ The largest of the lake islands, at 80 square kilometers (50 sq mi), **South Island National Reserve** is a striking feature on the Turkana horizon. The hostile rocky mass is home to herds of roaming feral goats. Visits by boat are best arranged through the lodges.

⑫ One of the area's main attractions is the El Molo community at **El Molo Bay,** a few kilometers up the lakeshore. Commonly and mistakenly referred to as the "smallest tribe in Kenya," the El Molo are one of the few hunter/gatherer societies remaining today. Although they once numbered fewer than 80, the present community numbers 500 as a result of intermarriage with the neighboring tribes, particularly the Samburu, whose language the El Molo have adopted.

The El Molo remain the country's poorest tribe. Interest in the El Molo and their rich cultural traditions have made tourism one of their principal sources of revenue. Visitors to the village generally pay the headman a small fee that goes into the village fund, and then they are welcome to snoop about and photograph freely. El Molo are skilled fishermen, and they use harpoons, nets, and lines from doum-palm rafts in the lake. They also hunt crocodile and turtles, and although it is forbidden, hippopotamus to supplement their diet.

The origin of the tribe is obscure. Some believe they originally inhabited South Island. Shared cultural beliefs with the Rendille lead some to think they are a splinter group of that tribe, who gave up a nomadic lifestyle to fish on the lake.

North from El Molo Bay lie Allia Bay and Sibiloi National Park, home to Koobi Fora (*see* Chapter 3). An alternate return route South takes you first up to North Horr and the Chalbi Desert, then to Marsabit, the Mathews Range (*see* Excursions, *below*), Isiolo, and on to Nairobi. The scenery on the drive through the **Chalbi Desert** desert alternates between crusted snow-white plains where the Gabbra nomads collect salt to sell in the Marsabit market, and exquisitely beautiful wind-sculpted sand dunes. Inquire at either North Horr or Maikona for current conditions.

⑬ You can get to **Ferguson's Gulf** by small plane from Nairobi on Air Kenya and on excursions from Koobi Fora and Loyangalani. From there the C47 north to Lokitaung and the main track

northwest via Lodwar to Kakuma and Lokichokio are dramatic
scenic drives, although the remote badlands can be dangerous.
Short drives along the shore in the Ferguson's Gulf area give a
good glimpse of the lifestyle of today's inhabitants.

The nomadic **Turkana** are of Nilo-Hamitic origin and are tradi-
tionally herdsmen. They can survive in these marginal lands by
living solely off their livestock: cattle, sheep, goats, and camels. (A camel will produce two or three times as much milk as a
cow in this harsh environment.) More recently, some Turkana
have turned to fishing; many still use the old method of catching
their prey in large seine baskets.

Turkana traditions stress marriage and individual independence, so young men marry and move away from their fathers'
home, a practice more important to this group than to the other
nomads of Kenya. The Turkana do not practice circumcision,
but they do have a series of equally important initiation ceremonies. Traditional ornaments and decorations are still evident and an important part of their lives today. The men wear
elaborate, blue-dyed mud-and-dung hair cakes, often further
adorned with an ostrich plume. To protect this headdress at
night, they sleep on wooden neck-stools, which are carried
along with their spears as symbols of manhood. Wrist and fin-
ger knives are also standard equipment for the young warriors.
Some men and women still wear ear and lip plugs, to which the
women often add necklaces made of ostrich-egg shells worn
into small discs. Women and girls wear the traditional leather
skirts decorated with colorful beads, or cowrie shells traded
from the coast over 1,000 kilometers (620 mi) away.

When conditions force the Turkana to move great distances,
the entire tribe loads their possessions onto donkeys; most of
the time, however, the men move with the animals while the
women remain behind at semipermanent manyattas.

In this region look for hippos and crocodiles, both plentiful
around Ferguson's Gulf. Mammals in the bush are not plentiful,
but look for Grant's gazelle, Beisa orix, striped hyena, golden
jackal, African hare, unstriped ground squirrel, and white-
tailed and dwarf mongoose.

Ferguson's Gulf has the largest concentration of waterbirds on
the west side of the lake; great white pelican, yellow-billed
stork, sacred ibis, and African spoonbill often nest there. From
October to April thousands of shorebirds and ducks appear,
many of which come from as far away as Siberia. For avid bird-
watchers, there is always the chance of seeing a truly rare species. The bush country around is the habitat of localized species
like the swallow-tailed kite, Heuglin's bustard, the Abyssinian
roller, and Somali fiscal shrike.

Trips to **Central Island** are arranged from Lake Turkana Fishing Lodge. The half-day trip allows one to two hours of walking
on the volcanic island, weather permitting. Here huge crocodiles, flamingos, African skimmers, and pelicans reside in
large numbers.

Excursions

Mathews Range Northwest of Samburu National Park lies the **Mathews Range,**
approached from Wamba either via Kisima from Rumuruti or
from Isiolo through Archer's Post. The dusty, corrugated road

between Archer's Post and the Wamba turnoff is at present in incredibly poor condition. It is an eight-hour journey from Nairobi to the Mathews via Wamba, but you can also fly to Wamba by charter from Nairobi.

The mountain range was named by Austrian explorer Count Teleki von Szek after the helpful general Sir Lloyd Mathews, then commander-in-chief of the Sultan's army in Zanzibar. The range is also known as Ol Doinyo Lenkiyio.

Today the Mathews Range remains isolated (four-wheel-drive only) and rarely explored. The area is a forest reserve, but the animals are difficult to see through the dense mountain vegetation. Access is easiest at Kitich Valley, an appropriate local name meaning "happiness," given by the local Samburu inhabitants. There are crystal-clear pools for fishing and swimming, and idyllic camping spots. Local guides are invaluable for those who want to explore this forested area.

Marsabit The trip north to **Marsabit** from the Wamba turnoff on Isiolo Road takes approximately six hours. You will travel through bleak plains with some striking volcanic-rock formations, and the Mathews Range in the distance, then through the Losai National Reserve with its Samburu settlements.

Along this road you will come to Ulanula, or "singing wells," deep, hand-dug wells where nomadic tribesmen form a human chain to draw water for their livestock. The rhythm of their song keeps time with their movements. It is advisable to ask before photographing.

Marsabit is a forest oasis of *gofs*, or craters, which rise 1,000 meters (3,280 ft) above the desert; it remains permanently green throughout the year in contrast to the dusty, flat plains that surround it. The town is a livestock trading center for the Gabbra, Boran, and Rendille herdsmen as well as for neighboring Somali and Ethiopians. Although it functions as a major administrative or trading center, the town is no more than a post office, police station, market, *hotelis*, and a couple of gas stations.

The Rendille people resemble the Samburu and share cultural traditions with both their Gabbra neighbors to the north and the Samburu to come south. Their livelihood comes from tending camels. They are one of the few nomadic tribes who practice monogamy and have a fixed bride price. Women with a male child wear a spectacular crested hairdo called a *doko*.

Marsabit's national reserve (*see* Chapter 3) is famous for its resident long-tusked elephants. Ahmed carried such an impressive (and valuable) load of ivory that he was placed under protection by presidential decree. He died in 1974. A fiberglass replica honors the big tusker at the Nairobi National Museum; you can see it in the garden to the left of the main entrance. There are no more elephants with tusks of this size; they have all been killed by poachers.

Most of the park is forested crater slopes, making the game difficult to view. The well-watered and densely forested area is home to greater kudu, Beisa oryx, buffalo, and Grevy's zebra, and attracts a variety of birds and snakes. The showpiece of the park is Gof Sokorte Guda, or Lake Paradise. The park's main circuit takes you along the crater rim for an unparalleled view and then down to the floor of the crater along the lake, where herds of elephant and buffalo come to drink. A special campsite on the floor of Lake Paradise can be booked at the main gate for Kshs. 300.

Lodging

Highly recommended lodgings are indicated by a star ★.

Category	Cost*
Very Expensive	over $125 (Kshs. 3,000)
Expensive	$83–$125 (Kshs. 2,000–3,000)
Moderate	$42–$83 (Kshs. 1,000–2,000)
Inexpensive	under $42 (Kshs. 1,000)

All prices are for a standard double room; excluding service charge.

Ferguson's Gulf **Lake Turkana Fishing Lodge** is on the end of a large sand spit. The breeze and shaded bar have given comfort to many weary travelers. The accommodations are adequate, and the meals feature fresh tilapia and perch. *Contact Ivory Safaris in Nairobi, tel. 2/78401. Facilities: boat trips, fishing, swimming pool. AE, V. Inexpensive.*

Loyangalani **Oasis Club.** This is a luxury lodge with 24 cottages, two pools
★ filled from the hot springs, a bar serving ice-cold drinks, and a breezy dining room featuring freshly caught lake fish, excellent Italian dishes, and home-baked bread. The rooms are comfortable, though hot and sticky on still nights, and noisy on windy evenings. The lodge operates as a club, charging a steep daily membership fee to nonresidents to ensure exclusivity. The club can organize fishing excursions on the lake, boat trips to Central Island, climbing expeditions to Mt. Kulal, or visits to Mt. Porr. *Bookings Limited, Box 56707, Nairobi, tel. 2/25255 or 336570. AE, DC, V. Expensive.*

Lake Turkana El Molo Lodge. Formerly a campsite, the lodge was recently expanded to include 20 self-contained double bandas. The facilities include outdoor showers and toilets for campers, a kitchen and dining area, a spring-fed pool, and a bar. The lodge's low rates, lack of daily membership fee, and popularity with the safari truck companies give it a casual atmosphere. *Across Africa Safaris, Box 30471, Nairobi, tel. 2/724384 or 332744. DC, V. Inexpensive.*

Maralal **Maralal Safari Lodge.** At first the Swiss-chalet-style cedar log cabins tucked into the forest glade seem out of place in Africa, but they are fully appreciated on a chilly night in Maralal. The cabins provide all the necessary comforts, including hot water and a blazing fire every evening. Meals are uninspired, but the service is friendly and willing. The dining room overlooks a salt lick. Leopards are baited each evening and can be viewed by floodlight from a hide near the lodge. The airstrip is located about 2 kilometers (1.2 mi) away, and if prearranged, visitors arriving by air will be met. Vehicles can also be hired for exploring the area. *Thorn Tree Safaris, Box 42475, Nairobi, tel. 2/28981 or 21761. AE, V. Moderate.*

Thomson's Falls Lodge. Located near the falls, the lodge is popular with tourists and locals. Picnic tables and curio kiosks carpet the area leading to the falls' outlook. Although rundown, the 1930s highlands-farmhouse-style lodge still retains charm. The lodge offers cottages and rooms with fireplace and bath, and there is a campsite on the grounds. The rustic dining room serves full English-style meals and the fire-warmed bar is a cozy spot to stop for tea and sandwiches on cold days. *Box 38, Nyahururu, tel. 0356/22552 or 22006. AE, V. Moderate.*

Yare Safaris Hostel. A recently opened hostel with dormitory rooms, private *bandas* (simple cabins), and a campground operates as a base camp for the company's safaris. The accommodations are very basic, geared to students and budget travelers. The camp is also something of a cultural learning center and organizes traditional Samburu events and dances. The restaurant features local dishes. A model *manyatta*, the traditional Samburu homestead, is located on the grounds and open to explore. *Box 63006, Nairobi, tel. 2/725610. No credit cards. Inexpensive.*

Marsabit   **Marsabit Lodge,** gracefully situated in the park on the rim of Gof Sokorte Dika, is a simple but comfortable lodge with a friendly staff. *Msafiri Inns, Box 42013, Nairobi, tel. 2/330820. No credit cards. Moderate.*

Mathews Range   **Kitich Camp,** overlooking the Ngeng River, is an old-fashioned camp with 10 well-spaced tents, private baths and toilets, and a swimming hole out of Eden. Walking tours are led by Samburu and Wandorobo guides. Transportation from the Wamba airstrip can be provided for Kshs. 1,600 round-trip for four passengers. *Let's Go Travel, Box 60342, Nairobi, tel. 2/34033. Closed Apr.–June. Very Expensive. No credit cards.*

Campsites   Those wishing to set up their own camp should take the wind, scorpions, security, and poisonous vipers into consideration. Check with local tour operators.

Sunset Camp established by the Turkana Bus is attractively set back in the doum palms and offers some protection from the wind, as well as basic bathing and dining facilities.

7 Western Kenya and Lake Victoria

Introduction

By Terry Stevenson

Terry Stevenson holds the world record for bird sightings in the 1988 Kenyan International Competition and works as a guide for Abercrombie & Kent.

Western Kenya is marked by the geological formation of the Great Rift Valley that runs roughly north–south through East Africa, creating spectacular vistas and an infinite variety of habitats for wild creatures. Considered by ornithologists a bird-watcher's paradise, it is also home to rare roan antelope with curved scimitar horns and long tufted ears. The diminutive potto, a small, furry monkey known as a bush baby, can be seen in the trees at night.

Western Kenya borders Africa's largest body of water, Lake Victoria, also known as Nyanza, where lateen sails power the fishing boats of the Luo people. The region features the only true tropical rain forest in Kenya, the Kakamega, an extension of the thick, lush vegetation of neighboring Uganda. The floor of the Rift Valley is marked by Lakes Baringo, Bogoria, Nakuru, and Naivasha. We outline several routes along the escarpments that line the valley, affording outstanding panoramas and a chance for a walk in the woods.

The region has both arid badlands—with basalt lava flows and hot springs that may vaporize into clouds or rush together into a warm waterfall—and vast mountains like Mt. Elgon, where only a few years ago elephants were discovered gathering a midnight snack in Kitum Cave, scraping salt off the cave walls with their tusks. Evidence of volcanic activity is everywhere: At the center of the dramatic crater of Mt. Suswa is a table of cedar forest, surrounded by a dry, steep moat that is 750 feet deep and 1,000 feet across at its narrowest point. The forbidding inner crater was not explored until 1980, when an international expedition of young people called Operation Drake mapped and surveyed the inner habitat. The only source of water in the central plateau comes from volcanic steam vents, which issue jets of hot vapor. The outer crater is easily accessible by four-wheel-drive and makes an exceptional picnic stop—a mere afternoon's journey from Nairobi. (There are no accommodations, however, so you should continue on well before midafternoon.)

We have chosen six starting points from which to explore Western Kenya: the Loita Plains, Lake Naivasha, Kericho, Kisumu, Kitale, and Lake Baringo. The routes can be taken in any order or approached from other parts of Kenya.

Beyond Lakes Naivasha and Nakuru, Western Kenya is not often included on a first-time visitor's itinerary, though it offers that tantalizing sense of being off the beaten path in unspoiled Africa, especially for the independent traveler with a vehicle. The area has good accommodations, such as the first-class island camp (very romantic and relatively expensive) on Lake Baringo; there are also opportunities for unusual bed-and-breakfast visits in Kitale, where your hosts are residents whose lifestyles tell you much about Kenya. The modern, recently built New Kisumu Hotel overlooks Lake Victoria, and tented camps have been built around Lake Bogoria, where you are likely to see kudu. There are also places where only camping with your own gear will get you on to the next stop, or where bandas afford little more than a roof over your head.

The people of this region are varied, their traditional lifestyle stronger than those you'd encounter on the more popular minibus itineraries. You will see traditional herdsmen and fishermen, *shambas* (small holdings), as well as vast tea plantations. Local tribes are described in the sections on the destinations where you are most likely to encounter them.

The main roads from Nairobi to Kisumu and Kitale allow you to reach western Kenya in five or six hours—should you picture yourself in the Kenya Safari Rally. Otherwise, slow down and enjoy not only the spectacular scenery, but also a few of the recommended detours—they may well become the highlight of your safari. The network of minor roads has been improved enormously, in part because the president of Kenya is from this region, the Tugen Hills. Most of the recommended roads in western Kenya are good; however, we note some on which you will need a four-wheel-drive vehicle, along with your own cooler for food, and plenty of drinking water. The distribution of gas stations is good as far north as Lodwar and Ferguson's Gulf. You should not go north of Ferguson's Gulf unescorted, and you should not drive the Nairobi-to-Naivasha Road at night.

To the Loita Plains

Arriving and Departing

This area is easily visited by taking A104 north out of Nairobi. After 40 kilometers (25 mi), turn left down B3, known colloquially as the old escarpment road; it is clearly marked to Narok.

A 650-yard airstrip was built on the outer crater of Suswa in 1980; charter pilots such as those with Air Kenya at Nairobi's Wilson Airport usually know its condition.

Exploring

Numbers in the margin correspond to points of interest on the Western Kenya and Lake Victoria map.

B3 west passes through ranching country, bypassing Suswa en route to Narok. For many visitors this will be their first view of the Great Rift Valley, and spectacular it is. There are several outlook points along the road with excellent panoramas of Mt. Suswa, the striking volcanic peaks of Longonot, and the western Rift Valley escarpment.

❶ The northern rim of **Mt. Suswa**'s volcanic crater, an afternoon's journey from Nairobi, can be reached in a four-wheel-drive vehicle and makes a pleasant day trip well away from the usual tourist route. It offers a chance to meet **Masai** people herding their cattle and living in dung-and-mud *manyattas*, as they have done for hundreds of years. The *morani* (warriors) are a marvelous sight as they stride across the hills carrying their heavy spears, wearing their ocher togas, and sporting long, plaited, red hair. Although they are friendly and inquisitive, it should be remembered that photography is not allowed without first obtaining their permission; this usually means negotiating some payment.

❷ **Narok** is the main trading center of the Masai people in southwestern Kenya. It is also a town of gas stations. Virtually everyone passing through the town stops for "petrol," and the

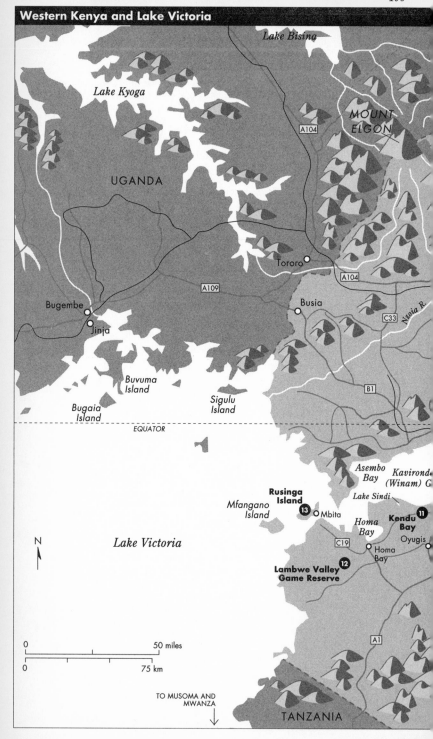

Western Kenya and Lake Victoria

Lake Bisina

Lake Kyoga

MOUNT ELGON

A104

UGANDA

Tororo

A104

A109

Bugembe

Jinja

Busia

C33

Ntoia R.

B1

Buvuma Island

Sigulu Island

Bugaia Island

EQUATOR

Asembo Bay *Kavirondo (Winam) G*

Lake Sindi

Rusinga Island

Mfangano Island

13 ○Mbita

Homa Bay

Kendu Bay **11**

Oyugis ○

N

Lake Victoria

C19

12 ○ Homa Bay

Lambwe Valley Game Reserve

A1

0 _____ 50 miles

0 _____ 75 km

TO MUSOMA AND MWANZA
↓

TANZANIA

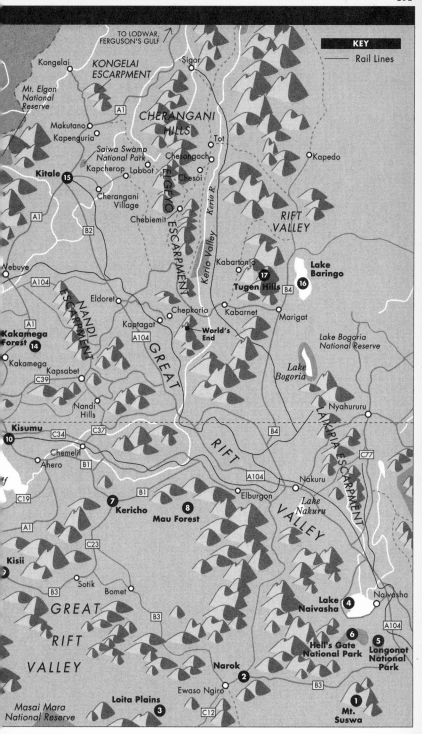

KEY
— Rail Lines

TO LODWAR,
FERGUSON'S GULF

Kongelai
KONGELAI
ESCARPMENT
Sigor

Mt. Elgon
National
Reserve
CHERANGANI
HILLS

Makutano
Kapenguria
Tot
Kapedo

Saiwa Swamp
National Park
Chesongoch
Kapcherop Laboot
Kitale 15
Chesoi

Cherangani
Village
RIFT
VALLEY

Chebiemit

Nebuye
Kabartonjo
Lake
Baringo

A104
Tugen Hills 17
B4 16

Eldoret
Chepkoria
Kabarnet
Marigat

Kakamega
Forest 14
Kaptagat
A104
■ **World's**
End

Lake Bogoria
National Reserve

Kakamega
Kapsabet
Lake
Bogoria

C39
GREAT

Nandi
Hills
Nyahururu

Kisumu
C34 C37
B4

10
RIFT

Chemelil
Ahero B1
A104
Nakuru

C19

A1
Elburgon
Lake
Nakuru

7
B1
8
Kericho **Mau Forest**

C23

Kisii

B3
Sotik Bomet
VALLEY

GREAT
B3
Lake 4
Naivasha Naivasha

A104

6
RIFT
Hell's Gate **National Park**
5
Longonot
National
Park

VALLEY
Narok 2

Masai Mara
National Reserve
Loita Plains
3
Ewaso Ngiro
C12
1
Mt.
Suswa

small shops clustered around these stations have become a major tourist attraction. There are literally dozens of shops selling thousands of artifacts: Necklaces, spears, knives, bracelets, animal carvings, masks, batiks, calabashes, and shields are but a few of the items for which one may barter. However the shopkeepers are expert salesmen, and you may not get quite the bargain you expect. These roadside stands are not shops in the everyday sense: They have no names and no posted hours, though they are likely to open when the gas stations do most of their business—midmorning to sundown.

The road beyond Narok continues southwest to Ewaso Ngiro, 18 kilometers (11 mi) away. Shortly after this village there is a **3** left fork, C12, which takes you fully across the **Loita Plains.** Although the plains do not have sanctuary status, they feature much wildlife, for the area is an ecological continuation of the famous Masai Mara Game Reserve. From the road, one usually sees large herds of wildebeest, zebra, giraffe, Thomson's and Grant's gazelles, and lesser numbers of buffalo, spotted hyena, rock hyrax, topi, warthog and impala. The open grasslands are particularly good for birds of prey: Six species of vultures occur, as well as martial eagles, bateleurs, and secretary birds. In the riverine forests look for Livingstone's turaco, Narina's trogon, and the double-toothed barbet.

The Masai people walk among the animals, but remember that lion, leopard, and hyena all live here, so do not venture far from your vehicle. There are no accommodations in the Loita Plains since most people pass this way onto the Masai Mara Reserve proper, where the wildlife is more abundant. For details on the reserve, see Chapter 3.

Lake Naivasha

Arriving and Departing

Naivasha can be reached from Nairobi on A104, which runs along the escarpment of the Great Rift Valley. To reach the lake, drive directly through town to Moi Avenue and turn left. Follow Moi Avenue (which turns into the Old Nairobi Road) for five kilometers (.6 mi); cross the railroad tracks of the Lunatic Express, turn right on South Lake Road, which was recently black-topped, to the relief of the world–it was terrible. There is a small airport in Naivasha and several small private strips near the lake, but no scheduled flights. Charters can be arranged from Nairobi through Air Kenya.

Exploring

Naivasha town is an old railroad stop, with little to slow you down except the meat pies at **La Belle Inn** (Moi Ave., closed **4** Tues.) **Lake Naivasha** is a freshwater lake with many hippos, fish eagles that perch in yellow-barked acacias, and a carpet of introduced salvinia that threatens to choke the lake. Many flower farms in the area use the lake water for irrigation, and there is great controversy about the lake's ecology, which is something of a mess because of many introduced species. It is nonetheless beautiful, especially with purple mountains like Longonot in the background, and many Europeans have ele-

gant houses on the lakeshore, including the Djinn Palace from
White Mischief, which is private.

Near the southeastern shore of the lake is **Crescent Island,** a
half-moon shaped island that's a sanctuary renowned for its
birdlife and small herds of antelope. It is reached by boat trips
that allow you an hour's walk on the island. *Book at the Lake
Naivasha Hotel; Kshs. 130.*

Elsamere. Formerly the home of conservationists Joy and
George Adamson (*Born Free*), this rambling colonial-style bungalow on the lake shore is now a museum open for tours. Tea is
served on the lawn, and you may inquire about a vacancy in one
of the limited number of rooms (which are usually occupied by
research scientists). *S. Lake Rd., 2 km (.3 mi) beyond
Fisherman's Camp. Open daily 3–5 PM.*

Time Out Eating Sunday lunch (a lavish cold buffet with traditional Sunday curry) at the Lake Naivasha Hotel and watching the sacred
ibis on the bright green lawns.

Lake Naivasha Vineyards produces a crop that, though small, is
memorable; its whites compete favorably with imported ones.
Do sample them if you find them on the wine lists in better
Naivasha and Nairobi hotels and restaurants. Small groups
and couples can arrange in advance by mail or through tour operators for a tour of the vineyards and a tasting. *Box 620,
Naivasha.*

There are two small national parks just south of Lake Naivasha
that are worth visiting. Both can be reached from the lake road
or by turning off A104 at the town of Longonot, about 20 kilometers (12 mi) south of Naivasha. There's a railroad station at

⑤ Longonot, but it's a long walk to the park. **Longonot National
Park** is a dormant volcano 2,885 meters (9,466 feet) with active
fumaroles. You can climb it in about 45 minutes from the head of
the track (it takes about 2 hours to walk around the rim). You
should pay someone to watch your car, or walk the extra 5 kilometers (3 mi) from the railroad station). *Park admission
Kshs. 220.*

⑥ **Hell's Gate National Park** (established 1984; 68 sq. mi), a beautiful and little-known park with great gorges and dramatic rock
formations, is like a small Grand Canyon with no minibuses in
sight. It is also one of the few parks in Kenya where you can get
out of your vehicle and walk. The pinnacle of Fischer's Tower,
favored by climbers, is named after a German geologist who
came here in 1883; it has a resident family of rock hyrax. There
is also a rarely seen species of mountain reedbuck,
klipspringer, small herds of zebra, and leopard, who prefer the
rocks. Bird life here is rich, including the rare lammergeyer, or
bearded vulture. Shortly before dusk you can see hundreds of
swifts flying to their nightly roosts in sheer rock faces; some
turn wing over wing to enter vertical cracks at great speed.

You will also see hot springs and geysers, a vast geothermal
project called Ol Karia sends clouds of steam into the air. The
volcanic lava at Hell's Gate is renowned for obsidian, a glassy
black stone used by early humans for making tools.

Kericho

Arriving and Departing

Kericho town, in cool, crisp air at 2,000 meters (6,560 ft), is reached by traveling north from Nairobi along A104 to the intersection with B1, a newly repaved road that's a beautiful drive west through Kipsigis farmlands and extensive tea estates. Kericho is 107 kilometers (66 mi) west of Nakuru.

Exploring

7 **Kericho** is the tea-growing center of Kenya, and cultivated fields surround the town. The tea estates are best visited in the morning, when the weather is clear and sunny and large numbers of pickers are at work. Weekday visits to a **Brooke Bond tea factory** can be arranged through Kericho Tea Hotel with 48 hours' notice.

The **Kipsigis,** part of the Kalenjin group, farm a large area of Western Kenya around Kericho, Bomet, and Sotik. Much of their land is fertile, hilly country at a fairly high altitude; good rains allow the Kipsigis to grow maize, tea, potatoes, and beans. They also grow the white-blossomed pyrethrum, the base for many insecticides.

A visit to a Kipsigis home can be arranged through the Kericho Tea Hotel. You can enter their traditional mud-and-thatch houses, see a variety of crops (depending on the time of year), and gather cows' milk the old-fashioned way; you may also be invited to sample the Kipsigis' own brew of sweet tea.

The well-maintained **Kericho Arboretum** is 7 kilometers (4 mi) east of Kericho on B1. A wide range of both exotic and indigenous trees flourish, and a beautiful small lake makes an excellent site for a lunchtime picnic. *Kericho Forest Station, tel. Kericho 20377.*

8 The **Mau Forest** is one of the largest undisturbed montane forests in Kenya, lying at an altitude of 2,000 to 3,050 meters (6,560–10,000 ft). Although much of it is inaccessible, a walk along its edges at the arboretum, or to the Kaptiget River, is a rewarding way to spend half a day. Elephant, buffalo, and bushbuck live in the forest, but they are seldom seen. Enjoy the atmosphere of the forest, the rich and varied birdlife, and a multitude of stunning butterflies. For the more adventurous traveler with a four-wheel-drive vehicle, there is an unfurnished rest house on the Kaptiget River, rentable through the KerichoTea Hotel. The accommodations are very basic, and you must take literally everything with you.

Drive south out of Kericho on C23 to Sotik, and then take B3 on
9 to **Kisii**, a total of 103 kilometers (64 mi) on a twisting, paved road. The settlement consists predominantly of shambas growing bananas, maize, and beans but is famous for its soapstone carvings of the same name. The carvings—of animals, birds, fruit bowls, dishes, candlesticks, and ornate ashtrays—come in a variety of pink, yellow, and white stone. Although these carvings can be purchased in many parts of Kenya, there is nothing quite like seeing the work being produced, then looking through hundreds of pieces for a particularly appealing one

before making your bargain. (Note: Kisii stone does break, so be sure to wrap your purchase in a T-shirt or a kikoi to protect it.)

Several stalls are set up along the main street of Kisii; however, it is far more exciting to go behind the scenes and watch the craftsmen at work. Because these carvings are produced in the artists' own homes, one must move from house to house. Do not feel as if you are imposing, for the Kisii are more than happy to see you, and a few hours spent meeting the local people in this way can be an unusual side trip from a safari. The main center of this industry is based around the village of Tabaka, about a 20-minute drive south of Kisii.

Near Oyugis, about 20 kilometers (12 mi) north of Kisii and 20 kilometers from Lake Victoria, there's a pelicanry, where pink-backed pelicans nest in large fig trees, and there is continuous coming and going as adults bring food from the lake for their young. The season runs from August to March, and the best time to visit is between October and January.

Kisumu and Lake Victoria

Arriving and Departing

By Plane and Train
Kenya Airways has daily service from Nairobi to Kisumu, and you can also make the journey by train.

By Car
The 80 kilometers (50 mi) of B1 from Kericho to Kisumu, on a paved road, makes a most enjoyable drive through varied country. After leaving the Kericho highlands, 20 kilometers (12 mi) west of the town, the road suddenly drops down an 800-meter (2,645-ft) escarpment to the Victoria basin. The view of the lake from the top of the Nandi escarpment with a foreground of acacia bush and sugarcane makes an outstanding photograph.

Exploring

➓ **Kisumu** is located on the eastern shore of Lake Victoria, the legendary source of the Nile and the largest lake in Africa. The lake is freshwater, but there is a history of volcanic eruptions whose effect can still be seen on such islands as Mfangano and Rusinga, where extraordinary fossils 16 million years old are preserved. The alkalinity from volcanoes helps preserve bones, and, when the alkalinity is extreme, even flesh and patterns of feathers. Findings at Rusinga include the breast-feather patterns of birds. Rusinga Island is special to the Luo people because Tom Mboya, a leading proponent of an independent Kenya, is buried here.

The **Luo** are the second largest tribe in Kenya after the Kikuyu, and they are hard workers. They are expert fishermen; mornings are the best time to see their brightly painted boats at work. The basic design of these boats has remained unchanged for centuries. Away from the lake, the Luo herd cattle and are subsistence farmers growing maize and beans. In recent years they have also made a success of growing rice at Ahero and sugar in the Chemelil area. The women, who also work the land, are known throughout Kenya for their large and expertly made clay pots.

Because much of this part of western Kenya is densely populated and cultivated, you should not expect to see much wildlife. There are usually some hippos about 3 kilometers (2 mi)
south of Kisumu in the area near Impala Park, which also has a
few Vervet monkeys, striped ground squirrels, and impala.

There are many boats for rent at the Kisumu town jetty; but it
is recommended that bookings for small boats be made through
one of the main hotels. A small ship leaves Kisumu every day
except Thursday for a cruise around the Kavirondo Gulf. This
ship stops at Kendu Bay, Homa Bay, and Asembo. The *Victoria*, a larger, well-equipped vessel, leaves Kisumu once a week
for a five-day safari, calling at Musoma, Mwanza, Bukoba, and
Port Bell.

The many bird sanctuaries near Kisumu make good side trips
to the area. The most interesting site is 11 kilometers (7 mi)
east of Kisumu on B1 toward Ahero. Because it is rather difficult to find, it is best to ask final directions from locals at the
signpost KSI 119–KER 78. The **great heronry near Kisumu** is
an "extraordinary spectacle" (to quote Sir Fredrick Jackson,
who visited it in 1901) and has been described as one of Kenya's
greatest birding sights. African spoonbills, sacred ibis, yellow-
billed storks, cormorants, and open-billed storks can all be seen
nesting in the same tree. Black-headed heron, great white
egret, cattle egret, and yellow-billed egret are also present,
though the number of birds and the proportion of species vary
from year to year. The nesting period coincides with the long
rains, beginning in March or April, and continues until July.
Outside this period, however, there are few birds.

Sixteen kilometers (10 mi) east of Kisumu on B1, a right turn
takes you down a rough road to a marketplace; a second right
here brings you to the **sacred ibis colony,** after about 2 kilometers (1.2 mi). There are usually several hundred pairs of birds,
with up to 30 nests in the same tree. The birds are very tame
and seem to pose.

The lakeshore immediately south of Kisumu is not accessible
via vehicle, but in areas off the usual tourist circuit, at settlements farther along the lake, you can see much of the way of life
of the Luo people on a rewarding detour. Take B1 from Kisumu
for 24 kilometers (15 mi), to Ahero; from here follow A1 for 10
❶ kilometers (6 mi) before turning right on C19 to **Kendu Bay.**

There are many small fishing communities along the shore of
the bay, and most of the people seem delighted to talk to foreigners. The boats leave at dawn, returning with the lake
breeze around midday. For a small payment (about $5) many
fishermen will be happy to take you with them; however, the
boats are not built for comfort (there are no toilet facilities),
and it is advisable to take drinking water with you. The brightly painted boats with large, triangular sails and upturned
prows make a striking sight.

The shore of Lake Victoria, especially the papyrus beds adjacent to Kendu Bay, is a fine area for some of East Africa's spectacular waterbirds, including fish eagles, hammerkops, yellow-
billed storks, cormorants, ibis, and a whole range of other species. Several local birds are found here, including the yellow-
backed weaver, swamp flycatcher, Papyrus canary, and the
stunning black-headed gonolek with a brilliant red breast. The
large fig trees in Impala Park attract western Kenyan special-

ties like the African hobby and the Eastern grey plantain-eater, and large flocks of bishops and weavers are seen around the many small farms just outside town; they wear their best plumage from April to November.

Lake Sindi, contained in a volcanic crater framed by wooded hills, is another area known to ornithologists. Rich in blue-green algae (the lesser flamingo's main food), this lake is home to thousands of these birds. To get there, drive west from Kendu Bay on C19, toward Homa Bay; after 4 kilometers (2 mi) turn left down D219 toward Pala; 3 kilometers (1.9 mi) along this road turn left again at the Lake Sindi marker; it is 2 kilometers (1 mi) to the lake.

About 27 kilometers (17 mi) farther along C19 from Kendu Bay is **Homa Bay,** which is the administrative center for the district; there is a small airstrip and regular motorboat service to Kisumu, and the Homa Bay Hotel offers an alternative base from which to explore the area.

The Lambwe Valley is easily accessible, approximately one hour's drive west along C19 from Homa Bay. The **Lambwe Valley Game Reserve** consists mostly of grasslands, acacia bush, and seasonal swamp. It is famous for its population of roan antelope, found virtually nowhere else in Kenya. Other local species include Jackson's hartebeest, oribi, and Rothschild's giraffe. Birds are colorful and abundant. One word of warning: Tsetse flies can be present in large numbers; take along a good insect repellent.

From Homa Bay C19 continues westward to Mbita and **Rusinga Island,** long known for its fossils. The remains of *Proconsul africanus*, a 16-million-year-old ape, were discovered here by Louis and Mary Leakey in the late 1940s. The ape is now thought to be a Miocene ancestor, a significant step in the course of human evolution. The island is also a major fishing center; hundreds of traditional Luo boats can be seen here.

A new fishing operation on Rusinga Island now gives sportsmen an opportunity to try for the enormous Nile perch in Lake Victoria (the record catch weighed 501 pounds). African Explorations Ltd. operates five powered fishing boats, and fish weighing well over 100 pounds are regularly caught. The boats depart from a base camp at the west end of the Island early each morning, returning around noon. Bookings should be made in advance through Signet Hotels (tel. Nairobi 723776). Daily flights from Masai Mara Game Reserve to Rusinga Island specifically for fishing trips can be booked through Kichwa Tembo, Signet Hotels; flights from Nanyuki can be arranged through Flame Tree Safaris (*see* Chapter 1).

Kakamega Forest

Arriving and Departing

The forest is reached by traveling north up A1 from Kisumu to a turning 9.5 kilometers (6 mi) south of Kakamega town, at a sign reading *Arap Moi Secondary Girls School*, and continue for 11 kilometers (7 mi) to the Kakamega Forest Station sign; turn left and drive 1 kilometer (.6 mi) down this track. Park

your car by the office and follow the grid system of footpaths
that begin here.

Exploring

🔞 **Kakamega Forest** is the only area of Central African rain forest
in Kenya, and to most of us that means *jungle*. It is of particular
interest to ornithologists, who travel here from all over the
world.

Bird-watching in a tropical forest can be most frustrating, as
their song is everywhere but few can actually be seen among
the dense tangle of leaves and towering trees. Perseverance is
the answer; the longer you look, the more you see. Almost 60
species of birds found here cannot be found elsewhere in Kenya, including the magnificent great blue turaco, black-billed
turaco, huge black- and white-casqued hornbills, Sabine's
spinetail, blue-headed bee-eater, brown-eared woodpecker,
shrike flycatcher, red-headed malimbe, bar-tailed trogons, metallic sunbirds, and many other colorful families such as barbets, wattle-eyes, and weavers.

A walk in this forest for the nonbirder is also a rewarding experience. Huge trees, tangled vines, and dense undergrowth offer a thousand shades of green. Three species of monkey can be
seen: blue- and red-tailed are often in close association with
each other, but it is the rare black and white colobus that are
the most spectacular as they leap and glide through the forest
canopy. If you're adventurous and lucky, a night walk with a
guide from the forest station might turn up such specialties as
bush babies (potto) and flying squirrels.

Mornings are the best time to visit this forest, when butterflies
can be numerous, hidden birds are singing everywhere, and the
far-carrying growls of the colobus reverberate through the
trees.

The town of Kakamega is a thriving center that began as a gold-
rush town. Today it is the administration center of the district.
The sprawling, open-air **Kakamega market** is a good place to
wander for an hour or so, observing the comings and goings.
The squawking chickens, jumble of household goods, baskets,
clay pots, and brightly colored clothes are typical of what many
of us imagine an African market to be. **Kakamega Pottery** is a
small local enterprise that makes modern-style plates, dishes,
cups, and saucers using an interesting and varied range of
glaze techniques. It is out of town just beyond the market.

Because Kakamega Forest is a scenic and unique part of Kenya,
many visitors spend two or three days there (*see* Dining and
Lodging, *below*). If you prefer to return to Kisumu, you can go
directly (50 km [30 mi] by C39) or take a longer route back by a
detour to **Kapsabet**. This choice offers good views of the Nandi
escarpment, and from Kapsabet a paved road—C37—winds
through tea and coffee estates to the town of **Nandi Hills**. From
here the road sweeps down the spectacular and beautiful
Nyando escarpment, giving splendid views of the valley below.
It then passes through the sugar estates around **Chemelil**, the
most important in the country. A right turn at the intersection
just after the Chemilil Sugar Factory leads to C34 and an easy
drive back to Kisumu. This road passes close under the peak

from which, according to legend, wrongdoers were hurled to their deaths.

Kitale and Luhya Country

Arriving and Departing

By Plane The Kitale airstrip accommodates regular flights to and from Nairobi.

By Train Kitale's is Kenya's most northerly railway stop.

By Car If you drive 60 kilometers (36 mi) north out of Kakamega on A1, you will come to Webuye, and 46 kilometers (29 mi) farther on, to Kitale—a total of about 110 kilometers (68 mi).

Exploring

⓯ The road to **Kitale,** after climbing the Nandi escarpment, passes through the undulating farmlands of the Luhya people. Many traditional homes are scattered among the hillsides, which are strewn with large granite boulders. Kitale, at an altitude of 1,900 meters (6,230 ft), is the center of an area often described as "the granary of Kenya" owing to the large acreage of maize grown there.

Luhya is a generic term for the 18 or more tribes of the Bantu people—more than 1 million of them—who farm this area northeast of Lake Victoria. Many families can trace their genealogy back more than 500 years (more than 20 generations). Luhya legend has it they migrated from Egypt and Sudan about 250 years ago, earlier than the Luo, who settled farther south. Like the Luo, they have a complex series of initiation ceremonies, which remain important events throughout their lives. Most of the subtribes practice circumcision, and some also remove two teeth from the lower jaw, again like the Luo. They are primarily farmers of maize, tea, coffee, and dairy products.

The small **Kitale Museum,** an annex of the Kenya National Museums, has been largely ignored by tourists; however, several recent developments make it well worth a visit. A new exhibit on human evolution in East Africa opened in 1989. An exhibit on biogas shows how waste matter from animals (in this case cows) can be fermented in a large vat, producing gases for cooking and heating. At the entrance note the colorful murals by American photographer Carol Beckwith.

The museum has its own 30-acre nature reserve, where the rare De Brazza's monkey can be seen (one of only three known sites in Kenya). Birds are plentiful, tree species are marked for identification, and an informative guide can show you around on request. The museum library is well stocked with books on natural history.

On land adjacent to the museum are traditional houses representative of western Kenyan peoples: the Turkana, West Pokot, Elgon Masai, Luhya, Luo, and Nandi.

Excursions from Kitale

Mt. Elgon National Park (described in Chapter 3), is about 25 kilometers (16 mi) west of Kitale. It is worth a visit for the view from Mt. Elgon's summit and to see its unique system of caves, including Kitum cave, mined by elephants for salt. Much of the park is dense montane forest where it can be difficult to see the animals, but if you drive around slowly and quietly, you should eventually succeed. The species most frequently seen are elephant, African buffalo, bushbuck, Genet cat, warthog, bush pig, tree Hyrax, Rock Hyrax, greater galage, Colobus, and blue monkey.

Saiwa Swamp National Park, a small park 24 kilometers (15 mi) north of Kitale on A1, is home to sitatunga, a rare, swamp-dwelling antelope with long hooves. For more details, see Chapter 3.

The **Kongelai escarpment** is a delightful place to spend a day; the escarpment road takes you from 2,000 meters (6,550 ft) down to 1,000 meters (3,280 ft). To get there, drive north along A1 from Kitale to Makutano for 34 kilometers (22 mi). Turn left through Makutano town on D344, the escarpment road. Although four-wheel-drive vehicles are not necessary for this safari, a sturdy, reliable car should be used.

The area is famous for its birds, and there are also enough rich vegetation, local tribes, and views to fascinate most visitors. From the farmlands, the road descends through open woodland and is crossed by several densely forested valleys, the habitat of the white-crested turaco. Farmlands give way to fields where herdsmen tend sheep and goats. The heat is noticeable at the bottom of the escarpment, but many fine fig trees bordering the *lugga* on the right of the road offer excellent shade for a picnic. Driving farther north toward Kongelai, the climate changes again, becoming hotter and more arid. Acacia thornbush dominates the landscape and nomadic herdsmen tend not only goats and cattle but also camels.

About 40 kilometers (25 mi) east of Kitale lie the **Cherangani Hills**, 80 kilometers (50 mi) long, 30 kilometers (18 mi) wide, and rising to more than 3,300 meters (10,825 ft). There are two interesting safaris to take: one traveling around the hills and the other over them.

The **Pokot,** who live north and east of the Cheranganis, are pastoralists and can be seen herding their cattle, goats, and (in the drier areas) camels. West of the Cherangani Hills, the Pokot grow crops, mainly millet. The hills are comparatively wet and fertile, and the success of crops is further ensured by terracing and irrigation.

In spite of their similarity to the Nilo-Hamitic Turkana, the Pokot are a Kalenjin tribe. Like other Kalenjins, they practice circumcision as part of their initiation ceremonies. Perhaps because of close contact with their Turkana neighbors, the Pokot have a similar style of dress; however, their language and customs are quite different.

The main attractions of the drive **around the hills** are the spectacular scenery, the feeling of being away from the normal tourist route, and the opportunity to meet the colorful Pokot people. Take A1 north from Kitale to Kapenguria. From here

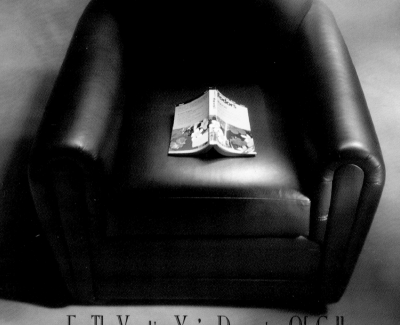

You've Let Your Imagination Go, Now Get Up And Follow Your Dreams.

For The Vacation You're Dreaming Of, Call American Express® Travel Agency At 1-800-YES-AMEX.*

American Express will send more than your imagination soaring. We'll fly you, sail you, drive you to any Fodor's destination and beyond. Because American Express believes the best vacations happen from Europe to the Orient, Walt Disney®World to Hawaii and everywhere in between.

For dependable service, expert advice, and value wherever your dreams take you, call on American Express. After all, the best traveling companion is a trustworthy friend.

It's easy to recognize a good place when you see one.

American Express Cardmembers have been doing it for years.

The secret? Instead of just relying on what they see in the window, they look at the door. If there's an American Express Blue Box on it, they know they've found an establishment that cares about high standards.

Whether it's a place to eat, to sleep, to shop, or simply meet, they know they will be warmly welcomed.

So much so, they're rarely taken in by anything else.

Always a good sign.

the newly paved road descends through the **Marich Pass,** leaving behind the rich farming country of the western highlands. The terrain is breathtaking. The forested Cheranganis rise steeply on the right, with panoramic views across the northern semidesert lands to the left and ahead. From the bottom of the pass, cross the new bridge and, after about 2 kilometers (1 mi), turn right for Sigor and Tot. From here the road is accessible only by four-wheel-drive vehicles, and you should be well equipped with plenty of food and drinking water.

Sigor is a market center for friendly Pokot, who are a pleasure to meet along the route. Continuing south along the foot of the Cheranganis, the road crosses small rivers where many large fig trees provide excellent shade for picnics and camping. The road passes through the tiny villages of Lomut, Chesogon, Cheblil, and Tot, where you may take a left fork through the Kito Pass and on to Lake Baringo, Nakuru, and Nairobi. However, our chosen route continues south to Chesongoch, along the bottom of the imposing Elgeyo escarpment. From Chesongoch, the steep and rocky road climbs the escarpment to Chesoi, a dramatic drive where scenes in the movie *Living Free* were filmed. The views to the east across the Kerio Valley and Tugen Hills are outstanding.

From the top at Chesoi the road becomes much easier and continues through farmland and forests of magnificent trees nearly 30 meters (98 feet) tall. The road through Laboot and Kapcherop is the main route to Kitale, but you may prefer to go south and then west through Chebiemit to Eldoret.

For a drive to the **World's End**—the highest point on the Elgeyo escarpment—take the road southeast from Eldoret for Kaptagat, through the Kaptagat Forest, as far as Chepkorio 32 kilometers (20 mi). Turn left along a narrow farm road (muddy and impassable in the rains) for 3 or 4 kilometers (2 or 3 mi) and follow a track bringing you to the rim of the escarpment. World's End is a rocky outlook next to a small, remote mission chapel. The view east from a height of 29,000 meters—of the whole Kerio Valley, the Tugen Hills and the 64-kilometer (40-mi) width of the Rift Valley to the Laikipia plateau—is unforgettable.

The route **over the Cherangani Hills** should be followed only in a four-wheel-drive vehicle. Drive north from Kitale on A1 5 kilometers (3 mi) to Mukatano; after Mukatano, turn right toward the village of Kabichbich. Travelers may stay in the sparsely furnished **Kabichbich Guest House** here; the key is available from the District Commissioner's Office, Kapenguria.

The road zigzags through montane forest to bare rocky summits, passing close to **Kipsait Peak** at 3,000 meters (9,840 ft), then drops toward Laboot, where there are patches of cultivation. From Laboot, a rough road leads northeast, giving access to the 3,340-meter (10,960-ft) peak of Kalelaigelat and the northern end of the range. This is a good route into the heart of the hills for those who wish to do some mountain trekking or visit the forests. The return to Kitale is via Kapcherop and Cherangani Village.

Lake Baringo

Arriving and Departing

Lake Baringo is easily reached in three hours from Nairobi by driving north through Nakuru and then straight up the newly paved B4. For those traveling from the west, a scenic and new paved road, C51, goes from near Eldoret and to Marigat, 18 kilometers (11 mi) southwest of the lake.

Exploring

16 Three tribes live around **Lake Baringo;** the **Pokot** (*see* Kitale and Luhya Country, above) inhabit the north and east, herding livestock. To the south, fishing the lake, are the **Njemps,** close relatives of the Masai. These people speak a language similar to that of the Masai, wear similar ocher clothing, and have many of the same initiation ceremonies. Like the Masai, they are herdsmen with large numbers of cows, sheep, and goats. But they also make small canoes from the ambatch plant and use these set nets and long lines to catch both tilapia and catfish. The third tribe, the **Tugen,** are part of the Kalenjin group; they live on the west side of the lake and in the hills that bear their name.

In the vicinity of the lake, at 975 meters (3,185 ft), the landscape is predominantly dry acacia thornscrub peopled with herdsmen. Climbing the hills toward Kabarnet, the land becomes more fertile; dairy cattle can be seen, and a wide variety of crops are grown, including maize and beans.

Lake Baringo is a freshwater lake covering approximately 168 square kilometers (104 sq. mi) on the floor of the Great Rift Valley. The imposing Laikipia escarpment runs north–south to the east of the lake; much smaller, but impressive, basalt cliffs are found to the west. Both escarpments are evidence of shifting faults. Beyond these the Tugen Hills climb to 2,500 meters (8,203 ft).

This is the area where geologist J. W. Gregory did part of his famous 1893 survey, which determined that this valley was not cut by erosion or water, like the Grand Canyon, but by shifting faults, the best example of which Gregory found at Baringo, on the Kamasia slab. The eastern branch of the Great Rift Valley is named after Gregory: the Gregory Rift extends through Olorgesailie and Olduvai. Of the eastern and western branches, the western rift is the more central pairing of fault lines, which is how a rift valley is defined. It is not the only rift valley in the world—more dramatic examples are underwater—but it is the most spectacular one we can see.

The lake is particularly well known for its birdlife; more than 460 species have been recorded. A boat trip along the shore and around the central islands gives a good opportunity to see and photograph a large variety of waterbirds plus hippos, crocodiles, and boiling volcanic springs.

New roads and expanded accommodations at Lake Baringo have recently attracted people to the area, though it is still unspoiled. Visitors tend to stay close to the two main lodges. For those with camping equipment, a rough road along the eastern side of the lake leads to many suitable sites. At Kampi ya

Samaki on the west side of the lake, **Authentic Goods** has a particularly good collection of local artifacts for sale. At the Roberts Campsite a cottage industry called **Dry Season** makes silk-screened fabrics, brightly colored shirts, shorts, kangas, and kikois. All items are original and handmade.

Not only is there a profusion of East Africa's waterbirds here, but during the northern winter both Baringo and **Lake Bogoria,** 30 kilometers (20 mi) to the south, are stopovers for hundreds of migrants as well. The acacia bush around the lakes is the habitat of hornbills, mousebirds, barbets, weavers, and shrikes. However, it is along the basalt cliffs west of both lakes that some of the most spectacular birds can be seen, notably the Verreaux's eagle. **Lake Bogoria National Reserve,** with the alkaline lake at its center, is described in Chapter 3.

At 975 meters (3,185 ft), Lake Baringo is hot and sometimes **⑰** humid; the **Tugen Hills,** at 2,500 meters (8,200 ft), a one-hour drive to the west, can be a pleasant, cool place to spend a day exploring or to stay overnight.

The route from Baringo heads due south to Marigat, 18 kilometers (11 mi); a right turn just outside the town leads up steep mountain slopes to **Kabarnet,** a total distance of 60 kilometers (37 mi) from Lake Baringo.

Kabarnet, on the summit of the Tugens, is the hometown of current Kenyan president Daniel Arap Moi, of the Kalenjin tribe. Once at Kabarnet, one may choose to turn left or right along the crest of the hills or to go down the steep, twisting new road that leads across the Kerio Valley and on to Eldoret. Whichever route you choose, the views are some of Kenya's finest. Originally thought of as the western side of the Rift Valley, the Tugen Hills are a further tectonic feature, running along the valley parallel to its main outer escarpments.

There are many places along the Tugen range where you can look west across a 1,220-meter (4,000-ft) drop to the floor of the Kerio Valley and the Elgeyo escarpment beyond. From the same spot look east to the lakes sparkling in the haze 1,525 meters (5,000 ft) below.

The new road north of Kabarnet passes through small Tugen farms and patches of montane forest to the village of Kabartonjo 19 kilometers (12 mi) away. An area of forest 3 kilometers (2 mi) before Kabartonjo is particularly good for bird-watching and pleasant, short walks. Beyond Kabartonjo the road is rough, but it eventually joins with B4 half an hour's drive north of Lake Baringo.

A safari into the **Kerio Valley** returns you to a hot climate similar to that of Baringo's, but it is a rewarding drive, with polite and friendly people; huge, castle-like termite mounds; and noisy, colorful birds. It is the closest many visitors will come to unspoiled Kenya.

Seventy kilometers (43.5 mi) north of Baringo, hot water springs emerge from barren ground near the town of **Kapedo** to join a mile-long river and flow over a 9-meter (30-foot) cliff, a hot waterfall. The water continues north as a broad warm river, eventually drying up in the Suguta Valley. Water is scarce in the surrounding country, so most animals are dependent upon this river.

Pelicans, herons, and storks compete with the Turkana children for small fish; farther downstream nomadic herdsmen bring their animals to drink. There is a profusion of frogs and insects, and in the evening baboons and lions come to drink. Dense groves of doum palms along the banks offer shade for picnics and camping, but few visitors to Kapedo venture far from the town, which, because of the local mission station, has grown into a regional center for the southernmost Turkana people. Here, visitors may see something of the way of life of the Turkana without having to travel much farther north. There is a shop in Kapedo selling soft drinks; otherwise visitors to this area should bring their own supplies.

Dining and Lodging

Category	Cost*
Very Expensive	over Kshs. 3,750 ($150)
Expensive	Kshs. 2,500–3,750 ($100–$150)
Moderate	Kshs. 1,250–2,500 ($50–$100)
Inexpensive	under Kshs. 1,250 ($50)

All prices are for a standard double room; excluding hotel tax.

Kakamega **Forest Station Rest House.** Situated at the edge of the forest, this rest house consists of four double rooms built on stilts. Running cold water, beds, blankets, and a kerosene lamp are provided. There are no dining facilities. *Contact Kakamega Forestry Dept., Box 460, tel. Kakamega 20020/20493. No credit cards. Moderate.*
Kakamega Golf Hotel. Located 20 kilometers (12 mi) from the forest, in Kakamega town, clean and comfortable, but take earplugs; at weekends the disco can be deafening. *Contact African Tours Hotels in Nairobi, tel. 2/336858. 62 rooms. Facilities: pool, use of golf course nearby. AE, DC, V. Moderate*

Kericho **Tea Hotel.** Set in attractive gardens, the Tea Hotel offers comfortable accommodations in the old style. *Contact African Tours and Hotels, Ltd., Nairobi, tel. 2/336858, or write Tea Hotel, Box 75, Kericho, tel. 20281. 43 rooms. Facilities: tennis, golf, pool. AE, DC, V. Moderate.*

Kisumu and Lake Victoria **Homa Bay Hotel.** Small and comfortable and located at the edge of Homa Bay town, it provides a reasonable base from which to explore this interesting area. *Contact AT and H in Nairobi, tel. 2/336858. 21 rooms. AE, DC, V. Moderate.*
Imperial Hotel. This new hotel in the center of town has an impressive lobby and comfortable rooms. There is a good selection of curries in the main dining room. *Contact Imperial Hotel, tel. Kisumu 41485. 70 rooms. Facilities: pool, health club. AE, DC, V. Inexpensive.*
New Kisumu Hotel. This modern hotel overlooking Lake Victoria has 75 rooms. *Box 1690, Kisumu, tel. 40559. AE, DC. Inexpensive.*
Sunset Hotel. This modern concrete-block hotel is 2 kilometers (1 mi) from the center of Kisumu, on the shore. All rooms are comfortable and have private bathrooms and excellent views of the lake. Whole grilled tilapia Luo style is an excellent fish

dish, which is served at poolside. Guests may use Kisumu golf course, 5 kilometers away. *Contact AT and H in Nairobi, tel. 2/336858. 50 rooms. AE, DC, V. Inexpensive.*

Kitale **Kitale Club.** Though worn, this is still the most comfortable place to stay in Kitale. *Box 3758, Kitale, tel. Kitale 47832. 25 rooms. Facilities: restaurant, bar; golf, tennis, squash. No credit cards. Moderate.*

For those who would prefer to stay in a farmhouse-type lodging and meet some long-standing Kenyan residents, there are two little-known alternatives.

Lokitela Farm. This working farm offers friendly and informal accommodations for about 10 guests. The hosts, Tony and Adrianne Mills, can give details about a wide variety of excursions in the area. They also offer a guided trip around the farm and a day safari with picnic up Mt. Elgon. There is a small, thickly wooded river on the farm where birds are abundant; large flocks of Eurasian white storks are often found on the open farm fields between November and March. The farm is reached on a rather rough road that starts by Marshall's Garage in Kitale town. The Lokitela sign is visible on the left after 18 kilometers (11 mi). *Write Box 122, Kitale. No credit cards. Moderate.*

Sirikwa Safaris, Guest House and Campsite. Along the A1 road to Kapenguria, 24 kilometers (15 mi) north of Kitale near Saiwa Swamp National Park, lies this small farmhouse run by the Barnley family. Although the land is no longer farmed, the house has much of the farm's character and hominess. There are two double rooms within the house (with shared bathrooms), and three double furnished tents in the garden. Camping is also allowed in the garden for those with their own equipment. Wholesome, locally grown food is served in the house. Guides are available for a wide variety of excursions, including visits to Saiwa Swamp, Kongeli escarpment, Kakamega Forest, the Cherangani Hills, and the Marich Pass. *Contact J. Barnley, Box 332, Kitale. No credit cards. Moderate.*

Lake Baringo **Island Camp.** This luxurious tented camp with private bathrooms and hot showers is located on Ol Kokwe Island, in the middle of the lake. A friendly staff and enthusiastic hosts offer personal attention. *Contact Abercrombie & Kent, Bruce House, Nairobi, tel. 2/506139, 2/502491, fax 2/502739; U.S., tel. 800/323-7308. 22 double luxury tents, 2 cottages. Facilities: pool, escorted boat trips, waterskiing. AE, MC, V. Expensive.*

Lake Baringo Club. Set on the western shore of the lake in beautiful gardens, the Club offers a high standard of food, service, and accommodations. A free welcome-drink is presented upon your arrival, and a resident naturalist is there to give you up-to-date information on all aspects of ecology of the area. There is an airstrip 2 kilometers (1.3 mi) away. *Contact Block Hotels, Box 47557, Nairobi, tel. 2/331635. 49 rooms. Facilities: pool, gameroom, guided boat trips, safaris to Lake Bogoria, escorted daily bird walks, camel rides, visits to a nearby Njemp manyatta. AE, DC,V. Expensive.*

Saruni Camp. This is a private camp on the north end of Ol Kokwe Island, with only 8 double tents. The camp is reached by canoe, and there are boats and guides available for hire, as well as waterskiing. A barge on the water is the setting for dinner and breakfast, and by prior arrangement it can be towed around the lake for private parties. *Flamingo Tours, Box*

44899, Nairobi, tel. 2/228961; fax 2/333262. Expensive. No credit cards.

Kabarnet Hotel. High on the Tugen Hills, 1 kilometer (.6 mi) north of Kabarnet town, Kabarnet Hotel offers clean, reasonable accommodations. *Contact AT and H, Box 30471, Nairobi, tel. 2/336858. 29 Rooms. Facilities: pool. MC, V. Moderate.*

Robert's Campsite and Bandas. Situated between the village of Kampi ya Samaki and Lake Baringo Club, this is a well-run campsite where you can watch hippos walking past your tent on moonlit nights. Showers, toilets, and drinking water are provided. There are also three two-person bandas and two large houses for rent. *Contact Mrs. Roberts, Box 1051, Nakuru. No phone. No credit cards. Inexpensive.*

Lake Naivasha   **Longonot Game Ranch.** This ranch has spectacular views of the lake and Hell's Gate, as it perches on a lower slope of Mt. Longonot. Formerly the home of writer Martha Gellhorn (one of Hemingway's wives), the ranch house has three elegant double rooms, a dining room, lounge, and veranda. Guests can be met at the Naivasha airport. Tented camping within the Longonot Game Reserve can be arranged here, and Grant Stephenson, the owner, organizes horseback riding, walking safaris, and game drives. *Box 43341, Nairobi, tel. 2/332132, 2/726209, or 2/891168; fax 2/22380. Very Expensive.*

Lake Naivasha Hotel. This long-established lodge is a popular luncheon stop, where lavish buffets are served between noon and 2 PM. The hotel's facilities include a swimming pool, a small health club, a gift shop, and horseback riding. You can also arrange for a boat trip to Crescent Island (130 Kshs. per person) or for a cruise on the lake (350 Kshs. per hour for 8 people). *Book at New Stanley House Arcade, Standard St., Nairobi, Box 47557, tel. 2/335807. Expensive.*

Safariland Lodge. This lakefront lodge offers standard double rooms, private cottages, and tented camping. Its facilities include a swimming pool and horseback riding. *Tel. 0311/20241. Expensive.*

Fisherman's Camp. In this lovely setting beneath yellow-barked acacias, the accommodations include four bandas and tents for rent, or you can pay a small fee to set up your own. Firewood and basic staples are for sale, and rowboats can be rented. *Book in Nairobi, tel. 2/720382. Moderate.*

8 Mombasa and the Kenya Coast

Introduction

By Richard Wilding and Delta Willis

Former curator of the Fort Jesus Museum in Mombasa, Richard Wilding is an East African historian.

While much of Kenya entices you with wildlife, the coastal towns exude the history of a unique culture. Arab traders who came to these shores thousands of years ago brought Islam to Africa, and the coastal streets are dominated by a different dress and architecture from what you see in other parts of Kenya. While the coast may also boast extraordinary wildlife and exceptional beaches, its essence is found in the people of these ancient ports, which gave rise to Swahili culture and language—thought to be a combination of foreign influences such as Arabic on the African Bantu. Millions of people in East Africa today speak Swahili, and it is the national language of both Kenya and Tanzania.

The merger of languages was based on another factor: Arab traders often married African women. The coast maintains a vastly international mix, with many residents from India and Germany, pastoralists from Somalia, and Southeast Asians. The excellent local cuisine reflects the rich maritime traditions of boat-building and fishing maintained by its inhabitants.

Ironically, water is a problem in these cities. Ancient towns have an abundance of wells; water for the city of Mombasa is piped all the way from Mzima Springs, in Tsavo West National Park.

Lamu town to the north is the best-preserved Swahili town; cars are not allowed in the inner city, where the "streets" are narrow, winding alleyways, a maze of houses set tight against one another, many with beautifully carved doors. Doors are built first, then the house constructed around them. By the same token, a mosque is built first, and the town constructed around it.

Islam spread from the coast to the inner cities, evidence of which may be seen in the predominance of the Muslim dress and customs. (Mosques are in daily use; wear appropriate clothing when visiting one. Men should cover their heads, and women their arms and legs. Remove your shoes. Generally, on the streets of coastal towns, revealing shorts and tops on either men or women are discouraged.)

Friday mosques (so called because the Muslim Sabbath is on Friday) are at the heart of every coastal town, and ruins of these mosques dot the coastline. You can see ruins north of Mombasa, including Jumba, a 15th-century Swahili town, and Gedi, a 45-acre site that is also a national park.

Just north of Lamu are the ancient ruins of Shanga, a town with a well-preserved Friday mosque at its center. The 21-acre site, cleared in 1980 as a joint project of Operation Drake and the National Museums of Kenya, uncovered the remaining coral walls of 160 houses, two palaces, three mosques, and hundreds of tombs. Archaeologists found pottery, glass, and gold by sieving hundreds of tons of soil from 15 excavation sites.

The origins of Shanga are still under investigation, but a legend among the people of neighboring Siyu Island is that the town was founded by Chinese traders from Shanghai—thus the name Shanga. The Swahili word for tea, *chai*, is the same in Mandarin, and Chinese porcelain has been found among the ruins. The best record of maritime trade, however, is from Arab historians.

The more recent influence of the Portuguese dominates in Mombasa, Kenya's second largest city. Mombasa was once the gateway to British East Africa, when people arrived and departed by ship. Mombasa now has an international airport.

Essential Information

Before You Go

Most international and Nairobi-based tour companies are well informed about facilities on the coast. During the peak season, and especially for the Christian New Year holidays and Christmas, hotel bookings should be made months in advance.

Arriving and Departing

By Train The journey between Nairobi and Mombasa is one of the most popular overnight train trips in the world. You can gaze out your window at gazelle and zebra on the plains and dine in elegance. Services are reliable and comfortable.

Two trains leave Nairobi for Mombasa every day. The first is the "slow train," which departs at 5 PM. The "express," departs at 7 PM. Both are punctual, arriving in Mombasa at 7:30 and 8 AM, respectively. A train also leaves Mombasa for Nairobi every day.

Accommodations include upright seats in third class; four or six seats that fold down into bunks in second class, and two folding seats in first class. Small lavatories are included in first and second class; toilets are at the end of the car. The beds are made up while you are in the dining car. You should expect to pay for extra bedding, which you may need since the nights are cool.

The dining cars are old-fashioned, cooled by ceiling fans, and paneled in wood; dinner is served on linen; and some of the silverware is marked with the initials of the railroad's previous names, such as East African Railway and Harbours. Buy tickets for your dinner from the employee who sit just outside the dining car before the train departs Nairobi station. There are two sittings, one shortly after the train leaves and another at 9 PM. The first sitting is better. British food is usually served; the portions are generous but overcooked. Drinks can be served in the cabins. Breakfast is between 6 and 7:30 AM. The price for a single bed in first class, one way, is Kshs. 500, or around $25; for a first-class two-berth compartment, Kshs. 454, or around $23, per person. Dinner, drinks, and extra bedding are additional.

There are taxis at the Mombasa station, or you can arrange to be met if you've made reservations with a hotel. Rental cars should be booked in advance, before leaving Nairobi.

By Bus Regularly scheduled buses make the six- to eight-hour journey to Mombasa from Nairobi. These are not luxury buses, nor are they always safe. It is, however, the most inexpensive way to reach Mombasa, at around Kshs. 120 one way. **Coast Bus, Malindi,** and **Tana River Services** have offices in Nairobi, Mombasa, and Malindi. Also try **R.V.P. Bus Service Ltd.** (Nairobi, tel. 2/26374).

By Plane **Moi International Airport,** 16 kilometers (10 mi) west of Mombasa town, is served by **Air Rwanda, British Airways** (tel. 800/247–9297), and **Sabena** (tel. 800/955–2000). It has banks, restaurants, car-rental and hotel booking services. Customs and immigration are here, as is a helpful information center. Hotels where you have made reservations will send a minibus to meet you. Taxi fees must be negotiated beforehand; they may be as high as Kshs. 250 per person. **Kenatco** is the most reliable.

Onward flights to Malindi and Lamu are offered by **Air Kenya;** Kenya Airways flies to Malindi only. You can also fly directly to both from Nairobi. The Lamu airstrip is on the mainland; passengers staying at Peponi's Hotel will be met by a dhow. Other boats are available for crossing to Lamu Island. Negotiate the fee before getting on; it should be about Kshs. 25.

International Airlines with offices in Mombasa: **Air Rwanda,** Biashara Bank Bldg., Nyerere Ave., Box 88660, tel. 11/26045; **British Airways,** Ambalal House, Box 90045, tel. 11/312427; **Sabena,** Moi Ave., Box 84972, tel. 11/26895, 21995.

Domestic and charter airlines include: **Air Kenya Aviation,** Moi International Airport, Box 84700, Mombasa, tel. 11/433320/32; and Lamu Rd., or Box 133, Malindi, tel. (town) 20524, (airport) 123/20888. **Kenya Airways,** Savani House, Digo Rd., Mombasa, or Box 90032, tel. 11/21251; and Box 634, Malindi, tel. (town) 123/20237, (airport) 123/20574. **Cooper Skybird,** Ambalal House, Nkrumah Rd., Mombasa, or Box 99222, Mombasa, tel. (town) 11/21443, (airport) 11/433548; Lamu Rd., Box 146, Malindi, tel. (town), 11/20860, (airport) 11/20981; Lamu office: tel. 121/55; and Ukunda office: tel. 1261/2096. **Skyways Airlines,** Moi Ave., Mombasa, tel. 11/432167; Lamu, tel. 121/3226; and Malindi, tel. 123/20253.

By Car The highway from Nairobi to Mombasa is good, and the scenery is beautiful. Also, car rental is often cheaper in Nairobi than in Mombasa. The drive may take from four to six hours, and there are good service stations near Voi.

Getting Around

By Taxi Taxis in Mombasa and Malindi are, by most standards, inexpensive. All prices are negotiable, and the difference between charges for locals and visitors can be outrageous. You must bargain. The drivers are friendly and helpful. They will wait or return to collect you if you ask. **Kenatco** offers good, if more expensive, services.

By Minibus There is a network of *matatus* (vans named after the three old pennies that used to be the fare). Matatus are numerous and cheap, but dangerous. They are also overcrowded and often have pop music blaring through loud-speakers. Matatus are not recommended.

By Bus A regular network of scheduled buses travels up and down the main coast roads, up to the Kwale area and back to Kaloleni and the hills behind the north coast. There are **Coast Bus Garissa Express** (Bondeni, Mombasa tel. 11/314528), **Malindi, Tana River Services,** and **Tawakal Bus** (Bondeni, Mombasa, tel. 11/3106).

Car Rental There are several good car-rental firms and this list is only a sample. Visitors will find the prices high, but the services good. **Budget,** Moi Ave., Mombasa, or Box 99483, Mombasa, tel. 11/24600, 24062, 24065; and Inside Africa offices at Severin Sea Lodge and Diani. **Avis,** Moi Ave., Mombasa, tel. 11/23048, 20465; and Sitawi House, Malindi, tel. 123/20513. **Hertz,** Moi Ave., Mombasa, tel. 11/316333, 316235; Nyali Beach Hotel, Mombasa Beach Hotel, Travelers, Bamburi Beach Hotel, Severin Sea Lodge, Whitesands Hotel, Diani Reef Hotel, Jadini Beach Hotel, Lagoon Reef Hotel, and Safari Beach Hotel, or Box 365, Malindi, tel. 123/20069. **Coast Car Hire,** Ambalal House, Mikindani Rd., Mombasa, or Box 99143, Mombasa, tel. 11/24891, 311225; Malindi office: Box 146, Malindi, tel. 123/20861. **Across Africa Safaris,** Moi Ave., or Box 82139, Mombasa, tel. 11/21951, 311453. **Ocean Car Hire,** Digo Rd., Mombasa, or Box 85798, Mombasa, tel. 11/312977, 313559.

Guided Tours

Excursions to game parks and museums are within a short drive of most hotels. Taxi drivers are often well informed on local attractions. Most hotels and the museums at Gedi and Lamu offer good guides, and the following tour companies can assist you with excursions:

United Touring Company, Moi Ave., Mombasa, or Box 84782, Mombasa, tel. 11/316333/4, 316235/6; Harambee Rd., Malindi, or Box 365, Malindi, tel. 123/20040; Hotel desks: Mombasa Beach, Travellers, Nyali Beach, Serena Beach, Severin Sea Lodge, Trade Winds, Whitesands, Diani Reef, Jadini Beach, Lawfords, Turtle Bay. **Pollmans Tours and Safaris,** Moi Ave., Mombasa, or Box 84198, Mombasa, tel. 11/316732, 314381; Lamu Rd., Malindi, or Box 384, Malindi, tel. 123/20128, 10820; Hotel desks: Robinson Baobab, Nyali Beach, Bamburi Beach, Whitesands, Travellers, Severin Sea Lodge, Watamu Beach, Diani Reef, Jadini, Safari Beach, Lagoon Reef, Neptune Village. **Flamingo Tours,** Ambalal House, Mombasa, or Box 83321, Mombasa, tel. 11/311978, 315635. **Gupta Tours,** Moi Ave., Mombasa, or Box 83451, Mombasa, tel. 11/311302, 311182; South Coast office: tel. 1261/2006. **Lofty Safaris,** Nkrumah Rd., Mombasa, or Box 80629, Mombasa, tel. 11/314397. **Ocean Car Hire and Tours,** Digo Rd., Mombasa, or Box 85798, Mombasa, tel. 11/312977, 313559. **Universal Safaris,** Ambalal House, Mombasa, or Box 99456, Mombasa, tel. 11/316576, 314174.

Many of the travel agents can also offer tours: **Bunson Travel,** Moi Ave., Mombasa, or Box 90291, Mombasa, tel. 11/311331, 24115; Malindi office: tel. 123/20095. **Eagle Travel,** Makadara Rd., Mombasa, or Box 80700, Mombasa, tel. 11/25445, 26437, 311965; **Inside Africa,** Moi Ave., Mombasa, or Box 99483, Mombasa, tel. 11/24600, 11/24062, 11/24065; Diani office: Diani Sea Lodge, tel. 1261/2114, 2060; and North Coast office: Severin Sea Lodge, tel. 11/485001. **Noor Travels,** Baluchi St., Mombasa, or Box 90012, tel. 11/313276, 313744.

Staying Healthy

A major danger is dehydration. You must drink several quarts of nonalcoholic beverages to maintain the level of body fluids. In general the tap water is potable and sweet. Ice creams and fruit juices can be eaten with confidence.

There have recently been two well-publicized scares on the coast: malaria and AIDS. Both exist, but neither is a good reason for not visiting the country. Do not have intercourse with prostitutes anywhere in Africa. Malaria is unpredictable: There are new strains, and some of them are not easy to recover from quickly. Any persistent fever, headache, or joint pain should be reported at once to a doctor. If you can reach medical care within 24 hours, don't take any antimalarial medicine, as it may mask the symptoms. Physicians on the coast are among the most experienced malaria doctors anywhere. Most hotels have their own contacts for physicians; all the major hospitals have experienced staff.

Communications

The telephone system works well internationally and locally. Some hotels have fax, telegram, and telex facilities. There are public telephones in most towns. Several reliable international couriers will deliver within Kenya. These include **DHL** and **TNT.** The main-line bus companies also offer a reliable internal delivery service. You must deliver and collect from their depots.

Mombasa

The best way to see Mombasa town is on foot, but you should not walk around at night. Purse-snatchers are common, and drug abuse exists up and down the coast. Beware of people who might approach you on Moi Avenue; they most often offer to become your guide. Tell them "No thanks" and move on.

Driving in Mombasa is an adventure; traffic and potholes rival those in Manhattan. Approach intersections and traffic circles with care; traffic lights do not always work. Outside Mombasa town the roads improve and they are well marked. Watch out for minibuses; the names painted on the back should give you a clue why: "Rambo Jet," "Rocket Rover" and the like.

Exploring

Numbers in the margin correspond to points of interest on the Mombasa Island map.

Mombasa Island, roughly 4 by 7 kilometers (2½ by 4 miles). The water east and north is Tudor Creek, where you'll find the Old Harbor; west is Kilindini Creek, leading to Port Reitz. To the southeast the Indian Ocean pounds against the reefs and the ships pick their way through the gap in the reefs; graceful dhows and rusty coasters bound for the Old Harbor, gliding under the battlements of Fort Jesus; trawlers and sturdy container vessels making for moorings or quays in Kilindini, swinging down the famous dog-leg channel, while the Likoni ferries lean
❶ back to make way. The **Oceanic Hotel** overlooks the channel between the island and the mainland and has fine sea views. The sculpted roof with the curved facade is intended to mock the ships that glide past.

❷ ❸ The **Outrigger Hotel,** in Liwatoni near the **Yacht Club** and the
❹ **Rowing Club,** overlooks the close reaches of the port itself. This is a good base for anyone interested in seeing town life. For visiting sailors, the Yacht Club next door has a lively social program as well as a full calendar of mixed-class dinghy sailing.

Mombasa Island

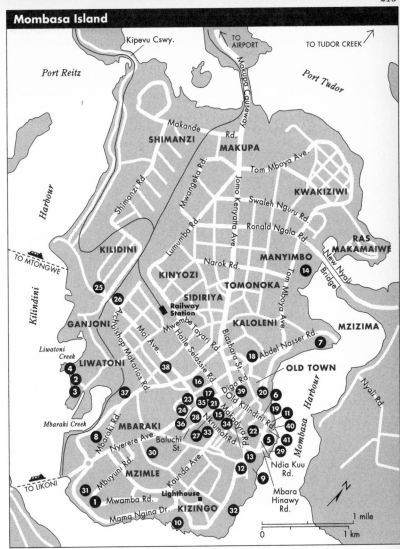

ABN Bank, **33**	Cuaca, **31**	Leven House, **11**	Old Police Station, **21**
Aga Khan Hospital, **30**	Datoo Auctioneers, **22**	Little Theater Club, **37**	Outrigger Hotel, **2**
Allidina Visram School, **14**	Dodwell House, **25**	Mackinnon Vegetable Market, **39**	Piggott Place, **41**
Ambalal House, **27**	Fontanella Cafe, **36**	Mandhry Mosque, **5**	Post Office, **17**
Baluchi Mosque, **15**	Fort Jesus, **9**	Manor Hotel, **24**	Rowing Club, **4**
Basheikh Mosque, **6**	Fort St. Joseph, **10**	Mbaraki Pillar, **8**	Salambo Club, **35**
Berkeley Place, **40**	Hindu Temple, **34**	Mombasa Club, **29**	State House, **32**
Bohra Mosque, **19**	Holy Ghost Cathedral, **28**	Mzizima, **7**	Stone Bridge, **26**
Bondeni Mosque, **18**	Ismaili Mosque, **20**	Oceanic Hotel, **1**	Treasury Square, **12**
Castle Hotel, **23**	Jundaan Mosque, **16**	Old Law Court, **13**	Tusks, **38**
			Yacht Club, **3**

The foundation of Mombasa as a port can be traced back to the 11th century, when there were several settlements around the creeks and on the island. Mombasa town thrived because of its deep harbor and its protected position.

The town was one of several small settlements that grew up along the East African coast between the 8th and the 16th century. It has always been involved with fishing and with deep-sea commerce. Nobody knows the origin of the word Mombasa, and very little from these early days is left. The **Mandhry Mosque** at the port end of Mbarak Hinawy Street, the mosque on Ndia Kuu, and the **Basheikh Mosque** on Old Kilindini Road near Piggott Place might be built on 11th-century foundations. Like other Swahili towns, Mombasa probably had a Muslim community from its beginning.

The earliest settlement was not located on the site of the present Old Town, which seems to be only a few centuries old. The earliest settlement was closer to the old Nyali Bridge, on the promontory called **Mzizima,** where there is still a small lighthouse. Here dhows are cleaned and repaired. Some of the earliest pottery that has been found was recovered from the area. On the beach below are pieces of 20th-century teacups discarded by sailors, beads from the 16th century, and colorful glazed bowls from Southern Iran, dating from the 11th and 12th centuries. This sense of continuity over the last millennium is noticeable everywhere. At Mbaraki, overlooking Mbaraki Creek leading off Kilindini, is the tall **Mbaraki Pillar** built of coral rag with a coral plaster finish. People leave rosewater and other offerings there and burn incense and pray to the spirits. It was originally a tomb; next to it was a mosque, built in the 14th century to serve a small Swahili village along the little creek. By the middle of the 18th century the village had been deserted and the mosque fell into disrepair. The area is now being redeveloped following many of the architectural precepts of the original buildings.

Another example of this "development archaeology" is in Ndia Kuu, just a few yards into the Old Town from the Fort Jesus parking lot. There, a 17th-century mosque lay for years under a rubbish heap outside a garage. It has been excavated and the remains recorded. The mosque has been rebuilt, following the original design, and put back into use. The mosque's history is obscure, and its architecture is unique on this coast. Take a short walk outside and see the two pilasters on the outer niche wall, perhaps an influence of northwest India or Baluchi.

The Portuguese left little along the rest of the coast, but in Mombasa, intent on consolidating their hold on the European trade with India and Southeast Asia, they built **Fort Jesus.** A way station for the vessels running between India and Europe, the fort was founded in 1593. The design is by Cairati, an Italian architect of note who worked for the Portuguese on several fort projects in the Indian Ocean region. The fort dominates the entrance to the Old Harbor. At the seaward end, a bastion carries the cannon which controlled the approaches from the open sea. This bastion also covered the beach just to seaward of the fort. Thus it was always possible, even if the fort was under siege, to bring shipborne supplies to the sally port in the wall under the cover of the fort guns. On the town side, the old square bastions were modified after the fort was successfully attacked from the town in the 1630s.

When the Omanis took the fort at the end of the 17th century, they made some adjustments. The fort captain raised the walls to deal with the improved distance and trajectory of small arms and small cannon. By the end of the 18th century, the fort was equipped with longer-range and more accurate guns. Turrets were erected. There is a house from this period on display. For water, the garrison relied on the well and on roof collections. There is a large pit cistern in the center of the compound, and an open one up on the northeast bastion. Some of the guides say this was the bath of the harem, an intriguing notion. The captain's house retains something of the old Portuguese building: Note the colonnade now filled in by a wall.

The collections on display at Fort Jesus include an important and much visited history of the ceramics of the coast, and the remains of a Portuguese gunner called *San Antonio de Tanna*, which sank outside the fort at the end of the 17th century. The sunken ship helps bring the period to life. There are sailors' shoes, glass bottles, a powder shovel, a cannon with its muzzle blown away, and jet pendants.

Fort Jesus is not only a national monument but also the headquarters for the regional services of the National Museums of Kenya. Here are the archaeology, preservation, and conservation facilities and a research library, generally regarded as the most comprehensive on coastal history. (The British Institute Library in Nairobi also has a very important collection.) If you seek in-depth information on the coast, this is the place to go.

The museum staff has excellent education and archaeology departments whose officers have a good grasp of the history and development of the fort and the significance of its collections. If you need expert help in interpreting this great monument, consult them. *Open daily 8:30–6:30; gift shop; snack shop. Nonresident admission Kshs. 100.*

The Portuguese also built several outforts, at **Makupa,** hidden under the mangroves near the causeway just where it grasps the island bank, and along the low cliffs overlooking the
⑩ Kilindini entrance. **Fort St. Joseph** is still standing on the divide of the two channels for Old and New Harbors, and can be seen by following the path from the lighthouse parking lot on the shore between the **Police Headquarters** and the **Mombasa Golf Club,** round to the front of the Police Headquarters and **Coast Guard** buildings. Guardroom graffiti of the 1630s confirm that the soldiers took seriously the notion of "His Majesty's most Christian Army." There is not a single literary infelicity and only one arrow through the heart, among all the ships, chapels, crosses, and soldiers in their helmets.

During the 19th century, Omani power in East Africa increased, and the newly established sultanate of Zanzibar extended its hegemony over the Swahili coast of Kenya. Baluchis with the Omani forces and Indians from the Indus and Bombay began to settle here as trade burgeoned across the Indian Ocean. This intensified as British interest increased. There was much building, with strong Indian influences. A walk down into "Old Town" reveals elaborate hardwood balconies; fine carved doors grace many an entrance. You might even hear an African Gray parrot shouting from behind a trellis.

Most of the buildings one now sees are not very old: They are
⑪ probably only a hundred years old or less. **Leven House** is one of

the exceptions. It is one of the few buildings which is documented to the early 19th century. It seems to have been built for a wealthy trading family and was occupied by a series of famous visitors. It served for a while as the headquarters of the ill-fated British protectorate in the 1820s, and Emery, Jackson, and Burton all visited. It was here that the wife and daughter of the famous missionary Ludwig Krapf died. It housed the Imperial British East Africa Company and was the building in which the Bazett sisters ran a mission school. It housed the German diplomatic mission at the beginning of the 20th century, and the building's facade dates from this period. The building is threatened with destruction, despite an urban conservation project.

There are several reminders of the early British occupation, such as the area called Buxton near the island end of the **new Nyali Bridge.** This was the site of a school run by the **Buxton** family, and there is still a school there. The Universities Mission to Central Africa established the **Anglican Cathedral** during the early part of this century. The influence of Middle Eastern Islamic architecture is clear in the frieze and archwork, the dome design, and the tall, narrow windows. The paneling behind the high altar is reminiscent of the glowing metal panels at Zanzibar Cathedral, also built by the UMCA. The walls of the nave are hung with brass plaques typical of British presence. The building is suffering from indifferent maintenance but retains much of its old character. The squat nave, dome and shuttered windows are partially hidden; the perspective of the building and its contribution to the beauty and interest of the neighborhood was upset by the recent building of a row of kiosklike offices.

⑫ Around **Treasury Square** there are several examples of early 20th-century architecture. The district administrative headquarters is one such building, with its heavy colonnade and balconied first floor and Mangalore tiled roof. Around the corner, ⑬ near Fort Jesus, is the dilapidated **Old Law Court** building. The building was erected during the early years of the 20th century, but it looks neglected, and there are now serious maintenance problems. The museum has recently taken an interest in the building, and there are plans to restore this important structure to its former elegance.

⑭ The **Allidina Visram School,** near the end of the Nyali Bridge, is another important early 20th-century building in Mombasa. Founded by a successful businessman of Indian origin, the school maintains high academic standards.

Islamic architecture has some notable examples here. In addition to the old mosques, there is a range of buildings from the past 150 years. The pastel walls and elegant dome of the new ⑮ **Baluchi Mosque** in the Post Office area, the comforting squat-⑯ ⑰ domed beauty of the **Jundaan Mosque** opposite the **Post Office** on the other side of Digo Road, the castellated angularity of the ⑱ **Bondeni Mosque** on the road to the old Nyali Bridge, the elabo-⑲ rate facade and soaring minaret of the new **Bohra Mosque** overlooking the Old Harbor, and the purposeful square facade of the ⑳ **Ismaili Mosque** all reflect the best in Islamic architecture. There are also several Hindu temples, alive and ablaze with color, images, murals, statues, and paneling.

Kizingo, the area between Treasury Square and the Light-house, has many examples of "Coast Colonial"-style houses. Coast Colonial style is characterized by spacious, high-ceiling rooms with deep arcaded balconies and red Mangalore tile roofs. Single story houses are often built on plinths. The floors are solid teak planks or imported Indian, British, or French red tiles. Banisters and balcony rails are finely finished teak. Some of these houses are now public buildings. The Aliens Office, a tattered but still recognizably handsome building, is near the Uhuru ni Kazi building on State House Road.

Many buildings are in disrepair. Hardwood floors are discolored and split, proud balustrades are insect-ridden, and roofs leak. Shutters hang drunkenly and gardens are grass and scrub jungles. Still, amid the decay and neglect, there is the exception. A stroll through Kizingo would reward anyone interested in architecture. Mombasa's seediness may stem in part from the dense humidity and the year-round high temperatures, neither of which are good for any townscape. Tucked into side streets are charming vistas, restful parks, and open spaces. A good way to experience Mombasa is to wander through the streets.

There are still many architectural gems, including several public buildings. The **Old Police Station** and the **Datoo Auctioneers** building on Makadara Road, home of the earliest auctioneers in East Africa, are examples. The **Castle Hotel** on Moi Avenue is a turn-of-the-century specimen, with high, arcaded, stone balconies and a very popular streetside veranda. The **Manor Hotel,** just round the corner, is from the same period, with cool pillars and shade patios. Down at the port end of the Moi Avenue is **Dodwell House.** Its fine Mangalore tile roof is still in excellent condition, and the interior is evocative of other times. The vast shipping hall still houses bustling clerks and their files on sturdy Mvule wood desks. The spacious entry hall with its massive columns leads to a long hardwood counter. Countless passengers leaned against this, conducting business that would take them to board the Union Castle boats; others stood a little breathless and flushed, savoring their first few minutes ashore after the journey from England or Bombay.

The **stone bridge** at the end of Moi Avenue is another monument of the past. It still carries the logo of the old Kenya–Uganda Railway; the original railway station was once on the other side of the bridge.

Not all new architecture is unimaginative. **Ambalal House** in Nkrumah Road, near the **Holy Ghost cathedral,** has a cool shopping arcade. On a more modest scale is the block of shops and flats next to the private **Mombasa Club** on Mbarak Hinawy Street.

Shore Walk From the patio of the Manor Hotel, a popular breakfast and lunch spot, walk down Nyerere Road away from town. The **External Communications Office** is along that stretch. At the roundabout is the excellent **Pandya Hospital.** Pass the prestigious **Star of the Sea School** and the Mombasa Women's Association, behind which is the highly respected **Aga Khan Hospital,** and go on to the roundabout above the ferry ramp. Turn left along Mama Ngina Drive, named after one of Jomo Kenyatta's wives. The road keeps to the cliffs overlooking the channel that leads from the sea into Kilindini. On the landward side of the

㉛ road is a large baobab glade, the site of the old town of **Cuaca** (as the Portuguese called it), now a popular park. There are good views of Likoni on the mainland from the park, and you may encounter vendors with fresh coconut milk. At the **Florida Club** you may choose to stop for a rest. At the end of the ocean view drive near the Golf Club House is a pleasant rest spot overlooking the buoys that lead ships through the reefs. This is the start of the path to Fort St. Joseph.

㉜ The road runs past the Police Headquarters and **State House.** Do not use cameras in this area. A 10-minute walk brings you to **Treasury Square,** near the site of the old railway station. In front is a peaceful park with seats and plenty of shade. There is also a bust of businessman and philanthropist **Allidina Visram.** Nearby, a **gazebo** has trees thrusting out of its dome. At the town end of Treasury Square you can walk back toward the Manor Hotel along Nkrumah Road or take a loop down Makadara Road.

Time Out Tucked behind the Anglican Cathedral, a bit west on Nkrumah Road, is the **Lotus Hotel,** with comfortable, moderately priced rooms and a fine courtyard. Here you can buy excellent inexpensive sandwiches and relax in cool, quiet surroundings.

Farther down Nkrumah Road, toward Digo road, are two well-preserved examples of **Indian classical facades,** and the new
㉝ **ABN Bank,** with an excellent example of the traditional carved
㉞ doors. Behind Barclays Bank on the right is a large **Hindu temple.** Nkrumah Road runs past Ambalal House to the commanding Italianate facade of Holy Ghost (R.C.) Cathedral.

The loop from Treasury Square down Makadara Road leads past the Datoo Auction House and the Old Police Station, up Baluchi Street past the new Baluchi mosque, and back onto Nkrumah Road at Ambalal House. This round-trip takes you past the Eagle Travel Office, Tasneems, a favorite snack place, the Crystal Ice Cream parlor, and Noors Travel agency.

Moi Avenue Walk Moi Avenue is 4 kilometers (2 mi) long and the main thoroughfare in town. It has a range of souvenir shops, boutiques and bookshops, travel agencies and car-rental offices, restaurants, and bars and clubs. At the cathedral traffic circle at Digo Road
㉟ is the **Salambo Club,** a good place for a drink later in the day. In the cool courtyard behind the shops on the other side of the
㊱ road is the **Fontanella Cafe,** a good, inexpensive, central place to rest and meet. A hundred meters (109 yds) farther down the road on the left is the Castle hotel, which has a cool veranda and the popular Bistro Restaurant. Almost opposite the Castle is the Istanbul, a cheap place for Middle Eastern–style snacks. A little farther down on the left, set back on a side road (Mnazi Maja Road), is the **Rainbow Bar.** The Rainbow serves delicious liver; it is also a nightclub, known for serious drinking. Two minutes from the Rainbow down Mnazi Mosi Road is the **Mombasa Sports Club,** offering a wide range of sports including
㊲ cricket and bowls. The **Little Theatre Club** is just down the road on the right, and the cemetery and **War Graves Commission Plot** is on the left. (If you come to the theater at night, do so by taxi from Moi Avenue.)

㊳ Dominating Moi Avenue are the famous **Tusks:** Two pairs of crossed elephant tusks made of sheathed metal tubing reach a considerable height across the highway. They were erected to commemorate the 1952 visit of Britain's Princess Elizabeth, now Queen Elizabeth II.

Just opposite the Wimpy and the Tusks is a large, shady open park with pleasant walks and seating. The Uhuru ("Freedom") monument is here. In this stretch, on the right, is the very helpful Information Center.

Time Out Turn right at the Moi Avenue roundabout, and 100 meters down Tangana Road, on the left is the Swahili Curry bowl. Its unassuming decor belies the stimulating choice of clean, cheap, delicious Swahili dishes.

Old Town Walk Old Town looks like a maze, but it is small and is easy to comprehend. All the streets leading off Nkrumah Road/Makadara Road run through Old Town and reemerge in the neighborhood of the **Mackinnon Vegetable Market** on Digo Road. The main thoroughfare is Ndia Kuu, which leads into the maze of alleys from Fort Jesus. Fort Jesus or the Mombasa Club are good places to start a tour. Fresh lime juice is sold on the bastion overlooking the harbor entrance in Fort Jesus.

There is always a willing guide outside Fort Jesus, but the walk can be accomplished without assistance. Take Mbarak Hinawy Street past the Mombasa Club, past some well-stocked souvenir shops to a series of very fine streetscapes and the conical tower of the minaret of the ancient Mandhry Mosque. Note the well on the other side of the road. Past the mosque the road takes a sharp left turn and deposits you in a little square. To the right is the gate to the Old Harbor, and just ahead is the new Bohra Mosque. The Old Harbor is an active port: Dhows sail from Abu Dhabi, Dubai, Iran, and Zanzibar, as well as from Lamu. Do not use cameras here: The police will normally let you past the railing overlooking the moorings to see the ships, but picture-taking is prohibited. The fee for harbor access is Kshs. 20.

There is another vantage point outside the Old Harbor compound, which you can reach by walking up immediately opposite the port gates. The alley passes a tiny little gap in the buildings called **Berkeley Place** and emerges onto the main Ndia Kuu. Turn right and walk down the street, past an old mosque, and turn at the third or fourth alley on the right (depending on definition), which brings you to a small square and the famous Leven House. In front of it, at the Leven steps, a short tunnel cut through the rock emerges on the water's edge at a **remarkable freshwater well.** Burton mentions climbing up from this well through the tunnel in the 19th century, but today it is best to take the open-air steps down to the waterside. The views of the harbor and the ships are well worth the deviation through the alleys.

Retrace your steps to Ndia Kuu, turn right and then left onto the Old Kilindini Road, past the Basheikh mosque, then turn left into **Piggott Place.** Here on weekends is an open-air market where everything from fine antique furniture to secondhand oilcans are sold. The major road out of the square takes you on a five-minute walk through the bazaar onto the main Digo Road at the Mackinnon vegetable market. Cross the road near Barclays Bank, turn right and then left. This is Biashara Street. Here are rows of shops filled with brightly colored kangas and kikois, the long cotton sarongs. Most of the material is light cotton; look for the heavier-weave white-cotton Benaadir cloth, heavy enough to be used as bedspreads and tablecloths as well as kikois.

Dining

By Kathy Eldon   Highly recommended restaurants are indicated by a star ★.

Category	Cost*
Expensive	over Kshs. 700
Moderate	Kshs. 350–700
Inexpensive	under Kshs. 350

*per person, excluding drinks, service, and sales tax

Expensive **Capri Restaurant.** Chic and ice cold, the Capri is one of the few elegant restaurants in Mombasa town. Situated in a high-rise building, the Capri is a dark and welcoming and features delicious fresh seafood. The service, however, is unbelievably slow. *Ambalal House, Nkrumah Rd., tel. 11/31156. Reservations not necessary. AE, DC, V.*

★ **Tamarind Restaurant.** Perched high above a waterway leading to the Indian Ocean, the Tamarind is probably Kenya's most beautiful restaurant. The Moorish-style place features high white arches, a simple airy interior, and an unparalleled view. The excellent food is served with enormous flair and a great sense of fun, and dhow luncheon cruises can be arranged. Especially worthwhile are the trout in banana leaves, prawns in a spicy butter sauce, fresh oysters, and fresh fish tartare. The seafood platter gives you the chance to try a bit of everything. The Tamarind is a 15-minute drive from downtown Mombasa. *Silo Rd., Nyali, tel. 11/472263 or 11/472263. Reservations required. AE, DC, V.*

Moderate **Bella Vista.** This relaxed, friendly air-conditioned restaurant is situated above the Agip gas station. Specialties include steak Akbar (sautéed with garlic and green chilies) and Chicken Bella Vista, marinated and served whole in a yogurt sauce. *Corner of Moi Ave. and Liwatoni Rd., tel. 11/313572, 25848. No credit cards.*

Chinese Overseas Restaurant. Competent Chinese fare is served in simple surroundings at this family-style restaurant run by Mr. and Mrs. Yu. The menu features sweet and sour jumbo prawns, ginger crab, and sizzling platters of meat and fish. *Moi Ave., tel. 11/21575. No credit cards.*

★ **Galaxy Chinese Restaurant.** Chinese lanterns hang from the high ceilings of this upscale eatery. Superb seafood dishes are featured, including ginger crab with black beans and steamed fish with soy sauce. *Archbishop Makarios St., tel. 11/26132. Weekend reservations advised. No credit cards.*

Inexpensive **Hermes Hotel.** The main redeeming feature of this gloomy little restaurant is excellent prawns—especially the prawn curry. The *chicken tikka* (chicken marinated and grilled over charcoal) is better than average, and the air-conditioning makes it an inviting haven on a steamy day in Mombasa. *Msanifu Kombo Rd., tel. 11/313599, 29744. No credit cards.*

Nawab. This dark, cool restaurant serves such Mughlai dishes as chicken *muree* (a rich spicy curry), garlic prawns, and *paneer* (cheese) corn. The lush upholstery and soft carpeting give the place a comforting, cozy feel, while the slow service allows patrons to relax into the coastal pace. *Moi Ave., tel. 11/ 20754. No credit cards.*

Rekoda. The place for experiencing Mombasa's nightlife, this *hoteli* is a gathering place for locals, backpackers, and would-be sociologists who come to observe coastal life. Join a shared table; order beans and rice, watery chicken curry, or leather *chapatis* (Indian bread); and enjoy the laid-back atmosphere. *Nyeri St., Old Town. No phone, reservations or credit cards.*

★ **Singh Restaurant.** For rich, freshly prepared curries served in air-conditioned comfort, try this family-style place, decorated with calendars and lurid Indian prints. Choices are severely limited, but all the dishes are delicious. *Mwembe Tayari Rd., tel. 11/83860. Reservations not required. No credit cards.*

Lodging

Most of the best Mombasa hotels are relatively widely dispersed and are located off the island on the beaches immediately to the north and south (*see* The North Coast Near Mombasa, *below*). The larger beach hotels offer shuttle service from the airport.

Highly recommended lodgings are indicated by a star ★.

Category	Cost*
Moderate	Kshs. 1,250–2,500 ($50–$100)
Inexpensive	under Kshs. 1,250 ($50)

*All prices are for a standard double room; excluding service charge.

Moderate **Castle Hotel.** Favored by business executives because of its central location, only 10 kilometers (6 mi) from Mombasa airport, this white Moorish-style four-story hotel, renovated in 1985, has a popular patio bistro near bustling Moi Avenue. *Box 84231, tel. 11/23403. 64 air-conditioned rooms with private bath, radio, phone, balcony. Facilities: garden bar and bistro, conference facilities, suites available; TV movies on request. AE, DC, V.*
★

Lotus. A charming hotel with wood shutters and a center courtyard, which at press time was in the process of being renovated. The rooms are air-conditioned, and its restaurant serves good, basic fare. It is a five-minute walk from the town center and is near the Anglican Cathedral. *Box 90193, tel. 11/313207. No credit cards.*

The Manor Hotel. This hotel is a rambling 1920s property that was renovated in 1987. *Box 84851, tel. 11/314543. 73 rooms, most of them air-conditioned. Suites and family rooms available. Facilities: à la carte restaurant with good, moderately priced food; conference facilities. 8 km (5 mi) from Moi airport, (Nyereie Ave. across from Holy Ghost Cathedral). No credit cards.*

★ **Oceanic Hotel.** This large, 220-room hotel was renovated in 1986. Among the three restaurants, the Tung King features Chinese cuisine and the Labanis serves Middle Eastern food; both are moderately priced. An apartment is available for monthly rates. The hotel is located on the Kilindi cliffs, near the Kizingo housing area, 11 kilometers (7 mi) from Moi airport. Courtesy transportation is provided into Mombasa town center. *Box 90371, tel. 11/311191/2/3, telex 21298. Facilities: meeting rooms, pool, gym, sauna, casino. AE, DC, MC, V.*

★ **The Outrigger Hotel** has 45 air-conditioned rooms, with a large patio, a swimming pool, and good moderately priced food in its terrace restaurant. There's a meeting room for 40, and fishing excursions can be arranged. *Overlooking Kilindi Harbor, near the Yacht Club. Box 82345, tel. 11/20822/3. Telex 21368. AE, DC, V.*

Inexpensive **Hermes.** This hotel has an unusual facade of curtained glass, a
★ cubby-hole reception area, and an earnest, if inexperienced, staff. The rooms have private baths; the food is good—with more character than most hotel food—especially the shrimp and seafood dishes. *Haile Selassie Ave., Box 94819, tel. 11/313599. No credit cards.*

Miramar. A renovated hotel, the Miramar offers comfortable rooms and a restaurant featuring fine Goan dishes. It is near the railway station. *Tangana Rd., Box 84819, tel. 11/313599. AE, V.*

New Carlton. Boasting comfortable rooms with private baths, this hotel features a moderately priced dining room. It is located near a tunnel on Moi Avenue. *Box 86779, tel. 11/23776, 11/315116. No credit cards.*

New Palm Tree. A palm tree set in a small "first floor" balcony is the hotel's sign. Rooms are quiet and have fans. The cavernous reception area leads to a bar and simple dining room, with a grill menu and adequate curries. *Nkrumah Rd., Box 90013, tel. 11/311756, 11/312169 or 11/312296. AE, DC, V.*

The Splendid Hotel. Featuring small rooms with private bath, the Splendid's antidote to claustrophobia is a rooftop bar and restaurant that serves good roast meat. *Msanifu Kombo St., Box 90482, tel. 11/20967. AE, V.*

Shopping

There are many shops on Mbarak Road in the Old Town near Fort Jesus that sell clothes, jewelry and antiques.

The **Sunshine Arcade** (tel. 11/227160) has brass, copper, antiques and Indian jewelry.

Nightlife

Cinema Films are a popular pastime in Mombasa; be prepared for audience participation. Cinemas such as the **Lotus** and the **Kenya** are clean and safe and also provide snacks. Consult *Coastweek*, the local newspaper, for times. You may find a film here that you missed in New York or London several years ago.

Theater The **Little Theatre Club** produces light comedy, farce, and the occasional African play. It is rare to hear good live Swahili, Indian, or Arabic music, or to witness dancing from those communities.

Nightclubs Nightclubs range from noisy smart dives such as **Tiffany's** (in Ambalal House) and **Toyz** (Casbah Post Office) to the floor show at the **Sunshine** (Moi Ave.) and the more basic **Rainbow** (off Moi Ave.).

Casinos The **Florida Nightclub,** on the cliffs overlooking the channel into Kalindini, has a casino. There is also a popular casino at the **Oceanic Hotel,** just a few minutes away from the Florida.

The North Coast Near Mombasa

Numbers in the margin correspond to points of interest on the Coastal Kenya map.

For many years there was a pontoon bridge over the Old Harbor entrance to Tudor Creek, operated by Nyali Estates, which controlled much of the land on the peninsula. During the 1970s, a graceful concrete bridge, the **Nyali Bridge,** was erected, but parts of the old bridge are still visible from the new span and from the Tamarind Restaurant. The Kenya Museums managed to acquire a small mooring anchor from the old bridge, and other parts of it can be seen all over town: Huge anchors stand outside hotels and restaurants, factories, and private houses.

In the days when the British Navy and missionaries were trying to thwart the slave trade, freed slaves settled around the area reached by the new bridge, in such towns as Kisauni and Kongowea, the latter a fishing village dating from the 11th century. On the Nyali side of the bridge, near the traffic-light corner, is a bell tower monument to the ex-slaves' freedom. African-Americans who come to Kenya in search of their roots should make a point of speaking with the elder villagers of Kongowea, for there are many who can impart much about their heritage.

After the Nyali Bridge, the road forks left to **Kisami** and right to **Kongowea.** Both communities are enthusiastically Christian, evidence of the 19th-century missionaries. At the far end of Kongowea, near the modern cement silos overlooking the Old Town, are the graves of the wife and daughter of Ludwig Krapf, a famous missionary and scholar.

Much of Nyali Peninsula is devoted to luxurious suburban estates, replete with gates and fierce dogs. Along the harbor are excellent restaurants and the Ratna shopping mall. Beaches around Nyali are not readily accessible to independent travelers, although you can approach them via the Nyali Beach Hotel, the Mombasa Beach Hotel, or the Reef Hotel. The public-access paths are not always safe.

At the northern end of Nyali, along Links Road is **Mamba Village,** featuring a crocodile farm. A brief tour is complemented by film screenings documenting both the conservation and commercial aspects of the operation. You can also arrange a special safari on the Tana River to watch crocodile catching. Camel rides are offered at Mamba village and there is an excellent restaurant. *Mamba Village, Box 85723, Mombasa, tel. 11/ 472709, 472341, 472361. Nominal fee. Open weekdays 9–5, Sat. noon–5.*

Farther up Links Road is the **SOS Children's Home,** (Box 90572, Mombasa, tel. 11/485789), an orphanage with a Montessori school, a livestock farm, and a small shop. **Bombolulu Craft Center** (Box 83988, Mombasa, tel. 11/471704), a cottage industry for the handicapped, produces a variety of brass, copper,

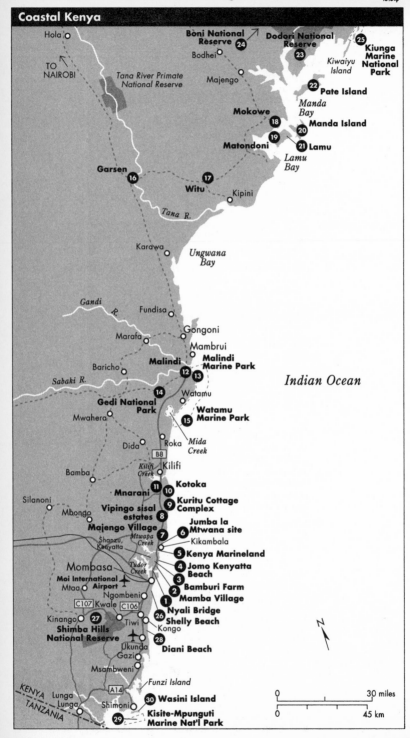

and seed jewelry in traditional patterns. You can visit the workshops, and the crafts are good value.

❸ Heading north on the road to Malindi, a dense casuarina forest on the left marks the famous **Bamburi Farm,** a hedge against the greenhouse effect long before it became a household phrase. Over a decade ago the executives at the Bamburi Cement Works began a reforestation program to repair the damage done by open coral mining, which left bare stone quarries. They chose one of the most innovative scientists/conservationists anywhere, Dr. René Haller, who developed a remarkable reclamation scheme that has attracted the attention of ecologists around the world. Dr. Haller's first task was to make the soil fertile for vegetation. To increase the mineral content in the soil, he imported and released millipedes, which produce excellent fertilizer. The experiment that began as a few trees on a white desert now shades a wildlife sanctuary. Dr. Haller organized a nature trail, a fish farm, a nursery, a crocodile farm, and domesticated a herd of eland. Haller is also an inventor. When driving around the farm, one crosses a cattle gap that triggers the gate to open. An animal orphanage attracts myriad wildlife, including "Sally the Hippo," made famous in the PBS documentaries by Alan and Joan Root. Sally welcomes visitors at feeding time, 4 PM daily. *Bamburi Farm, Box 90202, Mombasa, tel. 11/48529. Nominal admission fee. Open weekdays 10–6, Sat. 10–5, Sun. noon–5.* The **Kipepee Aquarium** opposite the Bamburi Nature Trail is also worth a visit.

❹ The stretch of coast between Nyali and Mtwapa Creek, 17 kilometers (10½ mi) north of Mombasa, is packed with beach hotels and private beaches. At the southern end of Bamburi Beach is the public **Jomo Kenyatta Beach.** For visitors wanting exercise beyond water sports, the Sunline Tennis School and Club offers instruction on some of the best surfaces in East Africa.

Mtwapa Creek, north of Mombasa, is crossed at the Shanzu end of Utange Village. The once-wealthy town of Mtwapa now languishes on the edge of a tall dark forest. Deep-sea fishing is available, but it is best to go fishing with an established firm: **James Adcock** (Box 95693, Mombasa, tel. 11/485527), **Francis MacConnell** (Box 82849, Mombasa, tel. 11/485230), and **Kenya Marineland** (*see below*).

❺ Mtwapa Creek is the home for the **Kenya Marineland** complex (Box 15050, Kikambala, tel. 11/485248, 11/485738, or 11/485866), with boat rentals and an underwater-view tank where sharks are fed. Nearby talented craftsmen carve ebony hardwoods, and there is a traditional Masai *manyatta* (settlement) where dances are staged.

Le Pichet Restaurant (*see* Dining, *below*) is surrounded by arts and crafts stalls, and you can take a dhow cruise from the jetty for a barbecue served on a sandy beach on the other side of Mtwapa Creek, followed by African dancing and music under the stars. The dhow dinner cruise is popular, so book early.

❻ Just north of the bridge at Mtwapa, 13 kilometers (8 mi) north of Mombasa, is a road leading east to the **Jumba la Mtwana site,** which is overseen by the National Museums of Kenya. The abandoned ruins of this 15th-century village, covering several acres, has walkways among the eight houses, three mosques, and several tombs. A printed guide is available at the ticket office for a minimal fee. You will see that little has changed in domestic architecture during the past millennium, and many modern versions of mud-thatch houses are visible today as you pass through the villages on the main road. Guided tours are available, and there is a pleasant picnic facility overlooking the sea. Jumba is a paradise for bird-watchers.

A short walk up the beach, or a longer drive by road, brings you ⑦ to **Majengo village,** where a track leads down to the shore at Kanamai village. There is a good campsite on Kikambala Beach, along with good hotels, among them Sun n' Sand, Whispering Palms, and Thousand Palms.

North of Kikambala and the hotels, the road runs through the ⑧ **Vipingo sisal estates.** Sisal has struggled to retain its niche in the market since the invention of synthetic fabric for rope, fabric, and mats. At the estate you can see fleshy spike leaves cut by hand and then loaded on trolleys that lead to the factory where the cortex is removed, dried, and packed into bales. Sisal is useful in emergencies in the bush. You can take the sharp tip from the top, and by carefully tearing it down the center of the long leaf, produce a needle and thread for making stitches.

Just beyond Vipingo, down 3 kilometers (2 mi) of easy track to ⑨ the shore, is the delightful **Kuritu Cottage Complex.** Beyond the sisal estates are mango, cashew, and coconut plantations surrounding the old town of Takaungu, once an independent sultanate. An easy drive from the main road, the complex is a good example of a modern Swahili village. On the bluff on the other ⑩ side of the creek are the remains of **Kotoka.** A house on the site was once owned by Denys Finch-Hatton, the erudite white hunter/pilot and lover of Karen Blixen (Isak Dinesen).

Kilifi Creek is about 30 kilometers (18½ mi) north of Mombasa, is traversed by a new bridge, completed in 1991. The Mnarani Club, just left of the bridge's apron on the old ferry road, is a good place for refreshment, and there is a small snake park nearby. A path from the snake park climbs across a mangrove-⑪ edged beach to the ruins of ancient **Mnarani.** The Friday mosque is a large, impressive edifice with one of the deepest wells on the coast. Just behind the mosque is a pillar tomb with carved decorations. The pillar of coral rag leans at a precarious angle. A short walk through the forest path leads to another little mosque, with the pillars still standing. Ancient Mnarani was deserted by the end of the 16th century.

Dining

See Mombasa's price chart, *above.*

Expensive **Harlequin Restaurant.** This, the newest of first-class seafood restaurants in the Mombasa area, has a commanding view of Tudor Creek. The cuisine is excellent at moderate to expensive prices. You can pick your own crab from the pool! *Kisauni. Tel. 11/472373.*
Le Pichet. Enjoy innovative seafood served by Belgian chef Willy Wainwiler, in this huge outdoor restaurant overlooking Mtwapa Creek. Try the oysters and the original and classic seafood dishes. Le Pichet is a 20-minute drive from town, but it's worth the trip. *North Coast, Kikambala, tel. 11/585923. Reservations recommended. AE, DC.*

Moderate **The Galana Steak House,** near Jomo Kenyatta Beach, overlooks the aces at the Sunline Tennis School and Club. *Tel. Mombasa 485572.*

Libbas Restaurant Featured here are excellent pastas and a range of pizzas, with special meals for children. *Ratna Shopping Mall, Nyali, tel. 11/471138.*

Rene's Restaurant. Excellent Italian food is served here. There is a disco in the evening. *Links Rd., Nyali, tel. 11/472986.*

Inexpensive **Mnarani Club.** Excellent food is served under a palm-thatch roof, overlooking Kilifi Creek. *Malindi Rd., Mnarani, tel. KIL 18, 26.*

Lodging

Most good-quality lodges and guest houses are located along the beaches, often isolated from the local culture. Accommodations range from first-class international chains to romantic, thatch-roof lodges, and self-contained cottages. Most face the sea and may feature a small balcony.

Package-tour groups are predominant, and almost every large hotel has sophisticated conference facilities and health clubs. Basic services are offered in English, Swahili, and Arabic, and most hotel menus are "international," while also featuring such local favorites as excellent curries and seafood dishes, with an abundance of fresh coconut, mango, and papaya. Most hotels can arrange snorkeling, windsurfing, waterskiing, parasailing, and tours in glass-bottom boats. Some specialize in deep-sea fishing and cruises by dhow or canoe. We denote hotels offering radio and video, and discos.

Topless sunbathing is not permitted in the hotel beach areas, and it is not a good idea to wear only your swimsuit to hotel meals. Kikois and kangas, sold locally, provide a handy cover.

Category	Cost
Very Expensive	over Kshs. 3,750 ($150)
Expensive	Kshs. 2,500–3,759 ($100–$150)
Moderate	Kshs. 1,250–2,500 ($50–$100)
Inexpensive	under Kshs. 1,250 ($50)

Expensive **Inter-Continental Mombasa.** This hotel features 192 rooms in the first-class tradition of the Inter-Continentals, with 8 acres of beachfront. Air-conditioned rooms include balcony, minibar, and movies upon request. *Shanzu Beach, 8 mi north of Mombasa, Box 83492, Mombasa, tel. 11/485811/2. Facilities: bars, nightclub, casino, meeting facilities for 260, 24-hour room service, 2 pools with bar, 2 tennis courts, 2 squash courts, health club. AE, DC, MC, V.*

★ **Mombasa Beach Hotel.** This first-class hotel built on coral cliffs overlooking the beach has 156 rooms, with air-conditioning, private bath, phone, and balcony facing the sea. 6 suites. *8 mi from Moi airport, Nyali Beach, Box 90414, Mombasa, tel. 11/471861. Facilities: grill room and snack bar, pool, meeting facilities for 60, 2 tennis courts, water sports and deep-sea fishing, golf nearby. AE, DC, V.*

★ **Serena Beach Hotel.** Above a courtyard set in Jasmine Garden, this superior hotel resembles an Arab village. All 120 air-conditioned rooms feature Swahili-style furniture. *20 kms (12 mi) north of Mombasa, on Shanzu Beach. Box 90352, tel. 11/485721. Facilities: disco, meeting rooms, pool with snack bar, 2 tennis courts, water sports. AE, DC, MC, V.*

Severin Sea Lodge. A lodge with 180 bungalows amid palm trees on Kenyatta Beach, the Severin Sea has air-conditioned rooms with minibar, bath, hairdryer, radio, and safe. The grill restaurant, the Imani Dhow, is a major attraction on Bamburi Beach. *6 kms (10 mi) north of Mombasa, Bamburi, Box 82169, tel. 11/21228. Facilities: windsurfing and Scuba diving school, 2 pools, tennis courts, nature trail, sailing. AE, DC, V.*

Moderate **Bamburi Beach Hotel.** An informal but well-managed hotel ren-
★ ovated in 1984 with 125 air-conditioned rooms with shower, phone, and balcony facing the sea; 25 suites. *12 kms (7 mi) north of Mombasa, Bamburi Beach, Box 83966, tel. 48561/8, telex 21181. Facilities: rooftop bar, nightclub entertainment, meeting facilities for up to 160, pool, sauna, gym, 2 squash courts, water sports, golf, tennis, and horseback riding arranged. AE, DC, MC.*

Giriama Apartments. Well-appointed maisonettes with garden and poolside restaurant. *Bambari, Box 86693, tel. 11/485726, 24997. AE, V.*

★ **Nyali Beach Hotel.** A vast colonial-style hotel with 235 rooms, 6.4 kilometers (4 mi) north of Mombasa. In addition to the rooms within the main building, there are cottages and a newer Palm Beach annex, all air-conditioned, most with minibar and balcony. *Box 90581, Mombasa, tel. 11/471551, 21241. Facilities: restaurant and grill room (service can be slow in the Mchana restaurant; the Mvita Grill offers excellent food and is a popular place to go in Mombasa, as is the in-house Blues Night Club), wheelchair access, meeting facilities, shops, pool with snack bar, 3 tennis courts. AE, DC, MC, V.*

Nyali Reef Hotel. A moderately priced hotel renovated in 1987, with half a mile of private beach. *19 kms (12 mi) from Moi airport, on Mwamba Dr., Nyali, Box 82234, Mombasa, tel. 11/471771. 161 air-conditioned rooms with balcony. Facilities: restaurant and snack bar, meeting room for 100, pool, sauna, tennis court. AE, DC, MC, V.*

Whitesands Hotel. One of the oldest hotels on the coast (renovated in 1986), it boasts "rooms for maids and chauffeurs available." *10 kms (6 mi) north of Mombasa, Box 90173, tel. 11/485926. Facilities: fountain gardens, pool, 2 tennis courts, conference facilities, entertainment. AE, MC, V.*

Inexpensive **Continental Beach Cottages.** Delightful rustic cottages are located on serene Kikambala Beach; though the cottages are difficult to reach, they are well worth it. *Box 124, Kikambala, tel. KIK 77. No credit cards.*

Kanamii Center. Clean and spartan single and double rooms are set in a rambling compound of dormitories by a beautiful beach. Meals are served in a dining hall. The staff is charming and helpful. *Box 208, Kikambala, tel. KIK 46, 101. No credit cards.*

Kenya Beach Hotel. Air-conditioned chalets with pool and garden. Scuba diving is available. *Box 95748, Mombasa, tel. 11/485821. DC, MC, V.*

Kivurtu Beach Cottages (Kurvitu). These are spacious and pleasant cottages at reasonable rates. Rooms have self-help kitchens, but the staff will prepare a grilled meal if you prefer not to cook. A quiet beach and a small hotel shop round out the offerings. *Box 81173, tel. 313378, 26729. No credit cards.*

Ocean View Beach Hotel. An informal hotel located on Kenyatta Beach, with 156 rooms, most of which are air-conditioned, with a balcony and a view of the sea. The hotel is a little out of date—as is noted in its offer to arrange hunting safaris. *Kenyatta Beach, Box 81127, Mombasa, no phone. Facilities: pool, disco, bar, waterskiing, snorkeling, deep-sea fishing. AE, DC, MC, V.*

Plaza Hotel. The well-appointed rooms here come with a view of the sea. The restaurant offers Indian cuisine. *Bamburi, tel. 485321, 485212. AE, V.*

Seahorse Hotel. Tucked away on a road running west from the northern slope of the old Kilifi ferry ramp, the Seahorse overlooks Kilifi Creek. It offers water sports and fishing charters. Delicious seafood is served in the informal Boat Grill or in the hotel restaurant. *Box 70, Kilifi, tel. KIL 90, 64.*

Malindi and Environs

12 **Malindi,** known as the Little Italy of Kenya, is a small town with picturesque parks and friendly people. Many explorers, including Vasco da Gama, have moored here. "Ma Lin De" is referred to in ancient Chinese maritime documents. During the 16th century the town thrived on long-distance trade; today it thrives on tourism, helped by its sandy beaches and vast stands of coconut palms.

The 14th-century tombs beside the main **mosque** near the south beach are among the oldest monuments in Malindi. There are two monuments from the Portuguese period: At the southern end of town, out on the point, a stone cross (*padrao*) commemorates a Papal Bull that authorized the King of Portugal to claim whole countries. On the seafront near the massive old baobab tree stands a little **chapel,** circa 1542, one of the oldest Catholic churches still in use in Africa. Should you wish to visit inside when a mass is not in progress, you can ask the *mzee* (elderly gentleman) in the house behind the chapel to let you in. He keeps the key and tends the flowers on the altar. (If he is not at home, he might be sitting with other elders under the baobab tree.) The little café across from the chapel is a fine place to rest in the shade. A **monument to Vasco da Gama** is near the District Commissioner's office.

The road past the chapel runs down to Silversand Beach, where there is an inexpensive camp site. A little farther along the beach is the famous Driftwood Club & Hotel, a good base for visiting the Marine Park—an unforgettable adventure. The Marine Parks of Kenya are highly successful in conserving tropical fish and encouraging research in marine biology. Don't gather shells on the beach, because the collection of shells, and their export and import into the United States, is prohibited.

You can take an "African Queen" tour, with a cruise on the tributaries of the Tana River delta and two or three nights at a private tented camp near the mouth of the river. The tents (with electric fans for hot nights) are in a picturesque setting, and by crossing the sand dunes you can have a swim in the Indian Ocean. The cuisine at camp is exceptional, as the manager/host is Renaldo Retief, who exports dried fruits to Europe. He imaginatively mixes fruit sauces with fresh seafood. Guests are collected in Malindi or at airstrips (by charter from Nairobi and Lamu) and taken by Land Rover to the river for transport to the camp by boat. Guests go bird-watching, take mud baths, and go game tracking on the sand dunes. *Tana Delta Ltd., Box 24988, Nairobi, tel. 2/882 826; USA: Lynn Glenn, Into Africa, Inc., 93 Doubling Rd., Greenwich, CT 06830, tel. 203/869–8165, fax 203/625–9648. Very Expensive.*

Fishing charters can be arranged through: the Malindi Sea Fishing Club (Box 364, tel. 20410), Malindi Sports Fishing Club (Box 163, tel. 20161), Kingfisher Safaris (Box 29, tel. 20123), Baharini Ventures (Box 435, tel. 20879), Peter Ready (Box 63, tel. 21292), L. Von Menyhart (Box 360, tel. 20840), and Slaters (Box 147, Watumu tel. Watumu 12).

The Kongoni Shop, a small shop on the bay road in town (tel. 20461) sells beautiful beaded sandals, belts and key rings.

The best way to tour the town is on foot, but you will need a car to visit the Marine Park or to go to restaurants and clubs. Most large hotels can arrange transportation, along with excursions to Tsavo and Gedi National Park, and you can also rent a car from Kotsman Car Hire (motorcycles and deep-sea fishing arranged also. Box 262, Malindi, tel. 123/20777 or 20988).

⑬ Malindi Marine Park is home to impressive populations of shellfish, conches, and cowries, and a great variety of corals. The fish life centers on two main reefs, with a deep, sandy-bottomed channel. The top of the north reef features a deep channel to sea, with pelagic shoals; the southern end is inhabited by kingfish and Kolo Koli. Glass-bottom boats and snorkel equipment can be rented from the boatmen in the parking lot. The cost is Kshs. 300 for a whole boat, or Kshs. 150 per tourist, depending on the equipment provided.

The road leading to the marine park features Mark Esterbrook's **Snake Park;** the entrance fee is Kshs. 30. Feeding times are Wednesday and Friday at 4 PM, when the mice and hamsters try to join the crowd. *Tel. 123/20121.*

Malindi Falconry is north of the Stardust Beergarden, on the left side of the road, down a mud track leading to the Catholic church—and worth the struggle to find it. You are met by a knowledgeable guide; the birds are well trained. It is said to be the only falconry in Kenya. *Box 65, Malindi, tel. 123/20383.*

A popular excursion from Malindi is to the ruins of Gedi National Park, followed by a trip to the beach at Watamu. Buses leave regularly throughout the day from the Main Bus Depot in Malindi.

⑭ Gedi National Park, 16 kilometers (10 mi) south of Malindi on Mombasa Road, features the ruins of an ancient village on 45 acres. At first glance, Gedi, which is located several kilometers from the sea, seems an unlikely candidate for a Swahili village. But in the 14th century Gedi was positioned along an inlet of the Galana River, which subsequently changed course to drain north of Malindi.

The town center was surrounded by a 10-foot wall; there is also an inner wall, apparently built later. Both are marked by the remains of ancient gatehouses. The Friday mosque is a large, well-built indication that the villagers were by no means paupers. During the 16th century, Gedi was deserted, perhaps as a result of an attack by the Oromo from the north. Gedi was soon reoccupied, but it never regained its economic footing. Many of the large houses were partitioned, perhaps by squatters, and the town was finally abandoned in the 17th century.

Many of the ruins remain intact, and Gedi is perhaps the best place on the East African coast to gain a glimpse of how these early Islamic towns looked. The artifacts and remains are under the auspices of the National Museums of Kenya; there are walkways to the various features of the ruins, including a palace. There are guides, a museum with artifacts, and a traditional Giriama village, partially occupied, where villagers sometimes perform dances accompanied by stupendous drumming.

Gedi is not only an important antiquity in Kenya's cultural history, but a wildlife sanctuary, home to the elusive elephant shrew, rare black-and-white colobus monkey, and a rich variety of birds including the harrier eagle, silver-cheeked hornbill, and Zanzibar shrike. The wildlife retreated to Gedi when the surrounding Sokoke forest, once vast and dense, occupying the coast between Malindi and Kilifi, began to be encroached on by farmers. The remaining patch is protected by strict control.

Watamu village and beach are east of Mombasa Road, 4 kilometers (2 mi) south of Gedi. After 5 kilometers (3 mi), the road forks, left to the village and right to the beach hotels. Here is superb fishing and sailing; for a real test of skill, try sailing into Turtle Bay at low tide. The Rangayambo coral caves at Watamu are interesting geological formations. The staff at the beach hotels or at the Gedi Museum have more details.

On a bluff at the southern end of Watamu beach road, next to the entrance for **Mida Creek Marine Park,** you will find the ruins of another Swahili village. The marine park is great for snorkeling, diving, and glass-bottom boat trips.

⑮ Watamu Marine Park runs from the reef to the coast and from Turtle Bay to Mida Creek. The coastline consists of low coral cliffs, with coral shelves and a rich spot for rock pool life. Beware the Moray eels, even the little ones. The bottom is covered with reeds and there are masses of brain coral, with exotic reef fishes, and octopus, which are shy of humans. A small reef at the mouth of Mida Creek has beautiful overhanging cliff gardens and impressive rock cod, up to 5 feet long.

Dining

See Mombasa's price chart, *above.*

Expensive **La Malindina.** Near the Eden Roc Hotel, this restaurant serves
★ good, simply presented food in no-fuss surroundings. *Follow the signs off Lamu Rd., tel. 123/20045. Reservations necessary. No credit cards.*

Moderate **German Beer Garden.** This is actually a patio bistro near shops, good for a cool beer, but the tea and sandwiches are expensive. *Lamu Rd., tel. 123/20533. No credit cards.*
I Love Pizza. Overlooking the bay road, moderately priced pizza is the attraction here. *Vasco da Gama Rd., tel. 123/20672. No credit cards.*
★ **La Gelateria.** A fine alternative to the Palm Garden, with good

ice cream and cappuccino taken in pleasant surroundings. *Lamu Rd., tel. 123/20710. No credit cards.*

Malindi Sea Fishing Club. This private club on the oceanfront, in a large, cool upstairs room overlooking the bay docks allows daily membership to its bar and lunch restaurant. Fishing charters can be arranged. *Box 364, Malindi, tel. 20410. No credit cards.*

Palm Garden Restaurant. Good curry is featured; seating is under thatch-roof bandas, within site of the Shell parking lot, so you can watch your car, which may be necessary in this neighborhood. The bar and ice cream parlor attached to the restaurant are described by one reviewer as "grubby." *Lamu Rd., tel. 123/20015. No credit cards.*

Lodging

See Mombasa's price chart, *above.*

Very Expensive **The Indian Ocean Lodge,** near Casuarina Point in Malindi, is an exclusive mansion built in the Lamu Arab style within a walled garden of bougainvillea, with a pool and private beach. There are 5 double rooms with four-poster beds and balcony. The cost of $500 per night, includes meals, and the rooms are enormous. The hosts, Peter and Johanna Nichols, arrange excursions to nearby Gedi and bird-watching, snorkeling, and fishing trips. *Box 171, Malindi, tel. 123/20394; USA: Anne Kent Taylor, Billings, MT, tel. 406/656 0706, fax 406/252 6353. 5 double rooms with baths. No credit cards.*

Expensive **African Dream Village.** Indian Ocean furniture made of hardwoods complement the spacious surroundings here. The service is friendly and efficient. At press time construction of a new restaurant was under way. *Box 939, Malindi, tel. 123/20442/34. AE, MC, V.*

Club Che-Shale is a popular luncheon place on a secluded beach 12 miles north of Malindi, near the ancient village of Mambrui. The 12 thatched *bandas* have colorful decor, baths and verandas; four cottages are new; the old ones have seen better days. The restaurant and bar are constructed of local material, and the host is a retired "white hunter." Deep sea fishing, snorkeling, sailing and boat rental. (Ask for explicit directions; it's not easy to find, and a four-wheel-drive vehicle is necessary. *Tourist Promotion, Ltd., Box 492, Malindi, tel. 123/20063, fax 0123/21257. AE, DC, V.*

★ **Eden Roc Hotel.** This superior 12-acre complex on clifftop comes with a view of the bay. *Lamu Rd., Box 350, tel. 123/20480. 157 air-conditioned rooms, all with bath or shower, balcony or terrace; some family bungalows. Facilities: 2 tennis courts, meeting rooms for 150, private beach, water sports, including scuba diving, horseback riding, deep-sea fishing, golf. No credit cards.*

★ **Hemingway's Hotel** (formerly known as Seafarers). Renovated in 1988, the hotel on Turtle Bay at Watamu is 14 miles south of Malindi. Family cottages are air-conditioned or cooled by fan, and come with bath and balcony. Two swimming pools and 4 miles of beach are added draws. Excellent cuisine—fresh vegetables from the fertile shores of Lake Naivasha, and seafood—is served. Hemingway's maintains its own deep-sea fishing fleet and excursions to Tsavo National Park can be arranged. *Box 267, Watamu, tel. Watamu 6 or 52, from Nairobi 0122/32624, telex 21373. AE, MC, V.*

★ **Ocean Sports Hotel.** Overlooking Turtle Bay, these private bungalows have their own gardens, and meals are served in a large thatched dining room. The Sunday brunch is famous; locals drive from Mombasa for a meal at what is colloquially known as Open Shorts. The clientele entertain with tall tales and public-school songs at the bar. *Box 340, Malindi, tel. Watamu 8. AE, DC, V.*

Moderate **Blue Marlin Hotel.** This international-style hotel with first-class staff is ideally located for exploring Malindi town. It is moderately priced and a good value. *Box 54, Malindi, tel. 123/20440 or 123/20441. MC, V.*

Coconut Village. Well-appointed two-story maisonettes here overlook a pleasant garden of palms and shrubs surrounding the pool and patio. *Box 886, Malindi, tel. 123/20928 or 123/20252. DC, MC.*

★ **Driftwood Club.** This popular seaview lodge has 29 cottages in a rock and shrub garden, with excellent seafood in the restaurant, and a poolside bar. The staff is charming and helpful. *Box 63, Malindi, tel. 123/20155. Facilities: pool, squash court, diving center, shop. AE, V.*

★ **Kivulini Hotel.** An innovative new hotel featuring thatch-roof chalets with traditional hardwood furniture and palatial bathrooms. Located down a long dusty road, south of Malindi, the building is set amid exquisite gardens rich in birds that extend to a private beach. The food here is excellent. *Box 142, Malindi, tel. 20898. AE, DC, MC, V.*

★ **Lawford's Hotel.** Fifty yards from Malindi town, this hotel was built in 1936, an old-fashioned retreat once favored by "upcountry" families on holiday. *Box 20, tel. MLI 6. 140 rooms in native-style bungalows and a 3-story balconied wing (built in 1978), some facing the ocean. Facilities: café and barbecues, meeting room, 2 pools with poolside bar, disco, glass-bottom boat. No credit cards.*

Malindi Cottages. These very popular thatch-roof cottages are at the north end of town, some overlooking the strand, others set inland. Most cottages feature four beds, with kitchen. There is a restaurant and a pool. Book early. *Tel. 123/20304. No credit cards.*

Scorpio Villas. First-class thatch-roof cottages with kitchens and traditional hardwood furniture are featured here, along with two pools and exotic gardens. The staff is experienced. Two minutes from Malindi Bay and the Vasco da Gama monument, its location is ideal for exploring the beach as well as Malindi town. *Box 368, tel. 123/20194, 20892. AE, V.*

Silversands Villas. Thatch-roof cottages in palm gardens and a central lodge area featuring Ethiopian carpets and beautiful carved doors make for a delightful stay. There is an excellent restaurant; the staff is efficient. *Box 91, tel. 123/20739, 123/20842, or 123/20385. MC, V.*

Tropical Village. This small hotel overlooking the sea at the southern end of Malindi town has beautifully appointed rooms with traditional hardwood furniture. Its pleasant terraces are built around the pool complex, and there is a rustic bridge running down to the shore. The facility is popular with Italians. *Box 736, Malindi, tel. 123/20888. AE.*

Turtle Bay Hotel. This hotel is relaxed, informal, and popular. *Box 457, Malindi, tel. Watamu 3, 80. No credit cards.*

★ **White Elephant Sea Lodge.** No, the name does not have the usual connotation, but pachyderms do assume the color of their surroundings, in this instance, a white-sand beach, and luxurious accommodations with beautiful gardens and a large pool. The individual cottages are furnished with traditional hardwood, and the Concourse is covered by two vast, conical thatch roofs. The outdoor restaurant is excellent. *Box 948, Malindi, tel. 123/20528 or 123/20223. No credit cards.*

Inexpensive   **Metro Hotel.** Simple, clean accommodations, shared bath, and an inexpensive restaurant make this a bargain. *Box 361, tel. 31,20400. No credit cards.*

Ozi Hotel. The simple accommodations behind the bay road are near the new Friday mosque. *Tel. 123/20218. No credit cards.*

Zinj Beach Cottages. *Zinj* is the Arabic word for East African coast, and these cottages with kitchen afford a view befitting the nomenclature. *No phone. No credit cards.*

Garsen, Lamu, and the Islands

For a taste of the bush before venturing back to the beach, independent travelers with a four-wheel-drive vehicle can take the road to Garsen en route to Lamu. Just outside Malindi, cross the Sabaki River and take the next right to the peaceful village of **Mambrui.** Mambrui, at least 600 years old, has an old mosque and a fallen tomb pillar, inset with Ming porcelain.

16 Although it is only a small cluster of shops and tea houses, **Garsen** is a welcome sight after a long drive through the desert scrub. Fuel and basic groceries are available. You can see Somalis and Orma pastoralists, who trade here. Just behind the town, cattle are herded across the Tana River, which has large crocodile and marabou stork populations. A new road is being built, with a bridge over the Tana.

17 En route to **Witu** you will see Orma houses with skins stretched over a frame, and perhaps ibis, carmine bee-eaters, and even lion. Witu was once an independant sultanate; Amad Simba is buried here, but little else of the era remains. The Old Government house is still standing, guarded by cannons. In the main square you can buy sweet bread (*hamri*), bottled soda, and tea.

From Witu you can venture north to Lamu Island, less than two hours away, or cut east to Kipini and the Bujras camp at Ungwana. For an idyllic view, try the Bujras thatched camp, which should be booked in advance for an overnight stay (consult tour operators).

The road to Lamu traverses black cotton soil lined with reeds and bogs dotted with *kongoni* (hartebeest). Past a huge agricultural settlement on the right, the road rounds a creek and
18 runs down to **Mokowe.** There is a new bridge in place of the old ferry. The channel stretches right toward the dhow-building
19 village of **Matondoni,** worth a day visit from Lamu, and left to Lamu itself. The narrow Makanda channel runs between the mainland and Manda island. At the south end of Lamu is **Kipugani,** where there is a new lodge with large bungalows and water sports.

20 You can get to Lamu (and also to Kiwayu) by flying to **Manda Island,** and then taking the boat taxi across to Lamu or being picked up by dhow from your hotel.

㉑ Few people are disappointed by a trip to **Lamu;** the old stone town is unique in Africa south of the Sahara. The elegant 19th-century Swahili and Indian houses with their beautifully carved doors reach down to the water's edge, where sailors and fishermen shout, and dhows draw out to sea. The narrow streets weave between their high, often blank walls, and inside the houses, high mangrove-beamed ceilings and finely plastered walls decorate narrow rooms that give onto cool, private courts. Lamu was one of many Swahili villages along the coast, although it is predated by Shanga, Pate, and Manda. During the 16th century, the Portuguese held sway over the Lamu archipelago, but in the 18th century the Omanis gained power. A group of islanders from Pate, supported by troops from Mombasa, attacked Lamu's southern Shela Beach in 1812. The islanders subsequently established a fort and garrison, with ties to the new sultanate of Zanzibar in the 19th century. Skilled shipwrights still practice their craft in Mantondoni, pressed by the scarcity of hardwood. They refer to the mangrove trees as "jungle crook," for they do not steam and bend the lumber but select trees in the shape they need for the hull in the mangrove forest. Their techniques and designs produced the hulls and rigs that dominated deep-sea commerce for 2,000 years.

Lamu has many mosques and is an important center for the study of Islam for the whole East African coast; students come from many countries around the Indian Ocean. Ironically, many tourists know Lamu from the swimsuit covers for *Sports Illustrated* (Cheryl Tiegs and Christie Brinkley were photographed on Manda Island) and as a playground for the rich and famous. But women in Lamu wear the black *bui bui* (veil) that covers all but their eyes, and donkeys are still the principal form of transport.

Lamu fort, formerly a prison, now features a rooftop restaurant with a spectacular view of the harbor, an exhibit hall, an air-conditioned library, and a gift shop.

The **Lamu Museum** (Kenyatta Rd.), part of the National Museums of Kenya, is exceptional and should be the starting point for your walking tour around town. (We do not recommend walking around at night.) It features a refurbished 18th-century Swahili house and informative exhibits on Swahili culture. The museum plays a central role in conserving old Lamu, including repair of the sea wall. The facility also has a good library. Archaeologists from the museum continue to work at excavation sites on Pate Island. (To get a feel for Lamu's past, you might take an easy trip by dhow over to Manda Island, to the ruins of Takwa, near Ras Kitau.)

To arrange for water-skiing, snorkeling, or fishing for tuna or sailfish through the **Lamu Broadbill & Barbill Club,** contact Niels Korchen, Peponi's Hotel (*see* Lodging, *below*); for windsurfing, contact Hussein at Peponi's Hotel; and for PADI scuba diving lessons and tented camping on Kiwayu Island through **Munira Safaris,** contact Mike Kennedy, at Peponi's.

From Lamu a ferry offers regular service around the islands. Hotels and private entrepreneurs also rent boats with crews.

㉒ On **Pate Island,** 30 kilometers (18 mi) northeast of Lamu, Faza and Siyu can be visited at any tide. The town of Pate is more difficult to reach. During the right tide it is possible to land there, but you must be prepared for an early start. Otherwise there is a long but fascinating hike from a landing area on the south end of the island.

From Lamu there is a daily boat to Siyu, a small fishing village, where you can see the Omani-style walls of the well-preserved fort and cannons lying in the grass outside. The village has a thriving leathercraft industry specializing in sandals, and you can watch craftsmen fashion furniture, doors, gold, and silver. Houses excavated in the 1970s show Siyu to have been an important cultural center for the archipelago during the 17th and 18th centuries.

From Siyu it is an easy hour's walk north to Faza, which shows signs of having been occupied in the 11th century. Note the beautiful qibla in the ruins of the Kunjanya mosque. Your boatman can collect you at Faza for the return to Lamu.

For a longer walk on Pate, venture from Siyu to Pate village itself, where narrow streets between the high stone walls of the houses are cool and full of interest. Pate village, on the island's southwest corner, is an authentic Swahili town, with strong Arabic and Indian influences. Once famous for silk, the island now grows tobacco. If you decide to take this walk, ask your boatman to collect you at Pate.

You can also take a boat directly to the Shanga ruins, where extensive excavations over the past decade have uncovered a wealth of artifacts from the 8th and 9th centuries. Most of the standing ruins are from the 14th and 15th centuries. If you want to make a day's journey of Pate Island, ask the hotel to pack a lunch for you. From the dropoff point at the Shanga ruins Siyu is an hour's walk north via a path.

㉓
㉔ ㉕ Northeast from Lamu, inland from the sea, are the **Dodori** and **Boni National Reserves.** The **Kiunga Marine National Park** runs along the coast, north of Lamu, and can be reached by a sandy road running across the Mundane Range. Before venturing to these three national parks, check with tour operators and/or the local police. Travel is not always safe, and the region may be closed for security reasons.

Dining

See Mombasa's price chart, *above.*

There are good restaurants in Lamu, most of them featuring Indian and Swahili menus at moderate prices.

Expensive **The Equator.** This waterfront restaurant is decorated with Swahili-style furniture. The specialty is crepes topped with sesame seed and wild forest honey. Try the smoked sailfish or delicious crayfish. *Kenyatta Rd., Lamu. No phone or credit cards.*

Moderate **Coral Rock.** European food with a Swahili touch is offered here. *Follow signs in Lamu town. No phone or credit cards.*

Lodging

See Mombasa's price chart, *above.*

Very Expensive **Blue Safari.** Consisting of thatch-roof bungalows on Ras Kinlindi a sandy spit on the northern shore of Manda island, the

Blue Safari has boat service for clients from the Manda strip. It specializes in water sports, especially scuba, and caters to a small and exclusive clientele. It is best to book through top tour operators. *Box 41759, Nairobi, tel. 2/338838. Closed May–Sept.*

Kipugani Sea Breezes. This new romantic and remote lodge has 12 large well-spaced thatched bungalows with huge beds, dressing rooms, and verandas. The open-air restaurant and bar overlook the mangrove channel at the southern tip of Lamu island. There are snorkeling and excursions to the dhow-building village of Matondoni. The hotel is owned and managed by the same people who run Kiwayu (below). Kipugani can also be visited by boat for lunch (Kshs. 1,300 for the boat from Peponi's, Kshs. 250 for lunch.) *Box 55343, Nairobi, tel. 2/503030, fax 2/503144. Courtesy boat transfer from Manda Island airstrip. AE, DC, MC, V.*

★ **Kiwayu Safari Village.** One of the most trendy and romantic destinations in Kenya is the renovated Kiwayu Safari Village, a collection of thatch-roof cottages, shops, and restaurant and bar located on Mkokoni inlet, facing the northern tip of Kiwayu island. With regularly scheduled flights via Air Kenya to its own private airstrip, Kiwayu offers a splendid beach and its own small fleet of well equipped deep-sea fishing boats. The hotel offers all water sports, and there are evening canoe cruises into the mangrove tributaries. The cuisine is exceptional, and the clientele sophisticated. *Box 55343, Nairobi, tel. 2/503030, fax 2/503144. AE, DC, MC, V.*

Expensive **Peponi's.** A legendary hotel on Lamu Harbor in the village
★ known as Shela, Peponi's is owned and managed with charm and efficiency by the Korschen family. The bungalows have private verandas, and there is a lively bar and grill. The restaurant features excellent lobster and a good wine list. Reservations are essential during the holidays. Peponi's also offer deep-sea fishing, water sports, boat transfer to Kiwayu, and excursions to Kipugani. There is regular dhow service to Lamu town for Kshs. 40. *Box 24, Lamu, tel. 121/3029. 21 individual cottages with shower in private bath, ceiling fans and veranda. Courtesy boat transfer from the airstrip on Manda island. 8 mi of private beach. Closed Apr. 15–June 30. AE, DC, V.*

Moderate **Petley's.** Established in 1862 by an English settler named Petley, this landmark hotel in Lamu town has 15 rooms, a decent restaurant and a dark, interior watering hole with bars on the windows. Petley's has seen better days, but is centrally located in Lamu town, next to the Museum. Sightseeing tours are arranged. *Petley's Inn, Kenyatta Rd., facing Manda island. Box 4, Lamu, tel. 121/7. AE, MC, V.*

Manda Island Village Resort. A secluded safari camp under the shade of baobab trees on Manda island, facing the village of Shela, this resort consists of self-contained cottages with a dining room, bar, lounge, and shop. The resort provides daily boat service to Lamu, deep-sea fishing, and snorkeling. *Box 78, Lamu, tel. 121/2751. No credit cards.*

Shela Rest House. This rambling, traditional house in Shela village on Lamu, five minutes from Peponi's, has several suites large enough for two couples or families at 3,000 Kshs. per night. *Coast Holdings Ltd., Box 199, Malindi, tel. 123/20182. Box 255, Lamu, tel. 121/3251. No credit cards.*

Inexpensive   Lamu has a number of lodging houses, often with beds laid out on the coral roofs. They are clean, but running water is sometimes a problem. Both the **Lamu Guest House** (behind the Lamu Museum) and the 36-room **Mahrus Hotel** (Box 25, Lamu, tel. 1) offer inexpensive bed-and-breakfast accommodations in traditional stone houses. Rooms may not include private bath and shower. Mahrus Hotel also has a private Arab house for rent. **Samahani Guest House** (Box 59, Lamu, tel. 121/3100) has 8 clean simple rooms, with shared bath and toilet, near Shela beach.

The Coast South of Mombasa

Kenya's coast south of Mombasa contains some of the country's most beautiful beaches. The A14 from Mombasa runs south about 80 kilometers (50 mi) to the Tanzanian border, giving easy access by sandy tracks to the reef and to the beach hotels, which begin shortly after the Likoni ferry crosses Kilindini Creek. The nearby Shimba Hills Reserve, a little-known but excellent game park, is a highlight of the area, as is the Kisite-Mpunguti Marine Park near the Tanzania border. Excursions can be arranged by most of the hotels along the coast.

㉖   **Shelly Beach,** closest of the beaches to Mombasa, is not as secluded and uncrowded as are those farther south, but the reef here, which is exposed for a long way at low tide, is a good place for diving. The road runs on through Ngombeni and Waa, where there are high and wild coral cliffs and interesting bat caves accessible at low tide. Near Ngombeni there's a turnoff

㉗   marked to Kwale, the entrance to **Shimba Hills National Reserve,** where you can see rare sable and roan antelope (*see* Chapter 3) and stay at either a "treetop" lodge or in self-service bandas. You can rejoin A14 at **Tiwi,** where there are inexpensive cottages and beach bungalows. At the mouth of the Mwachema River at Kongo, there is a **well-preserved mosque.**

㉘   The 20-kilometer (12-mi) stretch of **Diani Beach** is the most developed along the south coast, with a tarmac access road and a number of hotels, campsites, and villas. A casino, nightclubs, and a range of water sports take care of entertaining the visitors on packaged holidays, and the food is good. If you stay in one of the reasonably priced and delightful private cottages, local fishermen will take your order and deliver fresh lobster, and boys will bring fresh fruit to your door. The beach is shaded with palms, and at its southern end is the largely unspoiled **Jadini Forest,** the habitat of colobus monkeys, butterflies, and birds. It's a good spot to explore on foot or take a picnic.

On the road south you'll pass **Gazi,** where you can visit the 19th-century house of a Mazrui sheikh and a coconut-processing plant. At **Msambweni** there is a reputed slave pen and a fine, little-visited beach. The waters around the **Shimoni peninsula** are renowned for deep-sea fishing, and the snorkeling off the

㉙   **Kisite-Mpunguti Marine National Park** and Wasini Island is wonderful. You can visit the reef in a glass-bottom boat and take a trip to the superb coral gardens of the marine park (Kisite Dhow Tours, tel. Diani 1261/2331 or in Mombasa 11/311752). To the north is a shallow, sandy-bottomed reef, reached through an exhilarating choppy passage where dolphin play beside the boat; in the south end of the park are mangrove shallows, superb coral reefs, and a deep sea inlet with sharks. The shoreline, good for bird-watching, is famous among ornithologists as a nesting site for roseate tern. On this little excursion lunch is served in a gazebo at the end of **Wasini Island,** and you can take a walk to the ancient Arab settlement in Wasini village, where there are ruins of 18th- and 19th-century houses and an example of a Muslim pillar tomb with porcelain and shell insets.

Dining and Lodging

See Mombasa's price charts, *above.*

All the hotels serve good to excellent seafood. Nomad's is popular for Sunday brunch, and the Trade Winds has a huge buffet lunch.

Diani Area   **Diani House.** This private mansion is surrounded by 12 acres of forested garden on Diani beach. It is limited to 8 guests, and each double room has bath and veranda. All meals and safaris to the Shimba Hills Reserve are included in the rates. *Box 19, Ukunda, Mombasa tel. 1261/2412. U.S. Contact: A. K. Taylor, Billings, MT., tel. 406/656–0706; fax 406/252 6353. Very Expensive.*

Ali Barbour's restaurant features two dining sections; one open-air, the other in a coral cave. It serves excellent seafood. *Between Trade Winds and Diani Sea Lodge, tel. Diani 1261/2033. Closed Sunday. Expensive.*

Diani Reef Hotel. These pleasant, well-appointed air-conditioned rooms in a hotel with a shopping arcade, a craft gallery, and a hotel physician. *Diani Beach; Box 35, Ukunda, tel. Diani (01261) 2175/6/7. Facilities: disco, restaurant. Expensive.*

Golden Beach Hotel. This massive complex overlooking Diani Beach has 151 modern and attractive rooms with bath or shower, and 4 suites. *Box 31, Ukunda, tel. 1261/2054/9, and 2066/7. Facilities: restaurants, 2 lounges, boutique; pool with a bar, meeting rooms, gym, massage, 2 tennis courts, deep-sea fishing and water sports; wheelchair access. AE, DC, MC, V. Expensive.*

Jadini Beach Hotel. Located 4 km from Ukunda airstrip. This hotel's air-conditioned rooms, in 2- and 3-story buildings, all have a bath and a terrace or balcony. *Box 84616, tel. (01261) 2121/5. 152 rooms. Facilities: restaurant shared with Jadini and Africana Sea Lodge, disco and live entertainment, meeting rooms, health club, pool, 3 tennis courts, squash court, water sports, shopping arcade, bus to airport and town. AE, DC, V. Expensive.*

Lagoon Reef Hotel. These are spectacular thatched-roof accommodations with a large pool. *Box 83083, Mombasa, tel. 471 771, or Let's Go Travel, Nairobi 340 331. Expensive.*

Robinson Baobab Hotel. High on coral cliffs overlooking the Indian Ocean, this hotel, adjacent to an airstrip, has 149 air-conditioned rooms with showers, plus makuti-roofed bungalows with 2–4 rooms. In the Club-Med style, you pay for local services with beads. There is a good library, and Swahili language classes. *Box 32, Ukunda, tel. Diani (01261) 2026/7/8, telex 21132. Facilities: restaurant, pool, diving lessons, disco, shops, and hairdresser. No credit cards. Expensive.*

★ **Safari Beach Hotel** This hotel has 186 air-conditioned rooms with terrace, mini-bar, and telephone, divided in classic thatched white rondavels and grouped in 6 villages amid beautiful gardens. There is an excellent seafood restaurant shared with the Jadini and the Africana Sea Lodge. *6 km from Ukunda airport, Box 90690, tel. (01261) 2726 or 2131 or 2088, telex 22591. Facilities: meeting rooms, disco, pool, 3 tennis courts, squash court, water sports. AE, DC, V. Expensive.*

Africana Sea Lodge. On the Beach, 4 kilometers (2.5 mi) from Ukunda's airstrip, this lodge has air-conditioned rondavels with showers and terraces in a garden setting. There are suites available. *Tel. Mombasa (01261) 2021, telex 22591. Facilities: restaurant shared with Jadini Beach Hotel, meeting rooms; pool, tennis and squash courts, diving and water sports. AE, DC, V. Moderate.*

Leopard Beach Hotel. This is a comfortable well-appointed hotel overlooking a beautiful stretch of Diani beach. *Box 34, Ukunda, tel. Diani (01261) 2110/2111/2112/2113 or 2721. Moderate.*

★ **Trade Winds Hotel.** This is a pleasant, low-profile hotel with Arabian-style architecture, garden landscaping, and beach, near the Shimba Hills Game Reserve. *Box 8, Ukunda, tel. (01261) 2016/2116, telex. 21139, 103 rooms with air-conditioning, bath, shower and veranda. AE, DC, MC, V. Moderate.*

★ **Two Fishes Hotel.** This long-established hotel, renovated in 1984, has an excellent grill restaurant and 132 air-conditioned rooms with bath or shower and veranda. *Box 23, tel. (01261) 2101/2/3, telex. 21162. Facilities: meeting rooms for 50; pool, tennis court, deep-sea fishing, snorkeling, and sailing. AE, DC, V. Moderate.*

Vulcano serves fine Italian food. *Tel. Diani 1261/2004. Moderate.*

Diani Sea Lodge. These single-story chalets with balconies on Diani beach are good for families. *Box 37, Ukunda, tel. Diani 2060, 2114/5. Inexpensive.*

★ **Nomad's Beach Bandas.** These rustic thatched-roof huts are in a palm glade on Diani beach, with an excellent seafood restaurant that's popular at Sunday brunch. *Box 1, Ukunda, tel. Diani (0126) 2155/2156. Facilities: diving school, deep-sea fishing arranged. Inexpensive.*

Funzi Island   **Funzi Island Fishing Club.** This secluded fishing resort accommodates only 12 people in tents on an atoll of mangrove trees, with private outhouses and outdoor showers, and water heated over a campfire. Equipment for wind-surfing, water skiing, and snorkeling is provided, in addition to the charter boats and fishing gear. Transport, all meals, and drinks are also included in the rate. *Box 90246, Mombasa, telex. 21126. USA: Abercrombie & Kent, tel. 800/323–7308. Very Expensive.*

Shelly Beach   **Shelly Beach Hotel.** This high-rise hotel 2 miles from the Likoni
★   Ferry, has 111 simple rooms, plus new air-conditioned cottages with tile floors and bath or shower that are good for families. *Box 96030, tel. Mombasa 451011/2/3/4/, fax 315743. Facilities: dining room, coffee shop, lounges and dance veranda; pool, tennis court, private beach, water sports, and glass-bottomed boat trips; wheelchair access, and bus service to Mombasa. AE, DC, MC, V. Moderate.*

Shimoni   **Shimoni Reef Fishing Lodge.** Overlooking Wasini island, com-
★   fortable accommodations with excellent seafood. Dhow excur-

sions. *Reservations c/o Reef Hotel, Box 82234, Mombasa, tel. 471771, fishing lodge tel. Msambweni 5Y9. Expensive.*

Tiwi Beach **Diani Beachalets.** These fully equipped self-catering beach cot-
★ tages are good for privacy. They include the **Tiwi Beach Cottages,** the **Capricho Twiga Beachalets,** and **Fosters Cottages,**
overlooking Sand Island, a shallow paradise for children. The
restaurants and discos of the beach hotels are a pleasant walk
away. If you leave word that you are interested in buying fresh
fish and fruit, someone will come to take your order and deliver. *Diani Beachalets, Box 26, Ukunda, tel. Diani 2180. No
credit cards. Inexpensive.*

Twiga Lodge has double rooms for Kshs. 430 with breakfast,
and round thatched bandas with 4 beds for Kshs. 110 per person. There are also camping facilities, favored by the big overland trucks. Box 96005, Mombasa, tel. (0127) 4061. *Facilities:
restaurant, grocery store. Inexpensive.*

Camping A number of hotels and lodges at Diani Beach allow campers,
including Trade Winds, Jadini Beach, and Leisure Lodge. At
Tiwi Beach there's camping at Twiga Lodge.

9 Tanzania and Zanzibar

Introduction

By Ann Reilly

*Updated by
Delta Willis*

Since the Kenya-Tanzania border was reopened in 1985, it has been easier to venture south for some classic African experiences—climbing Mt. Kilimanjaro, camping on the rim of the Ngorongoro Crater (the floor of the crater is now closed to camping), and watching the great migration of wildebeest in the Serengeti—the Masai word for wide open space. For the most part, Tanzania provides this sense of space, and you will see fewer tourists than in Kenya's parks. This is especially true in the Selous Game Reserve, with over 54,000 square kilometers, the largest reserve in Africa. It is one of the few places in the world where you can gaze from horizon to horizon and not see a man-made thing. Nearly a quarter of Tanzania is classified as either wildlife or forest reserve.

Tanzania may well be the place where humanity began. It is home to the oldest evidence of our upright gait; four million-year-old humanlike footprints, preserved by volcanic ash, which were discovered by Mary Leakey and her team at a place called Laetoli, a few miles south of Olduvai Gorge. In Olduvai's interesting museum you can see exhibits on the Leakeys' discoveries, which included several skulls and bones of early humans, and hundreds of stone tools. One of Mary Leakey's former assistants, Arusha-based archeologist Peter Jones, now leads tours, demonstrating to visitors how our ancestors made stone tools.

While most people have their cameras trained on the wildlife, there are other spectacular natural forms here that will captivate you. The trees are extraordinary, and Ruaha, Mukimi, and Tarangire feature vast seas of baobab trees. There are a few giants in Dar es Salaam, on Ocean Road near the embassies en route to the Oyster Bay Hotel, and downtown, near the parliament building.

Like Kenya's, Tanzania's weather is under the influence of the monsoons, but the timing is somewhat different. July can be very wet in Kenya, while it is ideal in southern Tanzania. December and January are wet months in the Selous, while that is a peak dry season in Kenya. Insiders like to travel during the shoulder seasons, when you might have short rains, but you will have much of the terrain to yourself, and often a discount on prices. Some roads, like the climb up Ngorongoro from Manyara, can be treacherous with rain, but generally the roads throughout Tanzania have improved immensely. The graveled ones in the Serengeti enjoy good maintenance, and road graders in the Selous have come out of retirement.

The beautiful and uncrowded tropical coast was enticing to early maritime traders from China, Persia, and Portugal; the island of Zanzibar, perhaps the most exotic-sounding place in the world, was once the trading center for all of East Africa, with exports of ivory, slaves, and spices. It was the starting point for explorers Burton and Speke en route to the Mountains of the Moon and for journalist Henry Morton Stanley in search of David Livingstone. In 1880 the coastal region was acquired by Germany from the Sultan of Zanzibar. The mainland territory became German East Africa and Zanzibar became a British protectorate. After World War I, German East Africa was acquired by the British and renamed Tanganyika. It became independent in 1961, Zanzibar gained its independence in 1963,

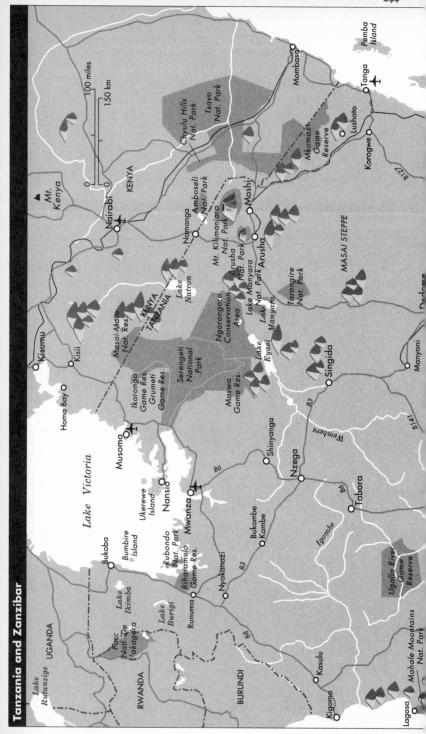

Tanzania and Zanzibar

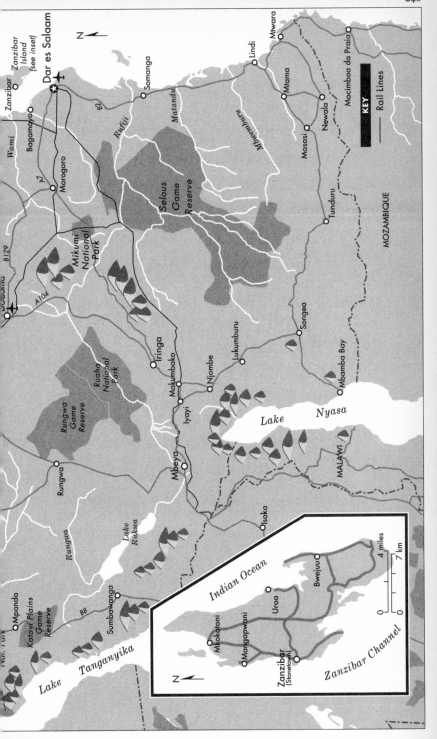

and in 1964, Tanganyika and Zanzibar joined to become Tanzania.

The people of Zanzibar are said to speak the purest form of Swahili, and the city of Zanzibar (often called Stonetown) is home to the Swahili Institute. While most people spend a couple of nights in Stonetown and then venture to the beautiful beaches, there is a small forest where you can see rare Kirk's red colobus monkeys. Accommodations for travel in Zanzibar were, until recently, for the truly rugged, but the island is now undergoing tremendous development (*see* Highlights).

Before You Go

Government Tourist Offices

These offices are useful for obtaining your visa but little else. Information on Tanzania is best obtained from established tour operators.

United States 205 E. 42nd St., New York, NY 10017, tel. 212/972–9160, or 2139 R St. NW, Washington, DC 20008, tel. 202/939–6125.

United Kingdom 43 Hertford St., London W1Y 7TF, tel. 071/449–8951.

Canada 50 Range Rd., Ottawa, Ont., Canada K1N 8T4, tel. 613/232–1500.

Tour Groups

These are tour operators that offer safaris to Tanzania, some in conjunction with safaris to Kenya.

A.K. Taylor International (2724 Arvin Road, Billings, MT 59102, tel. 406/656–0706, fax 406/252–6353).

Abercrombie & Kent (1420 Kensington Rd., Oak Brook, IL 60521, tel. 800/323–7308).

Caravan Tours (401 N. Michigan Ave., Chicago, IL 60611, tel. 800/621–8338).

East Africa Safari Company, Ltd. (250 W. 57th St., Suite 1222, New York, NY 10107, tel. 800/772–3274).

Jet Vacations (888 7th Ave., New York, NY 10016, tel. 212/977–4278).

Maupintour (1515 St. Andrew's Dr., Lawrence, KS 66044, tel. 800/225–4266).

Olson-Travelworld (5855 Green Valley Circle, Culver City, CA 90230, tel. 800/421–2255).

Overseas Adventure Travel (6 Bigelow St., Cambridge, MA 02139, tel. 800/221–0814).

Park East Tours Inc. (1841 Broadway, New York, NY 10023, tel. 212/765–4870 or 800/223–6078, or Box 42238 Nairobi, tel. 2/28168 or 2/334112).

Safariworld (40 E. 49th St., New York, NY 10017, tel. 800/366–0505).

Special Expeditions (720 5th Ave., New York, NY 10019, tel. 800/762–0003).

Wildlife Safari (23 Orinda Way, Orinda, CA 94563, tel. 800/221–8118).

Seasonal Events

The **Public Holidays** are Good Friday, Easter Monday, and Christmas; the **National Holidays** are January 12 (Zanzibar Revolution Day); February 5 (Founding of the CCM [Freedom] Party); April 26 (Union Day); May 1 (International Workers Day); July 7 (Peasants Day); and December 9 (Tanzania Independence and Republic Day). Holidays do not interfere with tourist services, even though banks and domestic shops close.

Currency

Tanzania shillings and cents follow a decimal system—100¢ equal 1 shilling, written Tshs. 1 or 1/. Coins are Tshs. 1 and Tshs. 5; notes are Tshs. 10, Tshs. 20, Tshs. 50, Tshs. 100 and Tshs. 200.

At press time the rate of exchange was Tshs. 301 to the U.S. dollar.

Every time you pay a hotel bill by traveler's check, you receive the change in shillings (you cannot pay hotel bills in shillings), so they accumulate. Tanzanian banks are reluctant to change any shillings back into foreign currency, and you are allowed to change no more than 6,000 Tshs. at the airport upon departure. So, to avoid getting strapped with extra shillings, use small-denomination traveler's checks.

The National Bank of Commerce is the only bank in Tanzania that deals with individuals and cashes traveler's checks. There are offices in almost every town and city and they are open weekdays 8:30–12:30 PM and Saturday 8:30–11:30. When the bank is closed, any hotel will cash traveler's checks.

Credit cards are not widely accepted in Tanzania except by the Tanzanian Tourist Corporation (TTC) (*see* Lodging, below). There are no American Express or Cook's offices in Tanzania. If you lose your traveler's checks, the National Bank of Commerce will act as an agent for you. If this does happen, you will have to survive on patience, for it could take up to a week or more to have your checks replaced.

When you cash traveler's checks, you must show your passport and currency form, and have the form stamped. Keep the receipts. You must show them at departure points, at the airports, and at the border into Kenya at Namanga.

If you are traveling independently, entrance fees to the national parks, room charges at all Tanzanian hotels, and certain other miscellaneous items must be paid in foreign currency; all foreign currencies are accepted except the Italian lire. Prices quoted in U.S. dollars in this chapter must be paid in dollars or the dollar equivalent in foreign currency.

Black Market There is an active black market in Tanzania, but you are at risk any time you trade, for currency forms are checked at the border as they are in Kenya. There are undercover agents in Arusha and Dar who will approach you on the street and offer black-market deals. **Never** accept a deal from someone who approaches you in the street, and be aware that while the black market thrives, your participation may land you in jail.

Passports and Visas

U.S. citizens need passports and visas to enter Tanzania. Visas must be used within six months and are good for a stay of one month unless other arrangements are made. Visas may be obtained from the Tanzanian Embassy in Washington, DC, or at the Tanzanian Permanent Mission to the United Nations in New York. A Tanzania visa is valid both for the mainland and Zanzibar. At press time visitors with a South African stamp in their passport are not permitted to enter Tanzania.

Customs and Duties

On Arrival   Personal effects and articles are duty-free. You may bring one pint of liquor and 200 cigarettes, or 50 cigars, or 250 grams of tobacco as long as you are 16 or older.

On Departure   Currency forms must be submitted with your passport, but often your safari guide will handle this formality. There is an airport tax of $10 on all international flights.

Language

The national language of Tanzania is Swahili, although there are many other languages throughout the country, and many Tanzanians in Arusha and Dar es Salaam and the lodges speak English.

Staying Healthy

In addition to the antimalaria precautions required for both Kenya and Tanzania, sometimes a yellow-fever vaccination is required for entry into Tanzania. When in doubt of this requirement, please check with the **World Health Organization** (tel. 404/329–3311), or with your local physician, who usually receives updates on the current requirements. You may also obtain advice on inoculations when you get your visa.

Insurance

In addition to regular trip insurance, you may want to consider joining the **Flying Doctors' Society,** which provides emergency rescue by air (*see* Staying Healthy in Chapter 1.) Most tour operators include this service as an option in their tour price, but you can make your own arrangements directly via **AMREF** (African Medical and Research Foundation) in New York (420 Lexington Ave., New York, NY 10170, tel. 212/986–1835) or at Wilson Airport, Nairobi. The pilot-physicians are contacted by radio in case of an emergency on safari. The story of flying doctors in told in Sir Michael Wood's *A Different Drummer*, Clarkson Potter/New York.

Arriving and Departing

By Plane

There are daily flights to Dar es Salaam from a number of European cities. There are no direct flights from the United States. **KLM Royal Dutch Airlines** (tel. 800/777–5553) offers twice-weekly flights into Dar es Salaam from New York, with a lay-over in Amsterdam. KLM also has one flight a week to Kiliman-jaro Airport near Arusha. **British Airways** has flights to Dar from London.

Kenya Airways flies to Zanzibar and Dar from Nairobi. There is a departure tax of $20 for international flights, and Tshs. 500–800 for domestic flights.

Staying in Tanzania

Getting Around

By Plane **Air Tanzania** (Tankot House, Sakoine Dr. near Pemba Rd., Dares Salaam, tel. 051/38300) has regularly scheduled daily flights between all of the major cities and towns using both jets and smaller prop planes. The prices are reasonable. There are no X-ray machines at any airport. Your carry-on baggage may be searched and you may be frisked. **Note:** It is forbidden to photograph at any airport, military installation, or harbor in Tanzania. Such restrictions are not always posted, but you may be detained for it.

There are air-charter companies out of both Dar es Salaam and Kilimanjaro airports that go to the game lodges and the is-lands. These are quite expensive and often booked far in ad-vance.

By Train **Tanzania Railways Corporation** has service three times a week between Dar es Salaam and Moshi. The fares are very reason-able, but the trains are unreliable. There is a new private train with service to the Beho Beho camp in the Selous, on the Great Uhuru Railway built from Dar to Zambia.

By Car Many tour operators from Kenya take their groups across the border at Namanga, but you must change vehicles. Driving a car without Tanzania plates requires special permits. There are no rental cars within Tanzania; you will always have to hire a driver unless you bring your own Land Rover from Kenya, which requires special paperwork, bonding, and taxes. For lo-cal drivers, figure Tshs. 95 per kilometer including fuel. You're better off with a driver, because he will change tires, repair the car if it breaks down, and fill you in on Tanzanian history and culture. All safari drivers have taken a three-month course run by the government on animals and birds, so they can be quite helpful.

By Taxi There are no metered cabs; negotiate the price first. The fare from the Dar airport to a hotel is 3,000 Tshs., as is the fare from the Zanzibar airport to Stonetown. A good place to get a cab in Dar is at the Kilimanjaro Hotel, or at the Agip Hotel.

By Bus There is daily bus service between Arusha and Moshi and Dar es Salaam and other points within Tanzania. The fares are inex-pensive, but travel by bus is not recommended. Long trips are usually scheduled at night. Matatus, unlike the ones in Kenya, are cars, and are very comfortable.

Mail, Telephone, and Telex

Postal service varies from place to place. Mail from Dar es Sa-laam is the quickest; from the game lodges, the slowest. It can take anywhere from five days to five weeks to get a letter from Tanzania to the United States. There is an express mail service that costs only Tshs. 10 more than a regular letter, but you will have to take your letter to the post office.

If you need to reach home in an emergency, there are radio telephones at the game lodges. They can radio a message for you to their main office in Arusha or Dar es Salaam, which have telephones and faxes. There are telephones in all towns and cities. Hotels will tack on a surcharge of about 50%; with the surcharge a three-minute call to the USA costs about $40.

To call the police, fire, or an ambulance, dial 999. There is no charge from a pay phone. The area code for Arusha is 057, for Dar 051.

Tipping

Most of the restaurants and hotels add a service charge to the bills, and no extra tipping is required unless you feel service was outstanding. If you do, Tshs. 50 to Tshs. 80 for a meal is sufficient. If the bellman carries a lot of luggage, a tip of Tshs. 200 is appropriate. Cab prices should be negotiated in advance, and no tipping is necessary. If you are on an organized tour, tip the driver $2 per day. If you booked your safari directly with a company in Tanzania, add $10 per day for the car. Drivers for organized tours receive tips from both the guides and the tour participants. Safari drivers receive very little salary ($20 per month) and rely on their tips.

Opening and Closing Times

Most businesses open at 8 and close at 3, although there are exceptions. Business offices are open on Saturday morning from 8 to 12:30. Many shops are closed between 12:30 and 2, and stay open until 6.

Shopping

Exceptional ebony wood carvings are found in Tanzania (most of the carvings in Kenya are mahogany). To make sure the ebony is real (and not mahogany painted or polished black) turn it upside down and scratch it on the bottom. If it remains black, it is the real thing. Other souvenir items are batiks, tie-dyed material, kangas, meerschaum pipes, and carved Zanzibar chests. Souvenirs from the Masai include beadwork, jewelry, and spears. The best place to shop for Masai items is at the border crossing at Namanga; you will be pestered to death, but the prices are very good. Tanzanite, the beautiful precious blue stone, is readily available. Ivory in any form is absolutely forbidden. Your purchases will be confiscated and you can be fined and/or jailed upon your return to the United States or Kenya.

Sports and Outdoor Activities

Golf Tanzania has three golf courses, all named the Gymkhana Club, in Arusha, Moshi, and Dar es Salaam. Arusha and Moshi have nine-hole courses and Dar has an 18-hole course. The greens fees are Tshs. 650. A golf course is being built in Zanzibar, at Magapwani, 12 miles north of Stonetown.

Ocean Fishing Ocean fishing is about as good as it can be in the Indian Ocean, particularly off Mafia Island, but also around Dar es Salaam. (*See* the sections on Mafia Island and Dar es Salaam, below, for more details on charters.)

River and Lake Fishing There is trout fishing in the rivers around Mt. Kilimanjaro and Mt. Meru, and lake fishing in Lake Victoria and Lake Tanganyika. The principle lake fish is tilapia, but you can also catch Nile perch, tigerfish, and yellow belly.

Dining

There are several good restaurants in Dar es Salaam and in Zanzibar's Stonetown, the old central section of the capital city, and food at the lodges is generally good, especially at Gibb's Farm. The local beer is Safari, and not bad (Tshs. 500 a bottle), but the local wine (Dodoma Pink and Red) is immature and sweet. Imported wines and liquor are very expensive. A mixed drink may cost $4–$7, a bottle of wine $25, and a bottle of unremarkable sparkling wine, $35.

Except at the better lodges, there is very little ice for drinks in Tanzania, and beer is generally served cool, but rarely cold. Sodas, on the other hand, are almost always cold. If you are on a diet or must restrict your sugar intake, keep in mind that there are no diet sodas in Tanzania. Bottled water is readily available, but soda is much cheaper. Bottled water can cost Tshs. 700 per liter. Bars in Dar es Salaam are often closed between 2 and 5 PM.

Lodging

The Tanzania Tourist Corporation (TTC) is a government agency that runs many game lodges, hotels, tours, and shops. You can count on any TTC operation to be of high quality and relatively expensive. TTC hotels are the only hotels that accept American Express and Diners Club credit cards. There is a 50% discount at all TTC hotels from the day after Easter until June 30. Non-TTC lodges of high quality include Gibbs Farm, Ngorongoro Crater Lodge, Mt. Meru Game Lodge, and Ndutu Safari Lodge.

Arusha

Arusha is an atypical Third World country center, with a marked contrast between old town streets and massive new hotel centers. There is a bustling feeling in town, and most places are undergoing renovation, including the Natural History Museum. Less than 80 kilometers (50 mi) south of the Kenya border, Arusha is the starting point of a Tanzania safari for most visitors, especially for those who come only to climb Mt. Kilimanjaro. Nearby Tarangire and Arusha National Parks, as well as the Mt. Meru area, are worth a visit.

Arriving and Departing

By Plane There are direct flights from Europe to Kilimanjaro Airport, 55 kilometers (34 mi) east of Arusha, and to Dar on KLM, British Airways, and Lufthansa. You can also drive to Arusha from Nairobi.

By Car If you have a rental car in Kenya, you can drive it into Tanzania; there is a fee of $75 per month to drive the car in Tanzania, and you have to obtain permission from the car-rental agency. If you are on an organized tour of Kenya and Tanzania, you will change cars and drivers at the border. If you are traveling on your own, you can arrange for a ride from any of the hotels in Nairobi to the Tanzanian border at Namanga. The fare may vary from Kshs. 350 to Kshs. 600 and depends on the number of passengers. The 150-kilometer (93-mi) trip takes from three to four hours over an excellent road.

By Minibus If you take a private minibus to Namanga, you will have to transfer to a second one to Arusha. There are always cars at the border during daylight hours. The cost is Tshs. 300 per person, and the drive takes about an hour over an excellent road. The trip passes meticulous Masai farms and is a good opportunity to photograph the colorfully dressed Masai. Be sure you ask their permission first; you will also have to pay them about Tshs. 100 to Tshs. 200 per camera depending on the number of people in the photograph.

You will go through both Kenyan and Tanzanian customs and immigration at the border, where you must surrender your Kenyan currency form and fill out one for Tanzania. There are no banks at Namanga, although one is being built on the Tanzania side. You are not allowed to take Kenyan currency into Tanzania.

If you do fly to Kilimanjaro, there is a State Travel Service bus that meets all flights and goes to Arusha for Tshs. 200. There are also cabs at the airport that charge Tshs. 2,000.

Getting Around

Once in Arusha, most places can be easily reached on foot, although the Mt. Meru Game Lodge and Hotel 77 are some distance from the city center. If you do need a cab, you can get one at the New Arusha Hotel.

Important Addresses and Numbers

TouristInformation
Tourist Office There is a **TTC Tourist Office** on Boma Road near the New Safari Hotel. It has information about safaris and will book rooms at the game lodges in the national parks.

National Parks The **National Parks Headquarters** is in the International Conference Center off Simeon Road (tel. 057/3134). It has small leaflets and excellent books on each of the national parks. Each is Tshs. 500. These are well worth the price as each contains detailed information about the park itself, the animals, birds, and plants found there, and accommodations.

Bank The Arusha branches are on Uhuru Road, on Sokoine Road near the Clock Tower, and in the Mount Meru Hotel. Banks are open weekdays from 8:30 to noon.

Medical
Emergency Shinatharia Hospital (Sekei St., Box 3092, tel. 057/6230). Your hotel can also call a doctor for you.

Post Office The post office is on Moshi Street at the Clock Tower. It is open daily 8–4:30 PM.

Exploring

The best stop to make in **Arusha** before heading out to the game parks and Mt. Kilimanjaro is the **Natural History Museum,** which was renovated in 1987 and has a new exhibit on human origins. The building is in the town center near the International Conference Center. It is a vast white structure—formerly a prison—and there is a pleasant garden in the rear with picnic tables. *Tel. 057/7540, admission is Tshs. 50 for adults; children are free. Open: weekdays 7:30–5, Sat. 7:30–4:40; Sun. and holidays 11–4.*

Shopping

The main shopping area is downtown between the Clock Tower and Ngoliondai Road. Shops sell wood carvings and other souvenirs, along with safari clothes.

Dining

At press time there were 225 Tanzanian shillings to the U.S. dollar.

Category	Cost*
Very Expensive	over Tshs. 3,500
Expensive	Tshs. 2,000–Tshs. 3,500
Moderate	Tshs. 1,000–Tshs. 2,000
Inexpensive	under Tshs. 1,000

*per person, excluding drinks, service, and sales tax (10–12%)

Expensive **Chinese Restaurant.** This is the most expensive restaurant in Arusha, but it is worth it. The prawns are excellent. For a better atmosphere, go upstairs. *On Sokoine Dr., near the bridge, tel. 057/7860. Closed Sun. No credit cards.*
Hotel Seventy Seven Restaurant. Buffet-style meals are served here with live music every evening. Lamb, beef, and chicken dishes are featured. There's an all-you-can-eat midday buffet on Sunday. *Moshi Rd., tel. 057/3800. No credit cards.*

Inexpensive **Safari Grill.** Next door to the New Safari Hotel on Boma Road is a casual, friendly place where everything is grilled in the open. Pork, steak, and fish are served. *Boma Rd., tel. 057/7782. No credit cards.*

For a taste of African food and lifestyle, try any of a number of cafés along Sokoine Road. There are also restaurants in all of the other hotels.

Lodging

Category	Cost*
Very Expensive	over $125
Expensive	$75–$125

Moderate	$45–$75
Inexpensive	under $45

All prices are for a standard double room; excluding 10–12% tax.

Very Expensive **Mt. Meru Game Lodge.** This is a cozy old-fashioned lodge on the foothills of Mt. Meru, about 15 minutes' drive south of Arusha. There are 14 cottages and a main dining lodge, with a lovely garden and a pond that attracts flamingos. The lodge was renovated in 1986. *Abercrombie & Kent, Box 427, International Conference Center, Arusha, tel. 7280, or 1420 Kensington Rd., Oak Brook, IL, tel. 800/323–7308. AE.*

Ngare Sero Mountain Lodge. Twelve miles south of Arusha near the Usa River is this beautiful estate, which you reach by crossing a small footbridge. Ngare Sero means "sweet water," and the local spring flows into a lake rich in tropical plants, birds and trout. The main house is beautifully decorated, and there are cottages that accommodate a maximum of 20 guests. Hosts Gisella and Michael Leach will arrange trout fishing and excursions. *Box 425, Arusha (turn left on the Moshi Rd. at Leganga Rd.), tel. 3629 or tel. Dar es Salaam 29325. USA: Jackie Allen, 7765 91st St., Cross Creek Villas, Plaza Del Ray, CA 90293, tel. and fax 213/823–2693. No credit cards.*

Expensive **Dik Dik Hotel.** Opened in 1990, this lodge south of Arusha near the Usa River was built in a contemporary design, with a small pool. The bedrooms feature sleek European design, and each has a fireplace, mini-bar, a telephone. The doors of Cypress wood, have bold animal carvings. *Box 1499, Arusha, tel. Usa River 73. In Germany: Dik Dik Ltd., c/o Gunter Diewald, Scheidter Strasse 52, D-6600 Saarbrucken, Germany, tel. 49/ 681–31565, fax 49/681–31582. 8 rooms with bath. Facilities: restaurant and conference space for 20. No credit cards.*

Hotel Seventy Seven. On Moshi Road about a mile from town, this is the largest hotel in Tanzania. It is laid out village style with numerous units, each containing about 10 rooms, all with private bath. *Box 1184, tel. 3800. 400 rooms. Facilities: bar, outdoor patio, entertainment. AE.*

Momela Lakes Wildlife Lodge. Formerly a hunting lodge built for the filming of *Hatari!* this renovated complex has 9 spacious cabins and 37 rondavels. There is a vast dining room where indoor barbecues are held, the lounge has a big fireplace, and there is a bar and veranda. The lodge is just outside the boundary of Arusha National Park, with spectacular views of Mt. Kilimanjaro and Mt. Meru. *Lion's Safari Int., Box 999, Arusha, tel. 057/3181, telex 42119 Lions. MC, V.*

Mt. Meru Hotel. This high-rise hotel built in 1973, has a busy lobby with the Themi Grill restaurant, bar, and shopping arcade. Offices for DHL and Air France are on the first floor, and a thorough renovation is being planned. *Box 877, Arusha, tel. 057/2711, 2871, telex 42065. Facilities: restaurant, bar, pool. AE.*

New Arusha Hotel. On Moshi Road by the Clock Tower, surrounded by lovely gardens, the New Arusha is a central meeting place, with a decent restaurant, and a busy lobby full of shops and the offices for Bushtrekker Safaris, has 67 rooms, all with private bath. *Box 88, tel. 057/3241, telex 42034; 67 rooms with bath. Facilities: grill restaurant, snack bar, 2 bars (1 in the garden), pool, sauna, gift shops, disco. AE, DC.*

Tanzanite Hotel. This hotel is 24 kilometers (15 mi) from town on the road to the airport. It has a restaurant, bar, game sanctuary, and pool. All rooms have private baths, but the supply of electricity and hot water is erratic. *Box 3063, Arusha, tel. Usa River 32. AE.*

Moderate **New Safari Hotel.** This older, but very comfortable hotel is on Boma Road and a center of activity. *Box 303, tel. 3261. Facilities: grill, restaurant, beer garden, disco, bar. No credit cards.*

Inexpensive **Equator Hotel.** A small hotel with 24 rooms, all with private bath. *Boma Rd., Box 3002, Arusha, tel. 3127. Facilities: restaurant, 2 bars (1 overlooks the river), gift shop. AE.*
YMCA. This dorm-style lodge has a restaurant, a lively bar, but no private baths. Rates: $5.25 single; $6.75 double. *India St., Box 658, tel. 6907. No credit cards.*

There is a **campsite** in Arusha between Boma Road and the Themi River near the Municipal Council Office. There are no facilities, water, or firewood and sites are $8 per person per night.

Nightlife

There is live music Monday–Saturday nights at the Mt. Meru and Seventy Seven hotels. There is no cover charge, but on Saturday night the dancing is for diners only. The **Equator Hotel** has disco dancing with live music, with a cover charge of Tshs. 275 on the weekends. **Arusha by Night,** in the hotel of the same name (on Swahili St.), has disco dancing every night, with a cover charge of Tshs. 200. It is very popular with locals.

Cave Disco in the New Safari Hotel is open every night and is popular. There is a cover charge of Tshs. 275.

New Arusha Hotel disco is open Monday, Wednesday, Friday, and Saturday and is a spot frequented by travelers. The cover charge is Tshs. 275.

Excursions

The main reason most people head to Arusha is that it is en route to the Northern Circuit of game parks and reserves in Tanzania: **Arusha, Lake Manyara, Serengeti,** and **Kilimanjaro national parks,** and the **Ngorongoro Conservation Area.** All five and several other parks near Arusha that deserve mention, including Tarangire and Mkomozi, are described in Chapter 3. It is best to make your arrangements before arriving in Arusha; lodges are booked far in advance for the Christmas holiday season and the wildebeest migration.

If you have not traveled to Tanzania with a tour group, it is possible to book directly with one of the many safari companies when you arrive in Arusha. You can also hire your own car and driver. The safari operators in Arusha can provide English-speaking drivers; many know a great deal about wildlife and botany; several were game wardens in the Ngorongoro Conservation Area. The cost for a six-day safari for the car and driver is approximately Tshs. 80,000 to Tshs. 100,000. The driver will pay his own hotel and food expenses out of this fee. You will also have to pay for lodging, food, and park entrance fees. Safari companies will charge you a flat, all-inclusive fee that will be more expensive, but you won't have the hassle of making the reservations. The safari companies require payment in foreign currency. The leading safari companies in Arusha, all of which have English-speaking drivers, are:

Abercrombie & Kent (Box 427, tel. 057/7280). One of the largest; located in the International Conference Center.

Bushtrekker Safaris (New Arusha Hotel, Box 3173, Arusha, tel. 057/3727).

Lion's Safari International (Box 999, tel. 057/8104, fax 8264; USA, Park East Tours, 1841 Broadway, New York 10023, tel. 212/765–4870. Also located in the International Conference Center).

Peter Jones Safaris, Ltd. (tel. 057/2664, fax 057/8215, or Nairobi fax 2/220–228). This Arusha-based archeologist leads walking safaris and special tours, including to the Olduvai Gorge. *USA: A. K. Taylor (see* Before You Go, *above).*

Ranger Safari (Box 9, tel. 057/3074). Its office is in the International Conference Center; it is also a large safari company.

Simba Safaris (Box 1207, tel. 057/3509). On Joe Maeda Road.

Star Tours (Box 1099, tel. 057/3181). Located on Uhuru Road, this is a small operation.

State Travel Service (Box 1369, tel. 057/3300), on Shule Road, is one of the largest and most expensive safari companies. It is a TTC subsidiary.

Tanzania Game Tracker Safaris (Box 2782, tel. 057/7700).

Wildersun Safaris (Box 930, tel. 057/3880), on Sokoine Road, has German-speaking tour guides.

Olduvai Gorge   Between the Ngorongoro Crater and the entrance to the Serengeti National Park is the **Olduvai Gorge,** one of the excavation sites that established the Great Rift Valley as the Cradle of Mankind because of the abundant fossils found there. The name of the gorge is derived from a Masai word for a tall, wild sisal (*duvai*) growing there, which you can see as you drive to the museum.

The gorge was discovered in 1911 by a Professor Kattwinkel, who was searching for butterflies and who accidentally stumbled upon fossils of prehistoric animals. The best-known finds are a hominid skull discovered by Mary Leakey in 1959, which was dated at 1.75 million years old; It was named Zinj, after the East African coast. The Leakeys also found skulls of *Homo habilis*, or Handy Man, and numerous stone tools. In 1986 a partial skeleton of *Homo habilis*, a precursor of modern man, was found by an American team. Thirty miles south of the gorge, the oldest evidence of our ancestors' upright gait was discovered, but these footprints have been covered with earth to protect them, in lieu of a museum.

From the rim of the gorge you can look down and see how the geology was ideal for revealing fossils. The guide can point out different geological eras evident by the different colors of the strata. It is possible to drive into the gorge to see the excavation sites if you have a four-wheel-drive vehicle. The charge for a guided tour is Tshs. 7 per person, and a tip of Tshs. 100 per group is in order. There is a small museum which takes about 20 minutes to tour; in it are dioramas explaining the dig sites and examples of stone tools and fossils found in the gorge.

If you want to take home photographs of the Masai, you can save all of your picture-taking for the gorge, because the Masai sometimes congregate there in large numbers for that purpose (and a small fee). They expect about Tshs. 100 to Tshs. 200 per camera for each group you photograph, depending on the size of the group.

Lodging **Gibbs Farm.** Located between Lake Manyara and Ngorongoro crater, this brick-and-stone German colonial house overlooking a coffee plantation has an exceptional garden, whose fresh vegetables and herbs contribute to the excellent meals. Many people stop here for lunch only, but the rooms are charming, and the gardens full of exotic plants and birdlife. (The pond in front of the lodge often has weaver birds, building and displaying their nests, a spectacle.) Short walks through the forest to a waterfall can be arranged. There is a pleasant lounge area with a fireplace in the main house and 15 double rooms (7 of them in garden cottages), which cost about $100 per night (50% surcharge Dec. 24, 25, 31). Lunch costs $14, dinner $16. Closed April, May. *Box 1501, Karatu, tel. Karatu 25. No credit cards. USA: Jackie Allen, 7765 91st St., Cross Creek Villas, Plaza Del Ray, CA 90293, tel. and fax 213/823–2693.*

There are no accommodations at the gorge, but Ndutu Lodge is on the border of Serengeti National Park, near Lake Ndutu, in the Ngorongoro Conservation Area, about 15 kilometers west of the main road. There is an old-fashioned-style lounge/dining room with excellent cuisine, all managed by Margaret Kullander, who was famous for her gourmet meals at Gibbs Farm. The setting is lovely, with many flat-topped acacias and the lake (Ndutu means "sound of the frogs"), which attracts flamingos. You should book far in advance to get a room during the wildebeest migration. Rates for a double are around $100 per night (50% surcharge Dec. 24, 25, 31), with lunch and dinner extra ($14, $16). *Box 1501, Karatu, tel. Karatu 25, telex 42041 Panker TZ. 32 double rooms with hot showers. AE, V. USA contact, same as for Gibbs Farm, above.*

Dar es Salaam

The capital city of Tanzania is a far cry from its neighbor, modern Nairobi. While you will spot a few 10- or 12-story buildings, most of Dar, as it's often called, is filled with three- or four-story structures painted in pastel colors and adorned with shuttered windows, looking much as they did almost a century ago. The streets are dusty and fortunately lined with shoeshine men.

Dar es Salaam means "haven of peace" in Arabic. It was a quiet fishing village founded by the Sultan of Zanzibar in 1857 until the German colonial government moved the capital there from Bagamoyo in 1891. Its population is now 1.5 million and growing. Besides being the current seat of the government (Tanzania has been building a new capital in Dodoma for 20 years, but no moving plans have been finalized), it is the country's busiest harbor, filled with both modern freighters and timeless dhows.

Arriving and Departing

By Plane Dar es Salaam's large international airport, 13 kilometers (8
Airports and mi) south of the city, is served by international carriers from
Airlines Europe, Asia, and the rest of Africa. KLM flies into Dar twice weekly from Amsterdam; British Airways flies to Dar from London. There are several daily flights to and from Kilimanjaro

Airport, which is between Arusha and Moshi. The flight is 45 minutes. Air Tanzania has two flights daily to Zanzibar, for $35 one way. The domestic airport is next to the international airport. Air Tanzania provides scheduled service to other cities and charters to other points.

By Bus There is a daily bus from Arusha to Dar es Salaam, terminating in Dar at the corner of Morogoro Road and Libya Street. The trip takes 12 hours. The bus leaves in the evening and arrives the following morning. Under no circumstances should you put your bag on top of the bus or in the overhead compartment; put it under your feet or sit on it, or it's likely to be stolen. Buses to Bagamoyo depart from the Kairakoo market on Swahili St. The price is Tshs. 175 one way, and the journey takes about 3 hours.

By Train There are trains from Moshi to Dar es Salaam, but there are many reports of robberies on the train, especially in the first-class compartments. Traveling in second class or third class, although less comfortable, is safer, because the passengers look out for one another. In second class you must share a compartment with persons of the same sex, six to a compartment, so couples cannot travel together. Third-class accommodations are seats with nowhere to sleep. The trip takes 16 hours. There is a new private train from Dar to the Selous Game Reserve and Mukumi National Park on the old TAZARA railroad (built by the Chinese to connect Tanzania with Zambia's copper belt). For reservations and schedule, go to the TAZARA station on Puga Road, midway between downtown and the airport, or contact Coastal Travels or the Oyster Bay Hotel (*see below*).

Getting Around

If you arrive in Dar es Salaam by plane, a cab to downtown will cost Tshs. 3,000, or you can take the State Travel Service van for Tshs. 450 per person. If you arrive by train or bus, you are already near the center of the city and cabs to most hotels would be Tshs. 500.

Once you arrive in town, you can travel most anywhere within the city for Tshs. 500. Always negotiate the price first. Look for one of the **CoCabs,** which have several taxi stands around downtown, as its prices are the best. A good place to find a cab is at the Kilimanjaro Hotel, where you can also get a useful street map of the downtown area (on their flyer).

Important Addresses and Numbers

Tourist Information **State Travel Service** (Box 5023, tel. 29291). Located on Samora Avenue near Maktaba Street, this is a TTC subsidiary travel agency that can make arrangements for tours, airline flights, and rental cars. It is open Monday–Saturday 9–5.

TTC (Tanzania Tourist Corporation) **Office,** in the I.P.S. Building (Box 2485, tel. 051/2485) has information on game parks, climbing Kilimanjaro, travel to Zanzibar, and other highlights of Tanzania. The staff will make hotel reservations for you at any hotel not in Dar es Salaam. The office has a limited number of brochures, and you will get more information from tour operators. It is open Monday–Saturday 9–5.

Banks There are many offices of the National Bank of Commerce in Dar. The main branch is in the NBC House on Sokoine Drive off

Azikiwe Street. Hours are weekdays 8:30–12:30, and Saturday from 8:30 to 11:30. For cashing traveler's checks, the bank rates vary slightly from the hotels, but the hotels offer faster service.

Communications The Extelecomms House on Samora Avenue near Mkwepu Street is open for international telephone calls 24 hours, seven days a week and for telex services from 8 to 7 PM, seven days a week.

Embassies **British High Commission** (Hifadhi House, Box 9200, tel. 051/29601). **U.S. Embassy** (36 Liabon Rd., Box 9123, tel. 68894).

Medical Emergencies **Aga Khan Hospital** (Box 2289, Ocean Rd. at Ukukoni Rd., tel. 051/30081). In an emergency, the hotel can call you a doctor. Drugstores carry most products with which travelers would be familiar; prescriptions from a Tanzanian doctor are required. There are no 24-hour drugstores in Tanzania.

Post Office The main branch is on Maktaba Street between Ghana Avenue and Garden Avenue. It is open weekdays 8–4:30 PM. If you want to send a package home, you'll have to take it to the customs department in the back of the building to be inspected before it can be mailed.

Precautions As we went to press, a travel advisory stated that Tanzanian officials do not immediately notify the U.S. Embassy when a citizen has been detained. Independent travelers (not traveling with a tour group) should register with the U.S. Embassy upon arrival. The best way to get yourself arrested is to trade currency in the black market or photograph a state installation (which includes harbors and airports, as well as military sites). Not all the sites are marked; save your film for the game parks. The beaches around Dar are considered dangerous even during the day; several robberies have been reported.

A flyer from the Kilimanjaro Hotel notes under Useful Hints: "Avoid walking on unlit streets after sunset. If at all a taxi is required use one from a respectable firm. Be ware about 'Hard Luck' stories from tricksters hanging around with their smooth talk and friendly persuasion. Do not venture to stroll about the harbour area, especially after dusk. Ladies always carry your bags securely under your arm preferably without valuable Ornaments too are very tempting for local snatchers."

Tour Operators **Richard Bonham Safaris** specializes in safaris to the Selous (3rd floor, Luther House, Pamba Road, Dar es Salaam, tel. 051/46862, fax 051/46863). Ask for Lizzy Theobold in the Lonrho Hotel offices.

Bushtrekker Safaris Ltd. (Upanga and Ohio St, Box 5350, tel. 051/31957, 051/32671, or 051/36811, telex 051/41178), manages hotels in Tanga and on Bahari Beach, north of Dar, and can arrange air charters and safaris.

Coastal Travels Ltd., a very efficient operation that arranges tours to Zanzibar, Bagamoyo, the Selous and Ruaha, as well as local bookings and charters, is agent for Alitalia Airlines. (Upanga Road near Ohio St., Box 3052, tel. 051/00255, 051/37479, or 051/37480, fax 051/36585, telex 41150 CSI TZ).

Charles Dobie, Selous Safari Co. Ltd. (Box 1192, tel. 28485/35638/26500, fax 28486) specializes in trips to the Selous.

Exploring

Go to the corner of Morogoro Road and Sokoine Drive and walk
down the hill. Pass through the security gates and walk over to
the **dhow wharf,** where men load and unload coffee, rice, and
sisal onto clustered dhows. If you're wondering about the
small, square area that hangs over the bow of the boat, complete with a small door, it's the "head." Unfortunately, no photographs are allowed of this port. The offices for **Sea Express**
hydrofoil services to Zanzibar are located at the pier called
Malindi Dock (no phone).

Between Mkunguni and Tandamuti streets, near Swahili
Street, is the large **Kariakoo Market,** consisting of two buildings and an outdoor selling area. Produce and fish are the most
commonly sold items, but you can purchase limited souvenirs
such as kangas, baskets, and wood carvings. There's a delightful ice cream bar across the street.

Local performers play musical instruments, sing, and dance in
Mnazi Mmoja Park, but the best sights are the medicine men,
known as local doctors, who man little stands and sell remedies
for everything from the common cold to stomach cramps, men-
strual irregularities, gonorrhea, syphilis, and impotence. Also
in the park is the **Uhuru (Freedom) Monument.**

In the **National Museum** are archaeological finds, memorabilia
from the German colonial period, and displays of wood carvings, jewelry, native dress, and musical instruments. *Botanical Garden between Samora Ave. and Sokoine Dr. at Shaaban
Robert St. Admission Tshs. 200. Open daily 9:30–7 PM.*

Nyumba Ya Sanaa, the House of Art, is a privately owned art
workshop where local craftsmen produce and sell wood carvings, paintings, tie-dyed material, batik, musical instruments
and clothing. *On the traffic circle at Upanga Rd. and Ohio St.
Admission: Tshs. 10. Open Mon.–Sat. 9–5.*

State House, off Ocean Road, is the president's home, a blend of
African and Arabic architecture built on the foundations of an
old German palace. There are no tours inside the house. The
plantings surrounding the house are colorful, and there is a
small animal and bird enclosure.

Shopping

Most of the shopping in Dar es Salaam is in the area bordered
by Samora Avenue, India Street, and Maktaba Street. You
won't find many stores selling inexpensive souvenirs and T-
shirts. The main items to look for are wood carvings, meerschaum pipes, jewelry, and fabrics. There are also many street
vendors selling wood carvings in this area. They are not hawkers and won't bother you as you wander by.

The **International Book Store** on Samora Avenue between
Maktaba Street and Pamba Road is one of the few places in
town that sells paperback novels written in English. There are
other bookstores along Samora Avenue, but these sell mostly
technical books. In the same area you will often find street vendors selling used paperbacks. If you are looking for tourist
guides, you can find them in the lobby of the New Africa and
the Kilimanjaro hotels.

Karibu Art Gallery, on Bagamoyo Road about 15 kilometers (9½ mi) north of Dar es Salaam on the way to the beach resorts, has an excellent selection of local art and handicrafts, and offers traditional dancing on Sunday afternoons from 3 to 5.

Music and Sports House on Samora Avenue between Mission Street and Morogoro Road is a good place to visit if you want to take home tapes of African music. What appear to be pirated tapes are sold for Tshs. 300.

Mwenge Curio Shops is 13 kilometers (8 mi) north of Dar es Salaam on Mlimani Road off Bagamoyo Road, halfway between the city and the beach resorts. If you want to buy makonde ebony carvings, this is the best place to shop. This is a large market with several dozen workshops where you can watch craftsmen carve, and bargain with them for good prices. Items carried are masks, carved figures, jewelry, and chests. The store is open daily 9–5. Expect to pay Tshs. 250 for a small item, Tshs. 800 for a large item.

Dining

There is a large variety of restaurants in Dar es Salaam. You can select from Continental, Arabic, Indian, Chinese, or African specialties. Fish is very popular at all restaurants. If you want to try Arabic food, *sambusa*, a slightly spicy ground beef in a pastry shell, is recommended. A typical African meal will include *ugali*, which is made from cornmeal rolled into a ball and dipped into a variety of sauces. Very few African dishes are spicy; Indian and Arabic dishes usually are.

Most expensive restaurants are located in hotels, while most lower-priced restaurants are located along Samora Avenue between Maktaba Street and the end of Samora Avenue at the Clock Tower. Many good restaurants have a minimum; for example, Tshs. 2,000 per person at the Karibu Hotel, or Tshs. 1,000 per person at The Alcove. Most restaurants add 10% tax and a 5% service charge. Unless noted, no reservations are needed and no credit cards are accepted. For prices, consult the price chart in Arusha Dining.

Very Expensive **Casanova.** A new open-air restaurant with shops and boutiques on Makami Road near the private Dar es Salaam Yacht Club, this Italian seafood place has à la carte menus and a brunch buffet on weekends for Tshs. 3,510. Cocktails cost around Tshs. 1,500 each. It is an attractive place, but the food, shortly after its opening in 1991, was not worth the price.
Oyster Bay Hotel Restaurant. With a pleasant view of the beach from the veranda, this restaurant is popular for Sunday brunch, priced at Tshs. 3,500. Cocktails cost Tshs. 300. There is a dinner barbecue and dancing in a second outdoor restaurant in back, with a second bar. *Toure Dr., tel. 051/68631.* (The management of Oyster Bay also runs lodges in the Selous [Beho Beho camp], the Mukumi Tented Lodge, and the new train on the TAZARA line.)

Expensive **Bandari Grill.** Here there is dinner dancing on Wednesday, Friday, and Saturday nights starting at 8. The specialty is pork, curries, fish, and prawns. *Box 9314, tel. 051/29611, in the New Africa Hotel on Maktaba St.*
Simba Grill. In the Kilimanjaro Hotel on Kivukoni Front, the

Simba has dinner dancing on Friday and Saturday nights with a prix fixe of Tshs. 1000. *Box 9574, tel. 051/21281.*

Summit Restaurant. Also in the Kilimanjaro Hotel on Kivukoni Front, with the bonus of a spectacular view of the harbor, this open-air rooftop restaurant is the place to dine. The menu includes curries, fish, chicken, steak and beef dishes. *Box 9574, tel. 051/21281.*

Moderate–
Expensive
Roof Garden. Charming outdoor rooftop dining with a good view of the city is the attraction here. Steaks, fish, and curries are served. *Box 1194, tel. 051/22561, in the Twiga Hotel on Samora Ave.*

Moderate
The Agip Café. Located on the street floor of the Agip Hotel, this is a clean, bright place, with music, decent lunches, excellent Samosas, and cold Safari beer. There is also an outdoor café on the upper level, good for meeting people. *Pamba Rd., tel. 051/23511. No credit cards unless you are staying at the hotel and put it on your tab.*

Alcove Restaurant. In addition to the popular dining room, which is air-conditioned and dimly lit, there is a takeout section, which is Dar es Salaam's first attempt at fast food, serving sandwiches and lamb burgers for Tshs. 300–600. The takeout is open until 6 PM every day except Sunday. The restaurant specializes in Indian and Chinese food and is open every night. A good lunch at the Alcove is around Tshs. 2,000. *Samora Ave. near Mkwepu St.*

Bruncherie. In the Kilimanjaro Hotel, this cafeteria-style restaurant has table service in the back. Hamburgers, fried chicken, and salads are served, as well as breakfast. The Kilimanjaro also has a moderate-priced rooftop restaurant with a view of the harbor. *Box 9574, tel. 051/21281.*

Bushtrekker Restaurant. It advertises itself as the most exquisite restaurant in Dar es Salaam. "Exquisite" is a bit of an exaggeration, but it is a charming place, even if it looks more as if it belonged in Barcelona. It specializes in fish, but pork and beef are also served. *Box 5350, tel. 051/25091, on the corner of Upanga Rd. and Ohio St., upstairs in the TDFL Bldg. AE.*

Hotel Mawenzi Restaurant. The air-conditioning comes in handy to cool you after partaking of the curry and fish dishes. *Box 3222, tel. 051/74592, in the hotel on Maktaba St. near Upanga Rd.*

Karibu Hotel Restaurant. There is a small private dining room as well as an outdoor Garden Café in this new hotel north of town; both serve classic Indian dishes and seafood. *Tel. 051/67761. Minimum: Tshs. 2,000. AE.*

Night of Instanbul. This restaurant, run by a Turk, features good kebabs and hummus. *Corner of Zanaki and UWT Streets.*

Salamander Restaurant. There is self-service breakfast from 7:20 to noon; lunch is from noon until 3; ice cream, snacks, and soft drinks may be purchased until 5. The outdoor café is a popular place to strike up a conversation with other travelers. *Corner of Samora Ave. and Mkwepu St., no phone.*

Sea View Restaurant. On Ocean Road near the Salander Bridge leading to the beach resorts, this restaurant has an outdoor grill and patio and a variety of meat and fish dishes in the Tshs. 250 range. *Box 2089, tel. 051/7881.*

Inexpensive
Dar Es Salaam Social Club in the Community Center in Mnazi Mmoja Park near the bus station for buses to Tanga and Iringa is the best buy in town, especially if you want to try African

food, including chicken, rice, chips, ugali, and roasted banana. It's an open-air, informal restaurant where you can watch the food being prepared.

Rendezvous Restaurant. This restaurant is air-conditioned and is open for breakfast from 7:30 to 10:30 AM and for lunch from noon until 3. It gets very crowded, but you can join others if there are no empty tables. On the menu are sandwiches, hamburgers, fish, steak, and spaghetti. *On Samora Ave. near Samaki St.*

Cafés

Dar es Salaam Coffee Bar is an outdoor café in front of the Lufthansa Building, next door to the Extelecomms House on Samora Avenue. The café is run by the Tanzania Coffee Marketing Board, and it serves coffee and pastries weekdays 6:30–5, and Saturday 6:30–2.

Hotel and Tourism Training Institute on Kivukoni Front just east of the Kilimanjaro Hotel, overlooking the harbor, is a training school for hotel managers. A former country club, it has a delightful terrace with umbrellaed tables and serves cold soft drinks weekdays noon–5 PM.

New Safari Hotel on Maktaba off Samora Avenue has an outdoor café that is very popular with the locals as well as with travelers. It's in a busy part of town, and it's a fun place to sit and relax while watching the city go by. Alcoholic beverages are served only when the restaurant in the hotel is open, although you don't need to buy a meal to buy a drink.

Ice Cream

Dar es Salaam is one of the few places in Tanzania where you can buy ice cream, and locals love it. Many outdoor cafés have ice cream bars, and there are outlets for Azam Ice Cream, a soft ice cream usually served with fresh fruit, all over the city. **Sno Cream,** on Mansfield Street near Bridge Street, behind the Twiga Hotel, is open daily 10–6, serves traditional American sundaes and sodas and in a Disneyland atmosphere. Prices Tshs. 200 to Tshs. 250.

Lodging

Hotels are often booked a month in advance. Most hotels add a 17½% tax and a 5% service charge to the rates given below.

Category	Cost
Expensive	over $75
Moderate	$45–$75
Inexpensive	under $45

Expensive   **Hotel Embassy.** This is one of the most expensive hotels in Dar, but it has fewer facilities than many of the other first-class hotels. All rooms are air-conditioned and with private bath. *Box 3152, tel. 051/30006, on Garden Ave. off Maktaba St. near the main post office. Facilities: grill, coffee shop, Peacock Bar, pool.*

Hotel Karibu. Opened in 1991, this new hotel north of town has an elegant lobby with leather sofas, a helpful staff, and well-appointed rooms, each with a VCR. This is the nicest hotel in all of Dar, but about 15 minutes by taxi from the center of town. *Msasani Peninsula Hotels Ltd., Box 20200, tel. 677601/67940/ 68069, telex 81038, Malaik, TZ. Facilities: restaurant, garden café, bar. AE.*

Kilimanjaro Hotel. Half the rooms in this TTC high-rise hotel face the harbor, which makes it about the only safe place to get photographs of the bustling port. The lobby is very busy, with many shops and tour company and airline offices, and the roof-top restaurant is very popular. *Box 9574, tel. 051/21281, on Kivukoni Front with a rear entrance from Sokoine Dr. off Ohio St. 200 rooms with bath. Facilities: air-conditioning, coffee shop, bar, breakfast room, 2 restaurants, entertainment, pool, beauty salon. AE, DC.*

Motel Agip. Despite the name, the Agip is a hotel, and it is very clean and comfortable. Its bar, lobby, and roof-garden restaurants have the reputation of being among the best in town. *Box 529, tel. 051/23511, on Pamba Rd. between Sokoine Dr. and Samora Ave. 60 rooms with bath. Facilities: air-conditioning. AE, DC.*

New Africa Hotel. Right in the heart of the city, this TTC hotel has 160 air-conditioned rooms, all with private bath. *Box 9314, tel. 051/29611, on Azikiwe St. between Samora Ave. and Sokoine Dr. Facilities: grill, lobby restaurant, outdoor café, entertainment. AE, DC.*

Oyster Bay Hotel. This renovated hotel 6 kilometers north of town on Toure Drive, has a lively social scene. Many rooms have an ocean view, some have verandas. Live bands perform in the open-air restaurant in back of the hotel (cover: Tshs. 1,000), and the balcony restaurant is popular for weekend brunches. Inquire at the desk about trips to the Selous on board the new train. *Toure Dr., Box 2261, Dar es Salaam, tel. 051/68631. Facilities: 2 restaurants. AE.*

Twiga Hotel. It has 100 air-conditioned rooms, all with private bath. *Box 1194, tel. 051/22561, on Samora Ave. between Bridge St. and Zanaki St. Facilities: grill room, rooftop restaurant, coffee shop, video library (which doesn't do the guests much good as there are no televisions in the rooms). AE.*

Moderate **Hotel Continental.** This is a small hotel, but clean, air-conditioned, and with private baths. *Box 2040, tel. 051/22418, on Nkrumah St. near Libya St. Facilities: restaurant and disco. No credit cards.*

Hotel Mawenzi. Very clean and comfortable, with all rooms air-conditioned and with private bath. *Box 3222, tel. 051/74592, on Maktaba St. near Upanga Rd. No credit cards.*

Jambo Inn. There's a sign by the registration desk that states: WOMEN OF IMMORAL TURPITUDE NOT ALLOWED IN ROOMS. Very clean rooms facing the street have balconies. All have private baths. Some rooms are air-conditioned. *Box 5588, tel. 051/ 30568, on Libya St. near the Mnazi Mmoja Park. No credit cards.*

Inexpensive **Luther House.** The most comfortable of the low-priced hotels, this high rise is behind the church on Sokoine Drive near Pamba Road. *Box 309, tel. 051/32154. No credit cards.*

YMCA. This establishment is clean but simple. It doesn't have air-conditioning or fans. There are no single rooms; doubles, all of which have private bath, are $6, including breakfast. The facility also has a restaurant, a gym, and frequent discos in the adjoining hall. Women are accepted. *Box 767, tel. 051/*

26726, on Upanga Rd. between Ohio St. and Maktaba St. No credit cards.

YWCA. It's similar to the YMCA, and charges the same price, but is a little nicer. Men are accepted. *Box 2086, tel. 051/22499, on Ghana Ave. off Maktaba St. near the main post office. No credit cards.*

Nightlife

In addition to the hotels that have dinner dancing (*see* Dining, above) and the night spots at the beach, there are several other night spots and discos in the city.

Mawenzi Grill in the Hotel Continental on Nkrumah Street has music every Wednesday, Friday, and Saturday night. There is a Tshs. 500 cover charge, although ladies are often admitted free.

New Africa Hotel on Maktaba Street has live music every Sunday night on the top (7th) floor. This is a popular place with Dar es Salaam Yuppies. There is a Tshs. 500 cover charge.

Excursions from Dar es Salaam

Bagamoyo is about 60 kilometers north of Dar on the coast, directly west of Zanzibar. Coastal Travels arranges trips to Bagamoyo, or you can take the bus (*see above*). The name means "lay down the burden of your heart," for this ancient town was the destination of slave caravans from the interior. From Bagamoyo they were transported to Zanzibar by dhow and there loaded onto ships bound for America and elsewhere. The tree under which the slaves were sold still stands. There are **14th-century ruins** of graves of the Sultans and a **Catholic Mission** built in 1868. Burton, Speke, Stanley, and Livingstone passed through Bagamoyo on their way into the interior.

Dining and
Lodging
En route to Bagamoyo you might stay at the **Bahari Beach Hotel,** which is on a beautiful clean beach 25 miles north of Dar. The hotel features two-story coral-rock chalets with thatched roofs, each with 4 bedrooms, air-conditioning, one bathroom, and a balcony. Tours can be arranged to Mbudya Island and Bagamoyo. *Bushtrekker Safaris, Box 5350, Ohio St. at Upanga Rd., Dar, tel. 051/31957, 051/32671, or 051/36811, telex 051/41178; and in New Arusha Hotel, Arusha, tel. 057/3727. TK rooms with baths. Facilities: 2 restaurants, 2 bars; Tennis court, pool. Expensive.*

Mkonge Hotel Tanga. The hotel is near the Kenya border at the edge of Ras Kozoni overlooking the entrance to Tanga Harbor, 150 kilometers north of Dar. Tanga can be reached by car on the A14, and there is a small airstrip. *Box 1544, Tanga, tel. 40711, telex 45020, or Bushtrekker Safaris (see above). 47 double rooms with bath and 3 suites. Facilities: restaurant, bar, pool, tennis court, disco, meeting facilities for 50. Inexpensive.*

Zanzibar

This ancient Arab isle was once ruled by sultans of Oman; pirates and explorers considered it their stepping stone into the African interior. The first Europeans arrived with the Portuguese in the 15th century, and thus began a reign of exploitation that continued with the export of slaves and ivory. The Arab/Islamic influence is strong; the main village, Zanzibar (also called Stonetown because most buildings were made of limestone), looks very much like Lamu from the harbor.

You can easily get lost on the narrow streets, but Zanzibar is currently safe for wandering, and the architecture captivates the eye. Wooden Arab doors are ornately carved, some with pointed brass bosses (an Indian design meant to discourage soldiers on elephants). The streets are so narrow in places that you can touch buildings on both sides, and Islamic women still wear the traditional boui-boui veil. There is so much history to Zanzibar that you find acute juxtapositions. The Cathedral church was built over the former slave market, its high altar on the site of the whipping post. The Marahubi Palace, built by the third Omani Arab sultan for the 99 women in his harem, is now the province of grazing cows.

Zanzibar island, 97 kilometers (60 mi) long, is separated from the mainland by a channel 35 kilometers (22 mi) wide; the island has several small resort atolls, including Changdu Island, and miles of beautiful beaches. The western part has many clove plantations, with trees 30–40 feet tall. Zanzibar, known as the Spice Island, once produced most of the world supply of cloves. Now the biggest source of foreign currency is tourism, and development is occurring rapidly. June to October is the best time to go. There are short rains in November, and heavy rains fall from March until the end of May.

Try to find *Slaves, Spices & Ivory* (Ohio State University Press), a good book on the history of Zanzibar written by Professor Abdul Sheriff of the University of Dar es Salaam, a native of Zanzibar, and curator at Stonetown's Swahili Institute.

Arriving and Departing

Air Tanzania has two flights daily from Dar to Zanzibar. The fare is $35 one way, and the flight takes about 20 minutes. There is an airport departure tax of Tshs. 800. Air Tanzania is on Vugu Road, Stonetown. If Air Tanzania flights are full, there is a chance of getting on board the *Daily News* (a charter that delivers newspapers), which has seven seats; the office is behind the bookstore at the market.

Kenya Airways has a daily 45-minute flight to Zanzibar from Mombasa that costs about $35, plus $20 international departure tax. Kenya Airways offices are on Creek Road in Stonetown.

Sea Express Services, Ltd. has two new Russian-built hydrofoils that make two round-trips daily from Dar. First-class seats cost $30; coach, $20. The vessel is comfortable and generally takes 1½ hours, though rough seas can slow it down, and the wise would take Dramamine before departure. The Sea Express offices are at Malindi dock, in Dar (tel. 051/20712) and in Zanzibar, at the harbor end of Malawi Road on the right. It's best to buy tickets in advance, but if you go to the office around 8 AM, you can usually get one for that day. Sea Express accepts cash in foreign currency, but no credit cards, and no shillings from foreigners.

There is a slower boat nicknamed *Yongo*, which is Swahili for "millipede." The journey takes six–eight hours and costs $11. The ticket office is near Sea Express, or inquire at the Malindi Sports Club.

Getting Around

Airport taxis look like toy cars. The fare to Stonetown is about Tshs. 3,000. Buses marked *U* will take you for much less, but you may discover a good tour guide in your taxi driver; they tend to compete. In Stonetown, taxis can also be found on Creek Road near the market and near the gas station/garage. Reception desks at the guest houses will call one for you.

Small pickup trucks with benches and a wooden frame in the back transport visitors to the east-coast beach houses for Tshs. 1,000 per person, but the journey can be crowded and dusty. Minivans charge Tshs. 15,000 per van and hold eight passengers. Vans can be booked at **Triple M Tours** (Africa House Club, tel. 054/30708 or 054/30709) or **Chemah Bros. Tours,** with offices near the fort (tel. 054/31751). Both also organize spice tours and trips to Changdu Island.

Most hotels and guest houses can arrange for you to rent bicycles, and you can rent motorbikes near the market. Walking around Stonetown is the best way to see things, and its much safer here than in Dar es Salaam, even at night, but it's smart to carry a flashlight. The streets can be dusty or muddy, depending on the weather.

Important Addresses and Numbers

Tourist Information The **Zanzibar Tourist Corporation** (Creek Rd. between Malawi Rd. and Parajani St. and Livingstone House on Malawi Rd., tel. 54/32344) sells detailed maps of the town and the island.

Travel Agent For advance bookings: **Coastal Travels, Ltd.** (Upanga Rd., Box 3052, Dar es Salaam, tel. 51/37479 or 51/37480, fax 51/36585).

Banks The **Peoples Banks of Zanzibar** and the **Tanzania Commercial Bank** are both near the old Fort.

Exploring Stonetown

Some taxi drivers will give you a good tour of the town for about $15, and tours out of town for around $30. Inquire at the reception desk of guest houses or hotels, at the **Triple M Agency**, or **Chemah Bros. Tours** (*see* Getting Around, *above*). **John da Silva** (tel. 054/32123), a local artist, gives walking tours that focus on architecture.

The Africa House (Kaunda Rd., off Suicide Alley, tel. 054/30708). This was once a British colonial club that saw its fair share of handlebar moustaches. There is still a bar with a view of the harbor, and rooms to rent, but the place is in need of renovation. That said, you are likely to meet someone from your notorious past or your scandalous future here at the ritual Sundowner cocktail hour. The beer is cold but expensive, and the simple meals are served one flight up from the bar.

The City Hall (Creek Rd. and Malawi) and the **Dispensary** on Kenyatta Road, with their beautiful architecture and wood carving like a wedding cake, are undergoing renovation.

The Old Fort, built by the Portuguese in 1700, is a formidable structure near the harbor. Its interior is undergoing renovation, but the a good crafts shop is open. People gather in the **Jamitive Gardens** in front of the fort in early evening to sample the many foods cooked outdoors: corn on the cob, smoked octopus, freshly squeezed sugarcane nectar, curries, cassava, and peanuts. It is worth a stroll in the evening to experience the exotic smells and impromptu music.

The **House of Wonders,** near the fort, is one of the largest buildings in Zanzibar, with four stories and big verandas. Built in the late 1800s by the Sultan Barghash, it has exhibits on the fight for independence.

The **Jozani Forest Reserve** is the only place you'll find the rare Kirk's red colobus monkeys, named after Sir John Kirk, the British consul in Zanzibar from 1866 to 1887. This subspecies has a reddish-brown back and tail, white whiskers, and bushy brows.

The Natural History Museum is at Creek and Museum roads, less than a block from the **Mazimolja National Museum.** *Admission: Tshs. 100. Both are open Mon.–Sat. 9:30–12:30 and 3:30–6.*

Shopping

The **Chanda Curio Shop** on Mhunazini Street has Nakonde wood carvings and mahogony jewelry boxes. **The Market Place** off Creek Road is largely devoted to produce and fresh fish, but many shops behind it sell kangas, wooden chests with brass trim, and the traditional white embroidered caps and robes. **Rashid A. Nograni Curio Shop** has brass and copper coffeepots, old door carvings, wooden chests, and jewelry.

Dining

Restaurants in Zanzibar are few and far between, but Stonetown is developing fast. You seldom need reservations, and many places have no phone. Credit cards are not widely accepted. *See* price chart for Dining, *above.*

The Africa House Club (*see above*), near the waterfront, has simple fare and cold beers with a view of the harbor. No credit cards. *Expensive.*

Fadiman's Cafe, in the elegant lobby of Emerson's House (*see* Lodging, *below*), has beautiful inlaid mahogany tables at which to take your tea or drinks. Nonguests can book for dinner on the roof a day in advance; seating is limited. *1563 Mkunazini St., tel. 054/32153 or 054/30609. No credit cards. Expensive.*

Fisherman's. A small trendy restaurant within walking distance of the Africa House Club, this new seafood place is expensive, but the lobsters are certainly fresh (two live ones trying to make an escape watched us from the floor of the entranceway). There are also good salads and soups, and the decor is pleasant in this old private house. *Shangani St. near the Starhe Club (a disco with a flashing light.).*

Floating Restaurant. This open-air restaurant on a dock right on the water in front of the old Fort has decent lunches and dinners at reasonable prices. Beef burgers cost Tshs. 500, and the menu includes a banana split or a plate of calamari for Tshs. 100.

Narrow Street Motel. This charming place on Koroni Street may have the best food in town, and attentive but novice waiters. Light pancakes with real honey are among the options for breakfast; it's best to place an advance order for a seafood dinner. Dinners cost Tshs. 1,000–1,500. *Tel. 054/32620.*

Lodging

Hotels and guest houses will change traveler's checks. All rooms must be paid for in foreign currency. Most guest houses do not take credit cards. In many of the small guest houses and bed-and-breakfasts you must provide your own bed linens or towels, and throughout Zanzibar there is a lack of toilet paper. Every bed, however, comes with a mosquito net. Some of the simpler B&Bs on the coast have no running water but provide a barrel of water with a coconut-shell dipper to drench yourself and flush the toilet. Though it seems primitive (and credit cards are rarely accepted), it's just practical; these places, if simple, are spotless and charming. (*See* price chart in Lodging *above*.)

Expensive **Bwawini Hotel.** This hotel deserves Prince Charles's Global Award for Unimaginative Design, and it's some distance from the center of town. That said, it has a pool, tennis and squash courts, a restaurant, a bar, and a disco, and the rooms have private baths. *Funguni Creek, tel. 054/30200. AE, DC.*

Emerson's House. This sprawling old mansion in a central location was recently renovated by a New Yorker named Emerson. The bedrooms are different sizes and configurations, some have views and some have private bathes, but all are decorated with antique furniture and each has a color scheme that complements its Persian carpets and elegant draperies. The Red Room, with a kitchen, for example, costs $95 a night; there is a brass bed in the Purple Room, which rents for $50, and others range from $40 to $75. The small dining area on the roof has spectacular views of the city, plus a bathtub around a discreet corner, for those who like to scrub under the stars. Fadiman's Cafe is downstairs. *Box 4044, 1563 Mkunazini St., tel. 054/ 32153 or 30609. 8 rooms USA: Members Afield, 217 E. 85th St., New York, NY 10028, tel. 212/879–2478, fax 717/477–2519.*

Inexpensive **The Malindi Guest House.** This wonderful old private mansion, one of the best values in town, is frequented by trendy people, although the single rooms and bathrooms are rather simple and bathrooms are down the hall. The interior lounges have bold Arab chairs and plenty of space to sprawl—floor pillows cover one corner that is studded with brass incense burners. The center courtyard, open to the sky, has lovely plants and a stairway. There is a breakfast room where service can be slightly disorganized (on a recent visit someone forgot to do the shopping, and a waiter ran to the market for milk and papaw.) The bathrooms are clean, and the brass sign out front is polished. The rates include breakfast. (New Gulf, a cafe, across the street, plays loud music at midday, but not in the evening.) *On Malindi St. at Funguni Bazaar near the dock. tel. 054/30165. No credit cards.*

Narrow Street Hotel. Don't be put off by the exterior: Inside are some of the sweetest rooms in town, with embroidered sheets and pillowcases and carved four-poster beds with mosquito nets. The rooms seem small, perhaps because they have so much ornate furniture crammed into them and (for some reason) TV sets. It's much more entertaining to go to a balcony off one of the sitting rooms for a view of the rooftops of Stonetown. All rooms have telephones and private baths with tubs. The restaurant downstairs is good value, and the staff is charming. *Koroni St., just off Creek Rd., Box 3784, tel. 054/32620, fax 054/30052.*

Spice Inn. As recently as 1990 this old mansion (near Emerson House and the intersection of Change Bazar and Mukunazini St.) was a highly recommended place to stay, but after reports of "seedy" and "unclean," a look in September, 1991, confirmed that things had gotten a little sloppy. If you can't find space elsewhere, check it out; it may have revived. The exterior has ornate balconies, and the interior has antique furniture in the best rooms, some of which have balconies. All the rooms are different value so ask to have a look. Single and double rooms with shared baths cost about $20–$28, and there are suites with private baths for $40 a night. *Box 1090, tel. 054/28826 or 054/30728.*

Victoria's Guest House. So this is Victoria's secret. An excellent place to stay if the Malindi Guest House is full, the guest house is located between Kaunda and Vuga roads near the Omani Consulate. This has surprising contemporary design and a very nice staff. *Victoria Rd., tel. 054/32861. No credit cards.*

Excursions

Changdu Island Once known as Prison Island, this is a lovely beach retreat, with good snorkeling, wind-surfing, sailing, and giant tortoises. You can arrange for transportation from Stonetown at the Triple M Agency or Chemah Tours (*see* Getting Around), and there are boats for transfer to the island. The price should be about Tshs. 2,000 (you may have to bargain), plus a docking fee to step on the island of $1 or £1. Lonrho Hotels plans a huge complex on Changdu Island to be completed in 1993. For information contact Lonhro at Luther House (tel. 051/46862 in Dar, fax 051/46863, or tel. 071/402–4141 in London).

Lodging **Changdu Island Resort.** This TTC lodge has simple rooms and reasonably priced meals (fresh lobster costs Tshs. 900). Wind-surfing costs about Tshs. 1,200 per hour, snorkeling Tshs. 500 per day for gear, sailing Tshs. 1,500 per hour. *Box 216, tel. 054/32344, telex 57144.*

Bwejuu This is a beautiful remote area on the eastern shores, where the beaches are clean and the water jade and aquamarine. In this traditional fishing village the men set out with dhows, and the women bury coconut in the sand to soften the fibers for making the twine that holds together a fishing net, or a bed, or a chair. The children will come by with baskets of hot potatoes or shells to sell, and you can rent bicycles or go fishing for nominal fees.

Lodging **The Palm Beach Inn.** This is a small, simple white house on the beach with a veranda and beach furniture, a couple of double rooms with private baths, and two dormitory-style rooms with an adjacent shared bath. There is no running water or electricity. Fresh water is provided in barrels for dipping with a coconut shell on a handle, and bottled water costs Tshs. 500 a liter. Kerosene lanterns are used in the evening.

Rates are $10 a night per person, including breakfast, but lunch costs about $6 and dinner $8. There is no alcohol for sale, but you can bring your own. The meals are good, with spicy curries and fresh fish; the cook and staff are friendly and helpful; and the owner, a Zanzibar woman of presence and character, plans to open a restaurant next door in 1992. There is no telephone, but you can book through Triple M Tours, Chemah Bros., or the Zanzibar Tourist Information Center in Stonetown.

Bwejuu Beach Hotel. Just north of the Palm Beach Inn is a slightly larger guest house, with a central courtyard, a bar, and a balcony. Most of the rooms are dormitory style, and each is named after a local spirit; bathrooms are shared. The rate is about $12 a night, with lunch and dinner extra (there is cold beer). It is a delightful place if you are on a budget, and the guests are interesting young Europeans and the occasional American. Book as for Palm Beach Inn, above.

10 Seychelles

Introduction

By Michael Pennacchia

New York City–based freelance journalist/ photographer Michael Pennacchia is an inveterate traveler in search of the exotic and unusual. His work has been published in the New York Times, *Travel-Holiday, Diversion, American Way, and* People.

Spread over 1,000 kilometers (600 mi) of the turquoise waters of the Indian Ocean, is the Seychelles archipelago. A tiny Socialist republic, this developing nation of 65,000 people consists of some 100 islands, only a quarter of which are inhabited. They are distributed from 4 degrees to 11 degrees south of the equator and are divided into four groups: the northern Inner Islands, about 1,800 kilometers (1,115 mi) east of Mombasa, Kenya; and the Amirantes, Farquhar, and Aldabra groups, extending southwest.

The 30 Inner Islands, except for the coral Bird and Denis islands, are the only mid-ocean granitic islands in the world. Of this group the three main islands, Mahé, Praslin, and La Digue, and also Frégate and Silhouette are of interest to travelers, as is Desroches, the largest of the coral Amirantes group, which opened to visitors in 1987.

Many things about Seychelles (SAY-shells) inspire awe in even the most seasoned globe-trotter: their variety of rare and endangered species, such as Frégate's magpie robins; botanical oddities such as Praslin's coco-de-mer, a double coconut that is the world's largest and heaviest seed of the vegetable kingdom; and George, the 90-year-old tortoise at the Cousin bird sanctuary, who enjoys having his leathery neck caressed. Some 180,000 giant tortoises roam on Aldabra Island. This, along with the variety of species, has led many to think of the Seychelles as the Galápagos of the Indian Ocean.

Clouds cap the granite peaks of Seychelles' larger, northern Inner Islands. Dense tropical vegetation blankets these mountains; below are blinding white beaches and gargantuan Pre-Cambrian outcroppings that hug intimate coves. Exotic seashells house hermit crabs, and multicolored coral parallels the pristine shores.

Although Seychelles' coral islands, flat, often bordered by limestone formations, and about 10 feet above sea level, are not as scenic as the granite islands, the coconut palms that grow on them are a boon to Seychelles' copra industry.

Since the 7th century, Arab traders, pirates, and such renowned navigators as Vasco da Gama have exploited these islands. Muskets, farm implements, and graves of pirates have been unearthed here. A search for sunken treasure is under way at the site of the skull-and-crossbones ensign at Bel Ombre on Mahé.

It wasn't until 1770 that the first French settlers arrived, with African slaves in tow. In 1811, Seychelles became the property of the British under King George III. When slavery was abolished in 1833 by the British Parliament, 6,521 of Seychelles' 7,500 inhabitants were slaves. Seychelles became independent from the British in 1977, when a new government was formed by a bloodless coup under the guidance of France Albert René, the current president.

Tourism to Seychelles is a recent phenomenon. In 1963 the U.S. Air Force, which had set up a satellite-tracking station at La Misère on Mahé, began a weekly flight from Mombasa with an amphibious Grumman Albatross. This heralded the air age in Seychelles and inaugurated regular airmail service to the rest

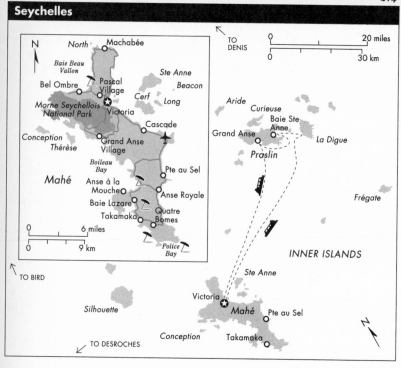

of the world. Regular passenger service started in 1970, operated by Air Kenya from Mombasa, and Mahé's international airport opened the following year.

More than half of the 2,000 annual North American visitors come via East Africa, usually as an addition to a game safari, although the unique character of these islands is reason enough to visit. Vacationers from Britain, France, Italy, and Germany constitute most of the 70,000 annual travelers to Seychelles. The nation has benefited from its innovative environmental and conservation laws, and from its commitment to limit development. The island nation has nearly 3,600 beds; officially the government has proclaimed a ceiling of 4,000 beds, but there was also once a promise that hotels would rise no higher than a coconut palm, and the Mahé Sheraton obviously does.

The Seychellois (Sey-shel-WAH) are of African, French, English, Asian, and Madagascan origins, evident in their black, mulatto, and white skin tones and their culture, language, and cuisine. Ninety percent of the population reside on Mahé, Praslin, and La Digue. The national language is Creole, but many speak French and English. Often, especially on the less populous islands, the Seychellois observe visitors with a bemused curiosity. Their welcoming smiles and easygoing nature are pleasant complements to the serene landscape.

The rare birds and unusual marine life, the variety of water sports, and the unsullied beauty of Seychelles' islands are the attractions. The islands are more of a destination for families and honeymooners than a place to meet singles. There is some nightlife—on Mahé in particular—but most visitors come to Seychelles to relax on deserted beaches and enjoy its pleasant climate and quiet.

Before You Go

Government Tourist Offices

Contact the Seychelles Tourist Office.

United States 820 2nd Ave., 3927 F., New York, NY 10017, tel. 212/687–9766, fax 212/808–4975.

United Kingdom Eros House, 2nd floor, 111 Baker St., London WIM IFE, tel. 071/224–1670, fax 071/487–5756.

Kenya Jubilee Insurance Exchange, 3rd floor, Box 30702, Nairobi, tel. 2/225103, 2/226744, 2/229441, fax 728696.

Tour Groups

Your air and land expenses will be reduced if you go on a package tour. Mahé's travel agencies and tour operators can arrange packages similar to those offered by your agency at home, and they may know the options more thoroughly, but planning your trip before you go will afford you more free time in Seychelles. Packages range from the general-interest island-hopping tours to the more specialized ornithology, walking/hiking, diving, fishing, and chartered-boat tours. If you choose an island-hopping tour, you can still sample the specialized attractions. The best way is to spend time on less populous islands such as Silhouette, Frégate, and Desroches, rather than only on Mahé, Praslin, and La Digue. Most North American travel agencies are not as well versed on Seychelles as those in the United Kingdom, where most Seychelles visitors originate. So you may have to plan your trip from a distance, unless you reside near a knowledgeable agency like African Holidays in Tucson, Arizona.

When considering a tour, be sure to find out (1) exactly which expenses are included (particularly tips, taxes, side trips, additional meals, and entertainment). Most lodging packages include breakfast. You may be wise to choose a breakfast-only option, and experience other hotels and restaurant cuisines. This will also free you from having to return to your hotel for every lunch and dinner, allowing day excursions around the island. (2) Familiarize yourself with the ratings of the hotels on the itinerary and the facilities they offer. Check to see if "soft" (nonfuel) water sports are offered free of charge. (3) Look into the cancellation policies, particularly the penalties, for both you and the tour operator. (4) Find out the cost of a single supplement if you are traveling alone. Most tour operators request that bookings be made through a travel agent, and there is no additional charge for the service. To phone Seychelles from North America, callers must go through the international operator. Callers from the United Kingdom may dial direct, using the area code (248).

General-Interest **African Holidays** (Box 36959, Tucson, AZ 85740, tel. 602/742–
From the 1161 collect from AZ or 800/528–0168) has a 13-day Island Hop-
United States pers Tour and honeymoon packages. **Abercrombie & Kent** (1420

Kensington Rd., Oak Brook, IL 60521, tel. 312/954–2944 or 800/323–7308). **African Safari Trails** (50 Water St., South Norwalk, CT 06854, tel. 203/866–0565 or 800/234–2585) has budget tours. **African Travel** (Glendale, CA, tel. 800/722–7755). **Sue's Safaris** (Rancho Palos Verdes, CA, tel. 213/541–2011 or 800/541–2011). **Wildlife Safari** (Moraga, CA, tel. 800/221–8118 or 800/526–3637 in CA).

From Canada **Mondorama** (5540 Côte des Neiges, Montreal, H3T 1Y9, Canada, tel. 514/735–5530).

From the United Kingdom **Abercrombie & Kent** (Sloane Square House, Holbein Pl., London SW1W, (tel. 01/730–9600).

The tour operators listed above can add a trip to Seychelles to an East African safari.

Special-Interest *In the United States* **Diving—Marine Biology: Fantasea Cruises Ltd.** (2409 23rd St., Santa Monica, CA 90405, tel. 213/392–8054, fax 213/392–5016).

Sea Safaris (Manhattan Beach, CA, tel. 800/821–6670, or 800/262–6670 in CA).

Walking: Check with the Seychelles Tourist Office (Independence House, Box 92, Victoria, Mahé, Seychelles, tel. 248/22881), which sells trail guides for the equivalent of $1.

In the United Kingdom **Tana Travel** (2 Ely St., Stratford-upon-Avon, Warwickshire CV37 6LW, tel. 789/414200). Besides the general island-hopping tour, Tana packages ornithology, walking, diving, fishing, and yachting tours.

When to Go

Seychelles' climate averages about 80°F year-round. During the northwest monsoon season, when winds blow from December until late March, heavy rains set in which fall with determination during sudden late-evening or overnight downpours. Between May and October, the Indian winter brings cooler and drier weather, when the southeast trade winds blow. During Indian winter, there may be a light, misty spritz, or sometimes a heavy downpour. The sun shines about seven hours each day, and the days last about 11 to 12 hours, with the sky darkening around 6:30 PM. There are often clouds in the sky, though they don't always conceal the sun. Conditions may vary from island to island and throughout Mahé, with one side of the island having different weather from the other. Weather patterns in Seychelles have been unusual over the past few years: The dry season hasn't always been dry, and the wet season not always wet.

Festivals and Seasonal Events

Seychelles will host the Indian Ocean Island Games in August of 1993.

Holidays in Seychelles include the two-day welcome to the New Year, on January 1 and 2; Good Friday and Easter in March or April; Labor Day on May 1; Liberation Day (June 5); Corpus Christi in May or June, observed with parades, floats, and musical celebrations, Independence Day on June 29, when schools compete in sporting events; the feast of the Assumption of Our Lady on August 15, when a large festival takes place on La Digue, luring visitors from many of the other islands; La Fête La Digue Annual Regatta in September; All Saints' Day on November 1; the Annual Deep-Sea Fishing Championship in November; the Celebration of the Immaculate Conception on December 8; and Christmas Day.

What to Pack

Lightweight, casual cotton clothing will be most comfortable in Seychelles. T-shirts, polo shirts, cotton blouses and short-sleeve shirts, slacks and cotton dresses, sandals, and canvas shoes or tennis shoes will suffice. Jackets and ties are rarely necessary for men, but women may be wise to bring a dress or two for evening dining. A light sweater, sweat shirt or windbreaker, sunglasses equipped with a strap, a strong sunblock, insect repellent, hat, umbrella, and light poncho will help to cope with the varied climate. Sturdy walking or light hiking shoes (*see* Exploring Victoria, below) will come in handy for nature walks and hikes through the sometimes rocky mountains. Bring a pack to tote your camera, towel, and such items as you will need for the day. Your feet will thank you for bringing a pair of old tennis shoes or diving boots to wear on rocky and coral beaches. Bringing your own snorkel and mask—though these are easily acquired at hotels and dive shops—will give you the opportunity to stop along the road and explore the coastline; they will also fit better. If you plan to visit the smaller islands, bring shampoo and other toiletries, which are not provided in hotels or easy to purchase. If you use a sugar substitute, pack that too, as it's hard to come by. A portable clothesline will also come in handy, as will a pair of binoculars for viewing the rare birds. You'll spend a lot of quiet time here, and evening activities on islands other than Mahé are limited, so bring a good book or two. If you're taking a 35-millimeter camera, use a polarizing filter to cut down on the glare when you photograph seascapes. Many hotels provide converters for the 200-volt-current, but bring one along just in case.

Taking Money Abroad

Traveler's checks and most major credit cards are accepted throughout Seychelles. You'll get a better exchange rate for traveler's checks than for cash, and if you use Barclays' checks and cash them at a Barclays Bank—the most widely represented, with seven branches—there will be no commission or service charge. If you're carrying traveler's checks, bring a list of offices along your route where you can get refunds for lost checks.

Getting Money from Home

Using an American Express or Visa card is the easiest way to get money from home. Barclays Bank represents Visa. Travel Services (Victoria House, Mahé, tel. 248/22414) is the local American Express representative.

Currency

The Seychelles rupee (SR) is the official currency. 1 rupee = 100¢. Coins are in denominations of 1, 5, 10, and 25¢, and 1 and 5 rupees. Notes come in bills of 10, 25, 50, and 100 rupees. Since 1987, the exchange rate has ranged from SR4.8 to SR5.2 per U.S. dollar. The rate in late March 1992 was SR4.4. The rates given by the banks are determined by the government, and published in the daily newspaper *Nation*. Most of the hotels change money, but the best rates are at the banks. Not all shops are equipped to cash traveler's checks, so carry some rupees when shopping. Prices quoted in this guide are in U.S. dollars unless noted otherwise, and are based on an exchange rate of SR5 to the U.S. dollar.

What It Will Cost

Most consumer goods must be imported into Seychelles. Travelers seeking a bargain meal may have a problem finding it. The majority of restaurants tack on a 10% service charge to your bill. There is no airport departure tax.

Sample Prices (1992): Cup of coffee, SR5 (US$1); bottle of beer, SR10 (US$2); soda, SR5 (US$1); toasted cheese sandwich, SR15 (US$3); 1-mile taxi ride, SR5.2 ($1.40); double room: budget, $70; moderate, $170; luxury, $300.

Staying Healthy

No single case of AIDS has yet been reported in Seychelles, but according to the Minister for Health, there is "the common practice of having multiple sex partners" and "a high incidence of gonorrhoea." With caution and care, the greatest dangers to your health are avoidable. Whether it is direct or overcast, the sun is very strong, so use a protective lotion and appropriate clothing. On the beaches, sea urchins, bits of coral, and broken shells may injure your feet, so protect yourself by wearing sandals or a pair of old tennis shoes. Mosquitoes are a problem in lush areas; ask your hotel for insect repellent or mosquito coils. Bring some of your own along. Oil of citronella is a good local repellent. It is safe to drink the water and eat fruits and vegetables. Intestinal parasites do exist, however, and some people prefer to drink bottled water.

There is no private medical practice in Seychelles. Treatment and hospitalization are free for the Seychellois and other residents, though visitors will be obliged to pay for them. Some of the larger hotels employ nurses to care for visitors when needed. If your illness is serious, either the Mont Fleri (tel. 24400) or the Anse Royal (tel. 71222) hospital can direct you to the nearest clinic. Your hotel management will assist you with this and will call an ambulance if necessary.

Language

A form of Creole is the national language, but half of the Seychellois speak English, and more than a third speak French. Most of the people in the tourist industry speak at least some English.

Car Rentals

There are 30 rental-car companies on Mahé and Praslin—the only islands where driving is permitted—with offices at the airport, hotels, and throughout Mahé. Major U.S. companies such as **Hertz** (tel. 800/654–3131), **Avis** (tel. 800/331–1212), and **Budget** (tel. 800/527–0700) are all represented. A standard car or jeep costs approximately $60 per day, including third-party insurance and tax, with no mileage charge. Rental cars include the Mini-Moke, an oversize go-cart, usually with open sides and open roof; Suzuki Samurai jeeps; Datsuns; Lancers; Toyotas; and Mercedes. Cars are rented with a near-empty tank. Renters pay only for the fuel they use, and gasoline costs about $4 per gallon.

The rate for a car with driver starts at $160 per day. Contact the Car Hire Operators Association in Victoria (tel. 248/23747).

Arriving and Departing

From North America by Plane

All international flights arrive at Mahé's **Seychelles International Airport,** 10 kilometers (6 mi) south of Victoria (tel. 248/76501).

Most North Americans reach Seychelles via East Africa. Others take American, or TWA to London, Zurich, Paris, Frankfurt, or Rome and connect with Air France, Air Seychelles, Aeroflot, British Airways, or Alitalia, which all fly to Seychelles. Air Seychelles also flies from Johannesburg and Singapore. Kenya Airways and Air Tanzania fly to Seychelles from Africa.

The flight from New York to London takes seven hours, and from London to Seychelles, 10½ hours. Flight time from Nairobi, Kenya, to Mahé is about four hours; the monthly Aeroflot flight from Dar es Salaam to Mahé takes four hours.

Between the Airport and Center City The airport is on the bus route into Victoria (fare is less than $1), where you can change buses at the station on Palm Street to reach your destination. A 15-minute taxi ride between the airport and Victoria will cost about $7 during the day.

Staying in Seychelles

Getting Around Seychelles

By Car Renting a Mini-Moke or jeep is a fun way to see Mahé, which is only 30 kilometers (18 mi) long. Local numbers for a few major car-rental companies are: **Avis** (tel. 248/22711 or 248/22542); **Budget** (tel. 248/73069, 248/44280, or 248/44296); **Hertz** (tel. 248/22447 or 248/22669). Foreigners must be over 21 years of age and have a valid driver's license to drive—on the left. The speed limit in Victoria and other villages is 45 kilometers (28 mi) an hour, 65 kilometers (40.4 mi) an hour elsewhere. Driving on the left is not as difficult as it may appear at first. The real challenge is driving across the island's two-lane corkscrew mountain passes, via La Misère (the quicker route) and Sans Souci. The passes afford spectacular mountain vistas, but if you want to sightsee, pull off the road. Guard rails are rare, and if you glance away from the road, you are likely to take a tumble down the mountain and spoil your holiday. The Seychellois walk and hitchhike along the narrow roads, so be attentive; they may be just around the next bend. Picking up hitchhikers is a harmless way to absorb some local culture, but you may have to set limits, since more people than your car can accommodate will jump in when you stop. If you're driving along Sans

Souci at night, don't be surprised if you encounter a road barrier, a bright light glaring in your eyes, and a young man in army fatigues wielding a shotgun. Seychelles' President René lives on this road, so this is no more than a protective measure. If you look more like a confused tourist than a mercenary, chances are the soldier will raise the bar and wave you on your way. There are only five gas stations on Mahé, and they close in the evening, so be sure you have enough fuel to get around, especially in the south, where the only station is at Anse Royal on the southeast coast.

A jeep is the most convenient mode of transportation on Praslin, where the roads are paved but not always in the best condition, and there are potholes in the dirt roads that lead to the island's most attractive spots.

By Plane Air Seychelles offers a network of scheduled interisland air services to the more popular islands. Many daily flights operate between Mahé and Praslin. There are two daily flights between Frégate and Mahé and one between Bird and Mahé; flights on Wednesday, Friday, and Sunday between Mahé and Denis; and flights between Mahé and Desroches on Monday, Wednesday, and Sunday. The flight from Mahé to Praslin or Frégate takes 15 minutes; between Mahé and Bird or Denis, 30 minutes; and between Mahé and Desroches, one hour. Extra flights operate according to demand, and charter flights can be readily arranged to other islands. Services are either on a 19-passenger or nine-passenger plane. If you are interested, you may ask to sit next to the pilot for a bird's-eye view of the islands.

Check-in for all interisland flights is 30 minutes before departure.

Reservations Contact the **Air Seychelles office** at Victoria House, Victoria, Mahé (tel. 248/21548/9), or at the **Domestic Terminal** at the airport (tel. 248/76501). Round-trip fares from Mahé: to Praslin, $60; to Frégate, $54; to Bird, $176; to Denis, $198; to Desroches, $160.

By Bus There is an excellent bus service on both Mahé and Praslin, with 24 routes on Mahé and four on Praslin. Buses run from about 5:30 AM to 7 PM, with reduced service on Sundays. Minimum fare is 40¢ and the maximum is $1. On Mahé some routes traverse the mountain passes, offering an inexpensive sightseeing tour. Most buses begin and end at the bus station on Palm Street in Victoria. On Praslin, many buses pass through the scenic Vallée de Mai. All hotels and guest houses are on bus routes; just let the driver know where you want to get off.

By Taxi There are more than 125 taxis on Mahé and Praslin, and day and night rates are fixed by the government. Updated fares are listed at the airport. Taxi drivers will also take visitors on sightseeing tours. On Mahé, taxis operate on a 24-hour basis (tel. 248/21703 or 248/47141). For further information, contact the **Taxi Association** (Olivier Maradam St., Victoria, tel. 248/23895).

By Boat Scheduled ferry services operate schooners that motor or sail between Mahé and Praslin, Mahé and La Digue, and Praslin and La Digue. Schedules may vary depending upon weather conditions. The three-hour trip from the Inter-Island Quay in Victoria to Baie Ste. Anne in Praslin operates Monday to Thursday at noon, and at 1 PM on Monday, Wednesday, and Friday. Return trips run on Monday, Wednesday, and Friday at 5:30 AM and 6 AM, and on Tuesday and Thursday at 6 AM and noon or 1 PM.

The boat for the 3¼-hour trip to La Digue departs Mahé at 6 AM weekdays, and departs La Digue weekdays at 1 PM. One-way trips for the above services cost $7. There is daily service between Praslin and La Digue. The one-way half-hour trip costs $5.

Charter Boats There is a wide selection of fishing boats and yachts that are available for day trips, overnight trips, or extended charters throughout Seychelles. The choice ranges from the 52-foot Sport Fisherman *Pasadena* to the 44-foot catamaran *Encounter*, which was used in the film *Castaways*. Charter packages may include diving, fishing, snorkeling, and water-sports equipment; full crew; and meals. A charter is one way to get off the beaten track and explore the more remote parts of the archipelago. Contact the **Marine Charter Association** (tel. 248/22126) or Seychelles' travel agencies (*see* Important Addresses and Numbers, below).

By Bike Bicycles and motorbikes may be rented on Mahé, at **Rent-a-Cycle** (Castor Rd., Victoria); **Tokio Rent-a-Cycle,** Mr. d'Offey, St. Louis (tel. 248/21179); and **Low Hong's,** Mr. J. Fontaine, St. Louis (tel. 248/22278). Bicycles are also available on Praslin at the **Flying Dutchman Hotel,** Grand Anse (tel. 248/33337); **Indian Ocean Fishing Club,** Grand Anse (tel. 248/33324); and **Maurice Payet,** Côte d'Or, on La Digue, at **La Digue Island Lodge** (tel. 248/34237/9), or at La Passe Harbor where the ferry docks.

Mail

Airmail letters to North America cost SR3.75 for the first 10 grams (⅔ oz); postcards cost SR2.6. Airmail letters to the United Kingdom cost SR3 for the first 10 grams; postcards cost SR2. Have mail sent to you at Poste Restante, Victoria, Mahé, Seychelles. Be sure to use your full name. Your mail will be delivered to the main post office in Victoria and held for pickup at no charge.

Important Addresses and Numbers

Tourist Information The **Seychelles Tourist Office** (tel. 248/22881), on the ground floor of Independence House in Victoria, is open weekdays 8–noon and 1:30–4. It also has a booth at the airport (tel. 248/76536).

Embassies **United States** (Victoria House, across from the clock tower, tel. 248/23921/2; emergency 248/23313, 248/41441, 248/24154). **United Kingdom** (Victoria House, tel. 248/23055/6).

Emergencies **Police** (tel. 999).

Ambulance (tel. 999).

Doctor: Call the **Seychelles Hospital** (Mont Fleuri, Mahé, tel. 248/24400), or check with your hotel manager for recommendations.

Pharmacies: Behram's Pharmacy (Mont Fleuri, Mahé, tel. 248/23659), **Fock Heng** (Revolution Ave., Victoria, tel. 248/22751).

English-language Bookstores **NPCS** (Independence Ave., Victoria, at the end of the arcade next to the Pirate's Arms Restaurant); **Jivan's Imports** (Albert and Market Sts., Victoria); **Seychelles News Service** (Kingsgate House, Independence Ave.).

Travel Agencies **Mason's Travel** (Box 459, Revolution Ave., Mahé, tel. 248/22670, 248/22643), **National Travel Agency N.T.A.** (Box 611, Kingsgate House, tel. 248/24900, fax 248/25111, **Travel Services Seychelles T.S.S.** (Box 356, Victoria House, tel. 248/22414).

Tipping

Though tipping is accepted in Seychelles, it is not expected, and indiscriminate tipping is discouraged because the tourism industry is trying to educate employees that improved service will be rewarded with cash incentives. Most restaurants and hotels will add a service charge to the bill, so there is no need to tip unless you feel that service has been exceptional. Ten percent of the bill is considered a fair tip.

Opening and Closing Times

Banks are open weekdays 8:30 to 1:30 and Saturday 8:30 to 11. Airport branches are opened for each incoming flight.

Museums are usually open weekdays 9 to 5 and Saturday 9 to noon.

Shops are open weekdays 8 to 5 and Saturday 8 to noon. A few shops are open on Sundays.

Guided Tours

Seychelles' three major travel agencies conduct tours similar to those listed below. Often there will be an agency representative in your hotel.

Orientation Tours The day-long **Mahé Explorer** coach tour offered by all the major tour operators picks you up at your hotel and proceeds to Victoria and its sights with time for shopping; then to the Botanical Gardens, Tea Plantation, and lunch at a creole restaurant, followed by a tour of south and west Mahé before returning to your hotel.

Special-Interest Overnight and day trips are available to nearby islands such as Silhouette, Frégate, Praslin/Vallée de Mai, and La Digue. There are only day trips to the bird sanctuaries of Cousin and Aride. An overnight stay on Bird Island can be arranged (*see* Tour Groups, *above*).

Excursions **The Marine Park:** Among the attractions here are glass-bottom boat trips to the Cerf, Round, and Moyenne islands, which include snorkeling and lunch.

Soirée Seychelloise: This evening entertainment consists of a music-and-dance performance at the National Theater and a Creole dinner at a local restaurant.

Seypirate: Sunset or day cruises along the coast of Mahé on a 92-foot brigantine schooner are featured. Lunch or beach barbecue with music is included. Book at the Yacht Club (Box 504, tel. 248/22362).

Victoria, Mahé

Victoria is a tiny, quaint town with a collection of brightly colored French colonial structures and modern buildings clustered beneath the peaks of Morne Seychellois and Trois Frères. It is the only city in Seychelles, the administrative and economic center for the archipelago, and it borders the nation's only port. With a population of 20,000, Victoria is one of the smallest capitals in the world. The city can easily be explored in half a day. The Clock Tower, a miniature reproduction of London's Big Ben, is at the point where all the city's streets converge.

Exploring

Numbers in the margin correspond to points of interest on the Victoria, Mahé map.

① At the **crossroads of Independence Avenue and Fifth of June Avenue,** which separates Victoria from the **New Port,** the **Interisland ferry departure pier,** the **Yacht Club,** and the **Marine**

② **Charter Association,** is the **sculpture of *The Three Wings,*** an imposing work that represents Africa, Asia, and Europe, the three continents from which the Seychellois originated. Across

③ from the Yacht Club is the bronze statue of *Zonm Lib,* or the *Free Man,* which represents Seychelles' liberation from colonialism. Behind the statue is the **People's Stadium,** where sports and national events are held. If you walk up Independence Ave-

④ nue toward the town center, **Independence House** is on your left. On the lower level are shops, boutiques, and the **Seychelles Tourist Office** information center. Across the road on your right is **Kingsgate House,** with more boutiques, the National Travel Agency, One-Hour Photo, British Airways, and electronics shops.

Time Out The **Pirate's Arms** restaurant, on Independence Avenue, is where locals, tourists, and expatriates gather for a cool SeyBrew, a baked-lasagna casserole, or a light snack. From the shaded open-air restaurant you can watch the light bustle of Victoria throughout the day, or you can relax in the garden at the rear. *DC, MC, V. Closed Sun. Inexpensive (under $10).*

Next to the Pirate's Arms is a long **arcade** with boutiques, a cash-exchange bureau, and **NPCS,** a bookstore and card shop stocking guidebooks, a few English paperbacks, daily newspapers, *Time, Newsweek*, stationery supplies, and children's books. Across from NPCS is a barbershop, and upstairs is the

⑤ **French Cultural Center,** which exhibits the work of local artists and has a French library and cinema. Films have English subtitles, change weekly, and admission is $2. They are shown on Monday at 8 PM, Wednesday at 6:30 PM, and Friday at 5 PM. Back on Independence Avenue to your left beyond Pirate's Arms is **Barclays Bank** and an **outdoor crafts market.** Across the road is

⑥ the **National Museum** (tel. 248/23653) where on display are shells, tortoises, local crafts, and historic exhibits, including the *Stone of Possession*, erected on Mahé by the French in 1756. Admission is free. The **post office** is on the corner, and a **taxi stand** is to the rear on Albert Street.

At the crossroads where Francis Rachel Street (and its many shops on the left, including **Seytels Cable & Wireless**) meets Al-

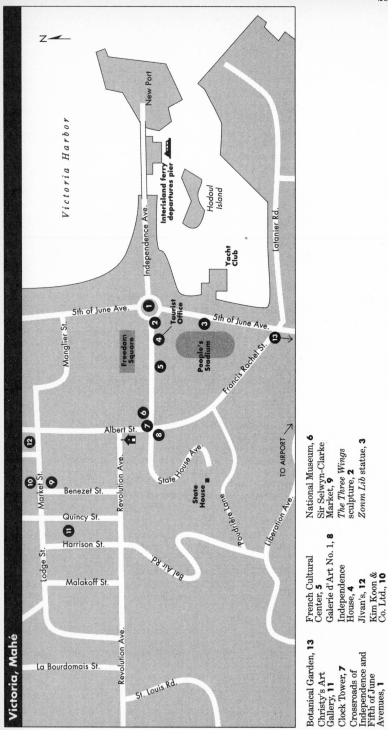

Victoria, Mahé

N

Victoria Harbor

New Port

Interisland ferry departures pier

Hodoul Island

Yacht Club

Latanier Rd.

5th of June Ave.

Independence Ave.

Manglier St.

Tourist Office

Freedom Square

People's Stadium

5th of June Ave.

Francis Rachel St.

Albert St.

State House Ave.

State House

Poudrière Lane

TO AIRPORT

Liberation Ave.

Benezet St.

Quincy St.

Harrison St.

Malakoff St.

Market St.

Lodge St.

Revolution Ave.

Bel Air Rd.

La Bourdomais St.

Revolution Ave.

St. Louis Rd.

Botanical Garden, **13**
Christy's Art Gallery, **11**
Clock Tower, **7**
Crossroads of Independence and Fifth of June Avenues, **1**

French Cultural Center, **5**
Galerie d'Art No. 1, **8**
Independence House, **4**
Jivan's, **12**
Kim Koon & Co. Ltd., **10**

National Museum, **6**
Sir Selwyn-Clarke Market, **9**
The Three Wings sculpture, **2**
Zomm Lib statue, **3**

bert Street (with more shops and **Barclays Bank** on the right) is
7 the **Clock Tower** and the center of the city. On Poudrière Lane
off Francis Rachel Street is the majestic **Hotel de l'Equateur,**
Seychelles' first hotel. Straight ahead is State House Avenue,
with the **U.S. and U.K. embassies** on the left in **Victoria House.**
8 Across the road is **Galerie d'Art No. 1,** where the works of local
artists are exhibited, and straight ahead are the **library** and the
offices of the president.

If you turn right on Albert Street and left on Revolution Avenue past shops, airlines, travel agencies, and **St. Paul's Cathedral** and **police headquarters** on your left, you'll encounter
9 **Benezet Street,** which leads to the side entrance of the **Sir
Selwyn-Clarke Market.** On Saturdays the crowded market is
abuzz with Creole cadence and haggling beneath the misty
mountain peaks of Mahé and the rusty tin roofs of turquoise,
red, and green colonial buildings. Women in bright flowered
dresses and straw hats shop at the many fruit and vegetable
stands and butcher stalls. Each butcher's name is posted
among the hanging meats and sausages, and the butchers stand
by with their bloodied aprons. Madame Patons, white birds
with long claws and yellow beaks, perch on mango trees waiting for scraps of food. Mounds of colorful fish decorate the fish
stalls, and the Seychellois spill out onto Market Street, toting
strings of snapper and dripping fish heads. The market is open
weekdays from 6 AM to 5 PM, Saturday from 5 AM to 1 PM, and
Sunday and holidays from 6 AM to noon.

Across from the market's main entrance, old men roll tobacco,
10 and disco music blares from **Kim Koon & Co. Ltd.** This is a good
place to buy lightweight plastic sandals for wearing with socks
when hiking on slippery trails, or for walking on rocky coral
beaches ($4). At the market exit, to the left on Quincy Street is
11 **Christy's Art Gallery,** where you can see and purchase the work
of local artists Michael Adams, Christine Harter, and Ron Ger-
lach. Oriental and Indian shops line Market Street.

Time Out Elbow your way into **Delite,** a small ice-cream shop on your left,
between Albert Street and the market, and cool off with a small
waffle cone of soft ice cream.

Farther along on your left, where Market Street meets Albert
12 Street, is **Jivan's** (*see* Off the Beaten Track, below).

Outside the city center, at the southern gate of Victoria at
13 Mont Fleuri, is the **Botanical Garden,** with displays of all of
Seychelles' endemic species, including the coco-de-mer. The or-
chid garden has species from all over the world. Take a break in
the Sapin Cafeteria, which overlooks the gardens.

Off the Beaten Track

You might like to seek out the works of the following Seychelles
residents:

Known as the country's master painter, Malaysian-born **Michael Adams** lived in Uganda for many years but has been in
Seychelles long enough to have created his own school of painting. His lush renderings are of the jungle that surrounds his
home and studio and the Seychellois performing their daily activities. Visitors are welcome to view and purchase his prints
and paintings in his studio at Anse aux Poules Bleues in

southwest Mahé near Baie Lazare Village (tel. 248/71106) and at Christy's Art Gallery (*see* Exploring Victoria, Mahé, above).

Christine Harter is one of the few native Seychellois artists painting in Seychelles today. Her watercolors of local scenes, seascapes, and houses can be seen at the Tec-Tec Boutique at the Paradise Hotel on Côte d'Or in Praslin and also at Christy's in Victoria. Her large mural of Praslin's Vallée de Mai can be seen in the lobby of the Beau Vallon Bay Hotel. Reproductions are available. Visitors may call for an appointment to view and purchase her works at her home on Côte d'Or in Praslin (tel. 32131).

German-born **W. Pit Hugelmann** a former biologist who created scent recipes for Revlon and Max Factor before settling in Seychelles in 1977, sells his two indigenous perfumes, Bwanwar and Bamboo, in many shops and boutiques, or at his home and laboratory at North East Point on Mahé (tel. 248/41329).

Kanti Jivan Shah is an internationally recognized expert on Seychelles' marine life, shells, birds, and natural history. You'll find him at the corner of Albert and Market streets in Victoria, at **Jivan Imports** ("where your rupee is worth more"), selling everything from Indian cottons to buttons, books, and shampoo. His family, from Bombay, has been in Seychelles for nearly a century, and he'll be glad to share his knowledge with you "to help you love Seychelles," especially if you're female. Nearly everyone in Seychelles knows Kanti, a psychic, healer, historian, botanist, naturalist, masseur, palmist, lecturer, entrepreneur, and self-promoter "interested in esoteric sciences. Nobody knows the Seychelles more than I do," he says. "All day, people come to visit from all over the world." Kanti's lectures can be heard at the Coral Strand Hotel on Sundays at 9 PM (tel. 248/47036).

Shopping

Shopping in Victoria is somewhat limited, although there are trendy shops on Mahé with lovely fashions. Packets of fragrant spices, bottled hot chilies, citronella and other teas, bamboo ashtrays, and kitchen utensils can be purchased at the **Selwyn-Clarke Market.** Many of the shops along Market Street carry colorful Indian cotton fabrics that may be used for clothing or for covering pillows. You'll also find fabric and batik clothing at **Oceana Crafts** in Kingsgate House. **Tic-Tac Boutique** in Independence House, **O-Trouloulou** in the Pirate's Arms Building, **Jivan's** on Albert Street, and **Julian's Souvenir Shop** at Anse La Mouche, as well as many hotel boutiques carry fabric and clothing. **Seypot,** a potter's cooperative in Les Mamelles, sells plates, ashtrays, mugs, and vases. Jewelry, and basketry sold at the **outdoor market** in the town center make nice presents, but the polished coco-de-mer nuts are heavy and expensive, so, unless you have your heart set on owning a specimen, take a photo of them instead. You'll also see shells and tortoise-shell items for sale at the market, but it's illegal to export shells and illegal to bring tortoise-shell back to the United States, so don't bother. Model sailboats or fishing boats handcrafted from the wood of the takamaka tree may interest model enthusiasts and children. These can be found at **La Marine Ltd.,** Le Cap. The postal authorities release five new issues of stamps each year, and these vivid collector's items are available at the **post office** in Victoria. Picasso-influenced abstracts by painter **Gerard Devoud** can be purchased at his studio gallery at Les Mamelles.

Beaches

It's easy to forget all else while lying on a Seychelles beach or, as most beaches here are called, Anse, French for "cove." The dance of the tides, light breezes, and the dramatic contrasts of turquoise water, puffy white clouds in a deep blue sky, and palm, takamaka, and casuarina trees or pink-and-gray granite-edged white shores, juxtaposed against misty mountains, will command all your attention. Depending on the season—southeast or northwest monsoon—some beaches, generally those on the windward side, may be swimmable only by very experienced swimmers. Others may be reclaimed by the sea. During the southeast monsoon, the leeward side of the islands is best for sailors, windsurfers, and water-skiers.

There are popular beaches such as Mahé's **Beau Vallon,** a 2-mile crescent with active surf, on the northwest coast, where the area's many hotel patrons and locals bask in the sun or drift by on parasails and Windsurfers. At **Anse à la Mouche** on the southwest coast, families enjoy the calm sea and shallow waters, and swimming and water sports are year-round attractions. The beaches are never overcrowded, and if you're looking for isolation, you'll find quiet coves or stretches of beach throughout Seychelles where the only prints in the sand will be your own and those of hermit crabs carting seashell domiciles around. Shelling on the less popular beaches can easily occupy an entire afternoon: About 320 species of marine animals live in the archipelago. Tempting as it may be, don't evict the hermit crabs from their attractive homes. The wealth of shells appears to be dwindling, though exporting them is illegal; leave them on the beach for the next person to enjoy.

Protected by granite outcroppings, **Baie Lazare** is a shady, tree-fringed beach on the southwest coast, in the village of the same name. Colorful fishing boats line the shore, and women hang laundry in the trees on the beach.

The beaches and coves along the north coast between Beau Vallon and the **North-East Point** are some of the most scenic, with their massive, imposing boulders, and lush vegetation reaching toward the sea. Those along the east coast south of Victoria to the airport, though least attractive, are calm and protected by reefs and offshore islands. Loners will enjoy the secluded **Anse Intendance** and **Police Bay** at the southern tip of Mahé.

Nude bathing is illegal in Seychelles, but topless bathing is accepted, and topless sunbathers often outnumber those with full suits.

Sports and Fitness

Participant Sports Water sports are the most popular activities, though there are also golf, tennis, biking, hiking, and bird-watching. Most hotels offer complimentary nonmotorized water sports, and there are water-sports shacks on some beaches such as Beau Vallon.

Bird-watching Active conservation of Seychelles' birdlife began in the late 1950s, and the establishment of nature reserves such as the

Morne Seychellois Park on Mahé, the Vallée de Mai on Praslin, and the island sanctuaries of Aldabra, Cousin, and Aride has done much to arrest the decline of many of the world's rarest species, among them the sacred ibis, black parrot, scops owl, and brush warbler. A visitor with a couple of weeks to spend in Seychelles can see most of the rare birds of the granite Inner Islands. Bird enthusiasts will enjoy Seychelles any time of the year, but the most dramatic sightings are in April, when a million migratory sooty terns swoop down on Bird Island in flocks of thousands to breed. They leave with their young in November.

Deep-sea Fishing This is a thrill for both beginners and experienced anglers, who hook tuna, marlin, sailfish, barracuda, and more. Though fishing is best between November and May, especially around the outer islands of Farquhar, Poivre, and the Amirantes to the south, and Bird, Denis, and Frégate to the north, you can have a satisfactory fishing trip just off the coast of Mahé. Contact the **Marine Charter Association** (tel. 248/22126) or inquire at your hotel.

Diving One of the most exciting recreations in Seychelles is diving, with more than 300 species of fish and 2,500 types of coral, 100 of them indigenous, making up the reefs. Though it's a year-round activity, the best times to dive are between October and December, and March and May. Dive centers offer PADI certification; dive packages; offshore charters; island-hopping trips; day, night, and adventure dives; underwater photography; and equipment sales, services, and rentals.

Contact **Seychelles Underwater Centre** (Coral Strand Hotel, Mahé, tel. 248/47357), **Marine Divers** (Northolme Bay Hotel, Mahé, tel. 248/47141, 248/47589), **Big Game Watersports** (Seychelles Sheraton, Mahé, tel. 248/78451), **Bernard Camille** (Praslin Beach, Praslin, tel. 248/32222), **Grégoire's Watersports** (Grégoire's Island Lodge, La Digue, tel. 248/34233), or **Werner Schulz** (Desroches Island Lodge, Desroches, tel. 248/44154, Mahé). **Fantasea Cruises** (3101 Ocean Park Blvd., Suite 302, Santa Monica, CA 90405, tel. 213/392–8054, fax 213/392–5016), which began in the Red Sea, offer a live-aboard fully equipped vessel that cruises to such sites as Aldabra and the remote Amirantes group. The vessel is 115 feet long and has 7 air-conditioned en suite cabins that can accommodate 10 passengers.

Golf The Reef Hotel Golf Club (tel. 76251) has nine holes.

Hiking This has become an increasingly popular diversion on the islands, where the scenery is lush with 250 indigenous species of plants, 75 of which are unique to Seychelles. There are 52 trails on Mahé, Praslin, and La Digue that vary in difficulty and length. Contact **Basil Beaudoin, Seychelles Tourist Board** (tel. 248/22881), for a leaflet and additional information.

Snorkeling Most hotels have masks, fins, and snorkels for their guests. You're likely to see marine life anywhere along the coast, but the areas near the rocks, along the reefs, and at the Ste. Anne Marine National Park off Mahé's east coast, northeast of Victoria, and those at Silhouette and Frégate are a sure bet.

Squash Contact **Seychelles Sheraton** (tel. 248/78541) or **Ecole Polytechnic,** Mont Fleuri (tel. 248/21330).

Tennis The **Equator Hotel** (tel. 248/78228), **Reef Hotel** (tel. 248/76251), **Beau Vallon Bay Hotel** (tel. 248/47141), and **Ecole Polytechnic** (Mont Fleuri, tel. 248/21330) all have courts.

Spectator Sports Soccer, boxing, volleyball, basketball, field hockey, and track and field events can be seen in Seychelles. Check the daily newspaper *Nation* for times and locations.

Dining

The phrase "dining out" can be taken literally in Seychelles. Most restaurants are open-air, constructed of timber, and often come with a thatch roof. Restaurants are located in hotels and scattered throughout Mahé. The cooing of turtledoves perched on banisters, and the sounds of the sea will soothe you, but the service tends to be slow and not very polished. There are exceptions, of course, like L'Archipel on Praslin, where service is attentive and timely. And since most dining is alfresco, flies, mosquitoes, and other insects are sometimes unwelcome guests.

The islands' cuisine revolves around three indigenous ingredients: fish, fruit, and endless variations on the yield of the coconut palm. Rice, imported from Southeast Asia or India, is readily available. Creole preparations are an often-spicy mélange of French, Asian, and African recipes. Generous use is made of spices, fruits, and vegetables such as breadfruit, sweet potatoes, and plantains. Some dishes lean toward the exotic, like the flying-fox pâté at Chez Plume, and octopus, squid, and cuttlefish curries. Turtle meat, turtle soup, and the "millionaire's salad," (so named because the palm heart requires felling a whole tree) should be avoided, and if you are conservation-minded, reported to the Seychelles Minister of Conservation and Environment. Sea turtles are endangered, and a new program restricts tree felling to protect wildlife and prevent soil erosion. *Chauve souris* (flying foxes or big bats) are not the least bit endangered and taste like tender quail.

The fish and seafood served are always fresh and range from substantial barracuda steaks and langouste, Seychelles' succulent lobsters, to the more common red snapper, poached in coconut milk and drizzled with lime juice, or served with a sauce of tomatoes, onions, and peppers, or a hot chili spread. Soups are often prepared with a seafood base. Grilled-chicken dishes are juicy, but chicken is not a staple, since grains for feed must be imported. Red meat is a rarity owing to the lack of pasture on the islands, though locals enjoy suckling pig.

Coconuts and bananas have infinite incarnations, from jams to pastries and cakes, and the fresh mangoes and papayas are a pleasant contrast to strong morning coffee or citronella tea.

The local beers are SeyBrew, a full-bodied lager, and Eku, which is more bitter. Wines are imported from South Africa, France, and Italy. The water is purified, but drinking bottled water is a cautionary measure that may prove to be wise.

Casual dress is usually acceptable during the day, but evening wear should be a bit dressier (no T-shirts or shorts). Men aren't required to wear jackets and ties. Lunch generally begins around noon and ends no later than 3 PM; dinner is served from 7 to 10 PM.

Highly recommended restaurants are indicated by a star ★.

Category	Cost*
Expensive	over $30
Moderate	$10–$30
Inexpensive	under $10

per person with tax and 10% service charge, not including wine or liquor.

Expensive
★ **Chez Plume.** French seafood dishes are featured at this small, open-air restaurant in the Auberge d'Anse Boileau. Candlelight, fresh flowers, and taped Creole music set the mood. The flying-fox pâté, made from *chauves-souris*, or fruit bats, caught with nets by locals, is a specialty, as are local fish fillets with saffron, shrimp, and passion-fruit sauces. *Auberge d'Anse Boileau, tel. 248/76660. Reservations advised. AE, DC, MC, V. Closed Mon. and June.*

Kyoto. Located on Anse Etoile, a 10-minute drive north from Victoria is this exquisite Japanese restaurant serving some of the best sushi found anywhere. *Tel. 248/41337, V. Closed Sun.*

Moderate
★ **Islander.** Granite pillars support the round thatch roof of this quiet, outdoor restaurant across from Anse à la Mouche on the west coast. Electric lanterns, candlelight, fresh flowers, and soft piano music or light jazz harmonize with the sea and a nearby mooing cow. Weekly specials include fish, scallops, and shrimp baked in dry sherry, or Creole dishes such as blackened redfish. *Anse à la Mouche, tel. 248/71289. Reservations advised. V. Closed Mon. and Sun dinner.*

La Moutia. Creole and international dishes are served at this restaurant, one of Mahé's first stone houses. The cozy veranda overlooks Victoria Harbor and several offshore islands. Occasionally, a local trio will play Seychellois favorites. The fricassee of gamba with saffron, a good bet, is made of large, savory prawns, scented with saffron, in a white-wine sauce. The peppered crab, chef style, is prepared with green, black, and white pepper, cream, and white wine. *La Misère, tel. 248/44433. Reservations advised. AE, DC, MC, V.*

La Scala. Fresh flowers, candlelight, and mellow taped Seychellois music complement the sound of the sea in this arched stucco dining room looking out on Beau Vallon Bay. Owner and chef Giovanni Torsi specializes in Italian and international cuisine. Try the clams stewed in wine for a starter, and progress to the tagliatelle Scala—homemade noodles with ham in a cream-and-tomato sauce. *Bel Ombre, tel. 248/47535. Reservations advised. AE, DC, MC, V. Closed Sun. No lunch.*

Lobster Pot Grill. This cozy seaside restaurant just north of Victoria features creole cooking and seafood. *Pointe Conan, tel. 248/41370. D, MC, V. Closed Sunday.*

★ **Marie Antoinette.** Mahé's most notable restaurant, situated in Victoria, is a 90-year-old, green wood French colonial house, formerly a nightclub. The fixed Creole menu features tec-tec soup, made from local clams and vegetables; tuna steak in Creole sauce; and a smorgasbord of Creole favorites. Lace tablecloths add a touch of elegance to a festive bright pink, green, and white candlelit room. The artificial flowers and wall of postcards from former patrons, however, are somewhat jarring.

Revolution Ave., Victoria, tel. 248/23942 or 248/22089. Children under 12 eat free. Reservations required. DC, V. Closed Sun.

Inexpensive
★

Baobab Pizzeria. Two women in aprons stand by in this laid-back eatery in the sand, rolling dough and baking pizzas in the open hearth, while Elton John carries on about Norma Jean. Diners sit in booths with checked tablecloths, drinking SeyBrew to the beat of crashing waves. The pizzas come out hot and crusty, and the steaming pasta dishes are cooked al dente. *Beau Vallon, tel. 248/47167. Reservations not necessary. MC, V.*

Chez Baptistas. Located south of Victoria, on Anse Takamaka, this is the place to go for grilled fish wrapped in banana leaves. Fresh catches are selected as they arrive and served shortly thereafter. It is a rustic place, popular for lunch, with a floor of sand and tables covered by coconut leaves. *Tel. 248/71535. AE.*

Lodging

Most of Mahé's hotels, guest houses, and self-catering cottages are situated on the shoreline, within sight or earshot of the soothing rhythm of the tides. Accommodations range from quiet, isolated hotels and guest houses, scattered about the island to lively hotels. The greatest concentration of hotels, restaurants, and activities is in Victoria and along the 2-mile crescent of Beau Vallon Beach in the northwest bay. Hotels between Port Glaud on the west coast and the southern tip of the island, such as the Sheraton and Equator, require a 30- to 40-minute trip through corkscrew mountain passes to reach Victoria or Beau Vallon.

The Seychelles Hotels Group is an association of properties such as the Northolme and Beau Vallon Bay Hotel on Mahé, and the Praslin Beach Hotel on Praslin. Guests of these member hotels receive Fun Cards, which entitle them to rooms and meals at other member hotels, discounted shopping at selected shops and boutiques, free access to "soft" (nonmotorized) water sports, and a free beginner's dive.

The following selection is representative of the recommended hotels and guest houses, organized by rate. Price categories are based on the year-round or peak-season price for a standard room at the rate of SR5 to the U.S. dollar. Although peak season varies among some hotels, it generally consists of a two-week period at Christmas and again at Easter, and the weeks from the end of July to the end of August.

Highly recommended lodgings are indicated by a star ★.

Category	Cost*
Very Expensive	over $250
Expensive	$200–$250
Moderate	$150–$200
Inexpensive	under $100

All prices are for a standard double room with breakfast unless otherwise indicated, including tax and service charges.

Very Expensive **Beau Vallon Bay Hotel.** This hotel has a new restaurant, renovated lobby, a new diving school, and the floor of the Chinese Restaurant has been raised to give diners a better view of sunsets over the pool. Beau Vallon, with a casino and disco, remains a hot spot for nightlife. *Box 550, Mahé, tel. 248/47532, fax 248/47809. 132 rooms with baths. Facilities: 3 restaurants, boutique, hairdresser; pool, tennis court. AE, DC, V.*

Le Meridien Fisherman's Cove. These thatch-roof one- and two-story units are positioned on a rocky cove at the end of Beau Vallon Beach at Bel Ombre. The air-conditioned rooms have rich wood ceilings, ceramic floors, bamboo furnishings, room safes, mini-fridges, TVs, and terraces with sea views. *Bel Ombre, Box 35, Mahé, tel. 248/47252, fax 248/47540. 48 rooms with bath. Facilities: pool, restaurant, poolside bar, 3 tennis courts, fitness room, hairdresser, game room, boutique, live entertainment, water sports, beach. AE, DC, MC, V.*

The Plantation Club. Located near a secluded cove, this massive new complex has 206 rooms and suites, each with a minibar, TV, direct-dial telephone and terrace or balcony. *Val Mer, Box 437, Mahé, tel. 248/71588, fax 248/71517. Facilities: 3 restaurants, pool, nightclub, hair salon and water sports. AE, MC, V.*

Northolme Hotel. With its own tropical garden overlooking a secluded beach on the coast of north Mahé, this 19-room hotel is an intimate resort for VIPs. There is a diving center and a restaurant featuring French and Creole food. *Glacis, Box 333, Mahé, tel. 248/47222, fax 248/47219. AE, DC, V.*

★ **Seychelles Sheraton.** This stark, seven-story curvilinear structure, built to resemble an ocean liner, sits atop a meticulously landscaped hill following the contour of the sea at Port Glaud on the west coast. Some locals don't appreciate the building's contemporary aesthetic, but it's one of the most dramatic settings in Seychelles. The commanding view of misty mountains and offshore islands from rooms 27 through 39 is one of the island's finest. Rooms are bright, with soft peach accents, TV, IDD (International Direct Dial) phones, terrace, and sea views. Formerly the Mahé Beach Hotel, opened in 1975, it was extensively renovated by Sheraton, which reopened it in September 1987. *Box 540, Port Glaud, Mahé, tel. 248/78451, fax 248/71512. 165 rooms including 11 junior suites, and presidential suite with bath. Facilities: pool, 3 restaurants, 2 bars, disco, daily transport to Sheraton/Thérèse Island, where the hotel's Creole barbecue restaurant is located, water-sports center, boutique, tennis, squash, game room, drugstore, hairdresser, sauna, massage, in-house video, live entertainment, excursions, secretarial services. AE, DC, MC, V.*

Expensive **Equator Grande Anse Residence.** Granite construction distinguishes this rustic seaside hotel, built in 1983 on the quiet southwest coast among tropical gardens. The air-conditioned rooms have ceiling fans, TVs with in-house video, and a decor in subtle earth tones, with ceramic-tile floors and bamboo furnishings. The standard rooms are dark and lack views, so it's worth paying extra for a suite with a terrace or balcony. The best sea views are from rooms 101, 209–216, 301–307, and 408–420. *Box 526, Mahé, Seychelles, tel. 248/78228. 49 suites with bath, living room, refrigerator, some kitchenettes, and room safes, and 8 standard rooms with shower. Facilities: restaurant, bar, poolside coffee shop, boutique, swimming pool, natural saltwater pool on the beach, lighted tennis court, free* *daily transportation to Thérèse Island, "soft" water sports. AE, DC, MC, V.*

★ **Sunset Beach Hotel.** Mediterranean-style intimacy and red clay roofs are the hallmarks of this hotel perched on a rocky promontory amid granite boulders in northwest Mahé, a few minutes from lively Beau Vallon. Shaded by towering dragon-blood trees, the breezy terrace/restaurant has north-coast views and a secluded beach. Air-conditioned rooms have ceiling fans and private balconies overlooking the sea. *Box 372, Victoria, Mahé, Seychelles, tel. 248/47227. 25 rooms with bath, including 6 on the beach, 6 junior suites, and a 2-bedroom villa with Jacuzzi, round bed, minibar, direct-dial phones, and dark bamboo-and-cane furnishings. Facilities: beach bar, restaurants, game room, boutique, day rooms, massage, beauty salon, pool, exercise room, beach, snorkeling, access to water sports. AE, DC, MC, V.*

Moderate **Coral Strand Hotel.** Located on popular Beau Vallon Beach in
★ northwest Mahé, 5 kilometers from Victoria, this three-story hotel faces Silhouette Island. The rooms were renovated in 1987 and have phones and programmed radio music, but the exterior could use a face-lift. Green bamboo-and-cane furnishings complement the carpeting and bright pastel appointments. Top-level center-block rooms have the best ocean views. Divers, expatriates, and visitors gather around the jumping seaside bar at sunset, when a mellow guitarist plays James Taylor tunes and Seychellois favorites. *Box 400, Mahé, Seychelles, tel. 248/47036. 103 rooms with bath. Facilities: restaurants, snack bar, live entertainment, pool, dive center, water sports. AE, DC, MC, V.*

Inexpensive **Auberge d'Anse Boileau.** This small thatch-roof hotel sits across from the main southwest coastal road among tropical gardens. Built in 1980, it has tile floors, simple wood furnishings, and sea-view terraces. There is abundant local activity here, with a grocery store nearby and fishermen bringing in their catch. Co-owner Jean-Claude Plumas holds the record for the largest marlin caught on the Ivory Coast. Chez Plume (*see* Dining) is the Auberge's highly recommended restaurant. *Anse Boileau, Box 211, Mahé, Seychelles, tel. 248/76660. 8 rooms with bath. Facilities: French seafood restaurant, bar, deep-sea fishing, diving, swimming at Anse Louis to the south. AE, DC, MC, V.*
Blue Lagoon. These spacious, self-catering duplexes are situated on the quiet southwest coast across the road from Anse à la Mouche. The airy bungalows have blond wood furnishings, full kitchens, living/dining room, two baths and a terrace. Guests renting half of a chalet may end up sharing common facilities. *Box 442, Mahé, Seychelles, tel. 248/71197. 8 rooms with bath. Facilities: water-sports center, yacht charter, maid service included in price, cook available. No credit cards.*
★ **Lazare Picault.** This guest house consists of thatch rondavels on a granite hillside among lush gardens and palms, overlooking Lazare Bay. "The steps do wonders for our beer sales," says Ian, the bartender. The compact rooms have ceiling fans, and two have air-conditioning. *Baie Lazare, Box 135, Mahé, Seychelles, tel. 248/71117. 14 rooms with bath. Facilities: bar, restaurant, TV room, snorkeling equipment. V.*

The Arts and Nightlife

Concerts Music and dance may be enjoyed in the form of **Sega** and **Moutia,** of Madagascan and African origin. The Moutia was a ritual prayer that was turned into a work song by slaves. Typically used in the Sega and Moutia are the *bom*, a bow instrument; the *zez*, a monochord sitar; and the *makalapo*, a string instrument with a tin can for a sound box. Both the zez and the bom use gourds as resonance chambers. Modern incarnations of the Sega and Moutia are performed before a bonfire on the beach to the beat of a drum, and the performers gather "rumors" about island residents (as on Silhouette) a couple of days before the performance in order to incorporate them into the dance. The beginnings of rap music? The Sega is similar, but the percussion instrument is the hollowed-out trunk of a palm tree. The traditional music and dance, **Komtole**—quadrilles or square-dancing—incorporates violins, banjos, bass drums, and triangles. It was brought to Seychelles by the French settlers and is performed at weddings and other family celebrations. Demonstrations of these island rhythms can be enjoyed at **Beau Vallon Bay Hotel** (tel. 248/47141).

Film and Theater **Deepam Cinema,** Victoria (tel. 248/22585). **Seychelles Artistic Productions,** Victoria (tel. 248/22731).

Bars and Nightclubs Though there is one casino at Beau Vallon Bay Hotel, and another at the Plantation Club, Seychelles is not renowned for its glamorous nightlife. There are some discos, and most hotels have attractive bars, and occasionally there is live entertainment, with bands playing regularly at Fisherman's Cove.

Jazz Clubs There's a jazz brunch on Sundays at the **Coral Strand Hotel** (Beau Vallon, tel. 248/47036), **Islette** (Port Glaud, tel. 248/78229), and the **Seychelles Sheraton** (Port Glaud, tel. 248/78451).

Discos Dance floors can be found at the **Auberge Club des Seychelles-Danzilles** (Bel Ombre, tel. 248/78228), **Equator Hotel** (Grand Anse, tel. 248/78228), **Katiolo Club** (Anse Faure, tel. 248/76453), and the **Seychelles Sheraton** (Port Glaud, tel. 248/78541).

Excursions from Mahé

Praslin

Aside from its scenic beaches, such as Petite Anse Kerlan in the northwest, and its pink granite formations, Praslin's most outstanding feature is the Vallée de Mai, a jungle of tropical rarities where black parrots mate, fruit bats hang in the trees, and the coco-de-mer palm tree grows wild. The trees are well over 100 years old and are enormous. The male tree with its three-foot-long "catkin" resembles the male anatomy, and fascination with the coco-de-mer has led to speculation that the thrashing of the tree's huge leaves on stormy nights is the union of the male and female trees. The Vallée de Mai's ecosystem, however, indicates that pollination is effected by insects, green geckos, or the wind. The germination period of the young coco-de-mer sprout lasts for three years, and the fruit matures only after seven years, when it weighs nearly 50 pounds. The palm first bears fruit after about 25 years, and doesn't reach its full height (the tallest in the Vallée is 102 feet) until it is about a century old. The landscape here, with its 650 million-year-old granite formations, is such that you expect to see a dinosaur at the next turn.

Getting Around The tour operators on Mahé can make arrangements for you on Praslin (*see* Important Numbers and Addresses, above), or your hotel can arrange for tours and taxis. Mini-mokes can be rented, but roads are under repair. The best boat trips can be arranged at **Praslin Beach Hotel** on Anse Volbert. Bernard Camille offers full-day and half-day excursions with picnics, fishing, scuba diving, and snorkeling.

Dining and Lodging Most of Praslin's accommodations are on the northeast coast on Anse Volbert, also called the Côte d'Or. Côte d'Or is a long stretch of silky white sand and turquoise water, safe for swimming year-round. Granite boulders, palms, and takamaka trees border the shoreline. The main water-sports center is located at the Praslin Beach Hotel, and other hotels also have water sports, though several are limited. Some small hotels are located across the island on the southwest coast at Grand Anse, where the tides get rougher and the beach is not as safe or attractive during the southeast monsoon. Accommodations range from small, simple beachfront bungalows and guest houses to more exclusive, deluxe properties like L'Archipel and La Réserve. The peace and quiet is sometimes disturbed by the Italian version of Club Med—Club Vacanze—which stages noisy evening cabarets that echo along the coast until around midnight. Mosquitoes and other insects may also be a nuisance. Any entertainment on Praslin is usually on Côte d'Or.

Restaurant choices are few on Praslin, except for those in hotels, most of which serve nonguests when space is available. Since there is not a lot of activity on the island, visitors may welcome the opportunity to dine out at the other hotels.

Highly recommended hotels and restaurants are indicated by a star ★.

Category	Cost*
Very Expensive	over $150
Expensive	$125–$150
Moderate	$100–$125
Inexpensive	under $100

*All prices are for a double room with breakfast unless otherwise indicated, including tax and service charges.

Very Expensive **Flying Dutchman.** With 13 thatched cottages facing Grande Anse beach, the Flying Dutchman's restaurant features international and Creole cuisine. Two meals are included in the rates, and day trips to local islands for fishing and barbecues can be arranged. *Grande Anse, tel. 248/33337, fax 248/47606. AE, DC.*
Praslin Beach Hotel. Located near Anse Volbert beach, this hotel also has its own swimming pool and watersports center. The cottages with a total of 86 rooms, create a semicircle around the pool. *Côte d'Or, tel. 248/32144, fax 248/32244. Facilities: restaurant, pool bar, big-game fishing, and excursions. AE, MC, V.*

Expensive **L'Archipel.** Surely Praslin's finest, these isolated French colo-
★ nial-style bungalows are built into a lush hillside among granite
boulders and a natural brook in Anse Gouvernement. Completed in April 1987, they offer magnificent views of off-shore
islands and distant peaks. Sunken platform beds, mosquito
nets, ceiling fans, bedside seashell lamps, rich woodwork, and
roomy terraces add to the deluxe ambience. Bungalows
Aldabra and Providence offer the best views, and Marianne is
directly on the beach. *Anse Gouvernement, Box 586, tel. 248/
32040 or 248/32242. 16 rooms with bath (shower). Facilities: direct-dial phones, minibar, restaurants, bar, water sports, boutique, game room, TV/VCR available on request. AE, V.*

La Réserve. These thatch-roof, private beachfront bungalows
are situated on a secluded bay along the Côte d'Or. Rooms have
standing fans, Van Gogh prints, arched louvered doors, roomy
bathrooms, minibar, and coffee/tea maker. Rooms 1, 2, 3, and 6
are closest to the shore. *Anse Petit Cour, tel. 248/32211. 30
rooms with bath, including beachfront villa and family bungalow. Facilities: pier restaurant, bar, lighted tennis court, water sports, boat charters, excursions, boutique, video room,
library. AE, DC, MC, V.*

Moderate **Paradise Sea Lodge.** These thatched chalets are situated on the
Côte d'Or across a dirt road. The "no-frills" rooms have green
tile floors, standing takamaka-branch lamps, mosquito coils,
ceiling fans, and phones. *Anse Volbert, tel. 248/32255, fax
32019. 42 rooms with shower. Facilities: water-sports center,
bicycle rentals, boutique, game room, restaurants, bars, excursions. AE, DC, MC, V.*

Inexpensive **Maison des Palmes.** With a roadside location on Grande Anse,
on the southwest side of the island, these thatch-roof bungalows are situated among coconut palms and jamalac fruit trees
whose yield is used in preparation of some of the hotel's meals.
The birds' sounds are a natural alarm clock heard against the
constant rush of the tides. The twin beds are firm and comfortable. Room 12 is closest to the beach; rooms 1 through 4 are
near restaurant chatter. *Amitié, tel. 248/33411, fax 33880. 16
rooms with bath (shower). Facilities: pool, beach, excursions,
water sports, catamaran yacht charter. AE, DC, V.*

La Digue

Touring vans have recently been introduced on La Digue
(meaning "dike"), an island where the ox cart was the main
form of transportation. The carts remain, but the vans have begun to transform the quiet charm of the island. The beaches,
especially Pointe Cap Barbi and Pointe Source d'Argent,
backed by huge granite boulders, are among Seychelles' finest.
The east coast has wilder, more remote strands such as Anse
Cocos and Petite Anse, where the currents are sometimes dangerous for swimming. Getting around by bicycle or on foot is
the best way to see La Digue. The old plantation house at
L'Union was the setting for the movie *Emmanuelle*, and the
film *Crusoe* was also set on La Digue. One of the world's rarest
birds, the black paradise flycatcher, has made its home here at
the bird sanctuary, a few minutes' walk from the lodge.

Lodging The **La Digue Island Lodge** consists of 22 bungalows, 10 of them
facing the beach, and 13 annex rooms across the dirt road, all
with showers. *Anse la Reunion, tel. 248/34232/3/7. Facilities:*

*pool, water sports, excursions, Creole beach restaurant, 2
bars. AE, V. Moderate.*

There are also two very inexpensive small guest houses on La
Digue: **Bernique** (tel. 248/34229) and **Choppy's Bungalows,** on
the beach next to the lodge (tel. 248/34224).

Bird Island

Air Seychelles has a 40-minute flight from Mahé to Bird Island,
the nesting site of thousands of sooty terns. They gather here
annually, then migrate elsewhere; a tag was once recovered
from Australia. The island is favored by ornithologists, including Roger Tory Peterson, who visited here several times. As
the phrase goes for the local lodge, "Three million birds can't be
wrong." Not only is it a phenomenal site for bird-watchers,
but the beaches are beautiful as well.

Lodging **Bird Island Lodge.** The only accommodation on the island has 25
bungalows with private showers, ceiling fans, and verandas
facing the sea. The restaurant serves Continental and English
breakfasts, a Creole lunch, and European-style dinner. *Box
404, Bird Island, tel. 248/24925. Facilities: Deep-sea fishing,
snorkeling, tennis. AE, DC, V. Very Expensive.*

Desroches

Desroches is located in the Amirantes group, about an hour by
plane from Mahé. This flat coral island five kilometers (3 mi)
long, is part of an atoll 50 miles in circumference and 10 miles in
diameter. The landscape, consisting mostly of coconut palms, is
not as interesting as that of the granite islands. If you walk past
the airstrip into the settlement, you'll smell the sweet scent of
coconuts and hear hollow cracking sounds as women sit around
heaps of coconuts, splitting them with a single stroke. The island's main products are casuarina timber and copra. Seychelles copra (coconut), exported to Pakistan—where it is used
for religious ceremonies, soap, candles, and oil—is some of the
world's finest.

Excellent diving and fishing are available off Desroches. The
island has a fully equipped water-sports center with a knowledgeable staff, where you can get a PADI scuba diving certificate in one week. You can spend mornings fishing for barracuda
(which the lodge will barbecue for dinner), and afternoons
skipping through wave trains in an 18-foot Hobie Cat, or lazing
on the beaches. All water sports are available.

Lodging The **Desroches Island Lodge,** with 20 duplex beachfront bungalows (40 rooms), offers some of Seychelles' finest accommodations. The large L-shape rooms have rich wood floors, ceiling
fans, and louvered windows that look out to the sea, silhouetted
through wispy casuarina trees. The airy lounge and restaurant
have stone floors that are polished each morning by local wom-
en "dancing" on coconut husks. *Tel. 248/24640. Reservations,
tel. 248/44154, Mahé. Expensive. AE, MC, V.*

Frégate

A small airplane touches down on a grassy strip by the crashing
blue sea. You catch a glimpse of the rare magpie robin before a
flock of fiery Madagascar fodys (cardinals) takes flight, and

within 20 minutes of arriving on magical Frégate, you'll see the giant tortoises, foot-long centipedes, exotic fruit and flower trees, lizards, and spiders that give the island its enchanted forest flavor.

Frégate's dense landscape may trick you with visions of Tarzan leaping from the suspended roots of the colossal banyan tree that dwarfs the Plantation House where guests stay, through this Garden of Eden past bamboo, mango, and breadfruit trees and into the arms of the strange dragon-blood tree, which "bleeds" when scraped.

You can circle this 1¼-by-¼-mile island in less than a day. Hiking to such beaches as Grande Anse and Anse Victorin is on rough and rocky roads, but the vistas of turquoise white-capped seas through the verdant palms are magnificent, and the creamy white beaches, superb. Occasionally, dolphins can be seen near Anse Bambous. Beware, though, the tides of the southeast monsoon, when you may be swept away to Madagascar, and the caves at the southern point, where a legendary headless woman is rumored to surface at low tide.

Lodging   **The Plantation House,** minutes away from the Marine National Park, opened in 1975, has 10 rooms, including four newer annex rooms near the shore. Rooms have ceiling fans, mosquito nets, and fresh fruit and flowers. *Box 330, Frégate, tel. 248/24789, 248/23123. Facilities: restaurant, seaside bar, free snorkeling and fishing equipment. AE, DC, MC, V. Expensive.*

Silhouette Island

Cheers, a 15-passenger Bertram yacht, leaves the Yacht Club in Victoria Harbor for Silhouette, 12 miles northwest of Mahé, each Monday, Wednesday, and Friday at 8:30 AM, and Sunday at 12:30. It returns at 10:30 AM and 2:30 PM. The round-trip, which can be a rough one, takes about one hour, and costs $80.

There are no cars or roads on Silhouette, just paths. After Mahé, it is Seychelles' most mountainous island, with its highest peak, Mont Dauban, rising nearly half a mile into the clouds. Silhouette's thick virgin forest is unprecedented in the Indian Ocean. The island's 250 inhabitants work on vegetable and animal farms or in the chicken slaughterhouse. Some fish, extract oil from copra, or work in the Island Lodge. Even "Dr. Kodule," the island's 77-year-old "witch doctor," has a job: sweeping the grounds for the island manager. Nearby, in the settlement, women pound laundry on rocks outside wood seaside shanties with tin roofs, some equipped with television antennae. Men gather around tables to play dominoes, and children play volleyball. They wave and smile and reach out their hands to touch you, as if to assure themselves that you are real, while jabbering chickens and roosters run amok.

A walk through the settlement will take you past the old plantation house and a mausoleum where the French Dauban family, former owners of Silhouette, are buried. If you continue along the path through palm thickets and granite peaks, you'll reach Anse Lascare, a quiet beach strewn with coconuts, seashells, and coral. Two trails join the north and south ends of the island, and it is advisable to hire a guide, lest you lose your way.

It's here that the oral tradition of the Moutia musicians (*see* Arts and Nightlife) is most alive, thanks to Silhouette's isolation.

The island remained inaccessible because of its reefs; it was opened to overnight visitors only in December 1986.

Lodging **The Island Lodge,** nestled among umbrella palms on La Passe beach and a freshwater lagoon, consists of 12 chalet-type thatch-roof bungalows built of indigenous takamaka and casuarina timber. The bungalows have louvered shutters, ceramic-tile floors, ceiling fans, bathrooms with showers, and a terrace looking out to sea. A large umbrella for rain or shine hangs from a wood peg in a wall of each bungalow, and rooms are equipped with mosquito coils. *Silhouette Island, Island Development Co. Ltd., Mahé, tel. Victoria 248/24003 or 248/24445, fax 248/44178. No credit cards. Very Expensive.*

Swahili Vocabulary

Words and Phrases

	English	*Swahili*
Basics	Hello	Jambo
	Goodbye	Kwaheri
	How are you?	Habari?
	Fine	Mzuri (pronounced like Missouri)
	Please	Tafadhali
	Thank you	Asante sana
	Yes	Ndio
	No	Hapana
	Mr.	Bwana
	Mrs.	Bibi
	Infant, child	Toto
	Elder	Mzee (one with wisdom
	Today	Leo
	Tonight	Leo usik
	Tomorrow	Kesho
	Wait	Ngojea
	Slow down (caution)	Pole pole
	Come in, near	Karibu
	May I come in?	Hodi?
	How much? How many?	Ngapi?
	How much is it?	Ngapi shillings?
	Bring me hot water, please	Lete maji moto, tafadhali
	Where is _____ ?	Iko wapi _____ ?
	May I take your picture?	Mikupige picha?
Numbers	One	Moja
	Two	Mbili
	Three	Tatu
	Four	Nne
	Five	Tano
	Six	Sita
	Seven	Saba
	Eight	Nane
	Nine	Tisa
	Ten	Kumi
Animals	Cheetah	Duma
	Elephant	Tembo
	Giraffe	Twiga
	Hippo	Kiboko
	Hartebeest	Kongoni
	Lion	Simba
Food and Drink	Beer or drinks	Pombe
	Chicken	Kuku

Coffee	Kahawa
Cold	Baridi
Finished	Quisha
Fish	Samaki
Ice	Baratu
Lamb	Kondoo
Maize with beans	Irio
Marinated and roasted	Kuchoma
Meat, usually beef or goat	Nyama
Milk	Maziwa
Plantains, fried green	Matoke
Porridge	Ugali
Shark	Papa
Sugar	Sukari
Tea	Chai

Medicines and Toiletries	Doctor	Daktari
	Insect	Dudu
	Insect repellant	Dawa ya wadudu*
	Laundry	Kufuliwa
	Market	Soko
	Medicine	Dawa
	Razor	Wembe
	Shop	Duka
	Soap	Sabuni

*Dawa *is also a strong cocktail;* dawa ya kopoza jua *is suntan oil; and* dawa ya meno *is toothpaste.*

WHEREVER YOU TRAVEL, *H*ELP IS NEVER FAR AWAY.

From planning your trip to providing travel assistance along the way, American Express® Travel Service Offices* are always there to help.

DAR ES SALAAM, TANZANIA
Rickshaw Travel
UWT Street
51-29125

MOMBASA, KENYA
Express Kenya
Nkrumah Road
11-315-898

NAIROBI, KENYA
Express Kenya
Bruce House, Standard St.
2-334-722

Index

Fodor's Travel Guides

U.S. Guides

Alaska

Arizona

Boston

California

Cape Cod, Martha's
Vineyard, Nantucket

The Carolinas & the
Georgia Coast

Chicago

Disney World & the
Orlando Area

Florida

Hawaii

Las Vegas, Reno,
Tahoe

Los Angeles

Maine, Vermont,
New Hampshire

Maui

Miami & the Keys

New England

New Orleans

New York City

Pacific North Coast

Philadelphia & the
Pennsylvania Dutch
Country

San Diego

San Francisco

Santa Fe, Taos,
Albuquerque

Seattle & Vancouver

The South

The U.S. & British
Virgin Islands

The Upper Great
Lakes Region

USA

Vacations in New York
State

Vacations on the
Jersey Shore

Virginia & Maryland

Waikiki

Washington, D.C.

Foreign Guides

Acapulco, Ixtapa,
Zihuatanejo

Australia & New
Zealand

Austria

The Bahamas

Baja & Mexico's
Pacific Coast Resorts

Barbados

Berlin

Bermuda

Brazil

Budapest

Budget Europe

Canada

Cancun, Cozumel,
Yucatan Penisula

Caribbean

Central America

China

Costa Rica, Belize,
Guatemala

Czechoslovakia

Eastern Europe

Egypt

Euro Disney

Europe

Europe's Great Cities

France

Germany

Great Britain

Greece

The Himalayan
Countries

Hong Kong

India

Ireland

Israel

Italy

Italy's Great Cities

Japan

Kenya & Tanzania

Korea

London

Madrid & Barcelona

Mexico

Montreal &
Quebec City

Morocco

The Netherlands
Belgium &
Luxembourg

New Zealand

Norway

Nova Scotia, Prince
Edward Island &
New Brunswick

Paris

Portugal

Rome

Russia & the Baltic
Countries

Scandinavia

Scotland

Singapore

South America

Southeast Asia

South Pacific

Spain

Sweden

Switzerland

Thailand

Tokyo

Toronto

Turkey

Vienna & the Danube
Valley

Yugoslavia

CNN TRAVEL GUIDE
PASSPORT TO THE WORLD

Join host Valerie Voss for an entertaining and informative program that takes you to the four corners of the earth. With expert advice from Michael Spring, Fodor's Editorial Director, *CNN Travel Guide* is the perfect companion for anyone planning a trip or just interested in travel.

Drawing on CNN's vast network of international correspondents, you'll discover an exciting variety of new destinations from the most exotic locales to some well-kept secrets just a short trip away. You'll also find helpful tips on everything from hotels and restaurants to packing and planning. So tune in to *CNN Travel Guide*. And make it your first stop on any trip.